FOOTPATHS OF
BRITAIN

FOOTPATHS OF
BRITAIN

p

This is a Parragon Book
This edition published in 2004

Parragon
Queen Street House
4 Queen Street
Bath BA1 1HE
United Kingdom

Ordnance Survey®   This product includes mapping data
licensed from Ordnance Survey®
with the permission of the Controller of Her Majesty's
Stationery Office. © Crown copyright 2003.
All rights reserved. Licence number PU 100039050.

Created and produced by
The Bridgewater Book Company Ltd,
Lewes, East Sussex

ISBN: 1-40544-076-7

Printed in China

Visit the Walkingworld website at
www.walkingworld.com

All the walks in this book are available in more
detailed form on the Walkingworld website.
The route instructions have photographs at key
decision points to help you to navigate, and
each walk comes with an Ordnance Survey®
map. Simply print them out on A4 paper
and you are ready to go! A modest annual
subscription gives you access to over 1,400
walks, all in this easy-to-follow format. If you
wish, you can purchase individual walks for a
small fee.

Next to every walk in this book you will see
a Walk ID. You can enter this ID number on
Walkingworld's 'Find a Walk' page and you will
be taken straight to the details of that walk.

CONTENTS

Introduction

Britain is a fabulous place to walk. We are blessed with a varied and beautiful landscape, a dense network of public footpaths and places of historical interest at every corner. Add to all this the many thousands of well-placed pubs, tea shops and visitor attractions, and it's easy to see why walking is a treasured pastime for millions of people.

Walking is the perfect way to keep fit and healthy. It is good for your heart, muscles and body generally, without making the extreme demands of many sports. For most walkers, however, the health benefits are secondary. We walk for the sheer pleasure of it – being able to breathe in the fresh air, enjoy the company of our friends and 'get away from it all'.

Equipment

If you take up walking as a hobby, it is quite possible to spend a fortune on specialist outdoor kit. But you really don't need to. Just invest in a few inexpensive basics and you'll be ready to enjoy any of the walks in this book.

For footwear, boots are definitely best as they provide you with ankle support and protection from the inevitable mud, nettles and puddles. A lightweight pair should be fine if you have no intention of venturing up big hills or over rugged terrain. If you are not sure what to get, go to a specialist shop and ask for advice. Above all, choose boots that fit well and are comfortable.

Take clothing to deal with any weather that you may encounter. Allow for the 'wind-chill' factor – if your clothes get wet you will feel this cooling effect even more. Carry a small rucksack with a spare top, a hat and waterproofs, just in case. The key is to be able to easily put on and take off layers of clothing at will and so keep an even, comfortable temperature throughout the day.

It's a good idea to carry some food and drink. Walking is exercise and you need to replace the fluid you lose through perspiration. Take a bottle of soft drink or water, and sip it regularly rather than downing it in one go. The occasional chocolate bar, sandwich or biscuit can work wonders when energy levels are flagging.

Walking poles – the modern version of the walking stick – are worth considering. They help you to balance and allow your arms to take some of the strain when going uphill. They also lessen the impact on your knees on downhill slopes. Don't be fooled into thinking that poles are just for the older walker – they are popular with trekkers and mountaineers of all ages.

Finding your way

Most walkers use Ordnance Survey® maps, rightly considered to be among the most accurate, up-to-date and 'walker–friendly' in the world. The 1:50,000 scale Landranger series has long been a favourite of outdoor enthusiasts. Almost all areas of Britain are also covered by the more detailed 1:25,000 scale Explorer and Explorer OL series. These include features such as field boundaries, farm buildings and small streams.

Having a map and compass – and learning how to use them – is vital to being safe in the countryside. Compass and map skills come with practice – there is no substitute for taking them out and having a go. Buy a compass with a transparent base plate and rotating dial; you will find this type in any outdoor shop. Most come with simple instructions – if not, ask in the shop for a guide.

If this all sounds a bit serious, I urge you not to worry too much about getting lost. We have all done it – some of us more often than we care to admit! You are unlikely to come to much harm unless you are on a featureless hilltop or out in very poor weather. If you want to build up your confidence, start with shorter routes through farmland or along the coastline and allow yourself plenty of time.

Symbol	Feature	Symbol	Feature
	Telephone		Lighthouse
	Start of route		Camping
	Viewpoint		Youth hostel
	Pylon		Bridge
	Triangulation point		Windmill
	Radio mast		Highest point/summit
	Church with Steeple	PH	Public house
	Church without Steeple	PC	Public convenience
	Chapel	1666	Place of historical interest
	Power		Embankment/cutting
	Golf course		Rocky area/sharp drop
	Picnic area		Building
	Car park		Castle
	Information		Tumulus
			Garden

There are plenty of walks in this book that are perfect for the beginner. You can make navigating even easier by downloading the routes in this book from Walkingworld's website: www.walkingworld.com. These detailed walk instructions feature a photograph at each major decision point, to help you confirm your position and see where to go next.

Another alternative is to join a local walking group

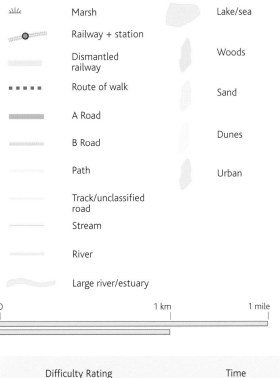

⁓⁓⁓	Marsh		Lake/sea
⊙	Railway + station		Woods
	Dismantled railway		Sand
▪ ▪ ▪ ▪ ▪	Route of walk		
	A Road		Dunes
	B Road		Urban
	Path		
	Track/unclassified road		
	Stream		
	River		
⁓⁓⁓	Large river/estuary		

0   1 km   1 mile

Difficulty Rating		Time
Gentle Stroll	Moderate Walk	Each circle = 1 hour
Easy Walk	Hill Scramble	Half circle = ½ hour

and learn from others. There are hundreds of such groups around the country, with members keen to share their experience and skills.

Enough words. Take the walks in this book as your inspiration. Grab your map and compass, and put on your boots. It's time to go out and walk!

Have fun.

DAVID STEWART *Walkingworld*

Scotland

Coastal & Waterside

Scotland's waterside walks take in wave-beaten crags, silent lochs and roaring waterfalls. Highlights include Dunskey Castle, Grey Mare's Tail, Herma Ness and Flowerdale Falls.

▲ Map: Explorer 309
▲ Distance: 9 km/5¼ miles
▲ Walk ID: 824 Tony Brotherton

Difficulty rating

Time

▲ Hills or Fells, Sea, Pub, Toilets,
Church, Castle, Wildlife, Birds, Flowers,
Great Views, Butterflies, Food Shop

Dunskey Castle from Portpatrick

From the port of Portpatrick this scenic walk heads south over the moorland byroad, passing by the ruin of Dunskey Castle with its dramatic cliff-top setting. The splendid coastal scenery, birds and flowers make this a walk to remember.

1 From the car park pass by the old lighthouse and walk round the harbour as far as Main Street. Turn into Main Street, then into School Brae. Follow the road uphill and across the old railway bridge to the junction with the Old Military Road.

2 Follow this road. It rises clear of Portpatrick and meets a junction. Keeping on the road, turn right across the moors, to reach the old railway viaduct.

3 Continue along this moorland road. At the stone wall, pause to view Dunskey Castle in the distance. The road switchbacks on, past a joining road at North Port O'Spittal, then drops and bends sharply before the turn-off to Knockinaam Lodge Hotel. Turn right down the lane towards the hotel.

4 At the top of the hotel car park, a sign points the way to Portpatrick via a cliff walk. The path climbs to the right. At the top cross two fields, exiting via the gate at the top corner of the second field. The curving path to the left leads down to Morroch Bay.

5 Follow the path along the top of the cliffs, crossing occasional stiles. Look out for abundant birdlife on rocks and cliff-ledges. Dunskey Castle comes into view again and the path descends to a bridge over the burn. Cross the bridge and ascend the steps. The path meanders over the headland to Castle Bay.

6 Follow the path round the top of the bay to Dunskey Castle. The path continues along the cliff top, with the old railway cutting below to the right. Portpatrick Hotel comes into sight. Follow the steps down to Portpatrick harbour. To return to the car park, retrace your steps by the old lighthouse.

A beautiful view of Portpatrick harbour, seen from the cliffs to the north.

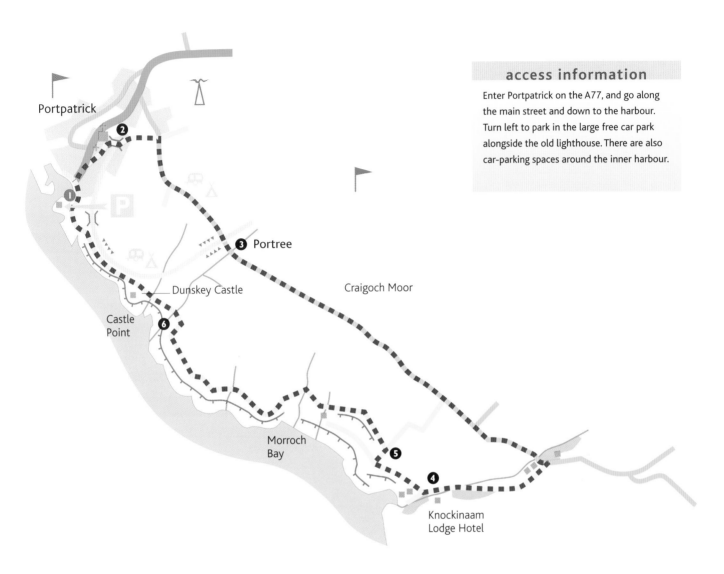

Portpatrick

②

⓪

③ Portree

Dunskey Castle

Castle Point

⑥

Craigoch Moor

Morroch Bay

⑤

④

Knockinaam Lodge Hotel

The ruins of Dunskey Castle stand out as a clear landmark at the top of the cliff.

0   1 km   1 mile

▲ Map: Explorer 330
▲ Distance: 11 km/6¾ miles
▲ Walk ID: 301 Simon Tweedie

Difficulty rating

👣👣👣

Time

●●●●

▲ Hills or Fells, Mountains, River, Lake/Loch, National Trust/NTS, Wildlife, Birds, Flowers, Great Views

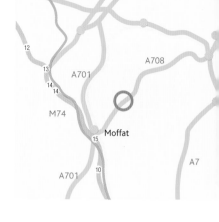

White Coomb from Grey Mare's Tail

This outstanding walk takes you to one of Scotland's highest waterfalls (known as the Grey Mare's Tail), a hidden glen and Loch Skeen. Listen out for the high-pitched call of the peregrine falcons which nest on the craigs.

❶ Leave by the steps on the north side of the car park. The path is steep and rises quickly to reveal spectacular views.

❷ When you reach the top of the falls, the glen above opens out. The path meanders, following the gentle flow of the burn. White Coomb looms high to the left with Lochcraig Head to the north. Continue on upwards until Loch Skeen comes into view to the left of the path.

❸ The route follows the eastern shore of the loch with no discernible path. Leaving the loch behind, the ground rises steeply. Follow a route to the east of the cliffs and up the steep grassy slope to the cairn at the top of Lochcraig Head. Follow the dry-stone dyke left towards White Coomb.

❹ At Firthybrig Head the dyke takes a sharp left to a southerly direction. Follow this through Donald's Cleuch Head to Firthhope Rig. Here the dyke takes a sharp left. Follow the dyke a short way until it bears left. This is the closest landmark to the summit cairn, which lies about 100 paces to the south west.

❺ Return to the dyke from the summit and follow it down the hill until you reach Rough Craigs. Scramble down to the left of the dyke until you pick it up again at the bottom. Follow the dyke over Upper Tarnberry and down to meet the Tail Burn.

❻ The dyke ends on the Tail Burn where you cross. Pick up the Tail Burn path again on the other side and follow it back down to the car park.

A stand of Scots Pine, seen from Moffat Water.

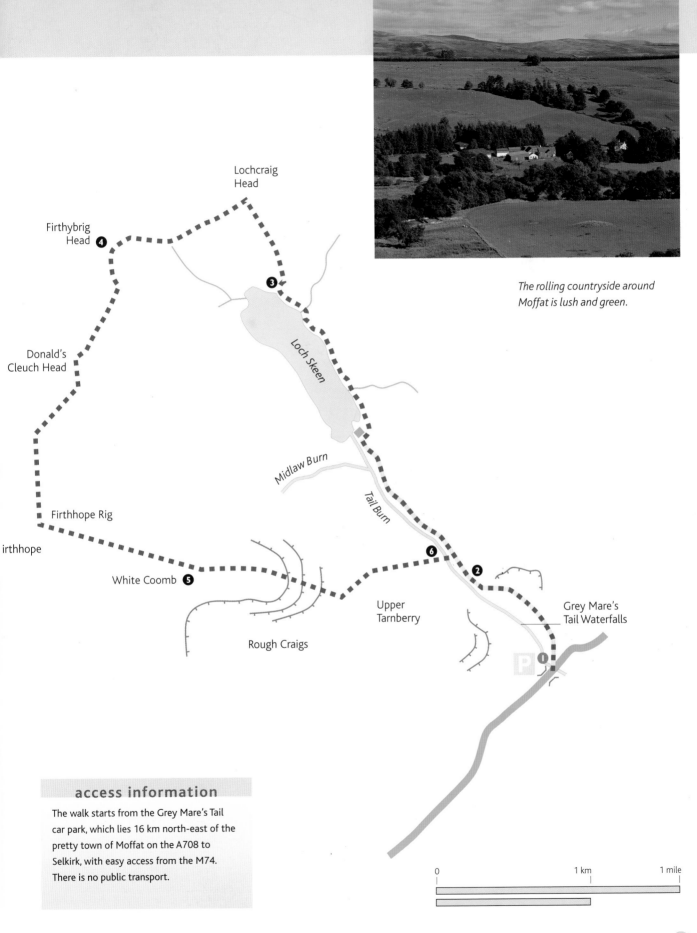

Lochcraig
Head

Firthybrig
Head ④

Donald's
Cleuch Head

Loch Skeen

③

Firthhope Rig

Midlaw Burn

Tail Burn

⑥

②

irthhope

White Coomb ⑤

Upper
Tarnberry

Grey Mare's
Tail Waterfalls

Rough Craigs

P ①

*The rolling countryside around
Moffat is lush and green.*

access information

The walk starts from the Grey Mare's Tail
car park, which lies 16 km north-east of the
pretty town of Moffat on the A708 to
Selkirk, with easy access from the M74.
There is no public transport.

0   1 km   1 mile

▲ Map: Explorer 326
▲ Distance: 6 km/3¾ miles
▲ Walk ID: 799 J. & D. Howat

Difficulty rating

Time

▲ Sea, Pub, Toilets, Museum, Play Area,
Castle, National Trust/NTS Property,
Wildlife, Birds, Flowers, Great Views

Maidens from Croy Bay

A linear coastal walk from Croy Bay through Culzean Country Park to reach Maidens, taking in part of the rugged headland by Culzean Castle. On a good day there are magnificent views towards Arran and the Mull of Kintyre.

1 Leave the top car park and follow the road down to the lower car park at Croy Shore. Turn left onto the beach to reach some small cottages. Continue the walk in woodland parallel to the shore.

2 At the next bay take the path away from the shore, past the Gas House and Gas Keeper's Cottage. Enter Culzean Park and follow the path up through the trees towards the castle.

3 Branch left towards the castle's forecourt. Take the gate to the left of the castle, and follow the path along the side. Descend the steps to the gardens and Fountain Court. Continue south through the gardens, through a gap in the wall, into a grassy field. Cut across the field towards the sea. Follow the steps and go past the cannons to the boathouse beach and Dolphin House.

4 Turn left, and continue carefully south along the rocky coast to the next bay. Take the steps and wooden walkway through a marshy area back to a T-junction on a well-trodden path.

5 Turn right, and follow the path. Turn right again at the 'Cliff Walk' sign. The path eventually turns inland and descends to the Swan Pond. Turn to the right at the side of the pond, and walk a few metres to reach a junction with a smaller path off to the right.

6 Leave the main path for a smaller one signposted to Port Carrick, Barwhin Hill. When you reach the edge of the park, fork left leading down to the beach at Maidens shore. Turn left and continue along the beach to reach the Maidens car park and the Wildings Hotel.

further information

The walk can easily be altered to become a circular walk if this is preferred. Once you reach the Swan Pond in Culzean Country Park, take any of the paths signposted towards the Home Farm, then return along the coast.

Watch out for the rocks and rising tides while you are walking along the shore beyond the castle.

access information

Take the A719 south from Ayr. Soon after Croy Brae take the road to the right to Croy Beach. Park either at the top or bottom of the hill. As this is a linear walk, you will have to retrace your steps unless you have a companion prepared to meet you at the end of the walk. To drive to the finishing car park, continue south on the A719. Turn right at the T-junction (towards Culzean Country Park). Continue past the park entrance to reach Maidens. At a sharp bend in the road to the left, take the small road to the right. Car parking is along this road.

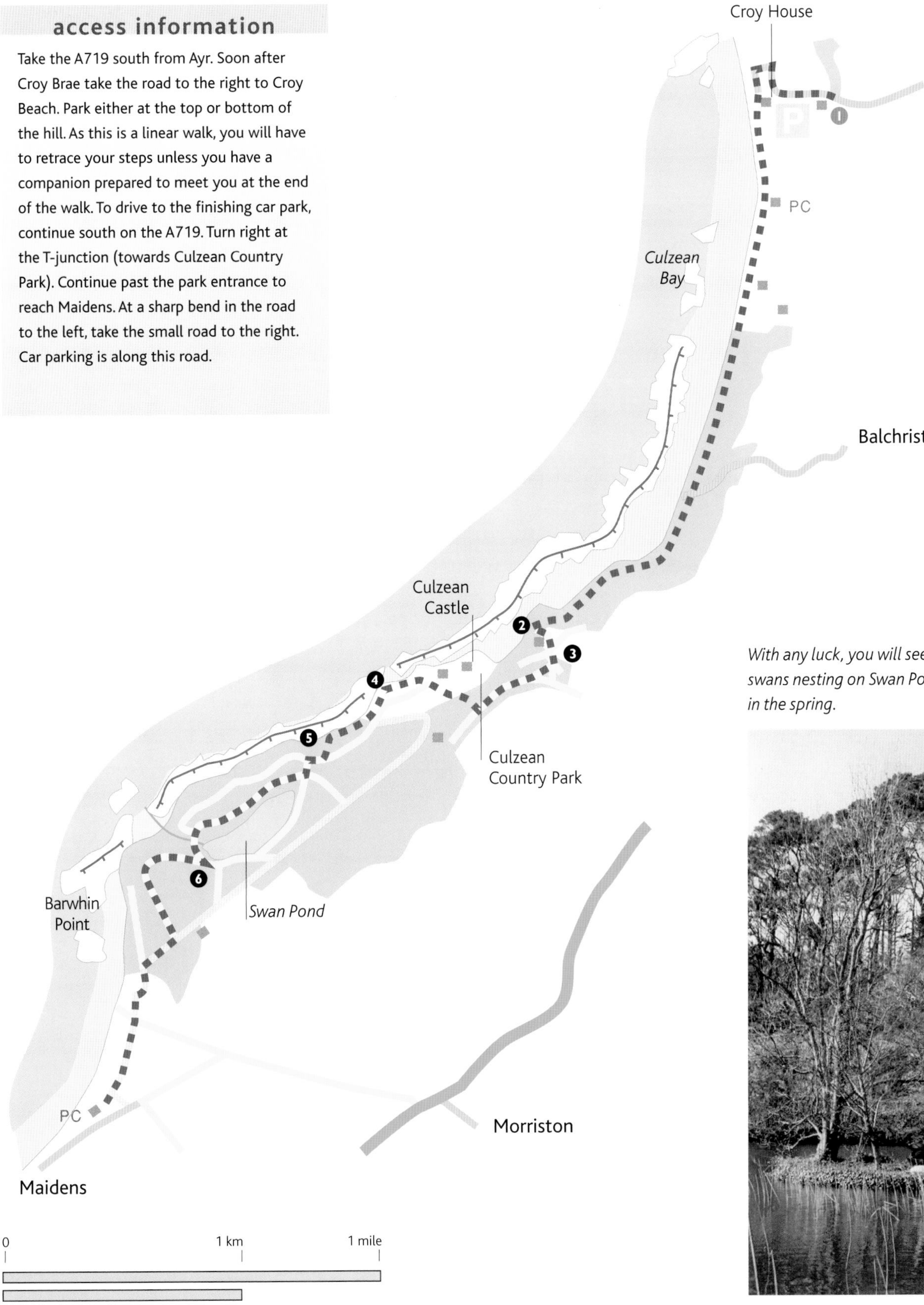

P

PC

Culzean Bay

Balchriston

Culzean Castle

2

3

4

5

Culzean Country Park

With any luck, you will see swans nesting on Swan Pond in the spring.

6

Barwhin Point

Swan Pond

Morriston

PC

Maidens

0   1 km   1 mile

▲ Map: Explorer 463
▲ Distance: 4 km/2½ miles
▲ Walk ID: 1528 C. & J. Simpson

Difficulty rating
👣👣👣

Time
⬤⬤⬤

▲ Sea, Wildlife, Birds, Flowers, Great Views, Moor

Birsay to Marwick

Amazing cliff views.

This linear walk traverses the top of the cliffs of the west coast of Orkney. This coast possibly has the best sea cliffs on Orkney and there are excellent views. Of particular interest are the seabird colonies on the cliffs, which include puffins, guillemots and fulmars.

① Approaching from the B9056, start by following the track that heads straight on between the field gate and a standing stone that forms the corner of a fence. (This is the track heading due west from the corner, not the one heading north.) After 300 m and an open area (sometimes used for parking) the track bends to the left and starts to follow the coast. From the bend in the track there are good views back over the bay to the Brough of Birsay.

② Continue parallel to the cliff edge, now rising gently, along the path which is fairly indistinct at times. As you continue to climb, the cliffs to your side become larger.

③ After about a kilometre of going gently uphill, a path comes in from the left (this is the direct route to the headland from a car park). This path becomes much more distinct, running between a fence and the cliff. There are excellent views back along the cliffs.

④ When you reach the highest point, topped by the Kitchener Memorial, there are superb views south to the island of Hoy. The famous Old Man of Hoy is visible to the right of the cliffs. You can also see beyond to the Scottish mainland.

⑤ A path continues past the memorial to rejoin the fence and then follows the fence to the south west before turning the headland and dropping downhill to the bay of Mar Wick.

⑥ At the foot of the slope the path follows the water's edge to reach the road and the end of the walk.

access information

The route as described starts from the sharp left-hand bend on the B9056, where it overlooks Birsay Bay, and finishes on the shores of Mar Wick – another bay to the south of Marwick Head.

further information

If transport cannot be arranged, an alternative to the end of the walk is to turn back from the memorial and retrace your steps to the gate. Go through the gate and follow a path to a car park from where you can follow the minor road back to your start point. This gives a total distance of 7 km for the walk.

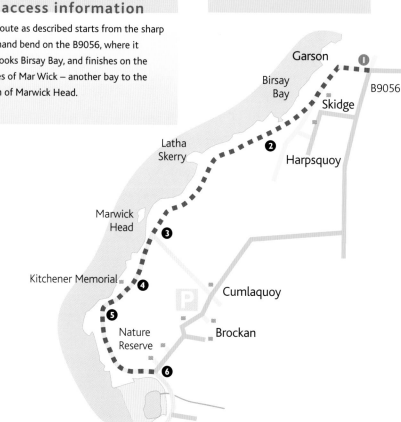

▲ Map: Explorer 326
▲ Distance: 12 km/7½ miles
▲ Walk ID: 759 Jude Howat

Difficulty rating

Time

▲ Sea, Castle, Wildlife, Birds, Flowers, Great Views, Good for Kids, Public Transport

Heads of Ayr from Seafield

A beach walk, to be undertaken at low tide, taking you from central Ayr along the seafront, eventually reaching the magnificent cliffs known as the Heads of Ayr, returning via the old railway line.

1 Follow the promenade along the coast and cross the footbridge at the River Doon. Walk down onto the shore past the ruins of Greenan Castle and on to Deil's Dyke. Continue along the coast, passing a caravan park to walk under the Heads of Ayr. Continue along the shore. The path is just before the waterfalls on the next set of cliffs.

2 Follow the path from the shore up the hill, taking in the glorious views up the Firth of Clyde. At the top of the hill the path widens to a track.

3 Turn left onto the track, into a caravan park. At the first crossroads turn left, then immediately right. Walk the length of the park along the route of the old railway embankment. At the far end of the site exit via a gate. Carry straight on through the next, rusty gate. It may be overgrown, but passable. The route leads between two sets of fields. Climb the fence and continue to reach a rough track off to the right.

4 Turn right onto the rough track to reach the main road. Turn left and walk along the road past the paths leading to Farm Park and the Holiday Village. Exit back towards Ayr. Follow the National Cycle Route sign off to the left.

5 When the road bends sharply right, continue straight ahead through a field back down to the shore.

6 Turn right and walk back towards Greenan Castle, then retrace your steps to the start of the walk.

The ruins of Greenan Castle are perched on the cliff edge.

access information

Free parking is available at the seafront just next to the Seafield roundabout. Ayr is also very well served by both buses and trains – follow signs towards the shore from either station to reach the start of the walk. The walk can be made shorter by parking at Doonfoot and starting at the footbridge over the River Doon.

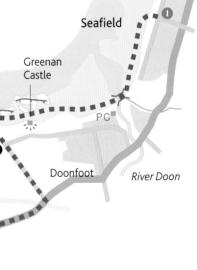

0   1 km   1 mile

Seafield

Greenan Castle

PC

Deil's Dyke

6

5

Heads of Ayr

2

Holiday Village

Doonfoot

River Doon

4

Farm Park

3

Low Glenayes

▲ Map: Explorer 11
▲ Distance: 17 km/10½ miles
▲ Walk ID: 171 Oliver O'Brien

Difficulty rating

👣👣

Time

⬤ ⬤ ⬤ ⬤ ⬤

▲ Hills or Fells, River, Lake/Loch, Pub, Toilets, Great Views, Public Transport

Loch Ard Forest from Aberfoyle

This long but easy walk, entirely on forest roads, tours Loch Ard Forest. The route includes a view of Loch Ard, an impressive Victorian aqueduct and superb views west to Ben Lomond.

1 Turn left out of the Visitor Centre and take the B829 west out of Aberfoyle.

2 At the restored mill, in Milton, turn left off the main road, cross a bridge and follow the road round, bearing right at the green Forest Enterprise signpost. Take the track to the right, past several houses. Cross a couple of gates, and continue along the track beside the loch shore. Bear right at the junction. Eventually Loch Ard opens out on the right. Here, the track meets the loch on the right again. Turn left at the junction and follow the track round to the left, climbing into the forest.

3 At the junction turn sharp right and continue to climb. After 200 m another track on the left joins this track. Bear right and follow the main forest track through the woodlands. Follow the main track, which starts to descend.

4 At the crossroads take a less distinct track to the left which swings back to the right and crosses under the aqueduct. Follow the track round beside electricity pylons, eventually passing another part of the aqueduct. The track passes under again before swinging back out. Continue along the track and follow the line of the aqueduct directly down the hill.

5 Cross Duchray Water on the bridge; there are stiles by both of its gates. Continue up the hill. Turn left and walk along the wide forest road, which crosses the Castle Burn three times.

6 Watch out for paths to your left that offer a pretty detour to Lochan Spling. Otherwise, continue along the main forest track, which eventually turns into a road, passing several houses and a hotel. Turn left and follow the road, crossing over a narrow bridge and back into the centre of Aberfoyle.

access information

Aberfoyle can be reached from Glasgow by travelling north on Maryhill Road and the A81. If you are coming from the east or north, travel to Callander on the A84, then take the A81 west to Aberfoyle. Aberfoyle is one kilometre off the A81, on the A821. There is parking in the square at Aberfoyle, by the Tourist Information Centre. First Edinburgh operates a regular bus service (Nos. 10/11/C11) from Glasgow to/from Stirling via Balfron and Aberfoyle.

further information

Loch Ard Forest is a working forest managed by Forest Enterprise, and some forest tracks may be closed. Be aware that areas which were forested at the time of writing may have been cleared.

The track passes under this impressive section of the Victorian aqueduct running from Loch Katrine to Glasgow.

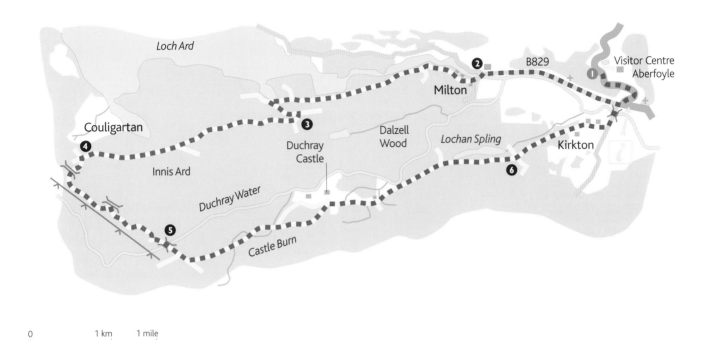

Loch Ard

B829

Visitor Centre
Aberfoyle

①

②

Milton

Couligartan

④

③

Dalzell
Wood

Lochan Spling

Kirkton

Innis Ard

Duchray
Castle

⑥

Duchray Water

Castle Burn

⑤

0   1 km   1 mile

*The outstanding features of this
walk are the beautiful woodland
setting and the waterside views.*

▲ Map: Explorer 470

▲ Distance: 7 km/4¾ miles

▲ Walk ID: 1508 C. & J. Simpson

Difficulty rating

Time

▲ Sea, Birds, Flowers, Great Views, Moor, Nature Trail

Herma Ness

This walk is a superb mix of moorland and coastal walking to the cliffs of Herma Ness with its fine arches and array of offshore sea stacks. The return over Hermaness Hill gives good views over Muckle Flugga and its lighthouse.

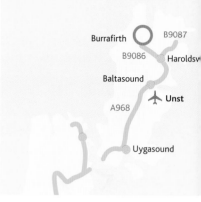

❶ From the car park, pass through the gate, uphill a few metres and through another gate to follow the path which traverses the hillside, rising gently as you go. In time this leads to and then follows the burn of Winnaswarta Dale.

❷ Shortly after you start following the burn you come to a fork and a marker post. Take the left-hand fork. (The return route comes in on the path on the right). There follows a gradually rising section across open moor, with occasional stretches of boardwalk to protect sensitive areas of bog.

❸ At the marker post the view along the cliffs is spectacular, with thousands of seabirds. The route turns right and follows the cliffs, dipping slightly before rising again.

❹ As you start to rise again the views over to the rock arch, the stacks and Muckle Flugga lighthouse open out.

❺ For the return journey, marker posts leading off to the right take you up a well-worn path to the top of Hermaness Hill. The top of the hill has some lochans (small lakes) and more boardwalk sections. There are good views from the top of the hill although, in contrast to the wilderness on this side of the Burra Firth, Saxa Vord, the hill on the other side, is topped by a prominent early warning station. The descent over more boggy ground with numerous lochans is

marked by a series of posts leading back to the junction.

❻ Rejoin the outward route further down the burn. Go back along the path to the car park.

The jagged rocks off the coast of Herma Ness are the northernmost point of Britain, and home to thousands of seabirds.

access information

The island of Unst is reached by two ferries from the Shetland mainland, including a drive over the island of Yell in between. On Unst follow the main road through Baltasound towards Haroldswick. Take the unclassified road on your left as you approach Haroldswick – signposted to Herma Ness and Burrafirth.

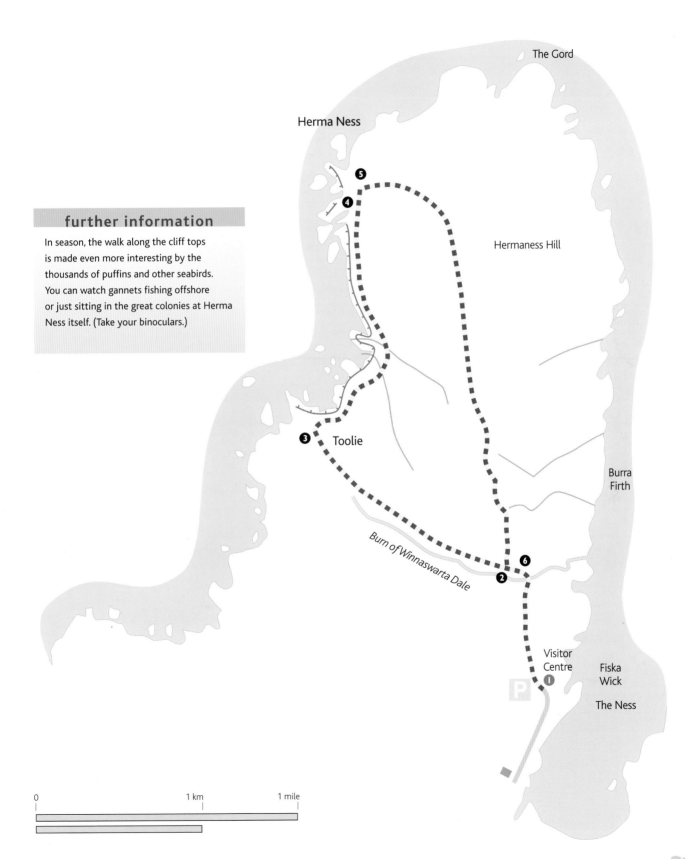

The Gord

Herma Ness

⑤

④

Hermaness Hill

further information

In season, the walk along the cliff tops is made even more interesting by the thousands of puffins and other seabirds. You can watch gannets fishing offshore or just sitting in the great colonies at Herma Ness itself. (Take your binoculars.)

③ Toolie

Burra Firth

Burn of Winnaswarta Dale

② **⑥**

Visitor Centre **①**

Fiska Wick

The Ness

0   1 km   1 mile

▲ Map: Explorer 396

▲ Distance: 7 km/4¾ miles

▲ Walk ID: 864 Ian Cordiner

Difficulty rating

Time

▲ Sea, Pub, Toilets, Museum, Castle, Great Views, Food Shop, Public Transport, Nature Trail, Woodland, Ancient Monument

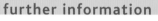

Dunnottar Castle from Stonehaven

A short walk through Stonehaven and on to the ruins of historic Dunnottar Castle, situated on dramatic sea cliffs. The walk returns to the scenic harbour area of the town and finally to the market square via a boardwalk by the seashore.

1 Leave the square in the town centre by going south along Barclay Street. At the end turn right. Cross to the other side of the street then go over the pedestrian bridge. Immediately take the path to the right. Turn right at the road junction, then turn left. Continue to the far corner between the houses to enter the woodland.

2 Follow the route to the right as you pass through the woodland gate. At the steps keep left and follow the sign to Glasslaw gate. Bear left here. You are going to take the route to the right, but first stop to look at Shell House (decorated inside with shells). Follow the track to the right until you come to the road. Cross here and follow the woodland path. At the first Y-junction bear left. Cross the bridge then turn right. Continue past this bridge until you reach a similar one further on.

3 From the next bridge you can view the stone structure of Lady Kennedy's bath. After a short incline turn left and follow the main track to the Glasslaw car park. At the exit keep left. At the main road turn left. Continue to the junction where you turn right to follow a country lane.

4 When you reach the main road at Mains of Dunnottar farm, turn right for a short distance, then left into Dunnottar Castle grounds, which leads to the right of the castle.

5 On the skyline you will see Stonehaven's War Memorial. Where the road narrows, look out for a narrow path leading to the right. Follow this steep path down towards the harbour.

6 Continue along the waterfront around the harbour. Take the road to the left and into a car park. Continue until you turn left at a boardwalk, which leads back to the town square. Cross the main road back to the car park in the square.

further information

From Dunnottar Castle, the route follows a cliff path back to Stonehaven. However, owing to coastal erosion this path may be closed for repairs. Instead, retrace your steps and follow the pavement back to Stonehaven.

access information

Stonehaven, 25 km south of Aberdeen, is served by frequent rail and bus services. It can be reached from the south by the A90 or A92.

A scenic harbour view welcomes the walker at the end of this route.

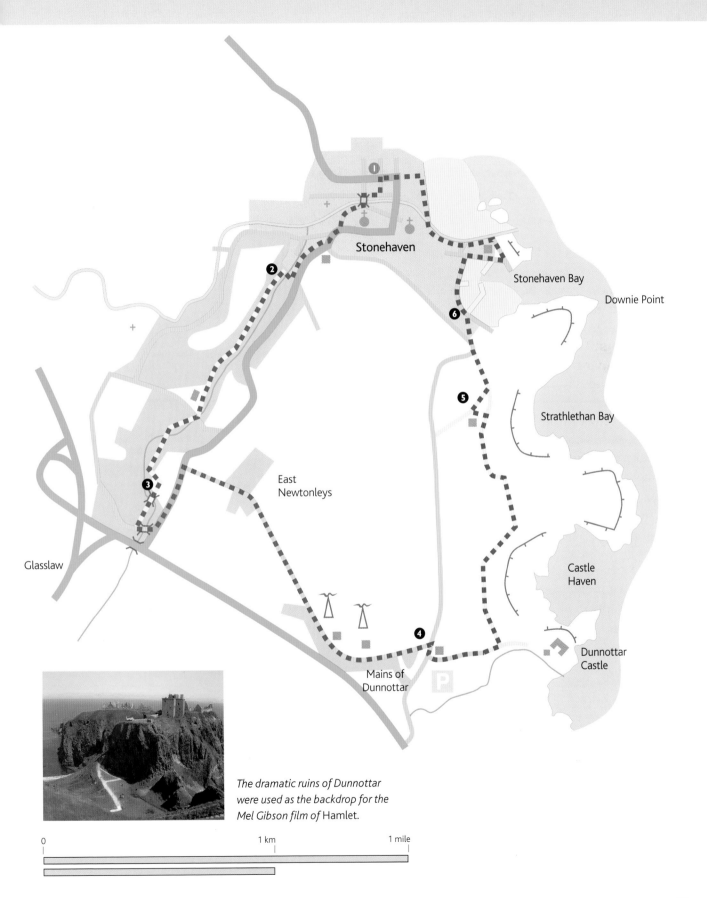

Stonehaven

Stonehaven Bay

Downie Point

Strathlethan Bay

East
Newtonleys

Glasslaw

Castle
Haven

Dunnottar
Castle

Mains of
Dunnottar

The dramatic ruins of Dunnottar
were used as the backdrop for the
Mel Gibson film of Hamlet.

0   1 km   1 mile

▲ Map: Explorer 421
▲ Distance: 12 km/7½ miles
▲ Walk ID: 1536 Ian Cordiner

Difficulty rating

Time

▲ River, Sea, Toilets, Wildlife, Birds, Flowers, Great Views, Food Shop

Collieston from Forvie Sands

This is a coastal walk of great variety. It starts at the estuary of the River Ythan and passes over sand dunes to the seashore. It then follows a coastal cliff path to the old fishing village of Collieston. The return route is more inland over old sand dunes.

1 On leaving the car park turn right and go along the track. Continue straight on, keeping the River Ythan to your right.

2 The path gives way to sand dunes. Follow the boundary markers until you reach the sea, where you turn left.

3 Continue along the sandy shore for about a kilometre. Look out for the grey hut on the left. Cross the stream and head up the sandy track ahead. The main path goes left, but you should turn right here. When you reach the ruins of Forvie Church, follow the path to the right. Bear right at the fork. Go through the gate and turn right.

4 The walk turns left but it is worthwhile taking the route straight ahead down into the old fishing village of Collieston. Continuing onwards takes you past the village shop to the harbour. Return to the walk by retracing your steps and rejoining the path.

5 Take the track to the left. Follow a grassy path to the left. Pass through the gate and follow the marked route to the right. The indicated route is to your left but you take the less well-worn track to the right at the marker post.

6 The path here is rather indistinct. Look out for a large sand dune then turn left. It does not really matter if you miss it, as you will eventually reach the main track again if you head straight on. Turn right at the larger track and follow it out of the nature reserve. Turn right and head back to the car park.

This walk is particularly attractive for the variety of landscapes and colours that you will see.

This walk takes you over sand dunes to the seashore at Forvie Ness.

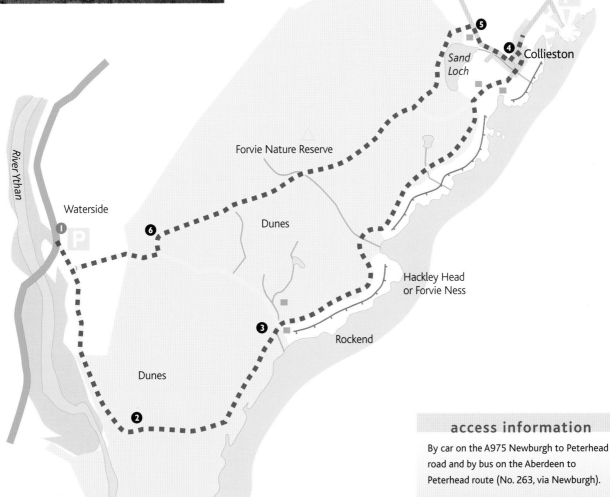

River Ythan

Sand Loch

❺

❹ Collieston

Forvie Nature Reserve

Waterside

❶ P

❻

Dunes

Hackley Head or Forvie Ness

❸

Rockend

Dunes

❷

0   1 km   1 mile

access information

By car on the A975 Newburgh to Peterhead road and by bus on the Aberdeen to Peterhead route (No. 263, via Newburgh).

further information

The sand dunes are rich in bird life. Parts of the sand dunes have restricted access, especially during the breeding season.

▲ Map: Explorer 425

▲ Distance: 11 km/6¾ miles

▲ Walk ID: 904 C. & J. Simpson

Difficulty rating

!

Time

● ● ●

▲ Sea, Pub, Toilets, Wildlife, Birds, Great Views, Food Shop, Mostly Flat, Public Transport, Ancient Monument

Portsoy
Banff
A98
A97
A96
Aberdeen

Sandend from Portsoy

This simple walk follows the coast from the historic harbour at Portsoy to the lovely sandy beach and picturesque village at Sandend, returning by an inland route along paths through farmland.

1 Follow the path away from the north-west corner of Portsoy's picturesque medieval harbour. The path soon goes round to the left past a barn and up the hill above the gate. Keep following the path between the houses and the sea. Soon after you pass the last of the houses, the path goes round a barrier and joins a single-track road. Ignore the turn to the right and follow the road.

2 After a distance of 100 m turn right along the track. There is a small waymark here. Keep following the track past a house until you reach a narrower path off to the right alongside a fence. Follow this for some way around the headland.

3 Beyond the headland start heading inland again towards Sandend beach. The prettiest route drops down a narrow path and behind a ruin to reach the little bay. At the far end of the bay follow the path up over the grass and on towards the beach. You can join the return route to Portsoy from here but it is worth crossing the beach to the lovely village of Sandend first.

4 After retracing your steps along the beach, join the faint path which runs along the back of the beach and across this grassy area to reach a track. Once you join the track, follow it through a strange little gate and on past a house to reach a single-track road. A couple of hundred metres along the road follow the turning left to North Arnbath.

5 Where you see a building take the track off to the right at the bend. Continue along this track.

6 Return to Portsoy along the outward route, which gives you good views of the village.

On the way back along the cliff tops, you get a good view of the beautifully restored buildings nestling in the village of Portsoy.

Portsoy's main attraction is its 300-year-old harbour, which was once a busy trading port during the herring boom in the 19th century.

Portsoy is on the main A98 trunk road between Fochabers and Fraserburgh and is well served by buses that ply the coastal route between Elgin and Banff, so access is easy. To reach the starting point follow the signs to the harbour from the A98. Sandend lies a short distance from the main road but it is still easy enough to reach it to get a bus back to your starting point.

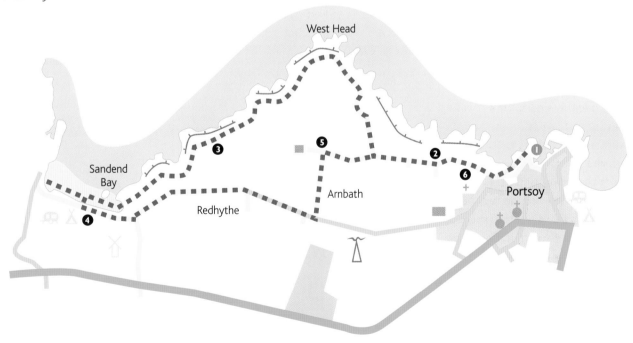

West Head

Sandend
Bay

③

⑤

Arnbath

②

①

⑥

Portsoy

Redhythe

④

0   1 km   1 mile

▲ Map: Explorer 382
▲ Distance: 10 km/6¼ miles
▲ Walk ID: 989 Alex Shepherd

Difficulty rating

Time

▲ River, Sea, Toilets, Museum, Wildlife, Great Views, Café, Food Shop, Nature Trail, Restaurant, Tea Shop

Montrose from Hillside

From Hillside, a good track follows the River North Esk upstream to the Morphie Dam and Salmon Ladder. Tracks and paths lead from here to the coastal sand dunes and back to Montrose.

1 From the centre of Hillside, follow the curve up the hill on the A937 Marykirk–Laurencekirk road. Turn right at cottages before the end of the speed restriction and follow the road to the old Water Station. Cross the lade over the bridge at the Water Station. This track leads to the North Esk. Follow the track upstream – the Morphie Dam and Salmon Ladder will be in view. Return downstream.

2 Take the grassy track which follows the river downstream to Kinnaber Bridge and the A92.

3 Go over the bridge that crosses the lade. Follow the path downstream and under the road bridge until the lade meets the river. Having followed the path past two sets of cottages, cross a stile and continue seaward. The path crosses a small bridge and a small lagoon appears on the left. Take the track to the right or continue to the beach.

4 At the salmon bothies take a diagonal track across to meet the main track. At the point where two plantations meet continue through a section of fencing opened to let walkers through.

5 At the end of the plantation cross the left-hand then right-hand stiles onto a track along the old wartime airfield. Just past the wartime pillbox go through a gate onto the golf course, which is common land, and continue past the Airfield Museum to Montrose.

6 If you have taken the beach route or continued from the golf course and the Links of Montrose, you will reach the facilities at Montrose Beach.

Montrose is famous for its tidal basin, where the mudflats are a wintering site for migrant waders.

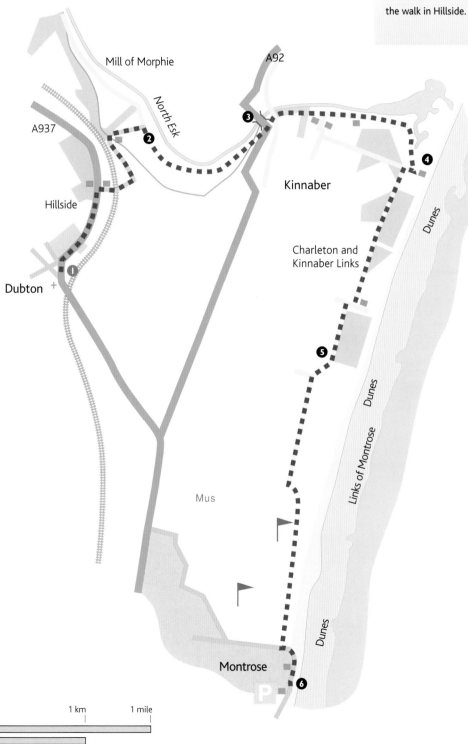

Mill of Morphie

A92

North Esk

A937

Hillside

Dubton

Kinnaber

Charleton and
Kinnaber Links

Dunes

Dunes

Links of Montrose

Dunes

Mus

Dunes

Montrose

0   1 km   1 mile

▲ Map: Explorer 416

▲ Distance: 4 km/2½ miles

▲ Walk ID: 794 D. B. Grant

Difficulty rating

Time

▲ River, Lake/Loch, Pub, Toilets, Birds, Flowers, Great Views, Public Transport, Nature Trail, Waterfall, Woodland

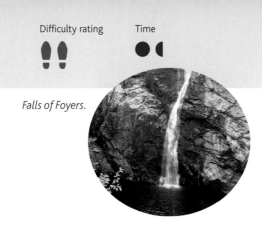

Falls of Foyers.

The Falls of Foyers

This is a short walk to enjoy at Foyers on the south shore of Loch Ness. Foyers is in two parts, Upper and Lower. The falls are best reached from Upper Foyers. The gorge descending into the Foyers River is narrow, wooded and very attractive.

❶ Start at the car park, next to the post office. Cross the road to the gate at the start of the walk.

❷ From the gate follow the signs 'Falls of Foyers', first to the Upper Viewpoint, then down to the Lower Viewpoint. From the Lower Viewpoint retrace your steps, passing the Upper Viewpoint, to a signposted junction.

❸ Take the path signposted 'To Path Network and Lower Foyers'. Keep to the main path, always going downhill. At a clump of rhododendrons there is another signpost.

❹ Take the 'Lower Foyers/Loch Ness' path (blue marker post). Stay on the main path; it eventually ends at a tarred road. If you go on to the lochside, return here. Retracing your steps you come to a wooden bridge over a pipeline.

❺ Cross the bridge and go left, up a few steps, to a junction. Turn left here for a few metres. Cross a wooden bridge and immediately turn right and retrace your steps to the car park.

further information

At Step 4, you can extend the walk by going on into Lower Foyers, on the lochside (this is one of the best areas for spotting the famous Loch Ness Monster!).

access information

Approach Foyers on the B852 from Inverness. Take the Upper Foyers road 1.5 km before Foyers. Park at the small car park next to the post office, on the main road. There is a limited bus service from Inverness to Foyers.

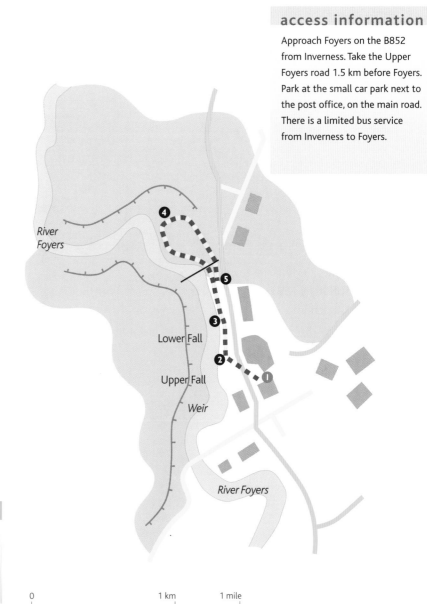

Difficulty rating

Time

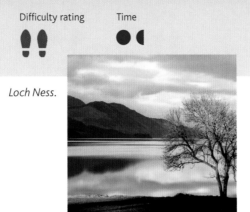

Loch Ness.

Aldourie from Dores

A short circular walk at the northern end of Loch Ness which goes partly along the loch shore and partly along a ridge. You can see Loch Ness from one end to the other.

❶ Cross the B862 at the Dores Inn and go through the gate. Beyond the green shed there is a narrow path leading to the children's playpark. Follow this lochside path, passing many viewpoints. Continue to reach the entry to a wood.

❷ From the wood go down to the beach, where there is a good path, and follow it for 400 m, passing Tor Point, to a turn off on your right. This path goes to a higher level and follows the loch for a while before joining the main forestry track.

❸ On the main track go left, to arrive at the pier and anchorage. At the pier take the path leading off right. Follow this path uphill to a T-junction.

❹ Turn right and continue to a fork. At the fork go left. The track follows a fence for a while, to a viewpoint. Continue, to a grassy fork.

❺ Take the left fork here, downhill. Here you will find a good view to Dores.

❻ After about 200 m there is a mini-crossroads. Go left, downhill, and head back to the car park at Dores.

access information

Dores lies 13 km south-west of Inverness, on the junction of the B862 and the B852. Park opposite the Dores Inn. If you wish to use public transport, there is a bus service from Inverness.

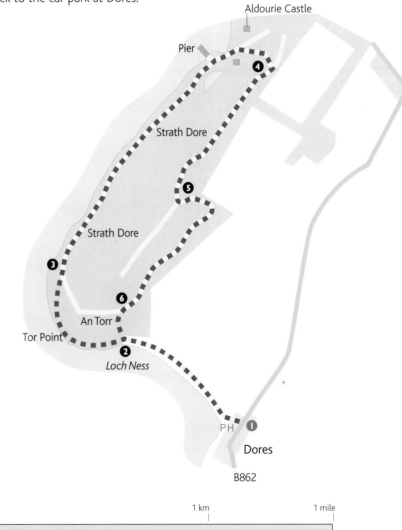

▲ Map: Explorer 433
▲ Distance: 6 km/3¾ miles
▲ Walk ID: 827 D. B. Grant

Difficulty rating

Time

● ● ◖

▲ Hills or Fells, River, Sea, Pub, Stately Home, Wildlife, Birds, Flowers, Great Views, Butterflies, Food Shop, Good for Kids, Moor, Waterfall

Flowerdale Falls from Gairloch

This pleasant family walk goes from sea level at Gairloch to 150 m at the falls. The walk can be made shorter by returning the same way, but the alternative return route offers splendid views of hills and sea.

❶ From the car park take the gravel path leading upstream. It soon joins a road to Flowerdale House. After passing the house there is a T-junction.

❷ At the T-junction turn right. Go straight on to reach Flowerdale Mains (trekking centre). Here go through the gate and continue on this path to a three-way junction. Keep straight on, following the red posts, to reach the falls. At the falls cross the bridge and take the narrow path up the side of the falls. At the top go on for 200 m to another wooden bridge.

❸ Cross the bridge and follow the path downhill to a junction. If you want to go back to the car park quickly go right, and return by the outward route; to continue on this walk turn left, uphill, for a kilometre to a wooden bridge.

❹ Cross the bridge and follow the narrow but delightful path for a short way, well marked with blue posts. When you reach the lowest point on the path, cross the little burn at the blue post and go left for 20 m.

❺ Here you will see two blue markers on your right, marking a faint track going uphill to a viewpoint. You may either go up to the viewpoint or carry on along the lower path; the two paths soon meet again. Continue on this path to a T-junction with a main path.

❻ At the junction turn right and go through the double wooden gates. Shortly, you arrive at a DIY store. Pass it and immediately go right. You should now be at the Old Inn, by the car park.

Gairloch is one of the most glorious and unspoilt wilderness regions in the whole of Britain.

access information

Charlestown (Gairloch) is on the A832. The car park is opposite the pier at the mouth of the river, conveniently by The Old Inn.

further information

Flowerdale is a glen sheltered from most winds. It has a microclimate of its own, supporting plants such as bog orchids, bog asphodels, butterwort and sundew. Animals and birds such as voles, pine martens, stoats, weasels and buzzards can also be seen.

This bridge above Flowerdale Falls is as far as you go as you follow the footpath upstream.

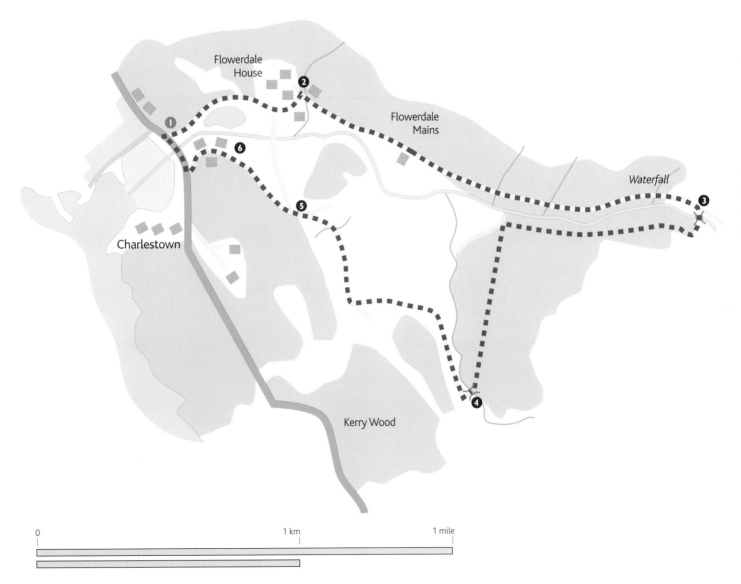

▲ Map: Explorer 434

▲ Distance: 7 km/4¼ miles

▲ Walk ID: 1261 C. & J. Simpson

Difficulty rating

Time

▲ Sea, Birds, Great Views, Café, Moor, Tea Shop

Camas Mór from Rubha Reidh

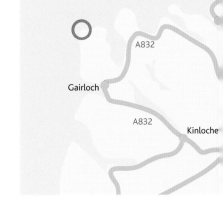

A wonderful coastal walk from the lighthouse at Rubha Reidh to the sandy beach of Camas Mór. Although the distance is short, the route can be steep in places.

1 The road drops quite steeply down to the lighthouse and round a hairpin bend to a parking area. The walk starts on the hairpin bend itself and goes through a 'gap' in the rocks. Follow the track until it starts to drop down towards a little jetty. Branch off right to cross the stream and head east, keeping parallel to the coast.

2 Follow the traces of path along the cliff until around the point where you get a view of the sea stack, then head uphill, still more or less following the line of the coast.

3 Keep following the coast and any path you can find to drop down to cross the stream before climbing back up the far side to reach the highest point of the route.

4 Coming down you start to get good views of the beach at Camas Mór.

5 To return to Rubha Reidh via the beach go down the long descending path. Go to the far (western) side where a rocky prow juts out towards the sea. Depending on the state of the tide you can go out round it on rocks and a boulder beach or through a little arch. On the other side is another bay.

6 At the back of this bay are steep cliffs. A path winds up below the cliffs to join the grassier slopes beyond – there are a couple of fairly steep and narrow sections before you reach the main stream that you crossed on the outward route. Follow the stream easily uphill for 200 m or so and you pick up the path, which is followed back to the starting point.

access information

The starting point is reached by following the B8021 north-west from Gairloch through Strath and Big Sand. The public road stops some way short of the lighthouse, but access is available to traffic visiting the lighthouse.

IMPORTANT: The route from steps 5 to 6 can only be followed when the tide is low.

From the top of the cliffs you get stunning views over the sandy bay at Camas Mór.

There's plenty of grand scenery to be enjoyed on this walk along the rocky headland of Rubha Reidh.

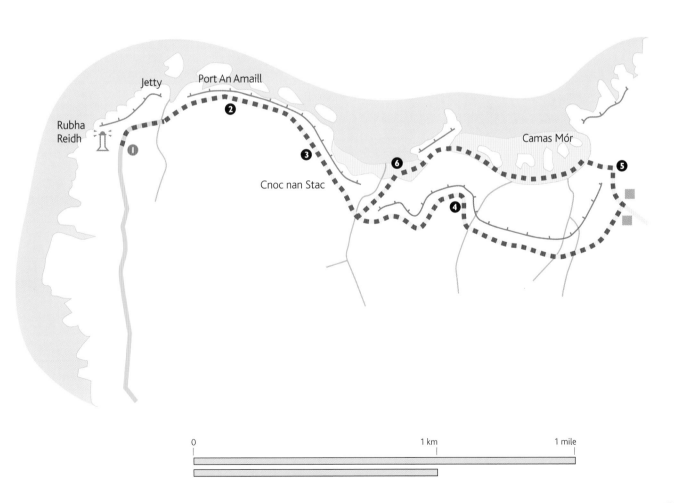

Woodland & Hillside

Scotland's woodland and hillside footpaths reveal soaring highlands, sweeping glens and forests, and ancient monuments. Highlights include Arthur's Seat, Edin's Hall Broch and Abernethy Forest.

▲ Map: Explorer 350
▲ Distance: 7 km/4¾ miles
▲ Walk ID: 892 Oliver O'Brien

Difficulty rating

Time

▲ Hills or Fells, River, Pub, Toilets, Stately Home, Wildlife, Great Views, Café, Gift Shop, Moor, Public Transport, Tea Shop, Woodland, Ancient Monument

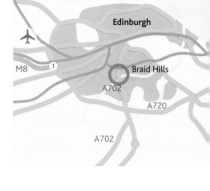

Braid Hills

From the pretty Hermitage of Braid, the route climbs, encircles a golf course and heads up to the highest summit of the Braid Hills. It finishes with a short and pleasant road section through Morningside.

1 From the top entrance to the Hermitage of Braid follow the road down past the Hermitage, keeping the stream on your left.

2 The route then takes a large, well-defined path to the right. Follow this path down through woodland. The path crosses over the stream three times as it meanders, and the sides of the valley become increasingly steep. Cross under the low footbridge and continue along the path.

3 You come to a clearing on the left and a prominent cliff face known as the Agassiz Rock. Shortly afterwards there is an obvious path junction. Turn right onto the 'Howe Dean Path'. The path crosses over the stream and climbs steeply up through the dean to the edge of the field. Continue along the route by bearing left, and upwards, to a large road.

4 Cross the busy main road, pass through the iron gate and turn left, to follow a path close to (but not on) the road. Continue, gradually descending, towards the golf course.

5 At the entrance to the golf course, turn sharp right and follow the large red track. Follow the track around to the right and continue along it, gradually climbing up to the top of the Braid Hills and the summit, at 208 m.

6 To descend, continue westwards, rejoining the red track. It quickly narrows into a path and becomes very steep. Take the left fork and continue down the hill until the path joins the main road. Turn sharp right and walk down the hill, beside the road. Continue straight ahead at a wide road junction. Continue along this road, passing by Morningside, back to the start.

Historic Edinburgh is laid out before you, with its famous castle towering over the city.

further information

Braid Hills is the name of one of Edinburgh's 'Seven Hills'. The other six can be seen on this walk. Directly north is Edinburgh Castle and the city centre, and directly south are the Pentland Hills.

access information

There is very limited parking on the road at the walk's starting point. Take care not to obstruct the entrance to the Hermitage. If there is no space, continue south uphill and park in the residential area or at the Braid Hills Hotel. Access by bus from the centre of Edinburgh is reasonably easy – catch any bus to Morningside, or No. 11, which passes the start of the walk.

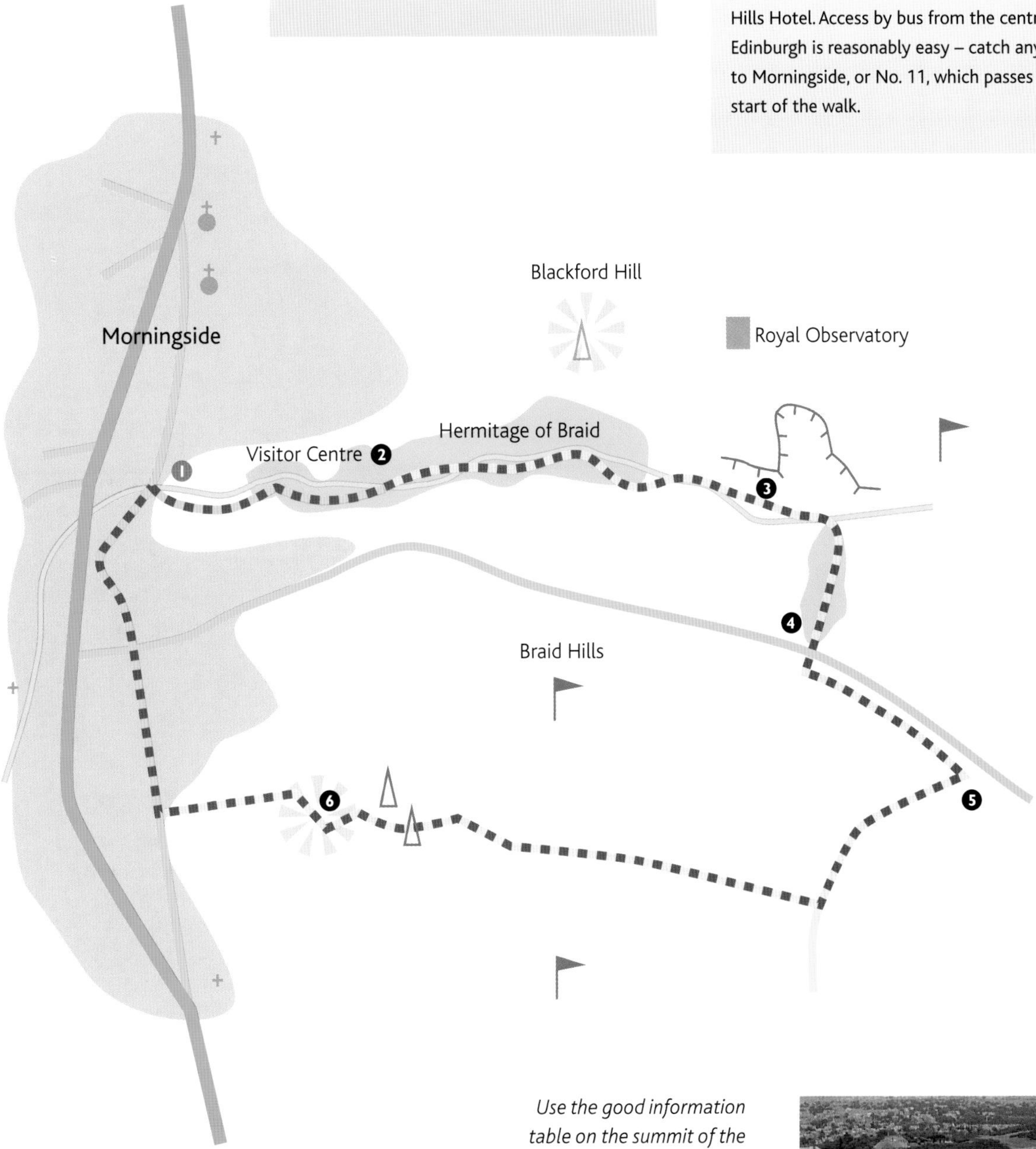

Blackford Hill

Royal Observatory

Morningside

Hermitage of Braid

Visitor Centre ❷

❸

Braid Hills

❹

❻

❺

Use the good information table on the summit of the Braid Hills to identify any landmarks you can see.

0   1 km   1 mile

▲ Map: Explorer 350
▲ Distance: 6 km/3¾ miles
▲ Walk ID: 110 Oliver O'Brien

Difficulty rating

Time

▲ Hills or Fells, Lake/Loch, Toilets, Church, Stately Home, Great Views

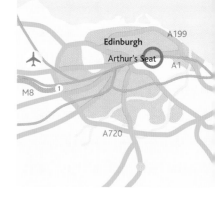

Arthur's Seat in Holyrood Park

A tour of the small but picturesque royal estate of Holyrood Park, in the heart of Edinburgh, climbing one of the city's Seven Hills – Arthur's Seat.

1 From the west (city centre) end of the car park, cross the road and climb a small flight of stairs. Turn right, and climb steeply on a good path with the crags (Salisbury Crags) on your left and dramatic views quickly opening up on your right. Follow the path to the end of the crags.

2 Before you get to the road, turn left and follow a smaller path, rising up slightly and over a brow. Take any of several paths down the broad, flat valley, going to the left of the water/marsh at the centre. Turn left and pass to the right of some small crags, then climb steeply but briefly uphill on a small path, aiming just to the right of the chapel remains.

3 Walk left to visit the chapel. Then turn back and follow a good path first back the way you came, walking straight ahead. Continue along the path into a smaller valley, parallel to the previous one. Follow the path up the right-hand side. The summit of Arthur's Seat is straight ahead. Continue up the path, climbing more steeply. The path peters out as it joins the main 'tourist' route up to Arthur's Seat. Turn right and follow it up.

4 On a fine day the views from the summit are magnificent. Turn back and head back down the tourist route, on a stepped path. Carry on straight down the tourist route, which becomes wide and grassy. Head down to Dunsapie Loch. Turn left and walk alongside the loch or follow a path around the left-hand side of the small hill.

5 Meet the path beside the road. Carry on down beside the road, to the bottom.

6 Take a small path to the left just after the set of barrier gates on the road. Follow this path around the left-hand side of the loch. Come back onto the road and walk back to the start.

Arthur's Seat is an extinct volcano in the heart of Edinburgh from where you have superb views of the city.

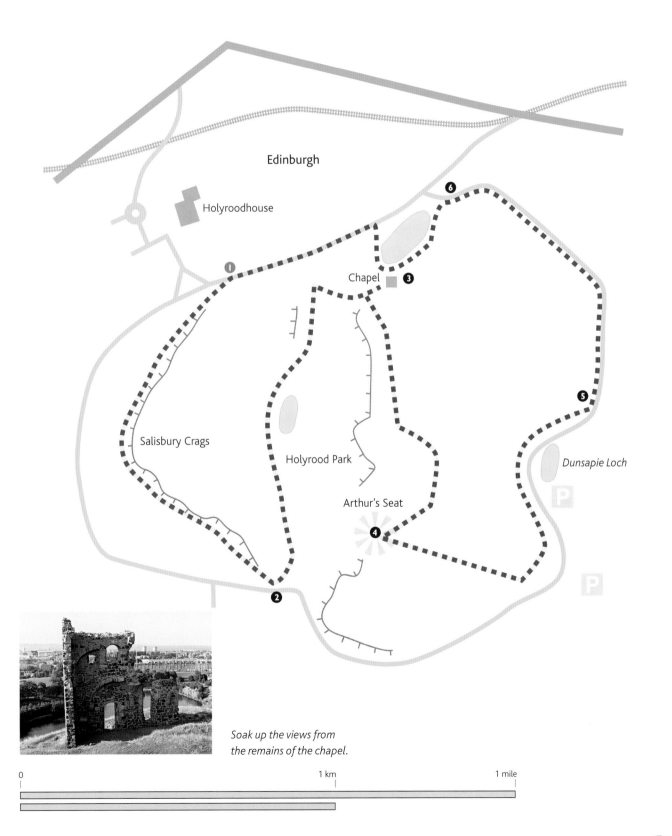

Edinburgh

Holyroodhouse

Chapel

Salisbury Crags

Holyrood Park

Arthur's Seat

Dunsapie Loch

*Soak up the views from
the remains of the chapel.*

0   1 km   1 mile

▲ Map: Explorer 344

▲ Distance: 11 km/6¾ miles

▲ Walk ID: 10 John Stewart

Difficulty rating

Time

▲ Hills or Fells, Lake/Loch, Pub, Toilets, Great Views

The Pentland Hills

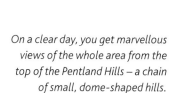

This walk lies in the heart of the peaceful Pentland Hills, just a few kilometres south of the hustle and bustle of Edinburgh.

❶ Take the path leading down the left-hand side of the Visitor Centre and follow it through the trees until it merges with the road.

❷ Continue along the road, skirting the reservoir and stream on the left. After passing a house with an adjacent white-posted gate, a second reservoir can be seen. At the far end of the second reservoir, make for a white house and cross the stream by the wooden bridge. Turn right onto a path in front of the house, entering a small field beyond.

❸ Walk towards the far left corner of the field and cross a stile adjacent to a wooden gate onto a well-defined track. Follow the steepish path upwards across several stiles, making for the saddle in the ridge just beyond. The path flattens out onto a broad ridge and soon crosses a well-defined ridgeway track.

❹ Turn left onto this track towards higher ground. Follow the track, which is fairly steep in parts, until you reach a large stone cairn surrounded by a stonefield. This is the highest point of the walk.

❺ Continue on the track running slowly downwards from the cairn until you reach a new ridgeway saddle. Cross the stile and continue on the path towards the top of the hill straight ahead, where there is a small stone cairn. From here, you can see most of the path leading all the way back down to the start of the walk.

❻ Follow the path down from the cairn through grassy slopes. Carry on towards the start of the walk among the trees beyond. The track finally descends to the stream on the left. Cross the wooden bridge onto the road and turn right to reach the Visitor Centre and the car park.

On a clear day, you get marvellous views of the whole area from the top of the Pentland Hills – a chain of small, dome-shaped hills.

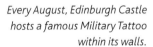

access information

The start of the walk is most easily reached by car. Take the main Edinburgh/Carlisle A702(T) road south out of the city to reach the Flotterstone Inn, which lies on the right side of the road about 5 km south of where the A702(T) crosses the Edinburgh by-pass (A720). Parking is available among the trees beyond the Inn and adjacent to the Visitor Centre.

Every August, Edinburgh Castle hosts a famous Military Tattoo within its walls.

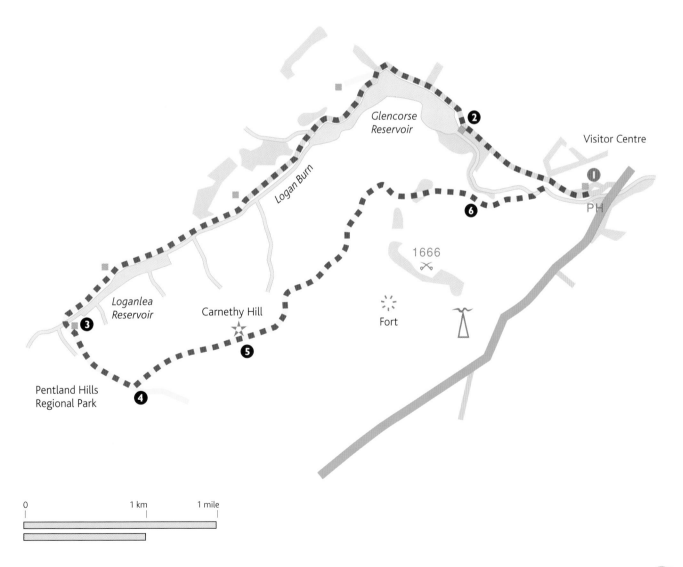

▲ Map: Explorer OL 32
▲ Distance: 11 km/6¾ miles
▲ Walk ID: 1463 Tony Brotherton

Difficulty rating

Time

▲ Hills or Fells, River, Toilets, Wildlife, Birds, Flowers, Great Views, Butterflies, Food Shop

Stroan Bridge Forest Trail

This route brings together various forest trails that start from the Visitor Centre at Stroan Bridge. It offers first-time visitors a sample of the superb upland scenery on offer without scaling the heights or plumbing the depths.

1 Take the path signposted 'Forest Walks', which goes gently uphill. Cross a forest track to reach a multicolour-ringed directional post. Follow the path, which goes right, alongside a stone wall. Continue as far as the forest track.

2 Follow the road left, eventually passing a yellow-ringed post, and arrive at a footbridge below Spout Head Waterfall. Continue along the path which runs pleasantly downhill to the road.

3 Cross the road, going left, and take the access road off to the right for Caldons campsite. Cross the bridge over the Water of Trool and go right, through the car park. Take the yellow trail off to the left, which is also part of the Southern Upland Way (denoted by a white thistle logo), soon to pass a signpost for Stroan Bridge.

4 The route follows the Water of Trool downstream, with duckboards in places, to reach footbridges. To return directly to the start, cross the footbridge and follow the path to the left, soon to accompany the Water of Minnoch upstream to Stroan Bridge. To complete the full walk, continue past the footbridges to reach the confluence of the Water of Trool and the Water of Minnoch. The walk proceeds alongside the riverbank to a stile and footbridge.

5 Continue on the riverside path as far as the bridge. Cross the river and go straight ahead on the track to reach the road at the sign reading 'Holm'.

6 Now turn right along the forest road leading back to Stroan Bridge and the start of the walk.

Spout Head Waterfall is one of the grander water features along your path through Galloway Forest Park.

access information

Turn off the A714 at Bargrennan, pass through Glentrool Village and then turn right (signposted 'Glen Trool'). Cross Stroan Bridge and park at the large car park near the Glen Trool Visitor Centre, where the walk starts.

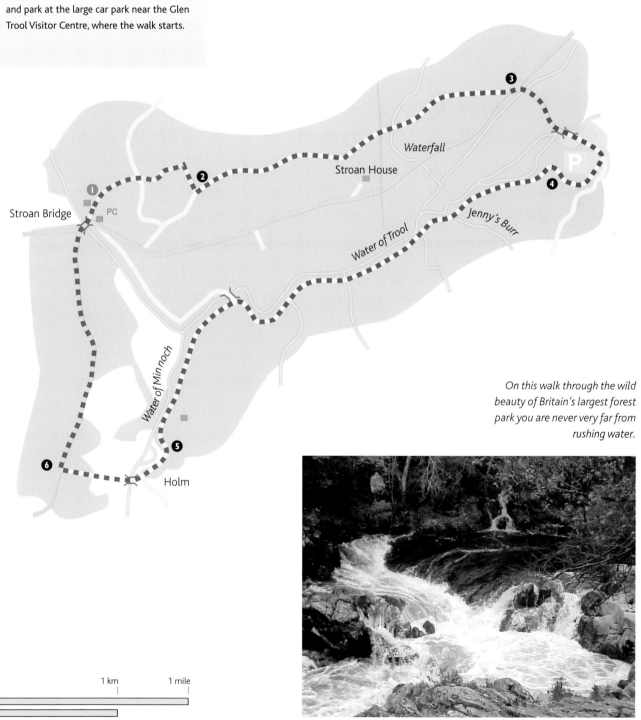

Waterfall

Stroan House

Stroan Bridge

PC

Water of Trool

Jenny's Burr

Water of Minnoch

Holm

On this walk through the wild beauty of Britain's largest forest park you are never very far from rushing water.

0   1 km   1 mile

▲ Map: Explorer 346

▲ Distance: 10 km/6¼ miles

▲ Walk ID: 121 Oliver O'Brien

Difficulty rating

Time

▲ Hills or Fells, River, Toilets, Church, Stately Home, Wildlife, Flowers, Great Views

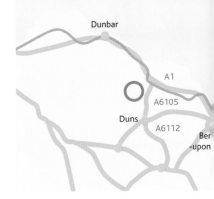

Edin's Hall Broch from Abbey St Bathans

This scenic circular walk starts and finishes at Abbey St Bathans, an historic estate village. Along the route there is a medieval broch, two suspension bridges, profuse oak woodlands, and a moorland, all in a 10 km walk!

You cross Whiteadder Water a couple of times on spectacular suspension bridges.

❶ Follow the road south-east through the village. Continue, bearing right and climbing. Take the small path that starts here to the left of the road and runs for a short way through woodland, before rejoining the road.

❷ The road turns sharp right. Take the path left dropping steeply to a stream. Cross the bridge and follow the path, gradually climbing. Turn left and go down beside a field. At the end of the field, turn right, and follow the path up, climbing steeply.

❸ Pass Edin's Hall Broch (the well-preserved medieval fort) to its right, then bear left slightly to pick up a well-defined path going steeply down the hill, through a gate. After crossing a wall with stone steps turn sharp left. Turn right at the bottom of the field, staying on top of a ridge above the river's flat flood plain. Follow it round to the right. At a small junction bear left into a thicket.

❹ Cross the gate and follow the path to the left passing some cottages on your right. Cross the suspension bridge above Whiteadder Water. Follow the track on the other side, through open land and then through a forest, passing two signposts. Turn left onto a very quiet country road, and follow it uphill.

❺ At the junction turn left, cross over a stile and follow a track beside a field, crossing two gates and gradually dropping down into a valley. At a signpost join the Southern Upland Way. Turn left and follow the track. Cross the gate and continue on the track.

❻ At Whiteadder Water turn sharp right (signposted) and follow a small path with the river on your left. Turn left off the path and cross a large and very long suspension bridge and back to the start.

access information

From the north take the A1 to Cockburnspath, then follow unclassified roads south and uphill, signposted to Abbey St Bathans. From the south take the A1 to Grantshouse, turn off left (S) on to the A6112 for 10 km to Reston, turn right (W) on to the B6355 for 4 km, then right (N) onto an unclassified road signposted to Abbey St Bathans. There is no regular public service to Abbey St Bathans — the nearest access by bus is at Grantshouse on the A1 – 6 km north of the halfway point of this walk. Start by the village church, opposite a red phone box.

further information

Much of the walk is signposted by small yellow arrows (for the first part) or Long Distance Path markers (for the last section).

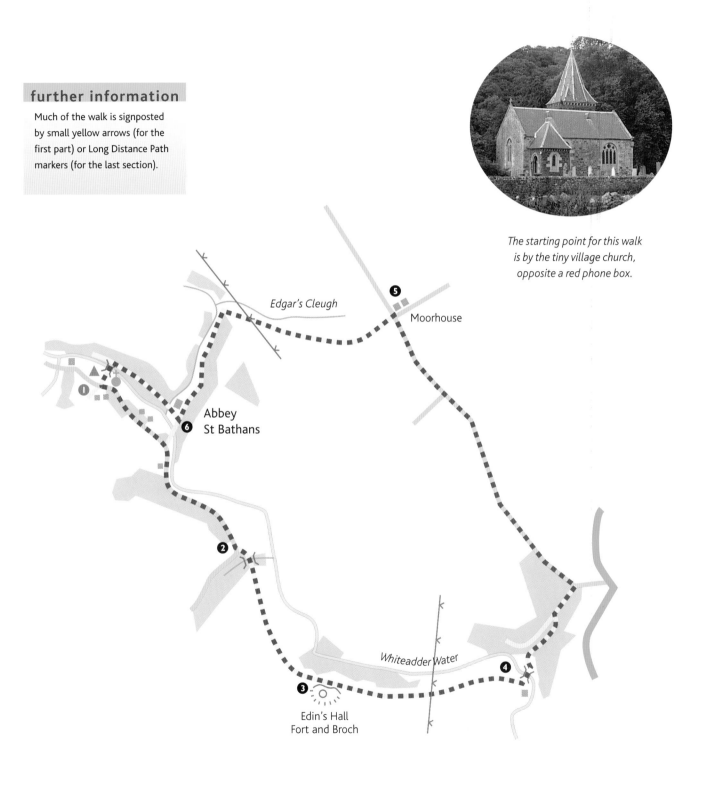

The starting point for this walk is by the tiny village church, opposite a red phone box.

Edgar's Cleugh

5 Moorhouse

1

6 Abbey St Bathans

2

Whiteadder Water

4

3 Edin's Hall Fort and Broch

| 0 | | 1 km | | 1 mile |

▲ Map: Explorer 326
▲ Distance: 5 km/3 miles
▲ Walk ID: 1201 Jude Howat

Difficulty rating

Time

▲ River, Wildlife, Birds, Flowers,
Great Views, Butterflies

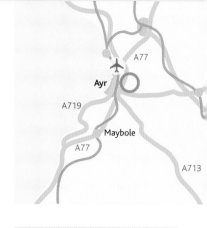

Wallace's Seat from Oswald's Bridge

The first part of this very pleasant walk follows the river through trees. At the turning point there is a seat by the river to enjoy the view (supposedly where William Wallace sat and contemplated his fight with the English).

1 Turn left to cross the bridge over the river. Turn immediately left at the post with the green robin sign and descend the stairs to the riverbank. The path is clear and takes you through some trees.

2 A steep climb leads to the top of Three Knights Field to a viewpoint. At this point admire the view – on a clear day you can see as far as the Isle of Arran. Continue to follow the green robin waymarks.

3 The green robin route crosses the stile here but this walk continues to the left, this time following red robin signposts which follow the path through Pheasant Nook Wood. Continue through Craighall Wood until high above the river where Wallace's seat can be seen.

4 There are steps down to the seat to enjoy the view. When you leave the river, care should be taken to double back. The path continues along the river but as you walk away from the river you should see a narrow path which turns back in the direction you have come by. Stay close to the fence until you meet the obvious cart track on the left.

5 Turn to the left out of the woods and walk along the broader cart track between fields and enjoy the pastoral views over Louden Law.

6 Climb over the stile, turn right and you are back to the start. If you wish you can enter Leglen Wood opposite and visit the monument to William Wallace.

River Ayr.

access information

Leave the A77 at the Heathfield roundabout, on the Ayr bypass, to take the B743 towards Auchencruive. After a kilometre take the minor road to the right labelled SAC Auchencruive, Leglen Wood. Just before Oswald's Bridge take the road to the left and park. If this car park is busy there is further parking closer to Oswald Hall.

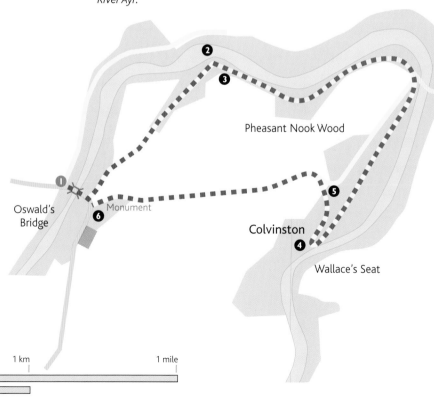

0   1 km   1 mile

▲ Map: Explorer 326
▲ Distance: 4 km/2½ miles
▲ Walk ID: 902 J. & D. Howat

Difficulty rating   Time

· River, Pub, Toilets, Play Area, Church,
Wildlife, Birds, Flowers, Great Views,
Butterflies, Food Shop

Lambdoughty Glen from Straiton

This walk goes along a country road followed by a picturesque scramble up one side of a fast-flowing burn and back on the other side, with wonderful views of waterfalls before returning to the picturesque village of Straiton.

1 At the start of the walk follow the green arrows. Go straight on to the path at the end of the road and follow it until you reach the burn. Cross by the bridge. Turn to the left onto the road. The road goes uphill for about half a kilometre, passing Largs Farm.

2 Turn to the left at the end of the trees to enter Lambdoughty Glen. A green arrow shows the way. The path to the left is easy to follow with steps cut in the earth, held in place by boards, and a bridge to cross the burn.

3 At the bridge you recross the burn and see the largest fall of all (known as the Rossetti Linn because the painter Dante Gabriel Rossetti was thought to have contemplated suicide here). Continue on the high path, now fairly level.

4 Turn right onto the road again as you leave the wood and walk back as far as the wooden bridge, to Straiton. Turn right at the T-junction. Continue past the church and back to the car park or parking place.

access information

From the A77 south of Ayr take the B7045 to Kirkmichael and on to Straiton. Park on the right or in the car park.

The grandest fall on your route is known as the Rossetti Linn, after the Pre-Raphaelite painter Dante Gabriel Rossetti, who is believed to have contemplated suicide at this point.

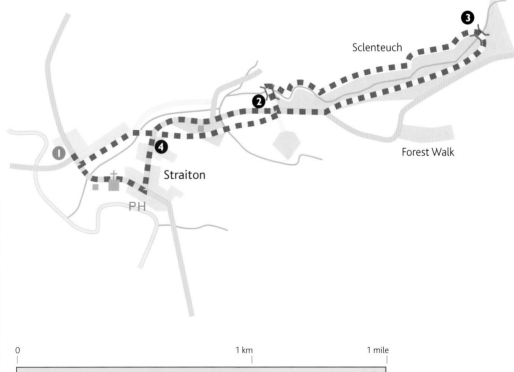

0   1 km   1 mile

▲ Map: Explorer 406
▲ Distance: 11 km/6¾ miles
▲ Walk ID: 585 Ian Cordiner

Difficulty rating

Time

▲ River, Toilets, Great Views, Food
Shop, Public Transport, Tea Shop

Peterculter from Aberdeen

A linear walk along the route of the old Deeside railway line, from Duthie Park to Peterculter (locally Culter). Although never very far from a main road, it is a very tranquil walk which also has some picturesque views over open countryside.

1 From the car park take the direction shown on the green sign, then turn left at the gap in the wall. Continue straight along the route of the old railway track.

2 A bridge has been removed, so you have to go down some steps and rejoin the route at the other side of a street. Where the same problem occurs further on, turn right at the steps, cross the busy main road, and rejoin the old railway route by climbing the steps. Continue along this path, which is well provided with seats to allow you to stop and admire the views.

3 Where yet another bridge has been removed, keep to the path which rises to the right. Admire the views to the south over a golf course. After passing the old platform, there are steps just beyond the next bridge. These will allow you to exit the walk here, should you wish. Turning right leads north to the A93 where it would be possible to catch a bus back into Aberdeen.

4 Continue across the main road. (Alternatively, turning right again takes you to the A93, which is about 200 m away, but doing so means you will miss some of the best views on the walk.) By now the walk passes much closer to the river.

5 You have now reached the platform for the old Culter station. Keep on until the track ends. Turn right up Howie's Lane. Continue up to the main A93 road.

6 At the top, turn left and cross the road to the bus stop where you can catch a bus back to the centre of Aberdeen.

Amazingly, it is possible to navigate a fairly peaceful, rural route through the granite city of Aberdeen.

further information

For those who enjoy railway history, it may be interesting to look out for old railway property and platforms. At one time, trains stopped at Holborn Street, Ruthrieston, Pitfodels, Cults, West Cults, Bieldside, Murtle, Milltimber and Culter.

The walk starts at the car park at the Polmuir Road entrance of Duthie Park in Aberdeen. It can be reached by car or city bus No.17. To return to Aberdeen it is a short walk from the old railway route to the A93, which is served by regular bus services (Nos.19, 24 and 201).

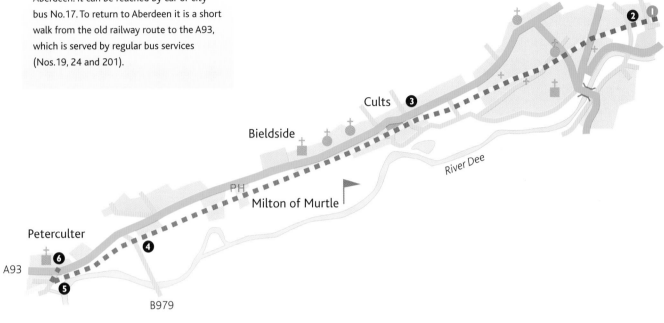

Aberdeen

Cults

Bieldside

River Dee

PH

Milton of Murtle

Peterculter

A93

B979

0   1 km   1 mile

▲ Map: Explorer 403
▲ Distance: 6 km/3¾ miles
▲ Walk ID: 1380 Ailsa Campbell

Difficulty rating

Time

▲ Church, Castle, Wildlife, Birds, Flowers, Great Views, Butterflies, Woodland

Inverness

A9

Grantown-on-Spey

A95

Aviemore

A

Abernethy Forest

This walk takes you through woodland and farmland, and near a former mill with its waterwheel and lade still intact. There are views and a spectacular castle.

1 Pass through the gate and follow the track. Cross the tiny bridge over the burn. Turn left at the pylons. Turn left at the road and walk parallel to it. Pass through the gate and cross the car park. Pass through another gate and follow the track.

2 Turn left at the waymarked post. At the fork in the track carry straight onwards. The path leads off to the right. Follow the pink arrows to a stile. At the stile cross the road. Follow the track leading to the left. As the track meets the driveway leading to Aultmore House, turn right.

3 Follow the trail leading downhill and to the left. Cross the footbridge over the burn and follow the path along the side of a field. Follow the path round to Milton Croft (the site of the former mill). Pass through the gate and carry on down the made-up road towards the church. Turn right and follow the path between the field and the road, near Castle Roy.

4 Pass through the gate and along the side of the forest. Continue up the forest road. At the top there is a T-Junction. Take the road to the right then take a smaller track leading off to the right, downhill through the trees. At the bottom of the track pass through the gate and cross the duckboards. Follow the track around the edge of the field. Pass through the gate.

5 Turn left and return towards the burn. When the track meets the road turn right and walk down the road. Pass through the gate on your left and continue through the woods.

6 Take the first track leading to the left and walk behind the school grounds. Cross over the stream and follow the track. Pass through the gate. Follow the pavement along the side of the road until you return to the starting point.

A hike through the Abernethy Forest, one of Britain's least-altered habitats, gives you a taste of what the Highlands were like 300 years ago.

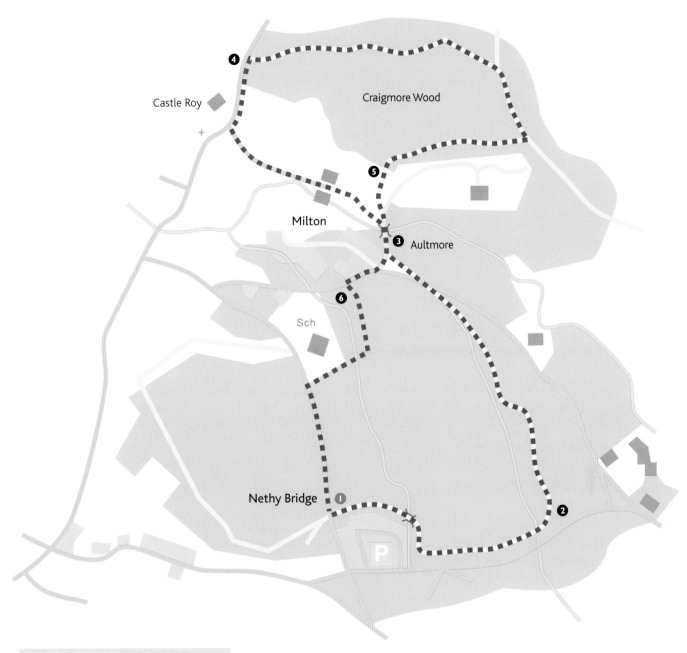

Castle Roy

Craigmore Wood

Milton

Aultmore

Sch

Nethy Bridge

access information

The village of Nethy Bridge is to be found east of the A95, about 15 km north-east of Aviemore in the Abernethy Forest. The start is found on the road south of the school.

0   1 km   1 mile

▲ Map: Explorer 419, 418

▲ Distance: 8 km/5 miles

▲ Walk ID: 839 D. B. Grant

Difficulty rating

Time

▲ Pub, Wildlife, Birds, Flowers, Great Views, Butterflies, Gift Shop, Food Shop, Good for Kids, Public Transport, Tea Shop, Woodland

Anagach Wood, Grantown-on-Spey

This is a popular walk with visitors to Grantown. Accessible from the town centre, the walk winds through pine woods, first following a military road then through glaciated scenery with old glacial lakes.

❶ Take the broad path (the Old Military Road indicated by a red arrow). Go through an iron gate. A few metres on there is a junction. Go left to the end of the old military road, ignoring all other paths.

❷ Turn off left on a narrow path and you immediately come to a fork. Go right at the red marker post and walk along the crest of a ridge to reach a fork. Keep left and you reach a junction after 20 m. The route goes right, to reach a crossroads after 50 m.

❸ At the crossroads go left through a birch wood to arrive at an open glade. A few metres into the glade go right on the broad path crossing it. Carry on to a fork near Craigroy Farm.

❹ At this fork turn left onto a gravelly track. When you arrive at another fork go left to a crossroads. Turn right at this crossroads. (Watch this one; it looks as though you should go straight on.) Keep on to reach a T-junction at a wire fence and burn.

❺ Turn left onto the Speyside Way. Follow it to a fork. At this fork go left, to reach another T-junction. Turn right and go on to another T-junction. Turn right at the T-junction to arrive at the edge of the golf course.

❻ At the golf course go left at the red/blue post on a narrow track, passing old glacial lakes to the left and right. When you come to an open glade take the right fork (red post) and cross the glade to the next red marker post straight ahead of you. From the second marker post you join a broad path. Pass the Curling Rink to a metal gate, where you join a wide track. When you join the wide track go straight on for 100 m to reach the car park.

access information

From the town square in Grantown go down Forest Road. The car park is at the road end. Public buses operate between Inverness, Aviemore and Grantown.

The heart of the Highlands, Grantown-on-Spey is a purple haze when the heather is in bloom in August.

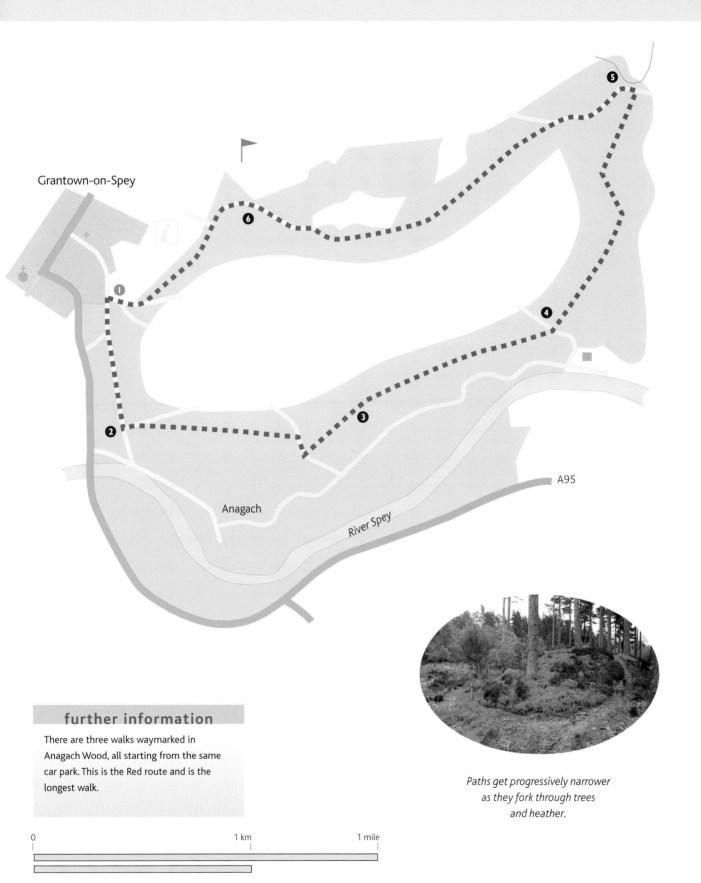

Grantown-on-Spey

Anagach

River Spey

A95

further information

There are three walks waymarked in Anagach Wood, all starting from the same car park. This is the Red route and is the longest walk.

*Paths get progressively narrower
as they fork through trees
and heather.*

0   1 km   1 mile

▲ Map: Explorer 406

▲ Distance: 11 km/6¾ miles

▲ Walk ID: 398 Ian Cordiner

Difficulty rating

Time

▲ River, Toilets, Castle, National Trust/NTS, Great Views, Public Transport

Crathes Castle from Banchory

A gentle walk along a former railway line, at first parallel to the River Dee. It enters the ground of Crathes Castle and returns along a wooded route.

1 Go to the east end of the car park. Enter Bellfield Park and walk across the grass to the opposite corner. Cross the rough car track and follow the tarred footpath, the old railway route. Continue under the bridge and take the path to the right. Again keep right, following a route parallel to the cemetery.

2 Turn right at the next main junction (parallel to the river). Again keep right. At the junction take the second road from the right (the first one goes down to the river). Continue past a fisherman's hut to a straight path which was once the old railway line. Continue straight on and bear right into the woods.

3 At the stream turn sharp left and climb a few steps up to the old railway line route again, then turn right. Follow the old railway route. Turn right at the Milton of Crathes sign. Enter the car park and follow the white signs to the end of the car park. Cross the old mill lade and go straight on, following the signs to Crathes Castle.

4 Follow the route through the castle grounds to the tree-lined road and out at the gate at the West Lodge.

5 Continue straight on across the new Hirn/Echt road and bear right along a disused loop road until you reach the next road. Turn right. Soon you turn left through an obscured metal gate through the wooded pathway.

6 Turn left and walk the short distance to the main road (A93). Turn right and walk towards the supermarket. Cross the A93. Walk away from the main road, past the main entrance to the supermarket. Turn right at the end of the buildings. Walk towards the south-west corner of the building where you find a small path. Follow this path towards the river. Turn right and retrace your route back to the car park.

access information

Easily reached by car or bus along the A93. There is a frequent bus service, No. 201 from Aberdeen. The walk starts at Bellfield car park, Dee Street, Banchory.

The picture of tranquillity, the River Dee winds along a broad valley, flanked on either side by pine forests, wild heathery moors and high hills.

One of the best-preserved castles in Scotland, Crathes Castle on Royal Deeside is a massive 16th-century fortress with fairy-tale turrets.

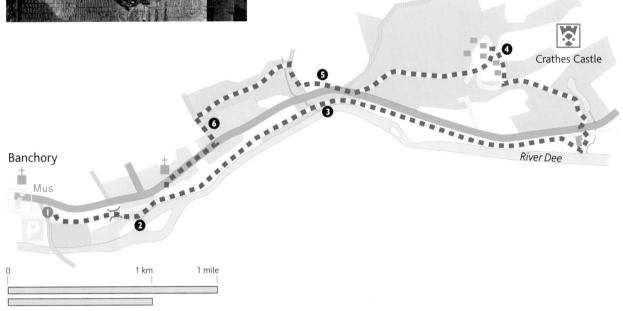

Crathes Castle

Banchory

Mus

River Dee

0   1 km   1 mile

further information

Crathes Castle dates from the 16th century, and has world-famous gardens with ancient yew hedges. Entry to the castle grounds and gardens is free all year round, but there is an entrance fee for the castle (open daily, April to October).

▲ Map: Explorer 395

▲ Distance: 8 km/5 miles

▲ Walk ID: 1069 Ian Cordiner

Difficulty rating

Time

▲ Hills or Fells, Mountains, River, Lake/Loch, Toilets, Church, Wildlife, Birds, Great Views, Nature Trail, Woodland

Knockie Viewpoint from Glen Tanar

This walk passes through pastoral scenery before entering a section of forestry plantations. It continues close by a stream for a large part of the route. Once past a small fishing loch the path skirts the Water of Tanar.

1 As you leave the car park cross the road to the bridge over the Tanar. Take the route to the right (if you wish to visit the Visitor Centre, go left). Follow this track away from the Visitor Centre and bear left.

2 Just off the track is the tiny St Lesmo's Chapel, built in 1870 and still in use today. Go through the gates at the cattle grid then turn right. Continue left up the rise. Continue straight on at the crossroads, into the forestry plantation. Turn right where the path forks.

3 Admire the view from the Knockie Viewpoint, before continuing down the hill where you take a left turn. Along this stretch there are some restful views along the waterside.

4 When you reach the bridge, turn right and cross it. Continue straight on. After crossing the bridge with the low walls, turn right.

5 Ignore the road from the left and bear right here. To the left of the path there is a small attractive fishing loch. Turn right at the next junction and continue to reach a bridge with rails. Cross the bridge and turn left.

6 Look out for a marker post here. Take the grassy path to the left and follow it along the riverside until you return to the previous track. There are some other grass paths and sheep tracks, but keeping to the left allows you to keep by the waterside. Retrace your route to the visitor centre and back across the bridge to the car park.

Part of the walk takes you through damp pine forest where the floor is lined with moss and ferns.

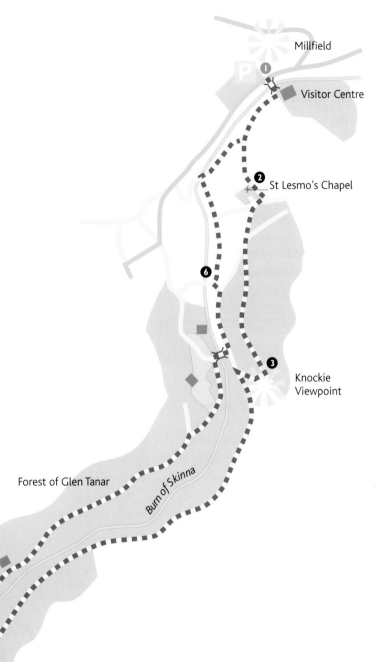
access information

Several kilometres west of Aboyne, on the South Deeside road B976, take the unclassified road west to Glen Tanar until you reach the car park for the Braeloine Visitor Centre.

further information

Many fine specimens of Scot's pine are found growing naturally through a carpet of heather and bracken. These trees are rare remnants of the old Caledonian pine forest which once covered the whole area.

Majestic Scots pines line the banks of the Water of Tanar flowing down the glen.

Millfield

Visitor Centre

❷ St Lesmo's Chapel

❻

❸ Knockie Viewpoint

Forest of Glen Tanar

Burn of Skinna

Glen Tanar

❺

❹

0   1 km   1 mile

North-east England

Coastal & Waterside

Waterside walks in North-east England unveil the coasts of Durham and Northumberland, and Yorkshire's scenic bays and reservoirs. Highlights include Beal Sands and Grassington.

Difficulty rating

Time

▲ Lake, Sea, Pub, Woodland, Wildlife, Great views

Howick Hall from Boulmer

This walk takes you from the fishing village of Boulmer, along the coastal path and into the wood of the Howick Estate, before rejoining the outward track back along the coast to Boulmer.

❶ From the car park, head north along a track to join the footpath alongside the road. Continue ahead past the Fishing Boat pub.

❷ At the junction, leave the main road and follow the 'No Through Road'. Follow the rough stone track through a series of gates and onto the beach. Turn left, continuing over a bridge and through another gate. Follow the track through the field and past a parking area. The track continues alongside the beach, rising over the dunes. Go through the next gate and cross the bridge.

❸ Turn left away from the beach and head along a grass track into the wood. Continue on the track labelled 'Long Walk'. Go through a turnstile, keeping left. The stoned track meets a grassed track going left. Follow this track as it bears left over a small bridge and continues alongside the stream.

❹ At the end of the 'Long Walk' go through the gate onto the main road. Turn right and pass the entrance of Howick Hall. Follow the road round a right-hand bend, past another gate out of the woods on your right and a turning to Howick village on your left. Continue to the corner, with the sea in front of you.

From seashore through woodland to grassy meadows, there is a wonderful variety of landscapes on this walk.

❺ Take the footpath towards the sea. Go through the gate and turn right, heading along the top of the dunes. Follow the track over three stiles, then past four marker posts. Cross the next stile and the bridge that you crossed earlier. Go through the gate and along the top footpath.

❻ Go through the next gate and cross the bridge. Go through the gate to your right and continue back along the outward track to the car park.

access information

Take the A1 to Alnwick, then from Alnwick take the A1068 signposted Boulmer, Alnmouth, Warkworth, Amble. At Lesbury turn left at the junction before the bridge, signed Boulmer. Continue on this road until you reach the village, parking in the car park on the right-hand side, on the dunes.

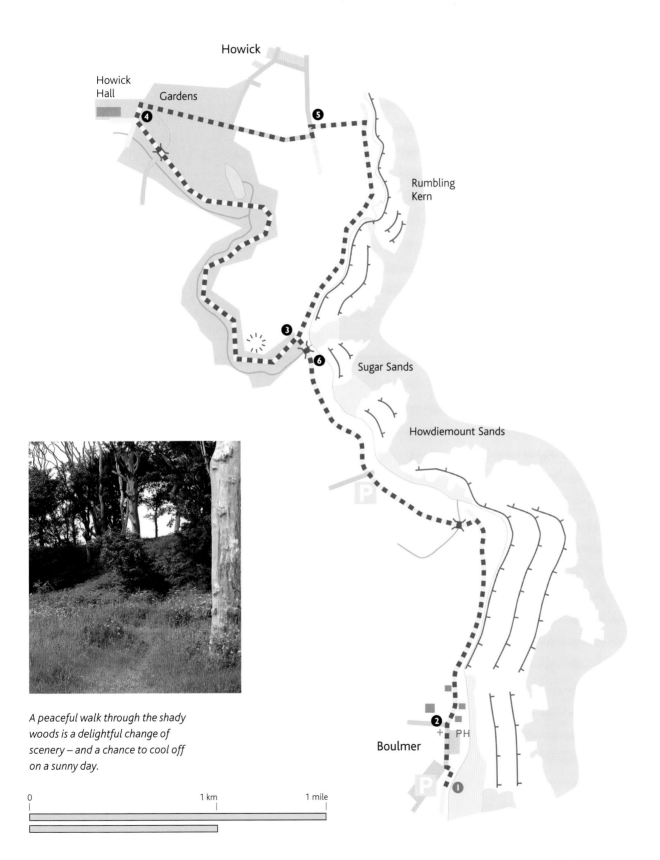

Howick

Howick
Hall

Gardens

❹

❺

Rumbling
Kern

❸

❻

Sugar Sands

Howdiemount Sands

P

P

❷

+ PH

Boulmer

❶

*A peaceful walk through the shady
woods is a delightful change of
scenery – and a chance to cool off
on a sunny day.*

0   1 km   1 mile

▲ Map: Explorer 339
▲ Distance: 16 km/10 miles
▲ Walk ID: 509 H. Weightman

Difficulty rating

Time

▲ River, Sea, Pub, Church, Castle, Wildlife, Birds, Flowers, Food Shop, Tea Shop, Ancient Monument

Tweed Walkway: Berwick from Norham

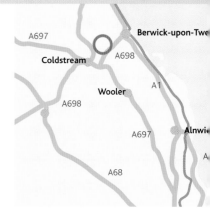

Starting at Norham Bridge, this linear walk passes Norham Castle and meanders along the river bank, passing one of the oldest suspension bridges in the country, to reach Berwick-upon-Tweed.

❶ The walk begins on the southern side of Norham Bridge. Climb over the wall, go down the steps to the River Tweed and follow the river bank round. Cross a footbridge, with Norham Castle directly ahead of you. Follow the path through the woods to the north of the castle.

❷ Leave the river bank and cross the stile. Follow the path, climbing gently through fields to enter a small wood. Turn left downhill at the signpost for Horncliffe.

❸ At Horncliffe, turn right at the T-junction and continue to the main street. Turn left to take the small road next to The Fisher's Arms.

❹ Bear left and follow the track, then the path, back down to the river bank. Continue along the bank for 1 km. The road swings left over the Chainbridge suspension bridge and into Scotland. Continue straight ahead past a house and through a gate to return to the river bank. The road leads to West Ord Farm — bear slightly left and cross a stile to continue on the river bank.

❺ Climb the steps through the thickets to cross a waymarked stile. Follow the field boundary to the left. Cross the A1 trunk road through a break in the hedgerow, making for the playground and picnic area. Go left behind the brightly painted play structure and then ahead for 50 m.

❻ Cross the stile and follow a path that dips to river-level, before climbing through woods to reach open fields. Bear left at the track junction and pass through a waymarked gate next to Berwick's sewage works. Follow the track around the plant and continue along the river. Passing under the railway bridge, bear slightly left towards Berwick. Turn left over Berwick Old Bridge to enter the town by Bridge Street.

access information

Buses run from Golden Square in Berwick-upon-Tweed to Norham. Berwick itself is on the A1, and is served by frequent trains, on the main Edinburgh to London east-coast line.

This walk takes you through woods and fields along the southern bank of the meandering River Tweed.

Berwick is the most northern town in England, and stands at the mouth of the River Tweed.

Chainbridge
suspension
bridge

A1

West Ord
Farm

④

PH

③ Horncliffe

River Tweed

②

Norham Castle, built of pink sandstone, is the subject of many paintings.

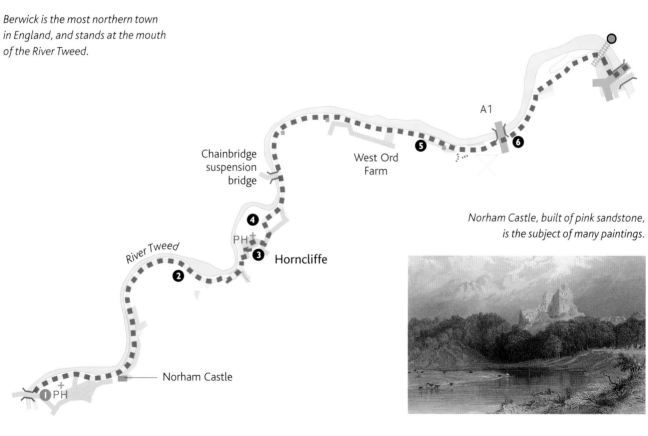

Norham Castle

PH

0   1 km   1 mile

▲ Map: Explorer 316

▲ Distance: 10.6 km/6½ miles

▲ Walk ID: 724 Jude Howat

Difficulty rating

Time

▲ Sea, Pub, Toilets, Museum, Birds, Great Views

St Mary's Island from Tynemouth

This coastal walk begins at Tynemouth and heads through the popular resort of Whitley Bay to reach St Mary's Island where, tides permitting, you can visit the lighthouse via a causeway. The walk returns along the headland.

❶ From the car park, cross the road and head north along the promenade, past Cullercoats Bay. Keep to the pavement until you reach the clock.

❷ Take the steps to the lower level and head for the slipway down to the beach. Walk along the beach towards the lighthouse (St Mary's Island). At the far end of the bay, take the steps and then the path. Tides permitting, cross the causeway to visit the lighthouse. Return via the causeway.

❸ After crossing the causeway, continue straight ahead and follow the road for a short distance. There is a nature reserve to the right, just beyond the car park. As the road bends sharply to the right, leave it and take the path to the left. This path is not shown as a public footpath on the map but is well used.

❹ There are many paths coming in from the right along the coast – ignore all of these and continue straight ahead. When you reach the hump-backed bridge, cross over to continue for a short distance along the coastal footpath.

❺ Take the left-hand path, towards the sea again. This takes you down to the lower level of the promenade. After a short distance you will see a path heading back up the dunes. Take this path to continue past a small outdoor auditorium. Take the left-hand fork along the coast.

❻ Towards the end of the bay, the promenade paths come to an end. Rejoin the promenade alongside the road. Retrace your steps along the coast and back towards the start point.

further information

St Mary's Island has a lighthouse, which was built in 1898 and remained operational until 1984. The island is now run as a visitor centre, with the surrounding area maintained as a nature reserve. It is advisable to check the tide table for the area before commencing this walk.

Tel: 0191 200 8650

Ideally, this walk should be done at low tide so that you can cross the causeway to visit the lighthouse on St Mary's Island.

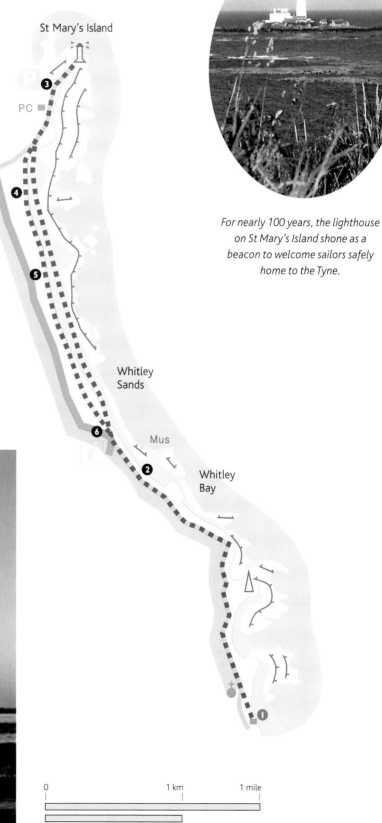

St Mary's Island

PC

Whitley
Sands

Mus

Whitley
Bay

access information

Parking is available along the
shore at Tynemouth, close to
the church. From Newcastle
follow the A1058 to Tynemouth/
Cullercoats. At the coastal
roundabout turn left and the
parking is about 200 m on the
left. Alternatively, take the metro
to Cullercoats station,
and walk the short distance to
the coast.

*For nearly 100 years, the lighthouse
on St Mary's Island shone as a
beacon to welcome sailors safely
home to the Tyne.*

0   1 km   1 mile

▲ Map: Explorer 308

▲ Distance: 8.86 km/5½ miles

▲ Walk ID: 400 Jude Howat

Difficulty rating

Time

▲ Sea, Pub, Toilets, Church, Birds, Flowers, Food Shop, Good for Kids, Industrial Archaeology, Mostly Flat, Public Transport

Easington Colliery from Seaham Hall Beach

This linear walk leads you along Seaham Beach and headland, along the shore of Hawthorn Hive, to climb up to Easington Colliery. On the way you pass through two areas maintained by The National Trust.

① Follow the yellow-chip path towards the sea. At the blue marker, turn right out of the car park. Follow the road to the next blue marker and climb the steps. Walk through another car park. Follow the road and the blue markers, crossing straight over the roundabout. Turn left into Foundry Road and pass the factory.

② Turn right, following the cycle route on to Ropery Walk. Pass under both bridges, cross the road, then pass back under one of the bridges. Take the next footpath and follow it back to the road. Turn left at the next junction and continue.

③ At the roundabout follow the rough path on the left, heading towards the sea. This opens out into a track, which leads all the way to Nose's Point car park. Just before the hill, take the path leading off to the left. Follow this down a steep bank, to rise again at the far side. This leads you into a National Trust area.

④ Cross the bridge and turn left. Walk through the grasses towards Hawthorn Dene. At the yellow marker continue straight ahead. This is another National Trust area. Cross the railway line. Follow the steps down to the shore. Turn right and walk towards the cliffs (Hive Point). Turn right at the end of the bay and follow the path, crossing the stream under the viaduct. Continue up the hill.

⑤ At the T-junction of paths, turn left and follow the coastal footpath underneath the viaduct again and along the railway. Just before the railway bridge, keep left and walk towards the edge of the headland. Follow the path along the cliff, then back inland.

⑥ Continue towards Easington Colliery, following the path under the railway bridge. Go through the car park and walk to the corner of the main road. The bus stop is straight ahead.

Much of the coastline near Easington is being eroded by the North Sea.

This impressive viaduct is a monument to the area's industrial history.

PC

1

Seaham Hall

Seaham

2

3

Nose's Point

Chourdon Point

Shippersea Bay

4

5

Easington Colliery

6

access information

From the A19, leave at the junction towards Seaham & Dalton-le-Dale. Follow the B1285 northwards towards Sunderland, which takes you through the westernmost edge of Seaham. Turn right at the traffic lights, where the A19 is signposted to the left, just beyond a school on your right. Follow the lane down towards the coast. There is good parking here.

0   1 km   1 mile

▲ Map: Explorer 305
▲ Distance: 10.5 km/6½ miles
▲ Walk ID: 1233 M. Parkin

Difficulty rating

Time

▲ Wildlife, Birds, River, Woodland

Whitworth Hall Country Park from Sunderland Bridge

The walk starts from the old Sunderland Bridge, passing through Coldstream Wood, over fields and lanes to Whitworth Hall Country Park, returning along the bank of the River Wear.

❶ Start from the old Sunderland Bridge, opposite the entrance to the Croxdale Estate. Follow the track to pass under the Croxdale Viaduct and along the riverside to a bend in the river. Take the left fork into the trees and keep to the edge of the wood.

❷ Bear right and cross a bridge over Nickynack Beck. Enter Coldstream Wood, looking out for roe deer. Leave the wood over a stile. Follow the path, crossing the track to Coldstream Farm. Continue over several stiles to reach a country lane. Turn left, then right, down to the end of a second lane. Outside the sewage works gates, head through the trees.

❸ Leave the main path, and take the path on the right. Cross Valley Burn over a bridge. Climb up through the wood and follow the track skirting the housing estate. At the end of the estate continue along the farm track past the drive to Burton Beck Farm. Follow the track through a band of trees and over Burton Beck. Where the track bends right, head along an enclosed footpath on the left.

❹ The footpath emerges onto a field. At a kissing gate follow the path as it passes to the other side of the fence. At the Whitworth Road turn right, passing the entrance to Whitworth Hall Country Park. Continue on the footpath to cross Page Bank Bridge.

❺ Take the footpath to the right and follow the river. Cross the stile ahead. Continue along the riverside to cross another stile. Leave the river going diagonally left. Cross a small beck and pass through the kissing gate.

❻ On the broad track turn right and pass under the Croxdale Viaduct. Walk along the track to the Sunderland Bridge, where the walk started.

access information

The old Sunderland Bridge spans the River Wear just off the A167 Durham to Croxdale road. Turn off the A167 near Croxdale Bridge and onto the B6300, then left down the lane, where there is ample parking before and after the bridge.

The handsome four-arched Sunderland Bridge over the River Wear is a good gathering point for the start of the walk.

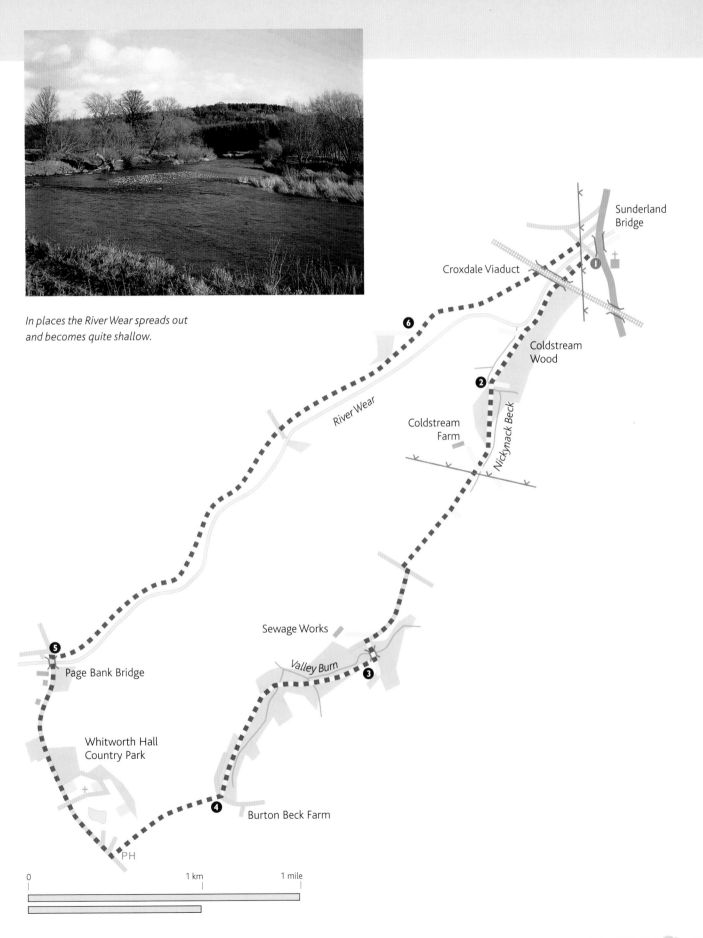

In places the River Wear spreads out and becomes quite shallow.

Sunderland Bridge

Croxdale Viaduct

Coldstream Wood

6

River Wear

Coldstream Farm

2

Nickynack Beck

Sewage Works

Valley Burn

3

5

Page Bank Bridge

Whitworth Hall Country Park

4

Burton Beck Farm

PH

0   1 km   1 mile

▲ Map: Explorer OL 30
▲ Distance: 5.6 km/3½ miles
▲ Walk ID: 492 Jude Howat

Difficulty rating

Time

▲ Hills or Fells, River, Pub, Great Views

Reeth to Arkengarthdale

This is a charming, easy-to-follow short walk, with some great views to enjoy along the way. The route starts in the Swaledale village of Reeth and goes along one side of Arkengarthdale, then returns on the opposite side.

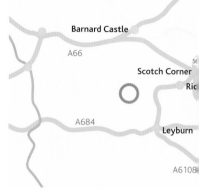

1 Starting by the village green with your back to the Black Bull pub, turn left and walk across the crossroads to follow the road out of the village.

2 Just after a sharp left bend in the road, watch out for a waymark by the trees. Follow the footpath across several small fields. You will need to cross lots of very narrow stiles between the fields, but the route is easy to follow, and each stile is marked with yellow paint. The path runs up the length of Arkengarthdale.

3 Follow the path first round to the right, then over Arkle Beck. The path then climbs on the other side of the dale. After a short climb, turn right and head towards the nearest of the farmhouses, following the yellow markers through the garden and beyond.

4 Continue on the path as it leads back towards Reeth on the opposite side of the dale. After a while the path drops to pass through a wood, close to the beck. Follow the bridleway slightly up the hill again. Continue to reach open countryside again, where there are good views of Reeth.

5 Pass through a metal stile on your right, just after some trees, take a sharp right bend and cross the field to the right of a barn. Head towards the trees in the distance to reach another stile. Continue again towards the gate by the road.

6 Pass through the gate, turn right and follow the road back up the hill to the village green.

access information

Take the A6108 west from Richmond. Reeth is on the B6270, which branches to the right before you reach Downholme. There is parking on the village green.

The glorious unspoilt beauty of Swaledale is the perfect antidote to the hurly burly of city life.

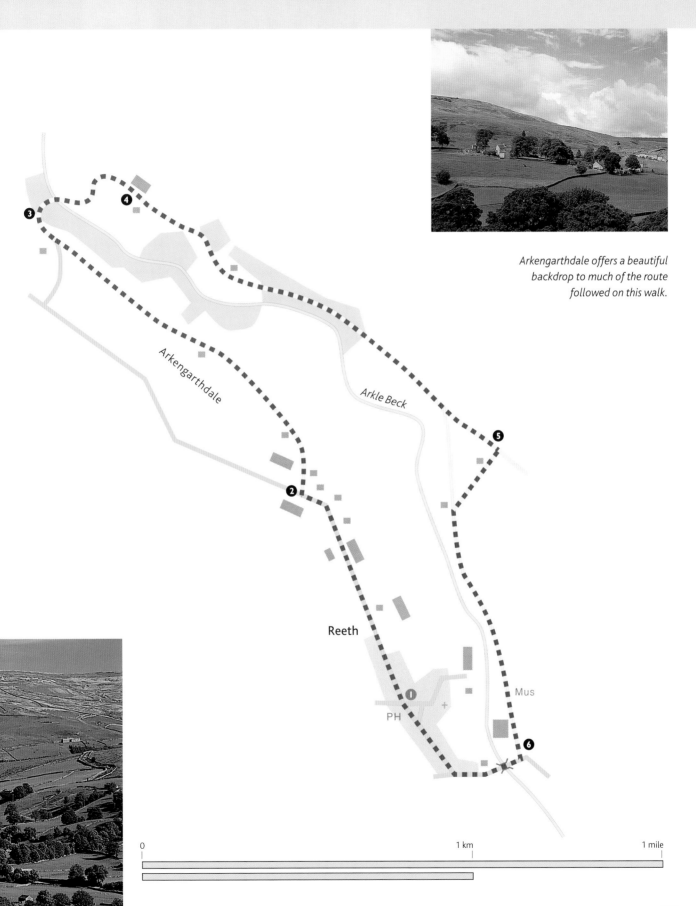

Arkengarthdale

Arkle Beck

Reeth

PH

Mus

③

④

②

⑤

①

⑥

Arkengarthdale offers a beautiful backdrop to much of the route followed on this walk.

0

1 km

1 mile

▲ Map: Explorer OL 21

▲ Distance: 8 km/5 miles

▲ Walk ID: 1130 W. Kembery

Difficulty rating

Time

▲ Hills or Fells, Lake/Loch, Birds, Great Views, Moor

The Gorple and Widdop Reservoirs from Hebden Bridge

From a remote spot above Hebden Bridge, the walk climbs steadily with views of both Lower and Upper Gorple reservoirs to reach Gorple Gate at the top of the moor. A steady descent takes in Widdop Reservoir and continues for a gentle return along its shore.

1 Turn right and walk down the quiet moorland road. Pass a house on the left and a road also on the left, to arrive opposite another lay-by. Turn right at the junction, following the route signposted 'Bridleway Lower Gorple'. Follow the track to a junction at the start of the reservoir.

2 Turn right, following the signpost marked 'Permissive Footpath Upper Gorple', still on a track.

3 Do not cross the dam. Turn right on a narrow path, signposted Widdop.

4 At the top (Gorple Gate), turn right at the sign marked 'Public Bridleway Widdop Road' and follow the broad track downhill. As the track swings sharply right, go straight ahead on a narrow footpath, indicated by a marker. The path follows a broken wall above the reservoir on the right.

5 At a fingerpost, turn right to cross a wooden bridge and walk up to join a broad green footpath. Turn right at the sign for Widdop Dam and continue with the reservoir on the right.

6 At the metal bridge keep to the right of the wall (this path is not marked on the map). Almost immediately you will arrive at a wooden bridge and a junction of footpaths. Turn right to cross the bridge and then turn left to follow a path to the left of the reservoir alongside the deep drain. After passing two houses, bear left to cross a bridge and go up to the road via a gate. Turn right along the road to return to the car park.

access information

The walk starts from a very remote location on the quiet, narrow unclassified road between Nelson and Hebden Bridge.

As well as being surrounded by lovely Yorkshire countryside, Hebden Bridge is fast becoming a lively cultural and social centre.

further information

There is no public transport near by. Park at the southern end of Widdop Reservoir by the dam on a large concreted area.

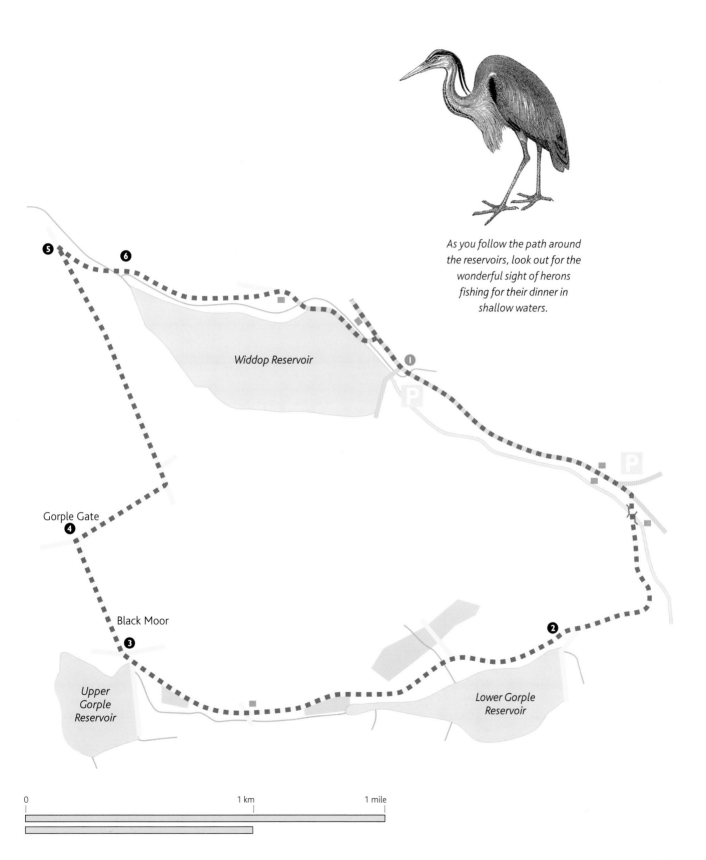

As you follow the path around the reservoirs, look out for the wonderful sight of herons fishing for their dinner in shallow waters.

Widdop Reservoir

Gorple Gate

Black Moor

Upper Gorple Reservoir

Lower Gorple Reservoir

0   1 km   1 mile

▲ Map: Explorer OL 2

▲ Distance: 11 km/7 miles

▲ Walk ID: 113 L. and D. Fishlock

Difficulty rating

Time

▲ Hills or Fells, River, Pub, Toilets, Wildlife, Birds, Flowers, Great Views

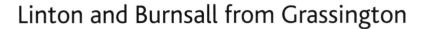

Linton and Burnsall from Grassington

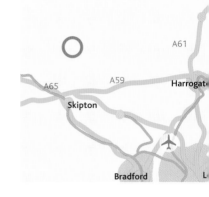

This undemanding walk takes you through the delightful little villages of Burnsall and Linton, ending with a visit to the beautiful Linton waterfall to complete a truly enjoyable family day out.

1 Go through the gate at the back of the car park. Turn right, following the sign to Linton Falls. At the junction before Linton Falls, turn left onto the riverside path. Follow the footpath sign away from the river to a stile onto the lane. Turn right.

2 At the junction, follow the signed footpath to Burnsall. Cross a field, a footbridge and a kissing gate, to follow the river again. Turn right to cross the Hebden suspension bridge and then left towards Burnsall. Cross a stone stile to continue along the riverbank.

3 Turn right before Burnsall Bridge. When the road turns right, take the left path, crossing a number of fields, lanes and stiles. Continue in the same direction, following the footpath signs and crossing Startan Beck. Go through the stile and straight on. Pass through a gate and exit the field through a stile in the corner. Turn left along the lane through Thorpe.

4 Take the left fork. Continue along the lane, then cross a gated stile on your right. Follow the path through the field. Just after the footpath sign, continue ahead and cross the next stile and field. Go through the farmyard, then turn right along the road to enter Linton.

5 At the T-Junction, turn left across the bridge and take the footpath on the right, along Linton Beck (signpost to

Threshfield). Follow the path to the right, in front of Linton Country Crafts and then between dry-stone walls. Take the right fork, continuing under the old railway bridge. Cross the field, over a small stream towards a small strip of woodland. Cross the main road. Take the path on your left to Threshfield School and turn right.

6 Turn left along Church Road. Take the path on the left to Linton Falls. Turn right just before a small bridge and cross Linton Falls Bridge. Retrace the route to the car park.

access information

The walk starts from the National Park Information Centre just off the B6265 Grassington-Hebden road (fee payable). Bus services to the park operate from Leeds, Bradford and York.

Grassington is a charming village of traditional stone cottages and cobbled streets in Upper Wharfedale at the heart of the Yorkshire Dales National Park.

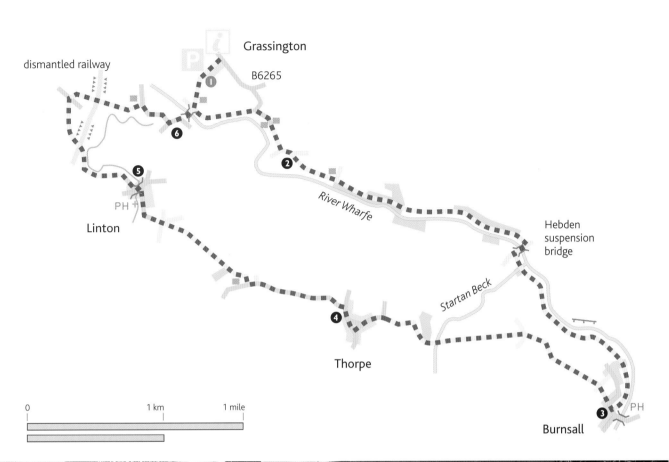

dismantled railway

Grassington

B6265

①

⑥

②

River Wharfe

⑤

PH

Linton

Hebden
suspension
bridge

Startan Beck

④

Thorpe

③

PH

Burnsall

0   1 km   1 mile

The woodland and hillside walks of North-east England reveal such wonders as Hadrian's Wall and the Yorkshire Dales. Highlights include Ilkley Moor, Simonside Crags and Hamsterley Forest.

▲ Map: Explorer OL 43
▲ Distance: 12 km/7½ miles
▲ Walk ID: 300 Jude Howat

Difficulty rating

Time

▲ Hills or Fells, Lake/Loch, Pub, Toilets, Museum, National Trust/NTS, Wildlife, Birds, Flowers, Great Views, Food Shop

Peel Crags from Housesteads

This hilly walk takes in an impressive section of Hadrian's Wall, from Housesteads to the end of Peel Crags. There are some spectacular views before the walk returns along more gentle slopes.

1 Follow the path through the arch and up the hill towards the Housesteads Fort. When you reach the museum continue up the hill on the outside of the fort, towards the trees on the brow of the hill. Pass through the gate and walk along the top of the wall. Stay on the path that follows the wall's route.

2 Cross the stile onto the farmer's road, then turn right and cross a second stile. Continue along the route of the wall on the northern side.

3 Descend from the wall and cross the field towards the house. Cross the stile and continue down the hill by turning left on the road. Cross the B6318 and continue past the Once Brewed Visitor Centre, close to Peel Crags.

4 Take the first junction on the left, towards Vindolanda. When you reach the Vindolanda car park, continue down the track on the outside of the wall. At the signpost, ignore its arrow and stick to the road up the hill. Turn left when you reach the T-junction, then follow the road.

5 At the next junction turn right and continue until you reach a bridleway on the left. Take this bridleway up to East Crindledykes Farm and continue over the field beyond. Beware – the field sometimes contains a bull!

6 Cross the stile, then turn right and follow the road back to the car park at Housesteads.

access information

Housesteads is on the B6318, which runs parallel to the A69 west of Newcastle. There is pay-and-display parking at the visitor centre for Housesteads.

A visit to Hadrian's Wall is a must for anyone living in or visiting the north of England.

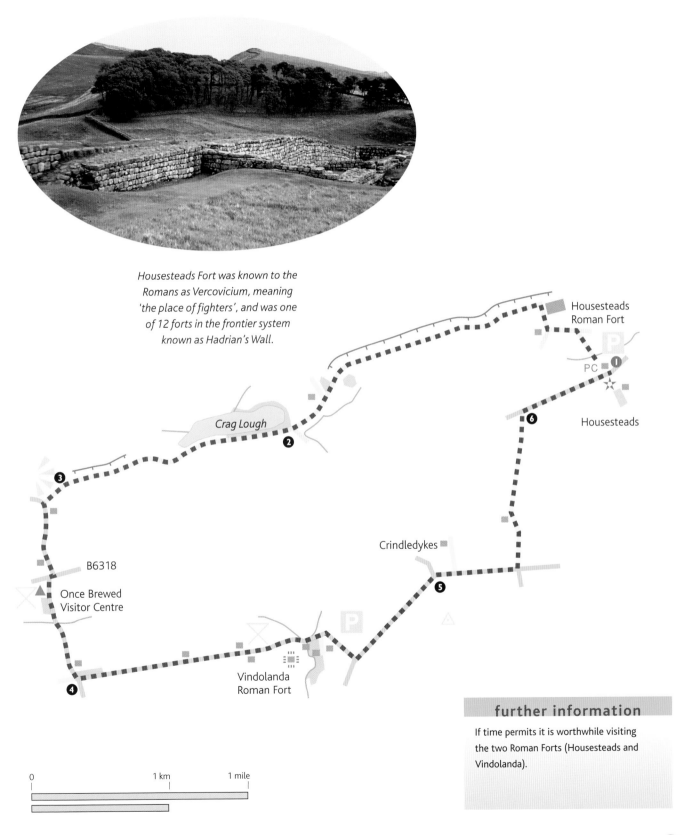

Housesteads Fort was known to the Romans as Vercovicium, meaning 'the place of fighters', and was one of 12 forts in the frontier system known as Hadrian's Wall.

Housesteads Roman Fort

Housesteads

Crag Lough

Crindledykes

B6318

Once Brewed Visitor Centre

Vindolanda Roman Fort

0   1 km   1 mile

further information

If time permits it is worthwhile visiting the two Roman Forts (Housesteads and Vindolanda).

▲ Map: Explorer OL 42

▲ Distance: 9.6 km/6 miles

▲ Walk ID: 427 Jude Howat

Difficulty rating

Time

▲ Hills or Fells, Great Views

Simonside Crags from Lordenshaws

This is a wonderfully bracing ridge walk, which takes in the four peaks of The Beacon Cairn, Dove Crag, Simonside Crags and Lordenshaws Fort, with breathtaking views along the way.

1 Follow the rocky footpath up the hill, and take the first right fork to continue towards The Beacon Cairn. The path follows a high-level ridge and offers superb views. Cross over the stile and continue uphill towards the summit of Dove Crag.

2 Just before you reach the summit, take the left fork and follow the broad track which leads to a cairn. Continue along the ridge-top path. The path passes to the right of Old Stell Crag, leading to the summit directly above Simonside Crags. At the summit, descend via a steep path down the face of the crag to join a forest track.

3 Turn right onto the track. It bends left sharply, then descends into the forest. At the marker, turn right. Pass by a bridge on the right and continue down the hill to reach a grassy picnic area.

4 Aim diagonally right across the grass to join a short path, which leads to the road. Turn left onto the bridleway, just beyond the cattle grid, and head up a small hill. Past the quarry the path turns to the right, through a gate. Continue along the path, and through a further two gates, to reach Whitton Hillhead Farm. At the farm, turn right onto the farm track.

5 At the next junction turn right. Follow the track up the hill to Whittondean and Lordenshaws Fort.

6 Near the top of the hill, take the left path to go up to the fort (then retrace your steps to this point). Continue straight ahead to reach the car park.

The views around Rothbury include stunning panoramas of peaks, crags and rolling countryside.

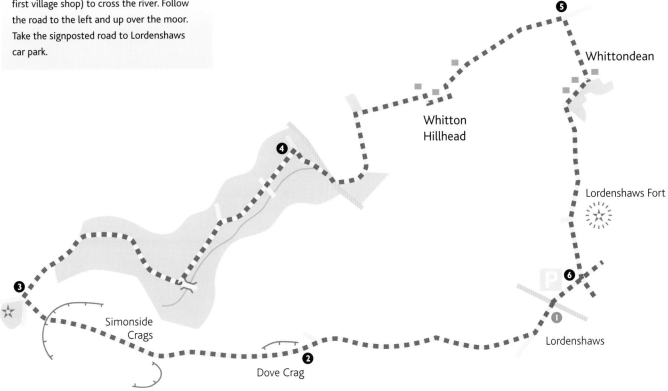

access information

From Alnwick, follow the B6341 to Rothbury. In Rothbury take the left turn (just after the first village shop) to cross the river. Follow the road to the left and up over the moor. Take the signposted road to Lordenshaws car park.

⑤

Whittondean

Whitton Hillhead

④

Lordenshaws Fort

③

⑥

Simonside Crags

Lordenshaws

②

Dove Crag

0   1 km   1 mile

Lordenshaws is an Iron Age hill fort surrounded by strange 'cup and ring' stone carvings. This site alone makes the walk one to savour.

▲ Map: Explorer 340
▲ Distance: 16.1 km/10 miles
▲ Walk ID: 362 Dave Lingard

Difficulty rating

Time

▲ Hills or Fells, Lake/Loch, Church, Great Views

Carey Burn from North Middleton

From North Middleton the track climbs steadily up and over moorland. The walk descends to the Coldgate Burn then climbs up to an old farmstead. The return is downhill or flat and takes in the magnificent Carey Burn.

This walk is set among the Cheviot Hills, an area of undulating hills and meandering streams.

❶ Head up the farm track to the top of the hill. Go through the gate and follow the path down over the burn. Cross the bridge. Follow the track across the field and over the stile.

❷ Take the right-hand track uphill. Go over the stile and turn right. Head downhill, over a bridge, and follow the path, taking the footbridge across Harthope Burn. Go over the stile and turn right.

❸ Cross the road and turn left, through the gate. Continue uphill on a farm track. Go over the stile and follow the grassy track, eventually heading downhill. Turn left onto the red-chipped farm track. At the waymark, turn right. Cross the burn and climb the bank, heading for Broadstruther.

❹ At Broadstruther follow the path to a marker, which directs you towards the red farm track in the valley. Avoid dropping down to the footbridge. Veer slightly left, above the burn, and head for the gate across another burn. Follow the path into Carey Burn, crossing over to the left bank. Keep to the right of the woods and follow Carey Burn as it bends.

❺ Climb up above the burn to just below the scree slope, and follow the track, just short of the bridge. Cross the stile and turn left onto the road. Go over the stile, then follow the track across an open area. When the track suddenly turns right, go straight ahead over the stile. Cross the field to the gate on the far side, which leads you through a wood.

❻ Cross the Coldgate Water by the footbridge. When you reach the road, turn right along it for a short walk back to the start point.

access information

North Middleton is 4 km south of Wooler, Northumberland. The unclassified road on which the hamlet stands runs parallel to the A697 trunk road and can be accessed at Wooler. Parking is available on the verge just south of the hamlet and close to the starting point.

The stunning slopes of the Cheviot Hills, on the border between England and Scotland, are famous as sheep-grazing land.

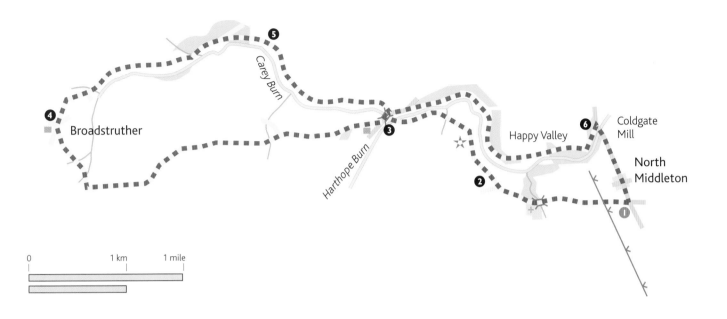

▲ Map: Explorer 305

▲ Distance: 13 km/8 miles

▲ Walk ID: 498 Karen Land

Difficulty rating

Time

▲ River, Great Views

The kissing gate in front of Barmpton Hall.

Brafferton to Ketton Country

The village of Brafferton lies in a small area of rolling countryside steeped in history, known locally as 'Ketton Country'. The walk is an easy ramble along old tracks, green lanes and ancient highways of outstanding beauty.

❶ Walk up the main street. At the end, follow High House Lane across Valley Beck. Just before it bends left towards High House Farm, go through a field gate on the right. Walk ahead through the field along a tall hedge. Continue on to reach a signed farm gate and stile.

❷ Climb gently between the hedges. The lane descends through several gates to arrive at Newton Ketton. Turn left at the junction. Just before reaching Fir Tree Farm, turn right into the ancient Catkill Lane and continue for 2 km.

❸ Soon after the entrance into Catkill Wood, take the footpath on the right, to cut through dense scrub. Proceed straight on, through the fields. At Moor House, head to the left of the buildings and follow the farm track to Barmpton.

❹ Pass through a kissing gate in front of Barmpton Hall. Walk along the River Skerne until you reach the farm bridge, then bear right to reach the old Ketton packhorse bridge. Behind the bridge take the right fork.

❺ Turn left at the access road. At the top of the hill, turn right to pass Ketton Hall. Just beyond a small wood, locate a green farm gate on the left. Follow the wood away. When it ends, continue straight on and through the bridle gate. Follow the left boundary fence to go through another gate. Veer right and stay near the hedge over the next two fields.

❻ At the far corner of the last field a pair of gates leads onto a quiet green lane that heads back to Brafferton.

access information

Brafferton is on an unclassified road off the A167 north of Darlington. Roadside parking is available in the village. There is also a regular bus service.

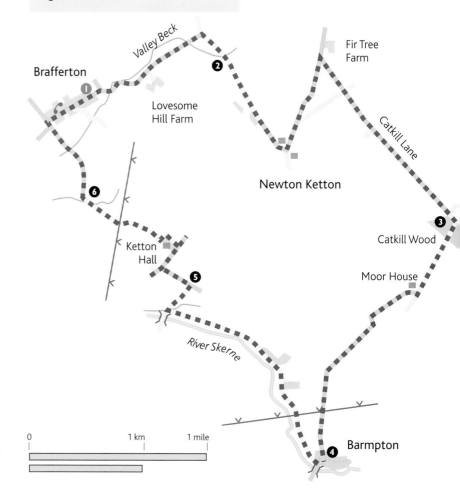

▲ Map: Explorer OL 43

▲ Distance: 4.8 km/3 miles

▲ Walk ID: 686 Jude Howat

Difficulty rating

Time

▲ Hills or Fells, Pub, Toilets, Castle, Great Views

Thirlwall Castle from Walltown

This short circular walk takes in part of Hadrian's Wall (between Walltown Quarry and Thirlwall Castle) and part of the Pennine Way. The walk provides lovely views, with relatively little effort!

1 Leave the car park and walk along the road to the T-junction. Turn right and continue for about 200 m, looking for a stile on the left.

2 Cross the stile and follow the wall along the hillside to join a farm track, heading steeply down the hill to the Tipalt Burn.

3 Cross the burn via the footbridge and follow the track up the hill on the far side, passing Thirlwall Castle on the way. Continue through the farmyard. Shortly after the farmyard, take the right fork and follow the path to Wood House.

4 At the junction, branch to the right and follow the road downhill towards the burn again. Cross the burn via the stepping stones, then follow the sunken track to the left and uphill.

5 Turn right at the marker and head through the field towards the Low Old Shields farmhouse. Exit the field in its far left-hand corner, then pass between the

shed and main farm building. Continue through the farmyard to join the farm track at the front of the farmhouse. Follow the track uphill as it joins on to a rough road. Turn right as it becomes a proper road again, and follow the route back down towards waymark 2.

6 This time, turn left on to the path at the end of the quarry picnic site. Follow the path, which runs parallel to the road taken at the beginning of the walk. The path leads back towards the car park.

This gentle walk takes in sights ranging from Hadrian's Wall to Tipalt Burn.

access information

From the A69 Haltwhistle to Brampton road, take the B6318 to Greenhead. In Greenhead, turn right up a steep hill for a short distance, then take the first road on the left (signposted to Walltown Quarry). Follow the quarry signs (turning right after a short distance) to the car park.

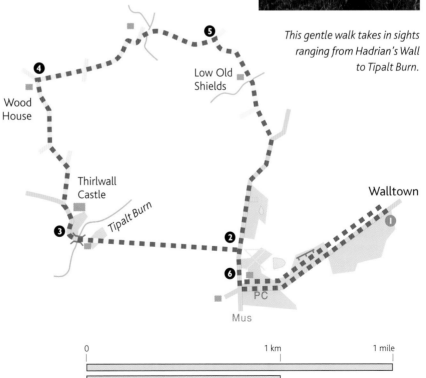

▲ Map: Explorer 308

▲ Distance: 6.5 km/4 miles

▲ Walk ID: 1063 Norman Hope

Difficulty rating

Time

▲ Pub, Stately Home, Birds, Butterflies, Woodland

Beamish Woods from Causey Arch

This is a picturesque walk over Causey Arch and around the woods of Beamish, taking in some of the industrial sights as well as the natural beauty of the surrounding area.

1 Park the car at Causey Arch picnic site. (The picnic area contains not only the famous arch, but also a magnificent embankment and culvert built in 1725.) Take the path to the left of the toilets at the bottom of the car park. Follow the path down, keeping the embankment on your left. Cross the Causey Arch and follow the main path. On reaching a footbridge on the left, cross it and follow the path to the railway.

2 Go through the kissing gate and cross the railway line, passing through the gate on the other side. Cross the open field and turn right at the main road. About 200 m down the road on the other side, the footpath continues up a flight of steps.

3 Go over the stile and keep going until the path meets a narrow country lane. Turn left. On the road, about 50 m on the left, go through the doorway in the wall. Walk through Carricks Hill Wood, keeping to the main path. When you reach the T-junction, turn left. This path joins a main road. Turn right and walk towards Beamish Hall.

4 About 200 m up the road, opposite Beamish Hall, follow the sign marked Coppy Lane.

5 The lane joins Beamishburn Road near The Causey Arch Inn, where you turn left. After about 50 m turn right to cross the fields by the public footpath.

6 The next road is the A6076. Cross it and go under the railway to return to the start of the walk.

further information

From the Norman Conquest the lords of Beamish were also the lords of Tanfield and Kibblesworth. The first records of a grand house on the estate were in 1309 when Bertram Monboucher took a wife who brought the Beamish estate as her dowry. The National Coal Board moved its offices here in 1954 but gave up the hall and grounds in 1974 to Beamish Hall College, which now shares the premises with the North of England Open Air Museum.

One of the most fascinating venues in this area is the Beamish North of England Open Air Museum.

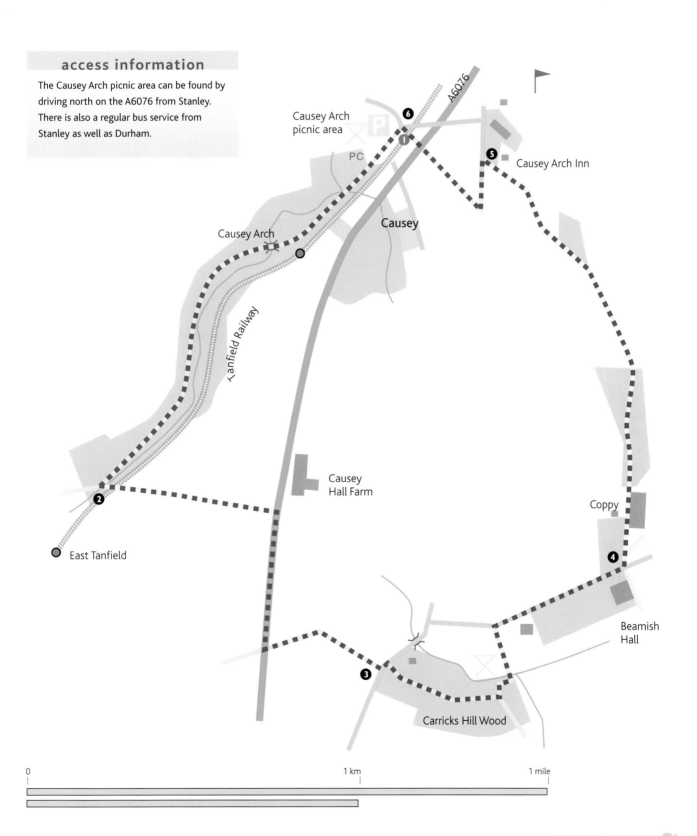

access information

The Causey Arch picnic area can be found by driving north on the A6076 from Stanley. There is also a regular bus service from Stanley as well as Durham.

Causey Arch picnic area

6

A6076

Causey Arch Inn

5

PC

Causey Arch

Causey

Tanfield Railway

Causey Hall Farm

2

Coppy

East Tanfield

4

Beamish Hall

3

Carricks Hill Wood

0   1 km   1 mile

▲ Map: Explorer 304

▲ Distance: 9.5 km/6 miles

▲ Walk ID: 1034 M. Parkin

Difficulty rating

Time

▲ Wildlife, Birds, Great Views, Woodland

Whitcliffe Scar from Richmond

This tranquil walk passes through woods and fields above the River Swale, before returning along the heights of Whitcliffe Scar with enchanting views over Applegarth, Swaledale, and Richmond.

1 Follow the track to High Leases and through Whitcliffe Wood. Stay on the track as it passes below Whitcliffe Scar, heading towards East Applegarth Farm. Continue straight ahead on a green track, passing through a gateway and a field. Cross the road and follow the path on the left. Cross the next road and the stile ahead. Cross another two fields and a small stream.

2 Head left to pass West Applegarth Farm. Follow the farm road, until it reaches the old Richmond to Reeth road. Turn right on Clapgate Bank and pass a junction for Whashton and Ravensworth. Cross the cattle grid on the right.

3 Almost immediately, leave the farm road, taking the green path to the left towards the top of Whitcliffe Scar. You will pass two monuments on the way. Carry on along the top of the scar. Keep to the breast of the hill, for marvellous views of the Hambleton and Cleveland Hills, and Richmond Castle.

4 Go down the hill to reach High Leases. Turn left along the track, back to the start of the walk.

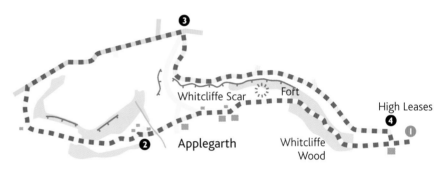

As you travel along Whitcliffe Scar, an enchanting view opens out before you.

access information

Heading out of Richmond on the main A6108 Reeth road, but before leaving the town at a sharp left, leave the main road and go up the avenue of West Fields. Follow the lane for just over a mile until the tarmac ends and park at the roadside between Whitcliffe and High Leases farms.

▲ Map: Explorer OL 31
▲ Distance: 3 km/2 miles
▲ Walk ID: 808 Jude Howat

Difficulty rating

Time

▲ River, Toilets, Play Area, Wildlife, Birds, Flowers, Great Views, Food Shop, Good for Kids, Tea Shop, Woodland

Hamsterley Forest from Bedburn

This short but enjoyable walk in Hamsterley Forest is ideal for when you need a breath of fresh air but time is limited. It takes you along both sides of the Bedburn Valley, through the forest, to return via the river.

1 Exit the car park via the small path leading into the forest. At the immediate T-junction turn right towards the children's play area, following the yellow markers. Turn left at the next T-junction to join the larger track. Cross over the burn (via a bridge) and follow the track uphill, into the forest. At the T-junction, turn right to follow the track along the hillside, until you reach a forest road.

2 Turn right, and descend for a short distance. Leave the road for the small path into the woods (signposted with a yellow marker). The path now begins to descend towards the river.

3 Do not cross the first bridge over the river. Instead, keep to the right and follow the path along the riverbank. The path does not follow the river, but meanders close by. Cross at the next bridge and turn right to follow the riverside path.

4 The adventure play area marks the end of the walk (the car park is just on its far side).

Both wild and arranged flowers add colour to the route as it heads off from Bedburn.

access information

Hamsterley Forest is close to the A68 near Bishop Auckland/Crook. There are brown tourist information signs from the junction close to Witton-le-Wear. Follow the signs, which lead into Hamsterley village. Keep following the signs through the village then out towards Bedburn. Park in the second car park.

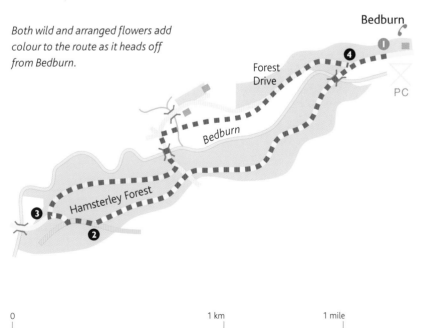

▲ Map: Explorer OL 26
▲ Distance: 5.5 km/3½ miles
▲ Walk ID: 1394 M. Parkin

Difficulty rating
👣👣👣

Time
⬤⬤

▲ River, Pub, Toilets, Church, National Trust/NTS, Birds, Flowers, Butterflies, Food Shop, Nature Trail, Tea Shop

Low Mill from Church Houses

This pleasant stroll in Farndale (famous for its daffodils) in the North York Moors starts in Church Houses, passing through Low Mill to return over fields and through farmyards.

❶ The walk starts from the lane behind the pub in Church Houses. Go through the gate and follow the lane to High Mill (The Daffy Caffy). Pass through the yard and exit through the gate. Follow the path near the River Dove's banks.

❷ At the junction, go through the gate and continue straight on, with the river on your right.

❸ Cross the footbridge. Follow the path up to reach a country lane in the delightful hamlet of Low Mill and stop for a visit. Retrace your steps to cross back over the footbridge. Go straight ahead and cross the field to the hedge. Keeping the hedge on your right, continue to High Wold House farm.

❹ Go through the gate and cross the yard, exiting onto a track on the left. Pass through a gate just below Cote Hill Farm. Cross the field diagonally left and climb over the stile. Pass the cottage on the right and cross the field to reach Bitchagreen Farm. Go through the gate and cross the yard to exit over the stile. Cross the field to climb another stile onto a track leading to Bragg Farm ahead.

❺ Go straight through the farmyard and exit through the gate. Cross the field and continue into the next one. Keep the wall to the left and cross the stile in the facing wall. Turn immediately right along the wall to reach a gate onto the road. Turn left and continue to Church Houses.

❻ At the crossroads outside the pub in Church Houses, turn left and down the lane to the start of the walk.

access information

Church Houses is in Farndale on the North York Moors. It lies about 14 km north of Kirkbymoorside, on the A170 Thirsk to Scarborough road.

There is parking for a handful of cars halfway down a 'No Through Road', behind the pub leading to the Daffy Caffy. There is also some parking on the grass verge.

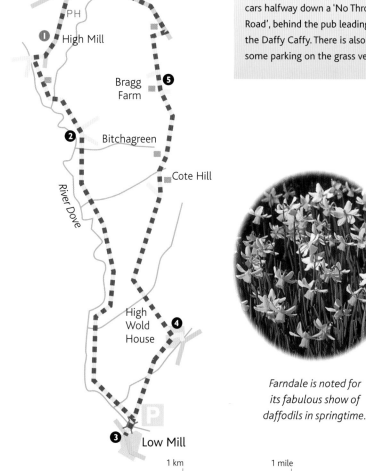

Farndale is noted for its fabulous show of daffodils in springtime.

▲ Map: Explorer 298
▲ Distance: 8 km/5 miles
▲ Walk ID: 1141 Graham Wilson

Difficulty rating

Time

▲ Pub, Toilets, Museum, Play
Area, Church, Castle, Wildlife, Birds,
Flowers, Butterflies, Food Shop

Low Kettle Spring from Ripley

This is a circular walk along the Nidderdale Way, through stunning Yorkshire woodlands and farmland. The route also passes through the formal estate of Ripley Castle.

1 From the car park head north through the village on the main road. Follow signs for the Nidderdale Way along Birthwaite Lane until reaching the B6165. Cross the road and follow the Nidderdale Way.

2 Turn right into the wood and follow the path down the hill. At the marker at the bottom of the wood turn right. Follow the path through the fields, looking out for the ancient inscribed stone.

3 Navigate the boggy ground and head left along the Nidderdale Way, passing along the edge of the wood. At the road, turn left and walk down the hill. Take the bridleway marked off to the right and follow it to the farm at the end of the track.

4 Just before the farm, the footpath crosses the field to the left. Drop down the field to the stream. At the stream, turn right and follow it round a bend. Cross the stream at the bridge and head to the right, into the field.

5 Follow the marker indicating the path across and up into the next field. Follow the path until meeting the road, and turn left. Go straight across the crossroads at Bedlam. The path goes through the garden gate alongside the main house gates. Walk through to a signed path across fields. Where the footpaths meet, head straight on

towards the stone estate wall at the top of the rise. At the wall, turn right and follow it round. Where the track meets a farm track, turn left.

6 At the next junction turn left and follow the track back into Ripley. The car park is to the right, back along the main road.

access information

Ripley is on the A61 north of Harrogate. Car parking in free car park. Buses from Knaresborough.

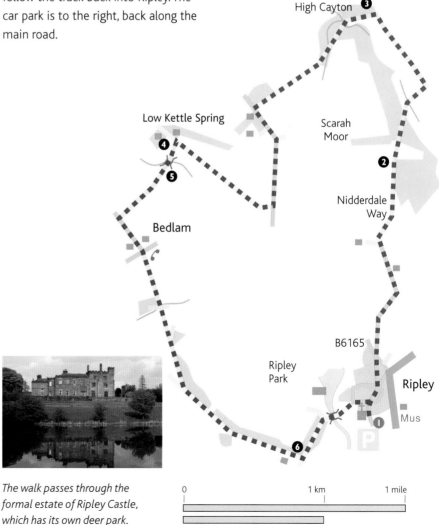

The walk passes through the formal estate of Ripley Castle, which has its own deer park.

WOODLAND & HILLSIDE **115**

▲ Map: Explorer 27

▲ Distance: 9 km/5½ miles

▲ Walk ID: 1019 Jean Hardman

Difficulty rating

Time

▲ Toilets, Birds, Great
Views, Moor, Ancient Monument

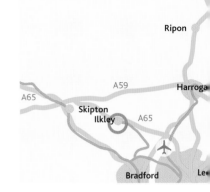

The Swastika Stone from Ilkley Town

Ilkley Moor is part of a large area of moorland, known collectively as Rombolds
Moor. This walk explores the area around the Swastika Stone, mostly on good
tracks and paths.

❶ Cross the road and walk up the steps
to the paddling pool. Turn left along the
path round the pool, then up the steps.
Follow the tarmac path to the right of
the shelter, then ahead up more steps
and along a deeply rutted path towards
the house. Take the steps down to the
track, which heads downhill. Walk over
the bridge and take the path to the left.

❷ Follow the path until it comes out
onto the road. Turn left up the road for a
short distance. At the signpost, turn right
and cross over the footbridge. Follow the
track along the moorside.

❸ Cross the bridge over Black Beck and
continue ahead on the path alongside
the wall. At the junction bear left away
from the wall. Continue on the main
path, crossing a series of three stone
stiles and one wooden stile, taking in the
extensive views across to Wharfedale.
Just before the next wooden stile, take
the narrow path on the left through the
bracken to a stone stile. Go through the
stile onto a path over the hill.

❹ At the wood, turn left and follow the
path, keeping the wood on the right.
When you reach the end of the wood,
continue up past East Buck Stones, then
on to Whetstone Gate.

*At Ilkley you will see not only the
famous moor, but also these
magnificent rock formations, the
Cow and Calf Rocks.*

❺ At Whetstone Gate, turn left and
follow the wide stony track, passing
Cowpers Cross on the left. Continue
downhill for about 2 km until the track
meets the road.

❻ Continue down the road, turn right
at the junction and walk back to the
car park.

further information

White Wells is a restored 18th-century
bathhouse. It is open to visitors most
weekends.

access information

There are regular bus and train
services from Leeds to Ilkley. If
using this form of transport you
will need to add an extra 1.5 km
to the distance for the walk up
Wells Road and back down at the
end of the walk.

By car take the A65 to Ilkley.
At the traffic lights turn towards
the B6382, turn left at the
roundabout then first right up
Wells Road, over the cattle grid
at the top and immediately right
into the large car park.

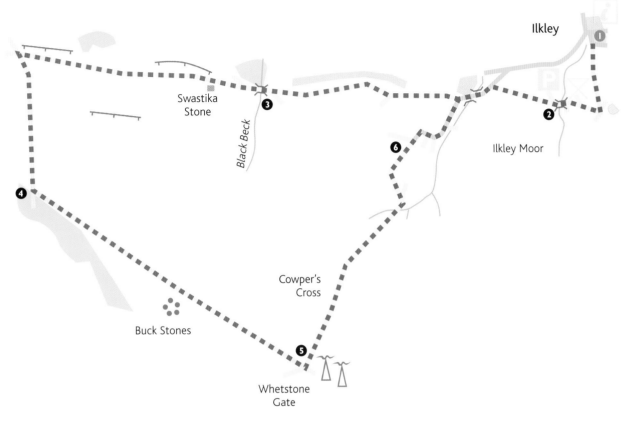

Ilkley

Swastika
Stone

Black Beck

3

6

Ilkley Moor

4

1

2

Cowper's
Cross

Buck Stones

5

Whetstone
Gate

0   1 km   1 mile

*The Swastika Stone is a magnificent
example of a Bronze Age swastika, or
follyfoot. The original is on the large
boulder, with a replica nearer the fence.
It is a version of the symbol of eternal life,
and dates from around 1800 BC.*

▲ Map: Explorer OL 10

▲ Distance: 13 km/8 miles

▲ Walk ID: 451 William Kembery

Difficulty rating

Time

▲ Hills or Fells, River, Pub, Toilets, Museum, Play Area, Church, National Trust/NTS, Birds, Flowers, Great Views

Barden Moor above Bolton Abbey

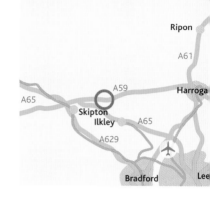

After a pleasant stroll along the Wharfe and a visit to Bolton Priory, the walk crosses the river and climbs up onto the grouse moors, with panoramic views of upper Wharfedale, before returning along the river.

1 Walk towards the river along the old road. Just before the bridge, turn left through a stile. Follow the signs to Bolton Priory.

2 Cross the river by the Priory. Turn left and keep to the lower path. Follow the river to enter the woods by a stile. Continue on this path through the trees. At the lane turn left down the hill to ford the stream. Turn left onto the footpath, signposted Pavilion.

3 Cross the bridge and the road. Head up the track to Bolton Park Farm. Take the left-hand track through a gate at the end of the farm, then across two cattle grids. Follow the track through the moor. At the next junction, take the right fork.

4 At the T-junction, turn right. Follow the track down the valley. Leap over the small ford and continue towards the farm. At the next junction, take the right-hand fork. Keep straight on, following the signs to Storiths. Cross over a stile to reach the next junction.

5 Turn right and continue straight past the farm access road. Keep to this track, leading into Storiths. Cross the road and continue ahead. Take the 'No Through Road' and follow it round a farm to arrive at a gate. Enter the ginnel and walk downhill.

6 At the T-junction, turn left towards Bolton Bridge. Follow this path over two stiles. Turn right and continue to reach the banks of the river. Cross several fields until you reach a track. Follow the track, climbing left. At the top, keep to the right of the gate to arrive at a stile giving access to a field. Continue on the track and enter the ginnel by a small gate to the right of the farm buildings. At the old road, turn right over the bridge, back to the car.

access information

Parking is off the A59 at Bolton Bridge to the east of Skipton.

Bolton Priory is a 12th-century Augustinian priory near the picturesque village of Bolton Abbey.

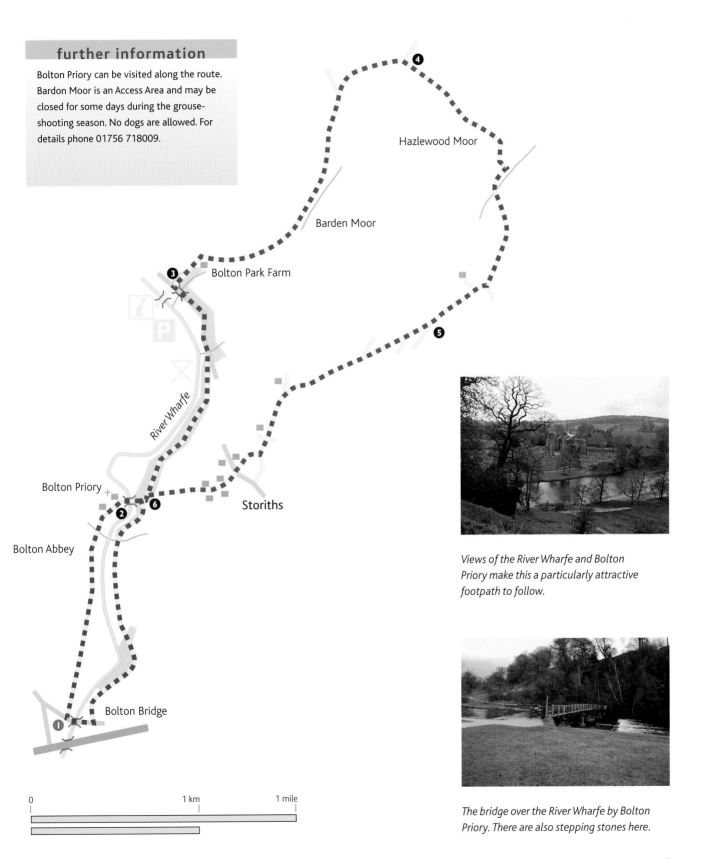

further information

Bolton Priory can be visited along the route. Bardon Moor is an Access Area and may be closed for some days during the grouse-shooting season. No dogs are allowed. For details phone 01756 718009.

Hazlewood Moor

Barden Moor

3 Bolton Park Farm

River Wharfe

5

Bolton Priory

2

6

Storiths

Bolton Abbey

Views of the River Wharfe and Bolton Priory make this a particularly attractive footpath to follow.

1 Bolton Bridge

The bridge over the River Wharfe by Bolton Priory. There are also stepping stones here.

0   1 km   1 mile

▲ Map: Explorer 298

▲ Distance: 9 km/5½ miles

▲ Walk ID: 321 Jim Grindle

Difficulty rating

Time

▲ Hills or Fells, River, Lake/Loch, Pub, Toilets, Museum, Play Area, Church, Great Views

Guise Cliff from Pateley Bridge

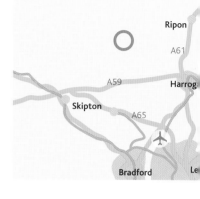

This walk, although relatively short, is wonderfully varied, rising through pastures and moorland, before descending through woods to the riverside. You even pass a very old and unusual folly.

1 Leave the car park and cross the road. Turn left alongside the playground. Turn left at the junction and then right at Bewerley Farm. Cross the stile and head uphill.

2 Follow the path to the top of the rise. Go through the stile and continue on the left, to the edge of the wood. Turn left, following the stream downhill, and cross the footbridge. At the lake follow the yellow marker to your right to reach a gravel track and a stile.

3 Turn right onto the lane. Cross the ford and continue uphill. Follow the lane as it bends left then right, and exit through the gate in the fence. Follow the path along the edge of the wood. Cross the stile and turn left. Go through a gate and turn right. Leave the wood for an open stretch and make for the stone wall. At a large beech tree in the corner, turn to the left and head downhill to a ladder stile. Follow the steep path down to a bridge, turn left to the stone wall and follow the path uphill.

4 Follow the track and cross the lane via a kissing gate. Head up the bank by the sign for Guise Cliff. Pass Yorke's Folly and cross the ladder stile. Follow the main track above the cliff top for 1.6 km, crossing numerous stiles on the way.

5 Go steeply down the track. Follow the path as it winds through the trees and forks left, towards Guisecliff Tarn. After the tarn, turn left. At the next junction take the muddy path to the right. Continue via a stile, steps, an enclosed path and another stile next to a cottage. Continue past the farm to a T-junction. Turn left, and then right to cross the bridge.

6 Turn left down the gravel track. Pass a reservoir. Just beyond the weir, follow the gravelled riverside path back to the bridge in Pateley.

further information

Yorke's Folly was built over 200 years ago under the instructions of John Yorke of Bewerley. There were originally three columns, but one was destroyed in a storm in 1893.

Brimham Stones, on the moor near Pateley Bridge.

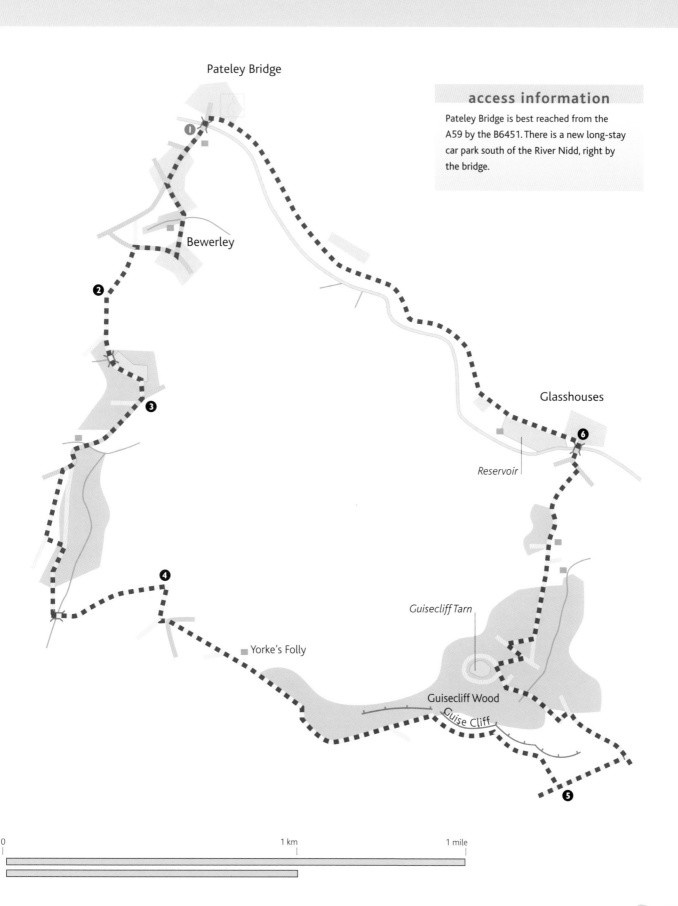

Pateley Bridge

❶

Bewerley

❷

❸

❹

Yorke's Folly

access information

Pateley Bridge is best reached from the A59 by the B6451. There is a new long-stay car park south of the River Nidd, right by the bridge.

Glasshouses

❻

Reservoir

Guisecliff Tarn

Guisecliff Wood

Guise Cliff

❺

0   1 km   1 mile

▲ Map: Explorer 27
▲ Distance: 8.5 km/5¼ miles
▲ Walk ID: 768 Jean Hardman

Difficulty rating

Time

▲ Great Views

Around Chevin Park

This is a favourite walk for weekend afternoons, with good tracks and superb views to Otley and Wharfedale. If you are lucky, you may spot some of the roe deer that live in Chevin Park – remember to keep dogs under control.

1 At the car park, go through the gap in the fence. Follow the path, bearing left to reach the main track. Turn right, then take the right fork along the broad track. Cross the stream, and take the right-hand track to the crest of the hill. Continue straight across the junction on a broad, sandy track. At the T-junction turn left, and head downhill. Bear left and go through the kissing gate. At the diverging paths keep straight ahead.

2 Turn left onto the main track and go through the gate. Follow the broad track to the top of Caley Crags. Continue straight ahead, then cross the bridge. Bear left over the walkway and follow the path on the right.

3 Take a small path to the right just before the car park, passing through a wooded area, running parallel with the road until you cross a stile. Turn right down the road, keeping to the verge, which becomes a footpath.

4 Cross the road and enter the East Chevin Quarry car park. At the far end, cross the stile and climb the broad track, which passes through the scrubland and then enters woodland. At the junction turn left. At the top turn right, keeping the woods on the right. Go straight ahead, passing the steps. Pass through a broken wall into a small wooded area. Follow the main path right and go through another broken wall.

5 Turn left at the junction, following the track uphill. At the top, turn left to reach the main path, and continue straight ahead. Take the next right-hand track, which goes above The Chevin with spectacular views. Continue past a car park.

6 Turn left at the gate and down the stony track to emerge on East Chevin Road. Cross the road and turn right to reach the car park.

A breathtaking view of Wharfedale on a glorious sunny day.

access information

Chevin Forest Park is south of the A660 Leeds to Otley road. If approaching from Leeds, when you reach the junction with the A658 (traffic lights at Dynley Arms), turn left up the A658 and at the third right-hand junction turn right onto East Chevin Road. The car park is on the right.

Beyond Caley Crags, the path meanders over bridges and through fields and forest.

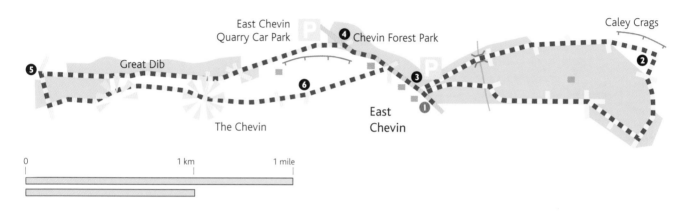

Caley Crags

East Chevin
Quarry Car Park

4 Chevin Forest Park

Great Dib

5

2

3

6

1

The Chevin

East
Chevin

0   1 km   1 mile

▲ Map: Explorer OL 1

▲ Distance: 10 km/6¼ miles

▲ Walk ID: 1137 Barry Smith

Difficulty rating

Time

▲ Hills or Fells, Pub, Toilets, Church, Wildlife, Flowers, Great Views, Moor, Woodland

Pots 'n' Pans from Binns Green

With superb views and plenty of inspiration and opportunities for taking photographs, this walk climbs over moorland then into small hamlets and green lanes for the return.

1 From Binns Green car park, cross the road and take the bridleway opposite, signed Oldham Way. Go to the second stile and turn right. Cross the next stile to start the climb up to the Pots 'n' Pans boulder, which comes into view over the crest of the hill. Follow this track and climb past (or through) the quarry to the summit, where you will come across the boulder with the memorial behind.

2 Go right, through a gap in the iron railings. A stone pillar will confirm you are still on the Oldham Way. Continue on the path ahead, forking left at the marker. Head for the ridge and Shaw Rocks. Looking down, St Chad's Church can be seen. Continue to Slades Rocks.

3 Here, take the lane to the left. After a stile, continue ahead. Pass a left-hand fork and follow the next left bend, cross a stile ahead of you and descend into Pobgreen.

4 Bear right and continue on the lane ahead. This soon turns into a path that follows the contours of the hill, crossing three stiles. At the fourth stile bear left, following the marker poles, and cross a broken wall. Keep the poles on your left. Continue by the wall to the corner where the poles meet the wall. Go straight ahead, passing a bench, then bear right slightly downhill.

5 Just before the stile on the right, turn left onto the lane towards Alderman Hill. Just before the farm, take the lane going sharply downhill to your right.

6 You will come out on Long Lane at Yars Hill. Turn left and this will take you to a waymark. Follow the lane back to Binns Green.

access information

From Oldham, take the A669 to Greenfield. Take the sharp right turn for the rail station and continue sharp left on the A669 to the roundabout. Turn left on the A635 and after 2 km turn right for Binns Green car park. This road also brings you from Holmfirth. The train stops at Greenfield from both sides of the Pennines, and is just 3 km from the start of the walk.

further information

Pots 'n' Pans gets the name from the hollows in the rocks that collect water, said to have healing properties for sore eyes!

Until you follow a footpath such as the Pots 'n' Pans route, it is easy to forget that Britain has some of the most stunning views in the world.

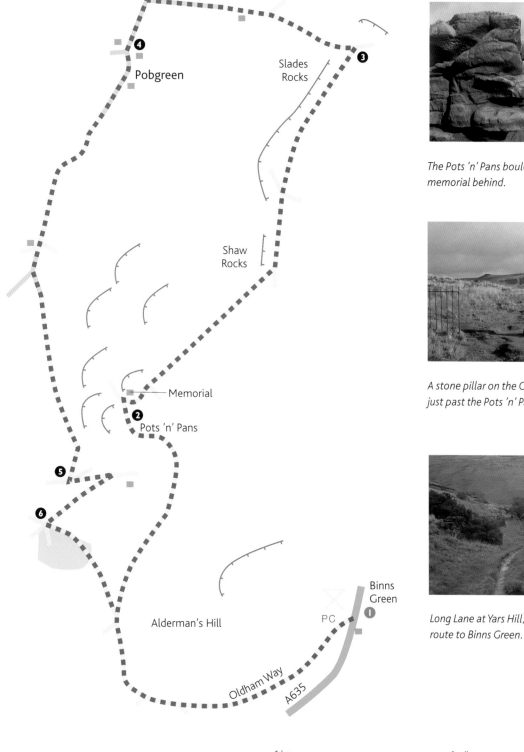

Pobgreen

Slades
Rocks

Shaw
Rocks

Memorial

Pots 'n' Pans

Alderman's Hill

Binns
Green

PC

Oldham Way

A635

The Pots 'n' Pans boulder with the
memorial behind.

A stone pillar on the Oldham Way,
just past the Pots 'n' Pans boulder.

Long Lane at Yars Hill, on the return
route to Binns Green.

0

1 km

1 mile

▲ Map: Explorer OL 21
▲ Distance: 9 km/5½ miles
▲ Walk ID: 244 Karen Walton

Difficulty rating

Time

▲ Hills or Fells, Pub, Toilets, Church, Great Views

Barkisland and Greetland from Stainland

This route shows Calderdale at its best, from open views over the surrounding countryside to period houses in local villages, and from hilltop to valley floor via tracks, country lanes and fields.

❶ From the car park turn right into Stainland Road. At the junction bear right, then turn left at the school. When you reach the crossroads, go straight down Coldwells Hill. At a signpost for Sonoco Board Mills, bear right. At a fork bear left over a bridge. Follow the curve of the road, then continue on a sandy track past a farmhouse. Go through a gate into a sloping field. Continue through two fields to a wooden stile.

❷ Turn right up a partly cobbled lane. Continue past Penny Hill Cottage and Park House Farm. Just before a row of houses, turn right. Follow the path into a field, passing through a series of stone stiles.

❸ Turn left into a lane and take the footpath on the right. Cross the field through a stile into a farmyard. Stick to the path through several fields, crossing a brook and a stony lane on the way. Go down the steps, over the beck and up the hill.

❹ Turn left into Stainland Road and pass the Griffin Inn. Turn right into Stoney Butts Lane. Follow the path to the road. Cross the road and continue on the path to Greetland Road. Turn right. Bear right past a farmhouse. Cross a lane and keep forward down a grassy track. At the bottom, turn right and cross Saddleworth Road. Turn left onto a signposted footpath.

❺ Follow the path ahead, turning right then left through a field. Cross the road and go through the mill complex. Continue into open fields, following the footpath signposted to Gate Head. Keep close to the brook. Climb the steps and turn right over a bridge. At the lane, bear left and climb the steps, following the sign to Stainland. Follow the yellow markers over the golf course. On reaching a wall, turn right.

❻ At the large boulder, turn left, then right to follow a walled lane to Stainland Road. Turn right back to the car park.

access information

The walk starts from the village of Stainland, on the B6112 to the west of the A629 between Halifax and Huddersfield. The car park is in the village centre next to the Red Lion. Stainland is easily accessible by bus from Halifax, Elland or Huddersfield.

The hills around Calderdale offer plenty of opportunities to fill your lungs with fresh air.

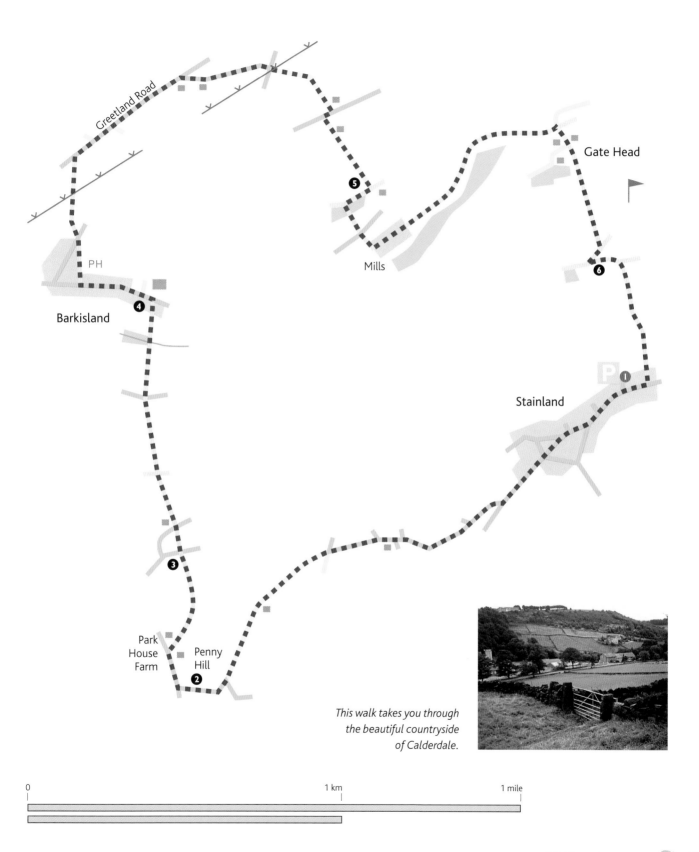

Greetland Road

Gate Head

Mills

PH

Barkisland

④

Stainland

P ①

③

Park
House
Farm

Penny
Hill

②

⑤

⑥

*This walk takes you through
the beautiful countryside
of Calderdale.*

0   1 km   1 mile

North-west England

Coastal & Waterside

The waterside walks of North-west England take in sea views and the inspirational calm of the Lake District. Highlights include Morecambe Bay, Elterwater and Buttermere.

▲ Map: Explorer 275

▲ Distance: 8 km/5 miles

▲ Walk ID: 256 Ian Darbyshire

Difficulty rating

Time

▲ River, Lake/Loch, Sea, Pub, Toilets, National Trust/NTS, Wildlife, Birds, Flowers, Great Views, Good for Wheelchairs

Hightown from Waterloo

This linear walk explores the seashore and sandhills that stretch between Waterloo Station, in the northern suburbs of Liverpool, and the Alt Estuary near Hightown. It is a rewarding route for bird-watching enthusiasts.

1 Turn left from Waterloo Station and walk down South Road to the distant promenade, past the Marine Gardens. Follow the path to the right of Sefton Coastal Park. Go between the two lakes to reach the beach side of the promenade. Carry on up the path towards the promenade. Turn right and follow the promenade, either along the path or along the beach.

2 Keep going until you reach the coastguard station at Hall Road. The stone wall at the end of the promenade is a favourite place for fishermen at high tide. If you wish you can cut the walk short here and walk inland along Hall Road West to Hall Road Station, about half a kilometre away. Alternatively you can take the little path from the car park.

3 To continue, remain with the shore beyond the end of the promenade, going along the path. Between the two beached lightships is a good place to look for wading birds such as oystercatchers, redshank and dunlin.

4 Just past the second lightship bear right at the waymark along a path through the low sandhills. This winds through growths of creeping willow, tough grasses and stands of sea buckthorn. Turn left where the path forks by a post. Follow the white-topped posts to reach the sailing clubhouse. Here a

board points the way to a viewpoint (at low tide) over the remains of an ancient submerged forest.

5 Rejoin the path through the dunes. Follow the white-topped posts leading to the Alt estuary and a boatyard. Keep an eye out for shore birds including the curlew and the bar-tailed godwit in the Alt estuary.

6 Walk up the path to the road and turn right. Go down the road, cross the roundabout and keep ahead along Lower Alt Road to find Hightown Station.

access information

Take a train to Waterloo Mersey Station. The suggested return is from Hall Road Station for a short walk, or Hightown Station for the longer walk – trains run every 15 minutes.

Liverpool's revitalized 19th-century dockside area now includes shops, restaurants, art galleries and commercial premises.

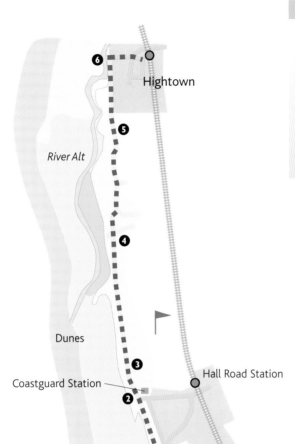

Waterloo to Hall Road is accessible to wheelchair users. For a longer challenge the Sefton Coastal Path links the entire length from Waterloo to Southport, crossing high sandhills and meandering through shady pine woods and rich farmland. It is waymarked throughout by yellow disks with a toad on them. Linking paths lead to all the stations on the Northern Line.

Hightown

River Alt

Dunes

Coastguard Station

Hall Road Station

Blundellsands

Waterloo

Marine Lake

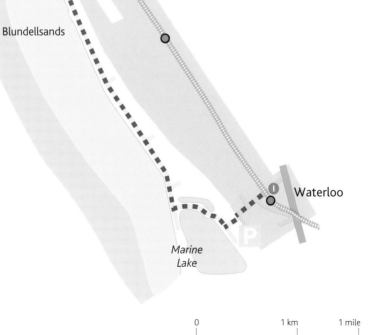

0   1 km   1 mile

▲ Map: Explorer 286

▲ Distance: 14.5 km/9 miles

▲ Walk ID: 732 Jim Grindle

Difficulty rating

Time

● ● ● ● ●

▲ Sea, Pub, Toilets, Play Area, Birds, Great Views, Good for Wheelchairs

Blackpool from Fleetwood

This is a linear walk along the Lancashire coast, from Fleetwood to the Pleasure Beach in Blackpool. By keeping to the beach where possible, and using the lower levels of the walks along the sea defences, you can keep well away from traffic.

① Cross the road from the North Euston Hotel and turn left on the promenade until you reach the pier 200 m away. Continue for another 50 m past the pier until you come to a turning on the right, beside a notice board, which brings you to the sea wall. Keeping to the beach or the embankment, turn and follow the promenade as it curves to the left. Simply continue south, with the sea to your right, until you reach Cleveleys.

② Continue on the promenade until the path curves up to the left to meet the main road. Continue to head south along the road.

③ At Little Bispham you can turn left if you prefer to catch a tram back to Fleetwood, or you can carry on south to Blackpool (you may have to walk

access information

You can take a train to Blackpool and then a tram to the terminus in Fleetwood. By road it is easiest to come by the M6 to junction 32; the M55 to junction 3 and then the A585 to Fleetwood. There is free parking near the North Euston Hotel which is right on the sea front at the very north of Fleetwood.

along the upper promenade for part of the way if restoration work is taking place). Carry straight on along the promenade until you reach Blackpool's North Pier.

④ If you wish to extend the walk, it is 3.5 km from here, past the South Pier, to the Pleasure Beach at Blackpool. You can then take a tram back to Fleetwood.

Blackpool's piers offer a delightful mix of nostalgia and scenic beauty for those walkers happy to continue to the end of this route.

▲ Map: Explorer 285

▲ Distance: 6 km/3¾ miles

▲ Walk ID: 257 Jim Grindle

Difficulty rating

Time

▲ Sea, Pub, Toilets, National Trust/NTS, Wildlife, Birds, Flowers, Great Views, Good for Wheelchairs

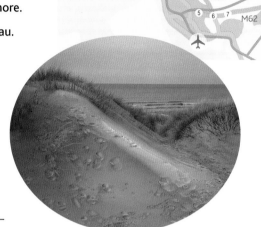

Fisherman's Path from Freshfield

This walk follows the railway line and enters pine woods before reaching the shore. Views from the beach take in the North Wales Clwydian Hills and the Carneddau. In clear conditions you can see the Lake District.

1 On leaving the station turn left and left again at the telephone box. Walk past a row of shops and then the station car park. At the end of the car park continue on the road which becomes a gravelled track. Take the wide left fork following the railway line as far as the level crossing.

2 Go over the railway line and follow the track through a golf course until you reach a metal gate at the entrance to the National Nature Reserve.

3 Take the left fork, which takes you for 1 km between the golf course on the left and the Reserve on the right. Go through a more open area and you reach a junction by the sand dunes.

4 Take the fork left, which has woods to the left and the sea behind the dunes to the right. After 1 km the path leads to the beach. Walk along the beach. The paths going off the beach are marked by posts. Continue as far as the fourth post, marked Victoria Road South, then turn left and climb by the fence to the top of the dunes.

5 A boardwalk leads down into the car park. Keep going until you reach a road leading to the Wardens' hut. Look on the right for 'Squirrel Walk' – this is the best place to see red squirrels.

6 Keep straight on and the concrete road gives way to tarmac – Victoria Road. It is now less than 1 km back to the station directly down this road.

The hills of North Wales can be viewed from the sand dunes of Formby Point.

access information

The walk starts at Freshfield Station on the Southport/Liverpool line. Access by road is from the A565. Follow the tourist signs to Formby Point (National Trust). The route crosses the railway line where there is parking.

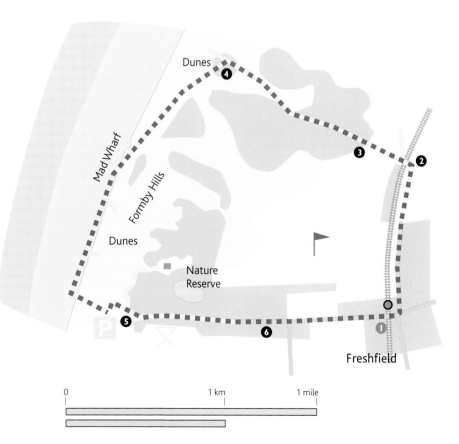

▲ Map: Explorer OL 7
▲ Distance: 11 km/6¾ miles
▲ Walk ID: 919 William Kembery

Difficulty rating

Time

▲ River, Sea, Pub, Toilets, National Trust/NTS, Wildlife, Birds, Flowers, Great Views, Food Shop, Good for Kids, Moor, Tea Shop, Woodland

Leighton Moss and Jenny Brown's Point

This is a varied walk through woods and along quiet lanes. The walk includes a stretch of Morecambe Bay's rich shores, and passes Leighton Moss bird sanctuary.

❶ From the car park take the little gate into Eave's Wood. At the first T-junction turn left. Soon take the right-hand fork going uphill through the trees. At the next junction keep straight on, swinging slightly left.

❷ Turn left off the track, but do not go through the gate. Turn right with a stone wall on the left and a hedge on the right. You will arrive at a lane by a bench and a signpost pointing right to Arnside Tower. Cross straight over, along a little lane opposite signed to Cove Road. Follow the narrow lane when it divides, towards a little gate to the left of a house.

❸ Go through the gate and onto the lane. Go straight on, to pick up the footpath again. Above Cove Road turn right and, when the footpath ends, cross the road and take the footpath on the other side. As it swings right, take the little road off to the left, signposted to the shore. Go through the gate and turn left along the shore, keeping near the base of the cliffs.

❹ After about 1 km, take a little road leading up from the shore. Go through the gate stile to follow the road. Soon take a right-hand footpath, signposted Lindeth Road. At the road, turn right and follow it until it forks with Hollins Lane going off to the left.

❺ Take the right-hand fork signed Jenny Brown's Point. Look out for a little gate on the right. Go through the gate and follow the good footpath across the heathland round to the left, parallel to the wall. Follow the footpath down into the bay. Continue with the footpath through the trees. Soon pass through two kissing gates. Turn right along the road. Just before Jenny Brown's Houses take the little causeway down onto the shore and past the old smelt chimney. Follow the base of the cliffs to a stile.

❻ Go through and continue with the fence on the right. At a metal gate go straight on. The footpath slopes gently uphill into the woods from a solid stone stile. At the road turn right and at the first junction turn right again. At the next major junction keep straight on towards the station. Soon a little lane goes off to the left. Take this lane to return to the car park.

access information

Silverdale is west of the M6, north of Morecambe Park. Begin the walk at Eave's Wood car park, north of Silverdale train station. If arriving by public transport, there is a regular train service from Lancaster or Carlisle.

The extensive tidal flats of Morecambe Bay are one of the most important bird reserves in Britain.

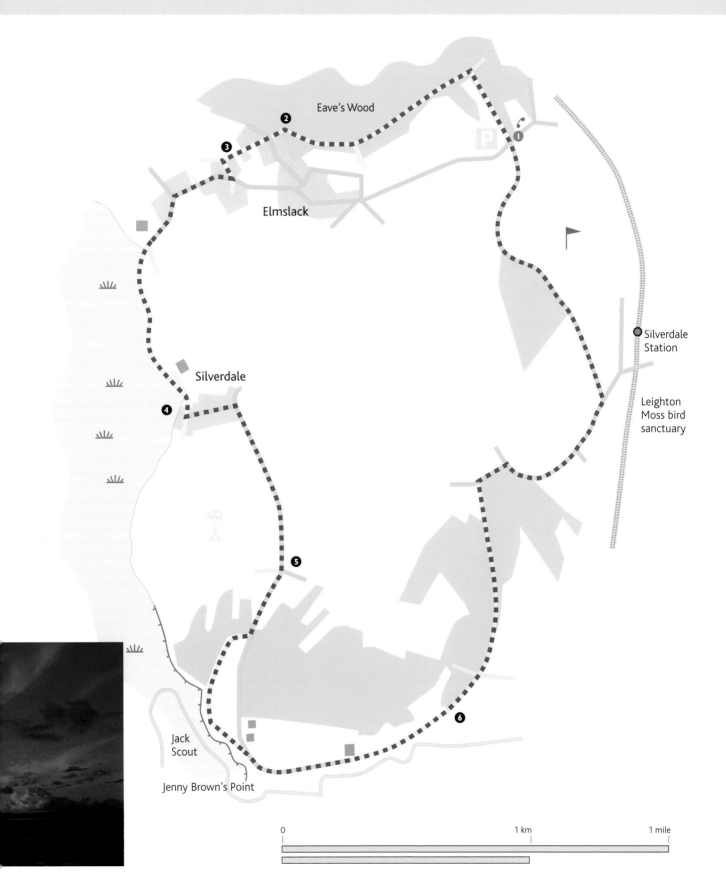

Eave's Wood

2

3

Elmslack

P

Silverdale
Station

Silverdale

4

Leighton
Moss bird
sanctuary

5

6

Jack
Scout

Jenny Brown's Point

| 0 | | | | 1 km | | 1 mile |

▲ Map: Explorer OL 7

▲ Distance: 14 km/8¾ miles

▲ Walk ID: 657 William Kembery

Difficulty rating

Time

▲ Hills or Fells, River, Pub, Toilets, Museum, Church, Birds, Flowers

Ulverston Sands and Birkrigg Common

A very scenic walk that takes in the Birkrigg Stone Circle and Conishead, a Buddhist priory. In the summer you can visit this retreat, but at other times stay on the track along the shoreline.

1 From the car park walk up the quiet lane and turn right at the top into Bardsea. Take the first road on the left. At the bottom of the hill, swing left towards Wellhouse and walk through the hamlet. Follow the road/track up the hill, now heading for Birkrigg Common. Continue until almost at a little unfenced road. Turn right and walk over the small rise.

2 Follow the stone wall, then the green track up the hillside. At the brow of the hill, curve around to the right to find the white trig point. From here head directly north towards the Hoad Memorial. Go back down on one of the grassy tracks. Follow the signpost to Far Mount Barrow and head for a gate left of the corner of a wall. This leads onto an enclosed lane, which you should follow. Turn right and then first left onto a farm track.

3 Go through the gate into the farmyard and pass to the right of the barn on a road and join the farm. Turn right at the Priory Road signpost and walk along the good track. Go through an iron kissing gate and continue between the hedges. Stay with the right-hand hedge to another iron kissing gate to join a track.

4 Soon you go through another kissing gate on the left. Keep the wall on the right. Left of a small wood go through another kissing gate. Head just left of the farmhouse to yet another kissing gate and join the farm lane down to the road. Turn right and 100 m down the road, turn left through a gap stile. Follow the right-hand fence as it turns right, over a ladder stile, then left until it emerges onto the road over another stile. Turn left along the lane and take a stile by the first gate on the right. Follow a faint track across the field to two stiles crossing a ditch.

5 Head half-left to the left of a row of houses, climb a stile by a gate and walk down the back road of the houses to a lane and turn left. At the T-junction at Sandhall turn left and in about 20 m go through a kissing gate on the right.

6 Almost doubling back, head for the left of a wood towards a gate. Through the gate walk with the trees on the right along a rough track and eventually via two further gates join a lane. Follow this round to the shore. Turn right on the track and walk along the shoreline past Conishead Priory. The path leads eventually back to the car park near Bardsea where you began.

Walking across Ulverston Sands at sunrise or sunset, the shore can be bathed in wonderful colours. As with all coastal walks, you should check the tides before setting out.

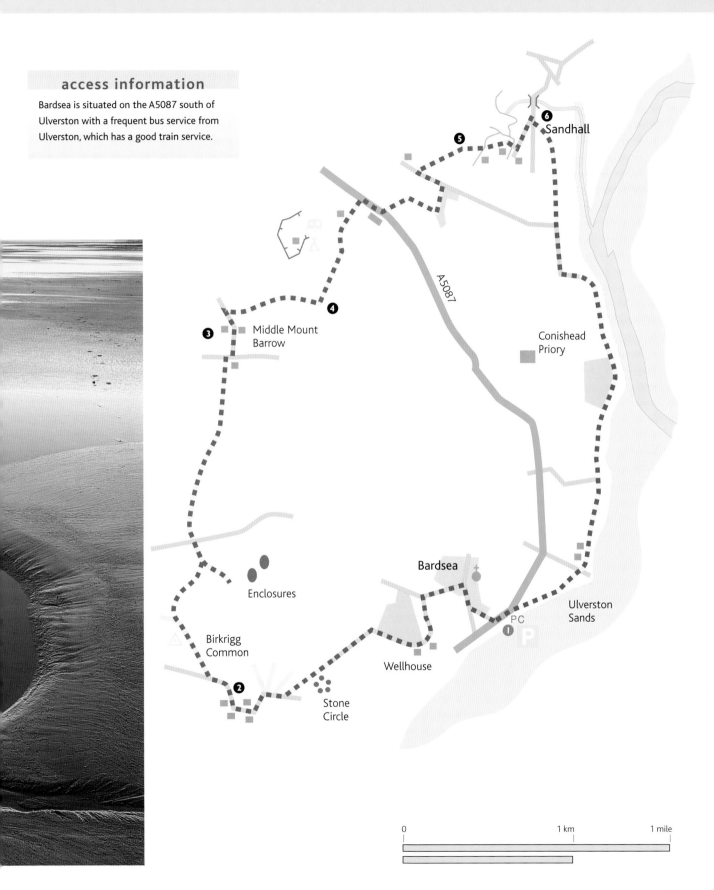

access information

Bardsea is situated on the A5087 south of Ulverston with a frequent bus service from Ulverston, which has a good train service.

6 Sandhall

5

A5087

4

3 Middle Mount Barrow

Conishead Priory

Enclosures

Bardsea

Ulverston Sands

P C

P

Birkrigg Common

2

Stone Circle

Wellhouse

0   1 km   1 mile

▲ Map: Explorer OL 7

▲ Distance: 6½ km/4 miles

▲ Walk ID: 447 William Kembery

Difficulty rating

Time

Hills or Fells, Sea, Pub, Great Views

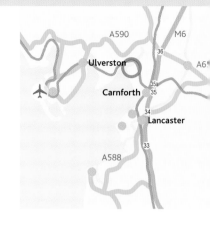

Arnside from Arnside Knott

From Arnside Knott, the walk passes through some woodland then drops down to the shoreline and along the promenade. After a stroll through the village the walk leads back up to visit the summit of the Knott for glorious views across Morecambe Bay.

❶ Go to the kissing gate in the wall of the car park. Head downhill through the trees until a major path crosses and then turn right. Go through the mini-gate and go straight over a crossing path and a ladder stile. Follow the fenced path to the road. Turn left and go down the lane. Just before a life belt, bear right to join the main path around New Barn's Bay. Continue along the shore to enter the trees beside another life belt.

❷ Follow the footpath to a gate, and climb the stile. Follow the left-hand boundary to reach another stile by the boatyard and cross it to join the shore again. Continue along the path into Arnside. Pass the station and take a track to the right signposted Silverdale Road.

❸ Cross Silverdale Road going slightly left to find an opening into a narrow ginnel. Go along this ginnel, then round some garages. Go up a path climbing steeply up to emerge through a gap in a wall onto Higher Knott Road.

❹ Cross the road and take a footpath signposted The Knott. Pass through the iron kissing gate and follow the footpath away, to arrive at a gate. Bear left to visit the summit. Walk up the hill keeping the wall on the left, and when a gate is seen in this wall, bear away to the right where the path splits into two. Head for the wicker gate seen in the wall ahead.

❺ Go through it and take the right-hand path, climbing uphill. Ignore all paths off until eventually arriving at the stone bench. Head back slightly right on a clear path, uphill to the trig point. Now return to the bench and go forward on a clear path going downhill. Ignore all minor paths off until a fork is reached and the path splits into two good paths. Take the right-hand path and go through a gate in a wall to reach a viewpoint.

❻ Turn left and follow the footpath down the hill with a wall over on the left, eventually to meet the wall at a gap. Turn right and follow the good path through the trees, keeping right on a good track to arrive at the car park.

further information

Morecambe Bay sands can be extremely treacherous. In the summer you can walk across safely, but only in the company of The Queen's Guide to the Sands, a traditional office held by an experienced local guide. At very high tides the beach section of this walk may not be passable.

There are some wonderful sites to visit around Morecambe Bay. At Heysham, you can see St Patrick's Chapel, where the saint is said to have been shipwrecked on his way to Scotland in the 5th century.

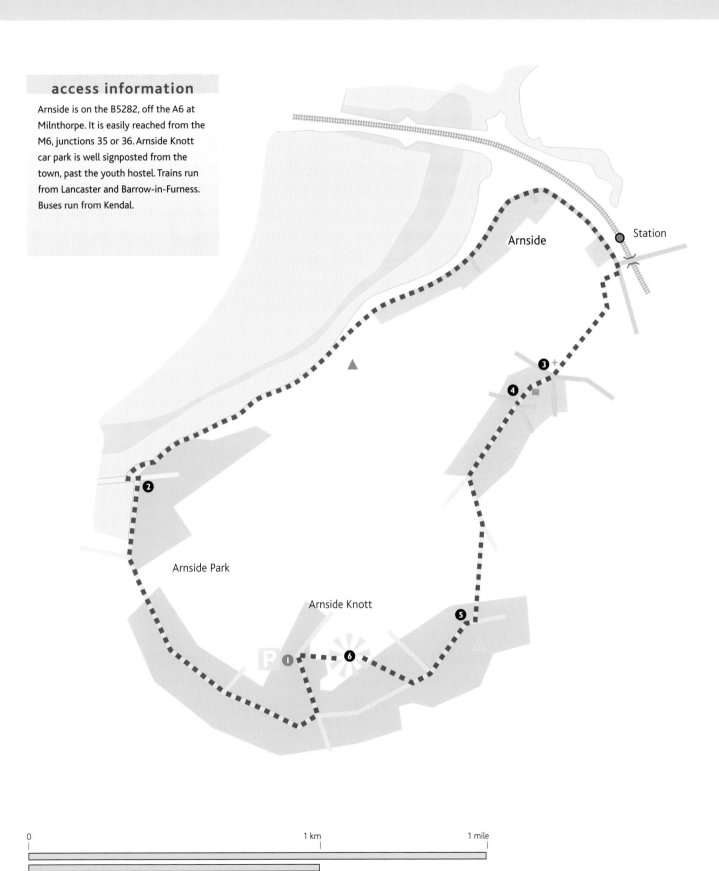

access information

Arnside is on the B5282, off the A6 at Milnthorpe. It is easily reached from the M6, junctions 35 or 36. Arnside Knott car park is well signposted from the town, past the youth hostel. Trains run from Lancaster and Barrow-in-Furness. Buses run from Kendal.

Arnside

Station

Arnside Park

Arnside Knott

0

1 km

1 mile

▲ Map: Explorer OL 7

▲ Distance: 6 km/3¾ miles

▲ Walk ID: 1299 Gary Gray

Difficulty rating

Time

▲ Lake/Loch, Pub, National Trust/NTS, Wildlife, Birds, Flowers, Great Views

Black Crag from Tarn Hows

This is a very pleasant, easy-to-follow, linear walk along Tarn Hows and up to Black Crag. The fantastic views include a panorama of nearly all the major fells.

1 From the car park walk out onto the road. The path down to the tarn is straight ahead. Take the right-hand fork towards the tarn. On reaching the gate, go through and follow the path alongside the tarn.

2 At the signpost (Arnside and Langdale), turn left. This is part of the Cumbrian way. This track leads you away from the tarn. On reaching a gate and stile, turn right onto a stone track. There are fine views of Tarn Hows to the right about two-thirds of the way up.

3 When you reach the plantation of Iron Keld on your left, look for a gate and a signpost marked 'Iron Keld'. Turn left through the gate and follow the track through the plantation.

4 As you emerge from the plantation, you will reach a gate and swing gate. Go through and walk on for a short way through an old set of stone gateposts. A path joins from the right at a sharp angle. Take this path which first doubles back then soon swings up to the left and towards the fell. Follow the grassy track upwards.

5 On reaching the summit there is a trig point at the top. You can continue over the stile and along the fell. However, there is no way down and you must return to the stile and the track. For your return journey, simply head back the way you came.

Tarn Hows is a man-made landscaped pool, surrounded by woodland.

access information

Access can only be gained by car. There is a National Trust car park with plenty of parking. To get to Tarn Hows, follow A593 out of Ambleside towards Coniston. After about 1km turn left towards Hawkshead, and follow the road (B5286) in the same direction. After about 1 km there is a junction to the right, signposted for Tarn Hows and Coniston. Make your way to the second car park, which is nearer to the tarn.

0   1 km   1 mile

▲ Map: Explorer OL 4

▲ Distance: 6 km/3¾ miles

▲ Walk ID: 173 David Stewart

Difficulty rating

Time

▲ Hills or Fells, Lake/Loch, Pub, Toilets, Church, National Trust/NTS, Birds, Great Views

Buttermere

A charming walk that takes you on a circuit of Buttermere, one of the prettiest and most isolated of the Lakes. The mere itself nestles at the end of its valley, with the steep sides of Red Pike, High Stile and High Crag rising up directly from it.

1 Pass down to the left of the Fish Inn and head for the lake. Immediately, you can see the waters of Sour Milk Gill cascading down the hillside. Head towards the waterfall, ignoring the path signed to Scale Force on your right.

2 As you reach the lake edge bear right and make straight for the base of the fall. From here it is a truly impressive sight, especially after a good rainfall. Turn left to follow the lakeside, taking the path which runs right by the water's edge. It is very difficult to go wrong, so all you need do is soak up the glorious scenery.

3 After a kilometre or so, the path runs beyond the end of the lake, and you will see a track to the left passing over Peggy's Bridge in the direction of Gatesgarth Farm. Follow the track, taking time to stop at the bridge, where you can admire the spectacular view along the lake. Continue up to the farm.

4 Turn left onto the road. There is a short stretch of tarmac here, but it is a quiet route. Shortly you come to a small bay and the lakeside path forks away from the road. The path follows closely along the lake edge.

5 Before you reach the village again, pass through a short tunnel hewn into the rock (mind your head as the sign here warns!).

6 Once you get beyond the lake, follow the well-signed paths back to the village.

access information

By car, take the B5289 from Keswick. From Cockermouth take the B5292, then the B5289. There are regular services by bus from Keswick and Cockermouth during the daytime.

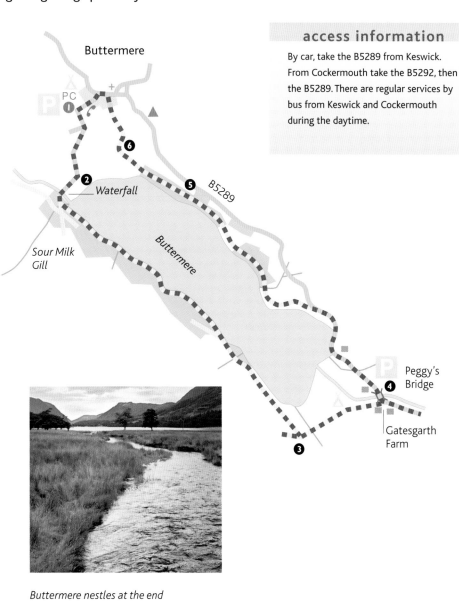

Buttermere nestles at the end of a steep-sided valley, surrounded by the peaks of Red Pike, High Stile and High Crag.

▲ Map: Explorer OL 7

▲ Distance: 11¼ km/7 miles

▲ Walk ID: 1268 Harold Toze

Difficulty rating

Time

▲ Hills or Fells, River, Lake/Loch, Pub, Toilets, Wildlife, Great Views, Gift Shop, Industrial Archaeology, Tea Shop, Waterfall, Woodland

Skelwith Bridge from Elterwater

This is a low-level walk with many interesting features to look out for along the way, including two waterfalls – Colwith Force and Skelwith Force – and an old clapper bridge at Slater Bridge.

1 From the car park entrance turn left to cross the bridge. Go along the road and take the lane that forks off to the right. Continue on the rough track. Go over the hill and down to the minor road through Little Langdale.

2 At the road junction cross diagonally down a farm track. At the farm buildings follow the footpath alongside the stone wall. Cross Slater Bridge and go up the track on the other side through a stile onto a wider track. Turn left and follow the stream. Go along the track ahead to the next footbridge/ford.

3 Follow the track away from the ford up the slope to the right. Follow the left fork signposted Skelwith and Colwith. Continue uphill to Stang End and along the road to High Park Farm. After the farm take the path leading off to the left. Go across the field and through a gate. Follow a small footpath downhill to arrive at Colwith Force waterfall. Continue alongside the stream to come out on a minor road. Turn right and after about 100 m there is a footpath signposted to Skelwith Bridge.

4 Turn left onto the footpath. At Park Farm take the right-hand path to the bridge. The path continues parallel to the road, eventually joining it. Continue down the main road to Skelwith Bridge. At the bottom of the hill turn left crossing the river by the road bridge.

Skelwith Force is a short distance up the stream. Pass by the Skelwith Bridge Hotel to the junction of the B5343 and the A593. Cross the B5343 coming from the left and go up the minor road. At the top of the hill turn right along the Ambleside road, then almost immediately left on a minor road. Turn right again at another minor road, which is marked to Loughrigg Tarn only.

5 Pass Dillygarth Cottage and turn left along a rough track. Follow the track around the north side of Loughrigg Tarn. At the Howe turn left through a wooden gate and down the hill to pass near to the end of Loughrigg Tarn. At the minor road turn left. Soon a track leads off to the right, signed back to Skelwith Bridge. Take this track, passing Crag Head Cottage on the left. Just before the dry-stone wall turn right and at the top of the next rise Elterwater should come into view through the trees. Continue downhill and go through a stile in the stone wall into the wood beyond. You will reach Langdale Road.

6 Cross Langdale Road diagonally and hop over the low wall alongside the wooden gate. Follow the track down the slope to join the main track beside Elterwater and continue along this track to return to the car park.

access information

Elterwater is on the B5343 to the west of Ambleside. There are two car parks in Elterwater. This walk starts from the lower car park.

The peaks of the spectacular Langdale Valley, which include Pavey Ark, Pike o'Stickle and Bow Fell, are a popular destination for hillwalkers.

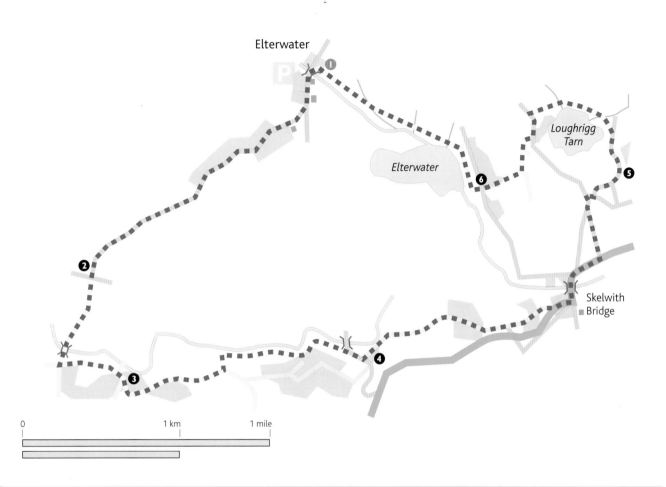

Elterwater

Elterwater

Loughrigg
Tarn

Skelwith
Bridge

0   1 km   1 mile

From picturesque woods to the dramatic fells of the Lake District, the woodland and hillside walks in this region are simply breathtaking. Highlights include the Sandstone Trail and Dungeon Ghyll.

▲ Map: Explorer 287

▲ Distance: 10 km/6¼ miles

▲ Walk ID: 1123 William Kembery

Difficulty rating

Time

▲ Pub, Toilets, Castle, National Trust/
NTS, Flowers, Great Views, Food Shop,
Good for Kids, Moor, Nature Trail, Tea
Shop, Woodland, Ancient Monument

Rivington Pike and Lever Park

Explore the many facets of Lever Park and seek out the half-hidden formal garden, the towers, the barns and a splendid folly of a castle.

❶ From Lowehouse car park, go over the stile. Follow the path to the bridge. Cross and turn right to another stile. Cross and follow the path. Go over the next stile, turning sharp left to join a path and walking downhill to continue straight on down a track. Follow this track. When a junction of tracks is reached a kissing gate can be seen on the left.

❷ Go through the gate and either follow the 'garden trail' up the hill or go directly up to Pigeon Tower via the flight of steps. Behind the tower go through the bridle gate and onto the wide track. Go through the kissing gate on the left and ascend Rivington Pike by any path.

❸ Turn right (across the front of the tower) and take the footpath that leads downhill. The track broadens out. At the next junction go straight across through the little gate and follow the grassy bridleway downhill. Go past the farm track. At the next junction, turn right (not sharp right). Follow this to a junction, before a gate ahead. Turn left downhill. At the main road, cross and head for Bridleway Castle. As the track swings right, carry straight on up.

❹ At the T-junction turn left. With the castle in view, follow the track round, turning right all the time. Beyond the castle, turn left away through the trees. At a junction of paths take the left fork and follow it parallel to the reservoir.

❺ At the fork take the left-hand path and follow along the banks of the reservoir, across the bridge to the small school car park. Turn left and at the main road turn right along it. Follow the road round to the right until you reach a footpath on the right signposted to the Great House Information Centre. Take this path through the woods, parallel to the road. Pass the arboretum and go towards the centre.

❻ Cross the main road and follow the path signed 'Rivington Hall Barn' alongside a wide road. Just before the hall gates, turn right onto a good track and follow it round to the back of the hall. Turn left, retracing the way out to arrive at the car park.

access information

Lowehouse car park is reached by taking the A675 north from Bolton, turning left in Belmont village, and turning first left after 4.8 km.

The views from Rivington Pike across to the Fylde coast are awe-inspiring. This was one of the heights on which beacons were lit to warn of the approach of the Spanish Armada.

Rivington Hall Barn

Pigeon Tower

Rivington Country Park

Lever Park

Rivington Reservoir

PC

Rivington Pike

The Castle

A stroll through the neglected gardens of Lever Park offers secret hideaways, bridges, towers and follies.

0   1 km   1 mile

▲ Map: Explorer 19

▲ Distance: 10 km/6¼ miles

▲ Walk ID: 786 Barry Smith

Difficulty rating

Time

▲ River, Pub, Toilets, Wildlife, Woodland, Flowers, Good for Wheelchairs

Tockholes Plantations from Abbey Village

A delightful walk that includes a lovely valley, with some breathtaking views at the start, then enters steep woodland, which includes the Tockholes Plantations. There are bluebells in the spring and early summer, wild garlic, fungi and native trees.

1 From the corner of the car park, go through the gateposts towards the reservoir. Ignore the stile to the farm on the left. Turn left at the footpath sign next to a house. Follow the track and cross the water run-off, using the bridge if the water is running. Follow the track to the embankment of Roddlesworth Reservoir. Go left at the concrete 'seats'.

2 At the other end of the embankment, bear right to enter the woodland. At the next signpost, bear slightly right to go downhill with the path to a gate and stile at the next embankment. Go left with the smaller path.

3 Keeping to the path by the wall and the reservoir, rejoin the main path and turn right. At the next junction, signed for the Visitor Centre, keep straight on and the same at the next, to go downhill once again and come out at a gate and bridge at the River Roddlesworth.

4 Turn right. Cross the bridge and go through the kissing gate in the wall. Follow the track by the river, in the most delightful part of the walk, over a small bridge and up and down steps, until you come to a fence and bridge where you bear left on a wider track through woods.

5 Go over a stile and continue straight on to the junction and bear right with the smaller footpath sign, to continue through woodland. When you reach a wall and gap, cross the footbridge and bear left again with the smaller footpath sign, on the path next to the reservoir.

6 Turn right at the footbridge to come to the concrete seats once again. Turn left and follow the footpath back to the car park at the start.

further information

If you wish to include a visit to Hollinshead Hall it will extend this walk by 2.5 km, but it is well worth the effort. Make the hall your first port of call if you start at Slipper Lowe car park or the Visitor Centre at Tockholes.

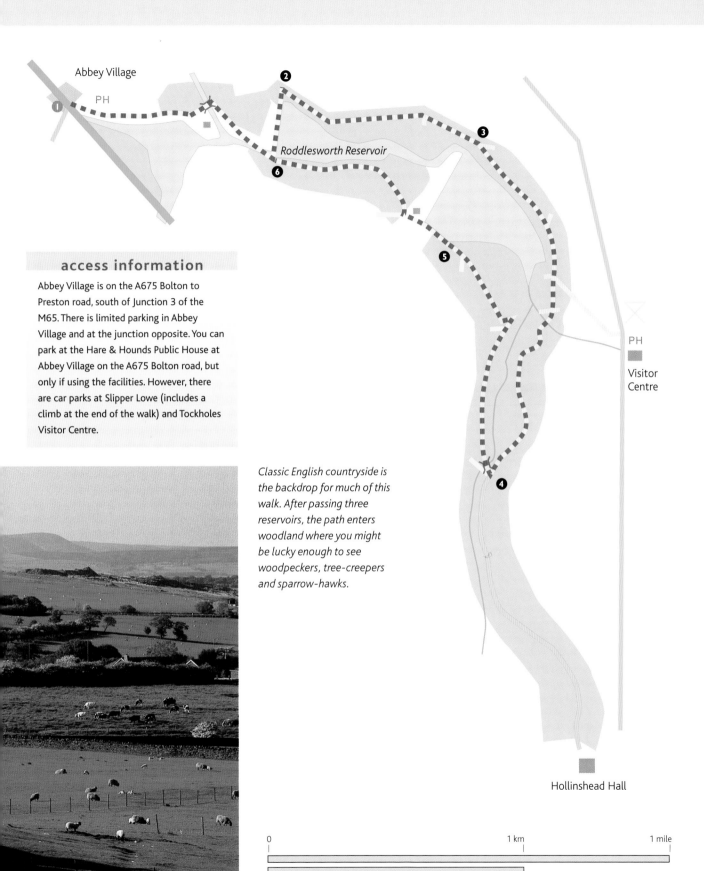

Abbey Village

PH

Roddlesworth Reservoir

PH

Visitor
Centre

Hollinshead Hall

access information

Abbey Village is on the A675 Bolton to Preston road, south of Junction 3 of the M65. There is limited parking in Abbey Village and at the junction opposite. You can park at the Hare & Hounds Public House at Abbey Village on the A675 Bolton road, but only if using the facilities. However, there are car parks at Slipper Lowe (includes a climb at the end of the walk) and Tockholes Visitor Centre.

Classic English countryside is the backdrop for much of this walk. After passing three reservoirs, the path enters woodland where you might be lucky enough to see woodpeckers, tree-creepers and sparrow-hawks.

| 0 | | 1 km | 1 mile |

▲ Map: Explorer 267

▲ Distance: 6 km/3¾ miles

▲ Walk ID: 234 R. & C. Jones

Difficulty rating

Time

▲ Toilets, Wildlife, Birds, Flowers, Great Views

The Sandstone Trail from Delamere

This walk starts from Delamere Station and follows country roads and the Sandstone Trail within the Delamere Forest. The Sandstone Trail runs from Frodsham in the north to Grindley Brook on the Shropshire border.

1 Leave the car park and walk towards the railway station entrance. In front of the station turn right and head for the main road. On reaching the main road turn right and walk along the footpath on the other side of the road for about a kilometre. There are good views to the left on a clear day. To the right is a hill on which was once a Saxon hill fort.

2 On reaching the road junction with Eddisbury Hill turn right, and climb the hill. Continue along this road until you reach the junction with Stoney Lane.

3 Cross over onto a sandy track and follow the path. You are now on the course of an old Roman road. On reaching the gate cross the stile and enter a large field. Keep straight ahead keeping the field boundary on your right, and head for the far right-hand corner of the field. Cross the stile and continue along a path bounded by trees. Cross this stile and enter Nettleford Wood.

4 On reaching the crossing path turn right on the Sandstone Trail. When you get to the footpath sign keep straight ahead, and cross the stile next to the five-barred gate. Follow the grassy track, which eventually starts to descend.

5 On reaching the junction with Eddisbury Lodge in front of you, turn right along the road. This will lead you past the Delamere Visitor Centre.

6 Just past the Visitor Centre is a bridge over the railway. At the side of the bridge is an alleyway, which leads back down to the car park.

access information

This walk starts at Delamere Railway Station. Access by car is via the A556 and then the B5152, which leads to the Lindmere Picnic site adjacent to the station.

A stirring view of Shropshire's beautiful pine forests.

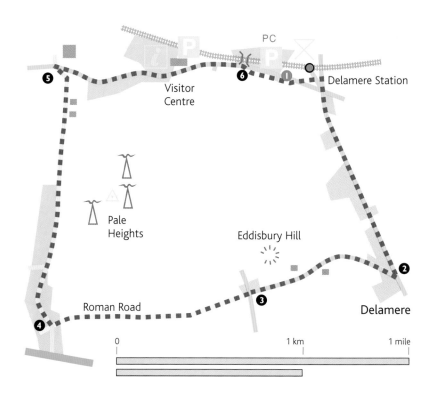

▲ Map: Explorer 285

▲ Distance: 4 km/2½ miles

▲ Walk ID: 255 Jim Grindle

Difficulty rating

Time

▲ Pub, National Trust/NTS, Wildlife

Freshfield and Dobson's Ride

Although this footpath is on the coast, we have classified it as a woodland walk because it is a very quick and easy stroll through tranquil Corsican pine woods. You may be lucky enough to see some of the area's red squirrels.

1 On leaving Freshfield Station turn left, and left again at the telephone box. Walk past the row of shops and then the station car park. At the end of the car park you can continue on the road or branch left onto the bridleway – they join up again further on. The tarmac ends at the last house and becomes a gravelled track.

2 Take the fork left on the wider track following the railway line as far as a level crossing. Go over the railway line and follow the track through a golf course until you reach a metal gate at the entrance to the National Nature Reserve.

3 Take the right fork, passing round the end of the golf course on a winding track until you reach a junction.

4 Go left at this junction, following the signpost for the Sefton Coastal Footpath. In 100 m the sandy path turns right by a white-topped post and in another 50 m it enters the wood. Do not go through the gate on the left – it is 'No Entry'. The track winds through the wood for 1 km

with white-topped posts to keep you on the right route. At the end of the wood you come to a broad, stony track – Dobson's Ride.

5 Turn right and follow the track for a further kilometre, crossing an open area and then entering the woods again. The path drops a little and you come to a fork with a white post.

6 Stay on the main track by turning left at the white post. In 50 m you will come back to the path to retrace your steps on the outward route.

This is one of the few areas of Britain where you may be able to see the native red squirrel, now an endangered species.

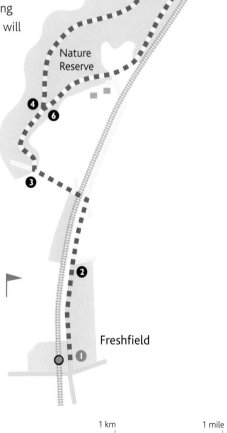

access information

The walk starts at Freshfield Station on the Southport/Liverpool line. Access by road is from the A565. Follow the tourist signs to Formby Point (National Trust). The route crosses the railway line at Freshfield Station where there is parking.

▲ Map: Explorer OL 6

▲ Distance: 10 km/6¼ miles

▲ Walk ID: 378 Samantha Asher

Difficulty rating

Time

▲ Hills or Fells, Pub, Toilets, Museum, Play Area, Castle, National Trust/NTS, Wildlife, Birds, Great Views

Eskdale Green to Muncaster Head

Take a walk from Eskdale Green to Muncaster Fell, stopping at Muncaster Castle if desired. The return journey, via a bridleway, cuts through a forest to Muncaster Head and back to Eskdale Green.

① Proceed down the road named Randlehow, which is opposite the post office. At the T-junction, turn right. Go through the wooden gate beside the cattle grid. Proceed to a gap in the dry-stone wall on your right, marked 'footpath'.

② Go through the gap. Follow the path across the field to a kissing gate beside the railway line. Pass through the kissing gate, cross the railway line and go through another kissing gate. Continue ahead. Cross a small stream and a kissing gate. Follow the right-hand perimeter of the field, until you reach a crossing track at its other side.

③ Turn left. Look for two arrows on a wooden post. (If you reach a stile beside a metal farm gate, you have gone too far.) Turn right up Muncaster Fell in the direction of the arrows. Continue uphill to a wooden gate beside a kissing gate. Go through it and climb the path over Muncaster Fell.

④ Pass through a gap in a dry-stone wall. Continue straight ahead. As you proceed, a triangulation point can be seen ahead and to your right. The River Esk is visible ahead where it meets the Irish Sea at Ravenglass, and to the right is Sellafield Nuclear Power Plant.

⑤ Keeping the triangulation point to your right, continue downhill to a forest. With the forest on your right, proceed to a kissing gate beside a wooden gate. Pass through and continue ahead on a track which runs between rhododendron bushes. Muncaster Tarn is visible to your right. Follow the track downhill to a track off to the left (signposted to Lower Eskdale) and a sign straight on to Muncaster.

further information

The triangulation point marks the highest point of Muncaster Fell at 231 m above sea level.

Dry-stone walls criss-cross the fells above Eskdale.

6 If you wish to make a detour to Muncaster Castle, go straight ahead instead of turning left. Otherwise, turn left and follow the path through woodland to a metal gate. Go through the gap to the left of the gate and continue downhill past a turning on the left and a house on the right, behind which you will see a monument. The path joins a tarmac road. Continue straight ahead past some houses.

7 Immediately after the last house, the tarmac road becomes a track. Pass through a wooden gate and continue ahead on the track for approx 2.5 km.

Look out for the Roman Tile Kilns, Cropple How plantation and Brantrake Crags (259 m) to the right of the track. Proceed to Muncaster Head farmhouse.

8 Go through a metal gate. Proceed down the track as it bends left just before the farmhouse and continue uphill between farm buildings on your right and a dry-stone wall on your left. Follow the track through a wooden gate beside a metal gate. Pass over a stile beside another metal gate. Proceed, following arrows on a wooden post, ignoring a path off to your left, back to Eskdale Post Office.

access information

Take the railway to Ravenglass and then take the narrow-gauge 'Ravenglass and Eskdale' railway to 'The Green' Station, walk uphill (i.e. away from the pub) to start the walk opposite the post office. By car, parking is available some 50 m before and after the post office.

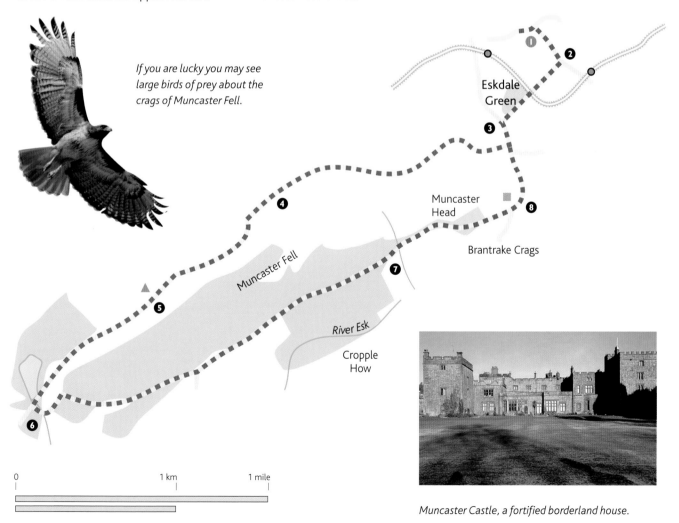

If you are lucky you may see large birds of prey about the crags of Muncaster Fell.

Muncaster Castle, a fortified borderland house.

▲ Map: Explorer OL 4

▲ Distance: 4 km/2½ miles

▲ Walk ID: 933 Craig Lannigan

Difficulty rating

Time

▲ Hills or Fells, Mountains, Lake/Loch, Toilets, Great Views, Food Shop, Moor, Nature Trail, Woodland

Dodd Wood under Ullock Pike

The walk takes you through eerie conifer corridors, which climb gently through Dodd Wood and onto the foothills of Ullock Pike. This allows perfect views of Bassenthwaite Lake and the fells beyond.

❶ From the car park at Mirehouse cross the wooden bridge and follow the footpath that gently rises ahead until you come to a junction with a forest track.

❷ Turn left and begin walking downhill. The path splits into a lower and higher path. Take the right-hand side path, which rises uphill. Follow this path through some lovely isolated pine-canopied aisles.

❸ Turn right at the junction and follow the path that gently rises ahead. Continue along the path, again through tree-lined aisles which are blanketed with pine needles. You will have spectacular views of Bassenthwaite Lake and the fells beyond. To your right is the summit of Skiddaw beyond Ullock Pike. This path comes to an end after a small descent and the path doubles back on itself to the left.

❹ Continue along the gravel track as it gently descends. The path ends once again in a double-back to the left. Follow this path until you reach the main A591. Turn right along the road and walk past the hotel.

❺ Cross over the road to a bus stop next to a series of stone steps descending along a dry-stone wall. Follow the path that bears to the right and cross the stile in front of you to an open field. From the field go over the

other stile and follow the path towards a copse of trees. The path then bears to the left and takes you over another three stiles until you reach the road at Green Hill. Turn left and head towards a junction with the A591.

❻ When the Keswick sign appears, turn right and cross over the road. The entrance to a path, which runs alongside the main road, will soon appear. The path ends at a small lay-by and a path ascends ahead towards a gate. Follow it until you come to a junction that takes you down to the bridge you first walked over and back to the car park.

further information

Exploring additional routes around Dodd Wood is well worth the effort, particularly as this route will take under two hours to complete. The nature trails are well marked out and they are very enjoyable.

Bassenthwaite Lake is an expansion of the River Derwent. Surrounded by wooded slopes and fells, it is an ideal centre for rambling and watersports.

access information

Mirehouse is on the A591 north of Keswick. There is a regular bus service from Keswick, stopping at Mirehouse. Parking is limited.

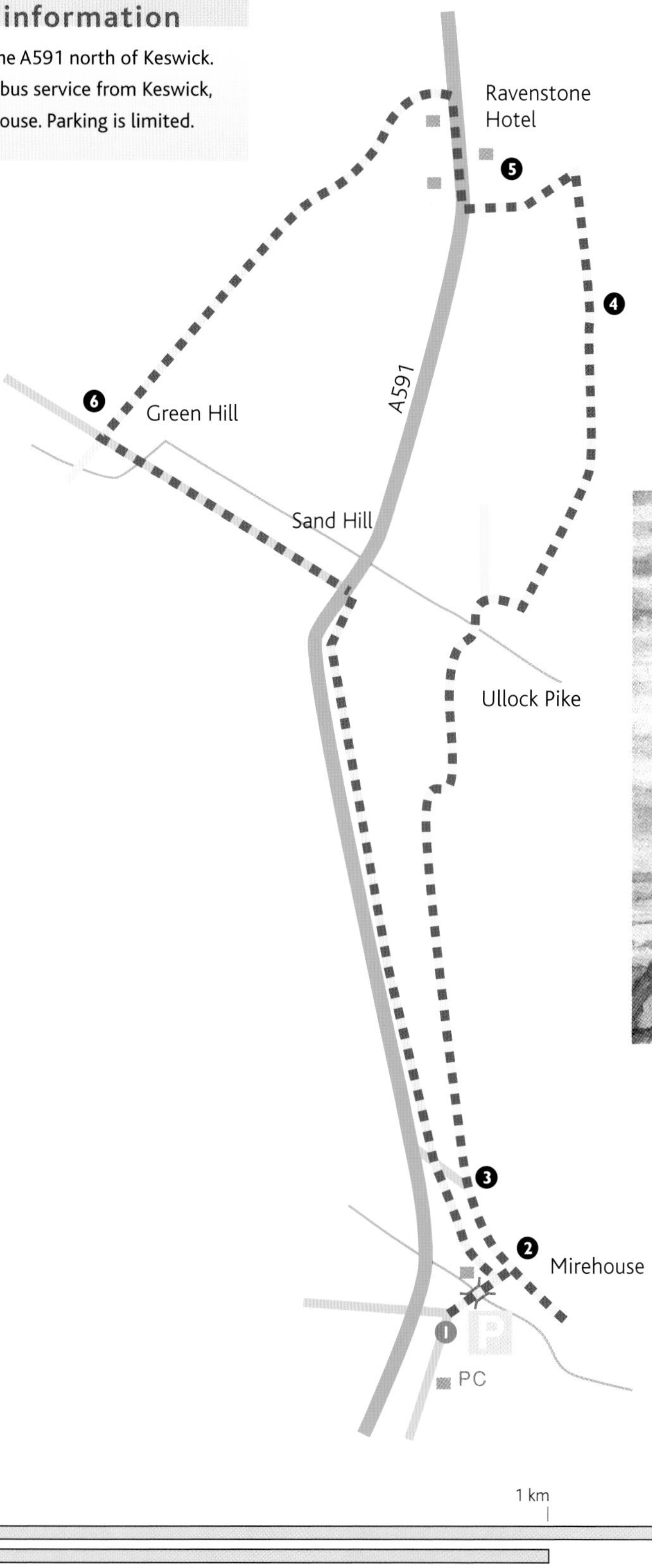

Ravenstone Hotel

5

A591

4

6 Green Hill

Sand Hill

Ullock Pike

Skiddaw, rising to the west behind Ullock Pike, is England's fourth highest peak (931 m). The Skiddaw Fells, many accessible only on foot, lie to the north of Keswick.

3

2 Mirehouse

1 P

PC

| 0 | | 1 km | 1 mile |

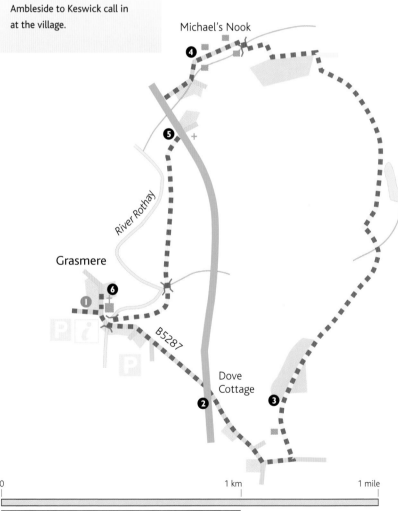

▲ Map: Explorer OL 7
▲ Distance: 6 km/3¾ miles
▲ Walk ID: 1390 Jim Grindle

Difficulty rating

Time

▲ Hills or Fells, River, Lake/Loch,
Toilets, Museum, Church, National
Trust/NTS, Wildlife, Flowers, Great
Views, Food Shop, Tea Shop

Alcock Tarn from Grasmere

In this walk a lane gives way to a track rising gradually above the Vale of Grasmere. The tarn itself is an attractive, quiet spot. The return is across beautiful meadows.

❶ Turn right as you leave the Information Centre and walk up to the junction by the church. Turn right and go past the main car park to the junction with the main road. Turn left to the new crossing point. Go over and turn right. A lane branches off from the main road. Follow signs for Dove Cottage.

❷ Take the left fork along the lane. At the top the lane forks again. Take the left fork and then watch for a track on the left signposted to Alcock Tarn. Where the track splits you will see a little gate.

❸ Go through the gate onto the track that leads up to the tarn. Go left of the tarn to a stile in the wall at the far end. Beyond the wall the track leads down to a beck. Cross the bridge and go through the gate onto a drive. This drops to a junction with a lane.

❹ Turn left to come to another lane on the left. Turn and follow the lane down to the main road. Just to the right on the main road is a crossing point. Go over and turn left to reach a gate 50 m away.

❺ Go along the enclosed track into the field at the end and then follow the right field edge to the first of a sequence of gates. You will reach a newly built bridge. Cross the bridge and turn left.

❻ This path will bring you out at the church in the centre of the village. Turn left and take the first turning on the right for the Information Centre.

access information

Grasmere is north of Ambleside on the A591 Ambleside/Keswick road. There are three large car parks in the village and some smaller ones. Buses from Ambleside to Keswick call in at the village.

A picturesque bridge across a lakeland beck is a good place to admire the views after visiting Alcock Tarn.

▲ Map: Explorer OL 6 & 7
▲ Distance: 10 km/6¼ miles
▲ Walk ID: 341 Jude Howat

Difficulty rating

Time

▲ River, Pub, Wildlife, Great Views

Dungeon Ghyll from Elterwater

This scenic low-level walk follows the course of the Langdale Beck up to Dungeon Ghyll, then returns part way up the side of the valley through some forestry to Elterwater.

1 From the car park, turn left and cross the bridge to the start of the walk. After crossing the bridge, take the road to the right at the T-junction. Follow the track until you reach a mine entrance in the rock face. Opposite this is a footpath heading down the hill towards the beck. Take this path and follow it over a footbridge.

2 You will come out into a car park in the village of Chapel Stile. Walk along the road for about 100 m and take the next footpath to the left. Follow this up a small hill. Continue straight on, keeping on the path just to the right of the white buildings.

3 Keep left. Soon you will cross a bridge over the beck. The path bends to the right. Continue along the track close to the water's edge. Cross the beck again at the bridge. Follow the path up to the main road.

4 Pass through the swing gate and turn left. Walk along the road for about 100 m, then turn left onto the track. Follow it until you rejoin the main road. Turn left and walk along it for 200 m.

5 Turn left onto the track over the bridge. Cross the field towards a farm house. Keep left. Pass through the swing gate, then cross the small bridge and turn left onto the path. Turn right by the disused barn. Follow the path over the hill, heading eastwards.

6 Continue straight on, following the main path all the way until you reach a road. Turn left and follow the road. Turn left again. This road will take you back down to the starting point by the bridge.

access information

Elterwater is on the B5343 to the north-west of Ambleside close to the lovely valley of Langdale. There is pay-and-display parking in Elterwater, where this walk starts, but you can start in Dungeon Ghyll, where there is also pay-and-display parking available.

A breathtaking overview of Langdale, showing the course of Great Langdale Beck.

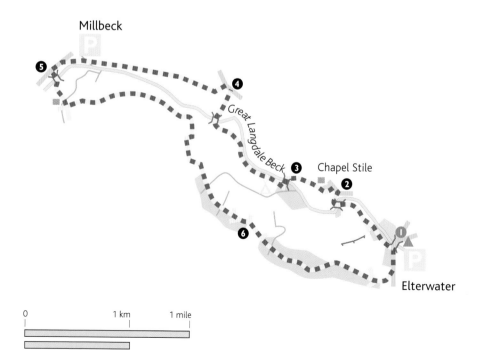

▲ Map: Explorer OL 7

▲ Distance: 8 km/5 miles

▲ Walk ID: 1340 Gary Gray

Difficulty rating

Time

▲ Pub, Toilets, National Trust/NTS, Wildlife, Great Views, Café, Food Shop, Good for Kids, Public Transport, Nature Trail, Tea Shop, Woodland

Latterbarrow from Hawkshead

A walk across open fields is followed by a short climb to the summit of Latterbarrow with its tall cairn visible from Hawkshead. The stroll back is through pleasant forest.

1 Starting from the Red Lion Pub in Hawkshead village, follow the path that runs down the side of the pub to the main road. Go across the road and down another path. The path dog-legs right and then left, and eventually leads to a small footbridge.

2 Turn left and walk alongside the fence to the corner of the field. Turn right and walk to the far corner where there is a kissing gate. Go through the gate and walk diagonally right across the field. Go through another kissing gate and turn left. There is a signpost for Loanthwaite. The path goes through two further fields and over two stiles. After the second stile follow the path right across the field up to a gate.

3 Go through the gate and left onto a track towards a large oak tree, which is on the right side of the track. Go over the stile next to the tree and follow the path. There is a fence on your right. Go through the gate and continue on the path, with the fence now on your left side.

Hawkshead offers fantastic views, not least from the summit of Latterbarrow, which looms over the village.

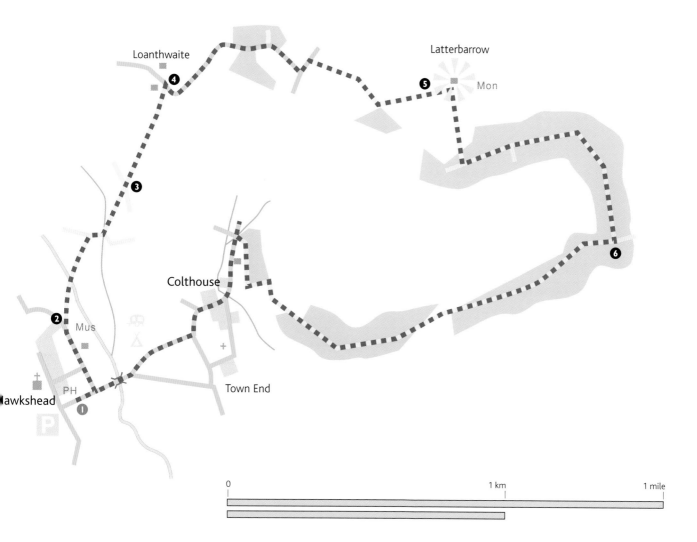

4 The path leads to the right of a farm. At the minor road (Loanthwaite Lane) turn right and follow it to a T-junction. Turn left onto this road and walk on for a short distance. On the right side of the road is a gate signposted Latterbarrow. Go through the gate and follow the track up through the trees. Follow the stone wall to your right and a grassy track to the left leads to the summit.

5 On reaching the summit, you will find the monument and good views. At the monument, go right. The grassy path leads you downhill to a corner and a stone wall and stile. Go left over the stile and follow the path into the forest. The path goes down a steep embankment. Keep to the well-defined main path.

6 The path reaches a gate in a wall, by a T-junction. Go through the gate onto a hard track and follow the signs for Hawkshead. The path leads to a road. Go left and follow the road towards Town End. Turn right at the T-junction and walk along the minor road back to the start at Hawkshead.

access information

The walk starts in Hawkshead, on the B5285 south of Ambleside. There are several large car parks, which are pay-and-display. These get busy at peak holiday times.

Wales

Coastal & Waterside

From glorious coastlines, to dramatic waterfalls and quiet canals, Wales has so much to offer the walker in search of waterside tranquillity. Highlights include the Devil's Kitchen and Colwyn Bay.

▲ Map: Explorer 255 or 256

▲ Distance: 10.6 km/6½ miles

▲ Walk ID: 312 Jim Grindle

Difficulty rating

Time

▲ Hills or Fells, River, Pub, Toilets, Museum, Castle, Stately Home, Birds, Flowers, Great Views

Llangollen Canal Walk

A walk along the canal with a return by bridleway, which snakes round the hillside offering outstanding views. The walk includes a climb to the top of Dinas Bran, the ancient castle overlooking the town of LLangollen.

1 Turn right from the car park entrance and walk to the main street. Turn left. Cross the bridge and go half-left across the main road to a passageway with a signpost for canal boats. Go up the narrow path or steps. On the towpath turn right and go under the road bridge. Follow the towpath for 2 km to reach another bridge.

2 Cross the stile by the gate and turn left on the lane, crossing the canal bridge. Go uphill until you reach Llandyn Hall. On the left is a stile. Go over and up to another stile by a gate 200 m away. Cross the two stiles near to each other. Go half-left across the field. Go through the gate and follow the hedge and then the buildings on the left until you reach a stile onto a lane. Turn right. You will reach a kissing gate and signpost for the castle.

3 Follow the signpost pointing left. Go over the stile at the end of the path and turn left. Go straight uphill to the castle. On the far side you will be able to pick up a broad, fenced track leading down. Turn right at the second tree. Continue until you reach a fence. Turn left and go down towards a stile. Cross the field to the far right corner to a stile by a lane.

4 Turn right and stay on the lane for 500 m. Turn right at the junction and look for the signpost for Brynhyfryd.

Turn left and pass a building close on your left and two others up to the right. Go through a gate and onto a grassy track for 1.2 km after which it drops and joins another. Turn left so that you double back. In 120 m you come to a ladder stile on the right. Cross and look for another one in the corner. Go over and follow the field edge.

5 Follow the sign towards Llangollen. You soon come to a gate. Follow an enclosed track to a road. Turn right. You come to a canal bridge on the left.

6 Cross the bridge, turn left and follow the towpath for 2 km back to Llangollen.

access information

Llangollen is just off the A5 and is signposted from the A483. There is a car park in the centre of town, again well signposted. There are regular buses to Chester, Chirk, Wrexham and Oswestry.

The Offa's Dyke Path, which runs along the hills above Llangollen, traces the border built between England and Wales in 770, when Wales effectively became a separate Celtic nation.

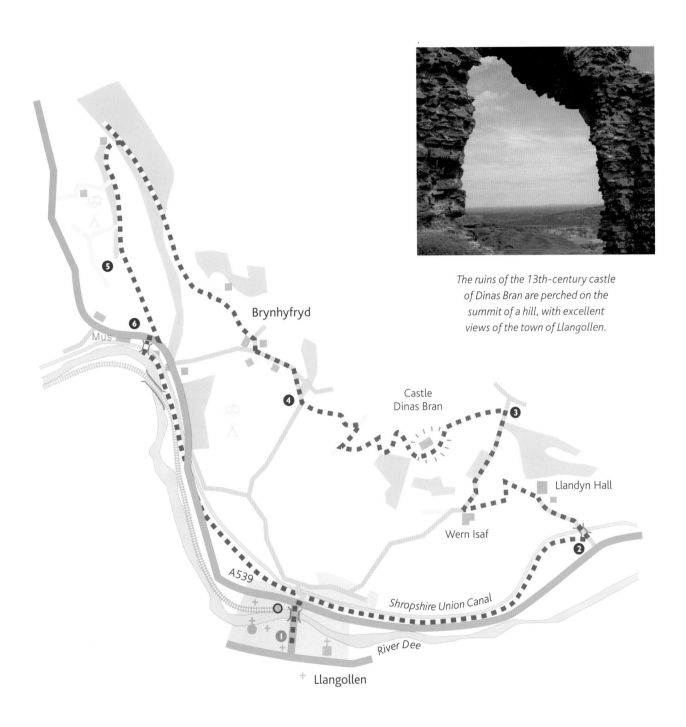

The ruins of the 13th-century castle of Dinas Bran are perched on the summit of a hill, with excellent views of the town of Llangollen.

Brynhyfryd

Castle
Dinas Bran

Llandyn Hall

Wern Isaf

Shropshire Union Canal

A539

River Dee

Llangollen

Mus

0   1 km   1 mile

▲ Map: Explorer 256 & 257

▲ Distance: 10 km/6¼ miles

▲ Walk ID: 139 Jim Grindle

Difficulty rating

Time

▲ River, Pub, Toilets, Wildlife, Flowers, Great Views

Erbistock from Overton

The 'Overton Yew Trees' walk follows the River Dee. The route then climbs and the views are spectacular. A further riverside walk is followed by a second climb to the village.

1 Go through the gate into the churchyard at Overton, with its famous 12th-century yew trees. Cross the road and turn left, passing the war memorial, and walk as far as the sharp bend left.

2 Turn right at the signpost for Maelor Way. Follow the road down the hill to where it curves right. The track goes into the field and makes a dog-leg onto the embankment. Follow this track to the river bank.

3 Turn left at a signpost and keep to the right of the field. The River Dee runs just behind the trees. A footbridge leads to a narrow path through the woods parallel to the river. Leave by another bridge and a stile into a small field. Keep to the right edge and make for the corner. Cross the stile and continue until you are opposite an inn on the far bank of the river.

4 Turn left, up the embankment, via some steps to a stile at the top. Turn left at the stile and then right to follow the line of some fencing uphill to another stile. This stile leads to some steps. Turn left and soon you will cross a stile by a cattle grid. Cross another stile on the left further on into a field. Follow the line of the hedge on the left to a signpost. This directs you half-right round two lines of trees. You must come back left again to a stile almost in the bottom left corner of the field.

The River Dee, with its rocky bed, swirls and eddies, and tree-lined banks, flows through peaceful villages and areas of unspoilt natural beauty.

access information

Overton is most easily reached from the A483 (Wrexham bypass). Turn onto the A539 (signposted Ruabon and then Erbistock). Continue on the A539 at the junction with the A528. There is a car park at the back of the church. The main street is wide and has ample parking.

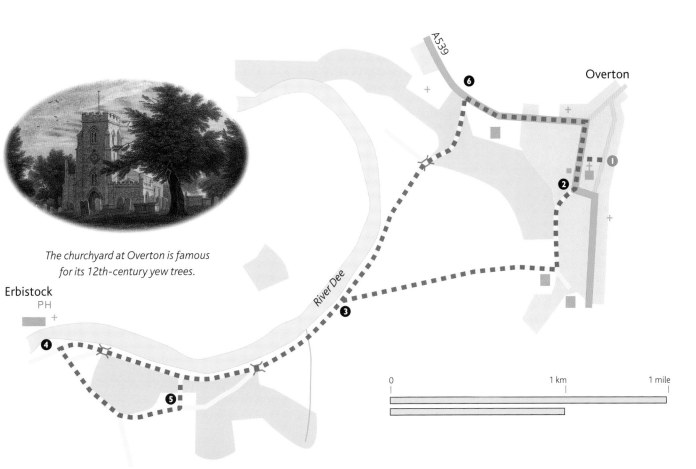

The churchyard at Overton is famous for its 12th-century yew trees.

Erbistock
PH

0   1 km   1 mile

5 Beyond the next stile is a path leading back to the riverside path. Turn right and follow your outward route. At the point where you joined the river, continue alongside the river on the left of the field until you come to a wire fence and a stile. Cross and turn right. Follow the line of the fence as it turns left and then sharp right. Look out ahead of you for a signpost by a gate and a bridge. The path beyond the bridge curves left and uphill. The path ends at the main road, the A539.

6 Cross to the pavement on the far side of the road and turn right for the centre of Overton, back to your starting point.

▲ Map: Explorer 256

▲ Distance: 6.5 km/4 miles

▲ Walk ID: 226 Jim Grindle

Difficulty rating

Time

▲ River, Sculpture Trail, Ancient Monument, Woodland

Alyn Waters from Gresford Bells

The walk begins and ends in Alyn Waters Country Park near Gresford Bells. The park has been created from the site of a large opencast mine and has a sculpture trail. Gradually it moves into tranquil fields by the River Alyn.

❶ From the gate at the lower end of the car park follow the path until you reach a silver sculpture. Take the right fork. When you reach a gateway on a lane, turn left. You will see a fork in the road. Take the right fork, downhill. The lane crosses the River Alyn and climbs again.

❷ At a sharp left bend go through the kissing gate on the right. Follow the path until you come to a junction with a path. Turn left and follow the path to a gateway. Turn left and go through a car park to the main road. At the road, turn right and continue until you reach the football ground.

❸ Go in, keeping near an embankment on the left. Turn left into a gap in the trees and pick up a little path leading down to Sherbourne Avenue. Turn right and in 120 m cross to a signpost. The path passes along the backs of houses to a kissing gate. Go through and turn left. Just after passing the pond on the left the fence takes a sharp turn to the left. Pass a gate with no fence round it to reach a broader track. Turn right here and in 50 m you come to a solitary tree. Turn left by the tree and pick up a path that follows the stream to a kissing gate and a main road. Cross the road to the path on the far side.

❹ Turn right into the lane. It goes sharp left after only 20 m to a group of farm buildings. Go between the buildings to

Majestic beech trees and deciduous woodland border the River Alyn, part of the Alyn Waters Country Park.

the bottom gate. Cross the metal stile and go towards a ruined building. Cross the footbridge over the River Alyn and turn right and follow the river. The route leads past two gates and stiles to a small lane by some houses. Continue to reach a T-junction.

❺ Turn left and follow the lane to a crossroads with the B5425. Cross to the lane opposite (Park Road) and walk as far as a sharp left bend, where there is a stile.

❻ Cross the stile into Alyn Waters Country Park. There is a narrow green path that you should follow. Cross the broader green path and continue until you come to a tarmac path. Turn right and you will see the car park.

further information

There has been a remarkable transformation of what was once a huge mining area. The latest development, and one which has added an interesting twist to the area, is the creation of a sculpture trail. A few of these witty and entertaining sculptures are passed on this walk, but a wheelchair user could stay in the park and track down many more.

access information

The start of the walk is in the car park of a public golf driving range less than 4 km north-west of Gresford. It is on the west side of the B5425. There are buses from the centre of Wrexham.

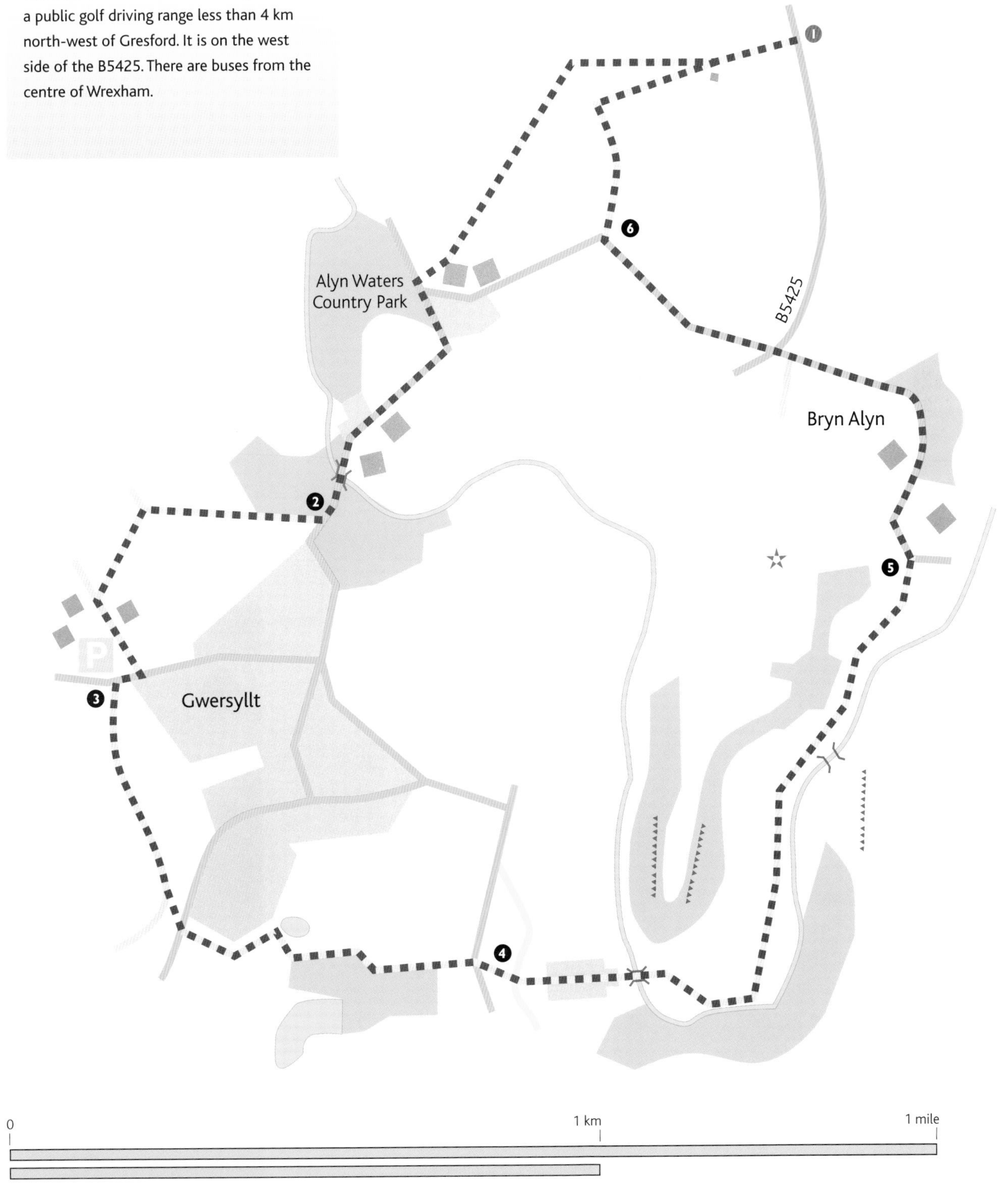

1
2
3
4
5
6
Alyn Waters Country Park
B5425
Bryn Alyn
Gwersyllt
P
0
1 km
1 mile

▲ Map: Explorer OL 17

▲ Distance: 8 km/5 miles

▲ Walk ID: 1419 Jim Grindle

Difficulty rating

👣👣👣

Time

⬤⬤⬤

▲ Hills or Fells, Mountains, River, Toilets, National Trust/NTS, Birds, Food Shop, Tea Shop

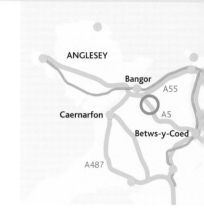

Ogwen from Bethesda

From Bethesda the walk descends into the valley and then offers an easy climb up to Ogwen Cottage and Ogwen Falls. An unusual landmark to look out for is a quartz stone by the side of the track.

The rugged, glaciated peaks of Snowdonia form a dramatic backdrop to this walk.

1 Start in the town centre and follow the A5 south. You will go over a river bridge and come to a crossroads on the edge of town. Turn left at the Snowdonia National Park emblem, then right into a street called Rhes James. Go through a gate at the end of this short street.
2 Follow the track and go through another gate. Follow the grass verge through to the woods. The path ends at a stile leading onto open ground. You will find a grassy track that soon turns sharply left. Follow the path. When it fades out, turn right near the remains of a sheepfold into a shallow valley. Make your way up the slope.

further information

A few minutes from the end of this walk is Cwm Idwal, a National Nature Reserve noted for its geomorphology and geology as well as for its rare Arctic-alpine plants.

3 Follow the higher ground until you see a wall on the right and then follow faint tracks alongside it. One kilometre from here you will cross the first of three streams and go through a gate in the wall leading you into the sheepfold. On the far side of the sheepfold is a stile by a gate – and a yellow arrow.
4 Cross the stile and turn left – there is another signpost on the far side of the wall. Follow the wall to another gate and stile about 100 m away. When you are over this stile look for posts with yellow arrows. They guide you onto a grassy track that leads gently downhill. After 1.5 km watch out for trees surrounding buildings below you on the right. By the track is a quartz stone.
5 The main track continues down to the A5. The right of way doubles back at the quartz stone to a gate in the corner. Go through the gate and follow paths down to the A5. Cross to a fingerpost. Go through onto a path leading to a bridge. The path goes over the bridge, left alongside the low wall and then passes a huge glaciated boulder and a smaller bridge to reach the old road.
6 Turn left and after a climb and 2.5 km you will reach the Youth Hostel at Ogwen. On the main road is Ogwen Cottage and the bus stop.

Accessible in any weather, this walk offers outstanding views of a number of Wales' 3,000 peaks.

Bethesda is on the A5 south-east of Bangor. Buses run from Betws-y-Coed to Bethesda and Bangor. There are several signposted car parks in the town. At the end of the walk you have several choices. You can walk back to Bethesda or wait for a bus if you are not being collected here.

Bethesda

A5

Ty Gwyn

Nant Ffrancon

Ogwen

0   1 km   1 mile

▲ Map: Explorer OL 23

▲ Distance: 8 km/5 miles

▲ Walk ID: 604 Chris Dixon

Difficulty rating

Time

●●●

▲ Mountains, River, Pub, Birds, Good for Wheelchairs

Mawddach Estuary from Penmaenpool

Following the route of a dismantled railway towards the sea, this walk takes in splendid views of the hilly countryside. The estuary at Barmouth Bridge is a haven for waders and other waterbirds. Parts of the walk pass unspoilt ancient woodland.

❶ At the car park you will see a hut and the toll bridge behind it at the start of the walk. From here, head downstream without crossing the river.

❷ Just over a small road is a hotel, converted from the old Penmaenpool railway station. The remainder of this walk is along the course of the old railway as it heads towards the sea.

❸ Pass through the gate, and after a slight bend the path heads for a kilometre straight across the marsh before reaching the estuary itself. After a further kilometre, you will cross a footbridge.

❹ About 2 km later, you may start to get views of the distant Barmouth Bridge.

❺ You can choose to take the road leading to Morfa Mawddach Station (formerly Barmouth Junction), or follow the route down the track on the right and past a disused platform. If you go to the station, a gate at the end of the one remaining platform links back up with the route.

❻ Barmouth Bridge can be crossed for a small toll, but since the tollbooth is at the far side, you can easily go half way for a view out to sea or back up the estuary. From here, retrace your steps to Penmaenpool.

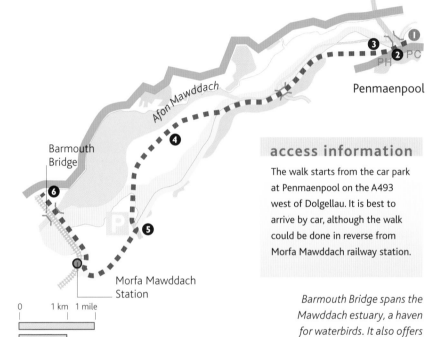

access information

The walk starts from the car park at Penmaenpool on the A493 west of Dolgellau. It is best to arrive by car, although the walk could be done in reverse from Morfa Mawddach railway station.

Barmouth Bridge spans the Mawddach estuary, a haven for waterbirds. It also offers fine views of Cardigan Bay.

▲ Map: Explorer OL 17
▲ Distance: 4.5 km/2¾ miles
▲ Walk ID: 757 Peter Salenieks

Difficulty rating

Time

▲ Mountains, Lake/Loch, Toilets, Great Views

Twll Du (Devil's Kitchen) from Ogwen Cottage

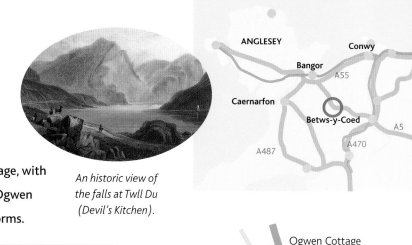

An historic view of the falls at Twll Du (Devil's Kitchen).

A short, scenic circuit of Llyn Idwal from Ogwen Cottage, with views up into Twll Du and across to Pen yr Ole Wen. Ogwen Valley is worth a visit for its splendid glaciated landforms.

1 The walk starts at the eastern end of the car park. Follow the stone path south, crossing a double stile and then a wooden footbridge. The path bends round to the left, before swinging back to the right after about 200 m. Follow the path to Llyn Idwal, go through a gate and continue along the eastern side of the lake. After passing Idwal Slabs, the path climbs towards the stream.

2 Cross the stream and continue more steeply along the path until you reach a path junction beside a large boulder.

3 For a better view into Twll Du, turn left at the large boulder and ascend a little further. When you have finished, continue along the path in front of the large boulder. Turn north and descend towards Llyn Idwal. Stone slabs bridge several small streams as the path goes along the western side of the lake. Bear right along the northern edge of Llyn Idwal, joining the path from Y Garn just before you reach a wooden footbridge.

4 Cross the footbridge and turn left at the footpath junction, finally rejoining your outward route back to the car park at Ogwen Cottage.

further information

This walk will take about 90 minutes. While it should present few difficulties in good conditions, this is graded as a moderate walk because the stream crossing can be awkward. Under winter conditions, the upper section is deceptively icy and should only be attempted by suitably experienced and equipped walkers.

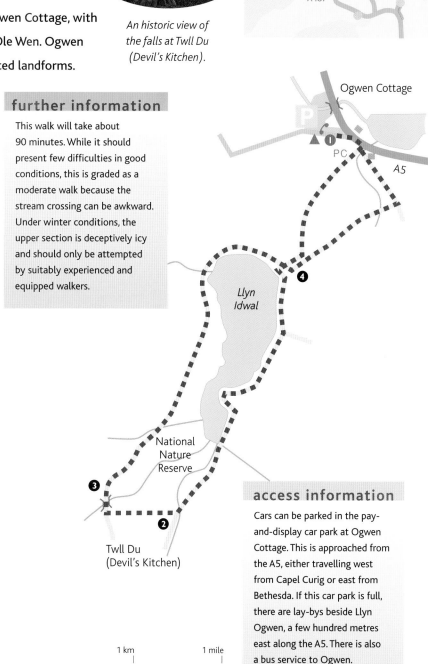

access information

Cars can be parked in the pay-and-display car park at Ogwen Cottage. This is approached from the A5, either travelling west from Capel Curig or east from Bethesda. If this car park is full, there are lay-bys beside Llyn Ogwen, a few hundred metres east along the A5. There is also a bus service to Ogwen.

▲ Map: Explorer 262

▲ Distance: 10 km/6¼ miles

▲ Walk ID: 635 Chris Dixon

Difficulty rating

Time

▲ Sea, Toilets, Church, National Trust/NTS, Wildlife, Birds, Great Views

Ynys y Fydlyn from Porth Swtan

This walk begins on the cliffs on Anglesey's north-west coast. After a view of the island of Ynys y Fydlyn the walk heads inland and there is an option to take in one of Anglesey's best viewpoints.

1 Leave the car park, and head towards the sea. Go through the gate, along the headland. When you reach a junction bear left and keep to the coast. When you reach a stile to the right, cross over it and continue. After a kilometre or so you climb up to a cairn.

2 From here, dropping down a fairly steep slope, you will reach a bridge. Cross the bridge and take the lesser of two paths, keeping to the left and to the cliffs.

3 Upon rounding the headland called Trwyn y Cerwyn there is a view of the island, Ynys y Fydlyn. From the beach, looking east, you will see a small marshy lake, and a track climbing to its right. Take the track and keep to the side of the forest. You soon join a track which leads to the road.

4 When you reach the road, turn left and after about 200 m, you should turn right onto a track to Hen-dy farmhouse. Continue through the gate. Follow the path round the pond in the marshy area ahead, and head for the white gate on the horizon, which will let you into

another farm. Go round the back of the building on the left, through another gate, and then up to the far corner of the field, where it meets the road. Turn right along the road.

5 After about 300 m, take the path to the left. Head to the left of Mynydd y Garn, then turn right across the bottom of the peak. Continue along the path back to the road, and turn left. After a few minutes walking, another road joins from the right. At the next fork turn right and continue on the road to the church.

6 Follow the road back to Porth Swtan, and turn right to return to the car park.

access information

Access to Porth Swtan is by car via the A5025, off the A5. Park in the car park at Porth Swtan.

A lighthouse perches on the barren island of Holyhead, which lies to the north west of Anglesey, and is connected to it by a rocky causeway.

further information

The island of Ynys y Fydlyn is easily accessible except at high tide. There is a small beach and a large cave.

Ynys y
Fydlyn

3

2 Cairn

Church Bay

4

Hen-dy

5

Mynydd
y Garn

1
PC
6
Porth Swtan

0   1 km   1 mile

▲ Map: Explorer 264

▲ Distance: 22 km/13¾ miles

▲ Walk ID: 753 Jim Grindle

Difficulty rating

Time

▲ Sea, Pub, Toilets, Church, Great Views

Rhyl from Rhôs-on-Sea

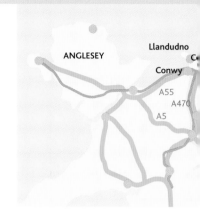

This is an easy-to-follow linear walk along the coast, using a specially made path as well as promenades and sea walls. It goes from west to east to take advantage of the prevailing wind.

Bodnant Castle boasts one of the finest gardens in Britain, famous for its display of rhododendrons, azaleas and magnolias. Perched above the River Conwy valley, the gardens offer fine views of Snowdonia.

❶ Keep Rhôs-on-Sea Information Centre building on your left to begin the walk. After 2 km you approach Colwyn Bay Pier. After another 2 km you have passed Old Colwyn, and the promenade now turns under the railway. A tarmac path branches off on the left. Follow this path.

❷ In 1 km the path rises by sea defence blocks. After another 3 km you cross a bridge. Keep going now for 5 km.

❸ Once you reach the front at Pensarn the railway station of Pensarn and Abergele is only 500 m further on, should you wish to return to Colwyn Bay. The footpath continues between the wall and the railway.

❹ Head towards Rhyl where there is a group of small buildings. Go through the metal kissing gate and onto a red shale path which winds through the dunes. About 300 m away there is a junction with a tarmac path.

❺ Turn right and go through a gate just in front of the bungalows. Go a little to the right to keep in the same direction down Betws Avenue. Turn to the left into Bryn Avenue. At the end of the road turn right and you will reach the Ferry Inn. The main road is just in front. Turn left and make for the bridge over the River Clwyd. Across the river there is a roundabout. Go straight over, following the sign to the railway station, which is still 2 km away. You can walk alongside the Marine Lake for a little. Keep going until you come to the traffic lights by the police station. The railway station is signposted again from here.

❻ From Rhyl you can return to Colwyn Bay by train or taxi.

access information

By car use the A55 Expressway, turning off at the signs for Llandudno and Rhôs-on-Sea. Turn right at the first two sets of traffic lights and right at the first roundabout. Go straight over the next roundabout and turn right at the next lights. This is Rhôs Road which leads directly to a T-junction by the Information Centre.

Views across Colwyn Bay make this a footpath to remember.

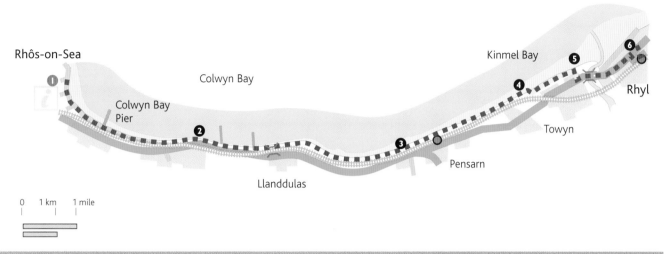

Rhôs-on-Sea

1

Colwyn Bay Pier

Colwyn Bay

2

Kinmel Bay

5

6

4

Rhyl

Towyn

3

Pensarn

Llanddulas

0   1 km   1 mile

▲ Map: Explorer 164

▲ Distance: 11 km/6¾ miles

▲ Walk ID: 981 John Thorn

Difficulty rating

Time

▲ River, Sea, Castle, Birds, Great Views, Café, Food Shop, Good for Kids, Moor, Public Transport, Woodland, Ancient Monument

Three Cliffs Bay from Penmaen

This is a circular walk from Penmaen through the woods and moorland to Three Cliffs Bay on the south coast of the Gower peninsula, a designated area of outstanding natural beauty.

1 Follow the track up the ridge. When you pass a stone marked 'Gower Way 12', bear right, following the track that skirts the woodland to your right. Just before the path divides, cross the stile on your right and follow the path into the woods as it opens out into a wider track. After a right-hand bend, go straight ahead at a crossroads (passing Gower Way stone 14).

2 At the crossroads at the bottom of a valley, turn right, following the track down. (Opposite on the left is Gower Way stone 15). The remnants of a prehistoric burial chamber will soon appear on your right.

3 Go through the gateway following a yellow arrow. Ignore the road on the left but turn left at the T-junction. On reaching the Gower Heritage Centre, continue straight ahead and cross the footbridge on the left. Continue along the road until you reach the main road.

4 Pass Shepherd's shop on your left and a house on your right. Turn right onto a path by a field gate. After 20 m, cross the footbridge and turn right, following a blue arrow. The path bears left over a hill. Ignore the left-hand path and continue ahead. The path opens out with a view of Pennard Castle. Continue down the left-hand side of the valley.

5 As you near the beach, continue ahead until you reach a ridge of pebbles, then turn right along the ridge and cross the stepping-stones. Do not take the path ahead marked by an arrow but turn left. Continue around the edge of the marsh with the hedge on your right. Go to the left of the sand dunes and emerge onto the beach.

6 Take the path to the top of the dunes. Follow the path that climbs up on the right-hand side of the holiday cottages. When you reach a stony track turn left, then turn right onto the road. Turn left at the T-junction. Cross the main road in front of the church and return to the start of the walk by following the narrow road on the right.

access information

Follow the A4118 along the Gower. Shortly after the Gower Inn at the Penmaen sign on the left-hand side, with the church in front of you, turn right on the narrow road. Follow this for about 200 yards, passing the care home on your left. When the road bears left, bear right onto the rough track and park on the grass.

Penmaen is accessible by bus, service 18 from Swansea.

The view from the cliffs at Three Cliffs Bay in Swansea makes the climb up the sand dunes worthwhile.

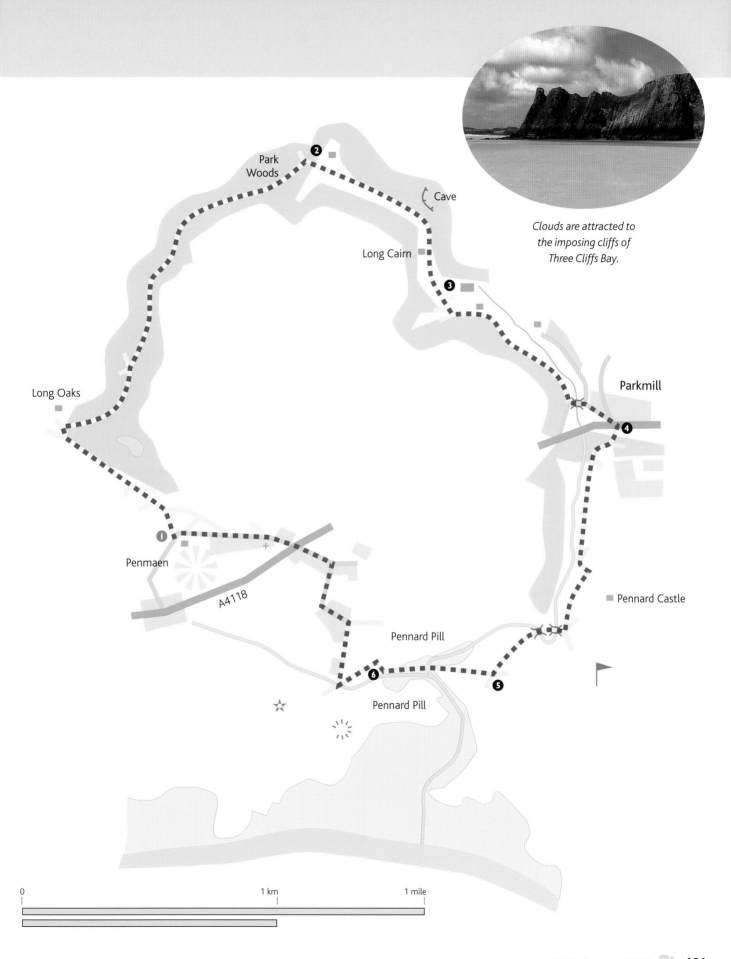

Park Woods

② Cave

Long Cairn

③

Long Oaks

Parkmill

④

① Penmaen

A4118

Pennard Castle

Pennard Pill

⑥ Pennard Pill ⑤

Clouds are attracted to the imposing cliffs of Three Cliffs Bay.

0   1 km   1 mile

Difficulty rating

Time

▲ Hills or Fells, Sea, Pub, Toilets, National Trust, Birds, Flowers, Great Views, Café, Gift Shop, Public Transport, Ancient Monument

Burry Holms from Rhossili

This walk demonstrates much of the natural beauty of the Gower. From Rhossili, climb the Beacon, descend to Llangennith, cross the dunes to the beach, explore Burry Holms and return along the beach.

① From the car park entrance, walk to the left of a house with a white garage door, then turn left and follow the path around the church. Turn left, following the lane slightly downhill. Go through the gate marked 'Rhossili Down' and bear slightly right up the hill. After about 250 m the track levels out a bit. Bear slightly right then left to reach the trig point.

② Continue along the grassy track in the general direction of Llangennith, bearing left along the ridge. Where the path divides, bear left, aiming for the hilltop ahead with a rocky crag. From the top, follow the grassy track ahead with the steep hill down on your left. Ignore the path on the left.

③ At a junction with a smaller path, turn right, heading in the direction of the large grey barn on the far hill. After 100 m, cross another path and bear left across the valley. Follow the path, making for the right-hand side of the small clump of trees to join a rough lane. Go through a gate, cross a stream and follow the road ahead into Llangennith.

④ Turn left on the road following the sign marked 'Beach'. At the junction go ahead, following the road towards Broughton.

⑤ At the entrance to the caravan park, cross the cattle grid and take the track on the left. After 150 m cross a stile. Just over the brow of the hill bear right. Cross another stile then fork right on the less well-defined path. Cross a fence at a stile and continue across the dunes. Turn right on the beach.

⑥ Burry Holms Island can be reached at low tide. Having explored the island, retrace your steps to the beach and continue along the beach towards Rhossili. Just before the end of the beach, climb the steps to the left. After 100 m, turn right through a gate and continue uphill. Pass between the buildings to return to the car park.

access information

The walk starts from the car park at Rhossili, at the end of the B4247 west of the A4118.

Buses 18, 18A, 18C, 18D run to Rhossili from Swansea; call Traveline for info on 0870 6082608.

Exploration of Burry Holms is possible when the sea retreats at low tide, although the island is inaccessible at high tide.

Do not follow this walk in poor visibility. Apart from missing the best views, some navigation depends on sighting far-away points.

As you climb towards the trig point (point 2), you may see Lundy Island. Left of this is Clovelly, Ilfracombe and Exmoor as far as Minehead. To the right of Lundy are Pembroke and Tenby.

Burry Holms has an Iron Age fort and various other relics.

This walk takes in a variety of interesting archaeological features including an Iron Age fort, as well as beautiful countryside.

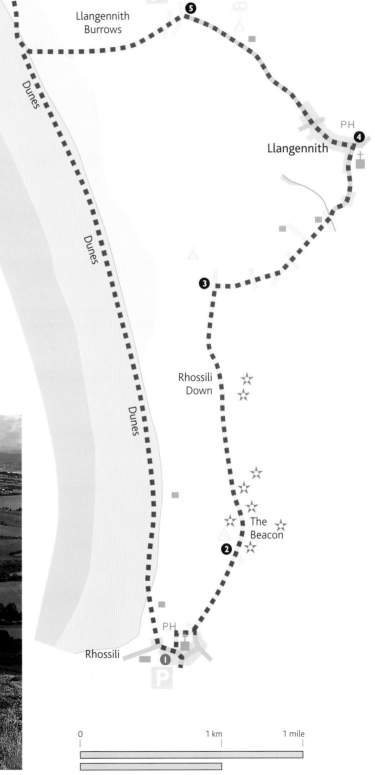

Burry Holms

Llangennith Burrows

Dunes

Dunes

Dunes

Dunes

PH

Llangennith

Rhossili Down

The Beacon

PH

Rhossili

0   1 km   1 mile

Difficulty rating

Time

▲ Sea, Toilets, National
Trust, Wildlife, Flowers, Great Views

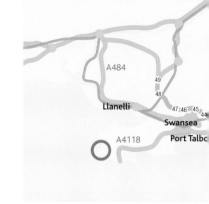

Mewslade Bay from Rhossili

This is a glorious walk combining cliffs with wild beaches and a bird's-eye view of the Gower peninsula from Rhossili Down. If conditions are right, you can visit the enticingly named Worms Head.

1 Turn left onto the path by the visitor centre. Go through the gate and head left towards Worms Head. When the path curves left, cross the grass to the building ahead. Take the grassy path to the southern cliffs. You will soon reach a corner of dry-stone wall on the left – keep alongside it.

2 Turn right just before the gate at the corner of the wall; turn left and follow the wall again. At the next corner turn left. At the junction continue uphill. At the top follow the path along the wall. Continue along the cliff, keeping the wall on your left. Ignore the path to the right above Fall Bay. On reaching a ladder over the wall, do not climb it – follow the middle path. Take the steep path next to the wire fence. Follow the wall towards Mewslade Bay.

3 At the sharp cliffs, head away from the wall. At what looks like a deserted stone shepherd's hut, head uphill. As the white house comes into view to the right, take the grassy path inland.

4 Take the right-hand path opposite the rocky outcrop. Do not cross the stile, but turn right. Continue uphill on the left-hand side of the path. Go through the gate into the woods. Pass through a farm and turn left onto a road. Turn right at the larger road and immediately left at the post box. At the fork take the left track past a house called Bramwood.

5 100 m before the large white house, climb the stile into the Nature Reserve. Follow the path across a footbridge, pass a house on the left, then another stile, to go uphill. Climb the stile and cross a minor road to take the track opposite. Skirt around the reservoir and follow the track left to Rhossili Down. At the fork stay on the wider track to the right to reach a trig point with spectacular views.

6 Retrace your steps for 50 m then take the right fork to Rhossili village. At the corner of the wall, head straight on. At the next corner take the path downhill to the gate. Follow the track. Just before St Mary's Church, take the path to the right. Follow the road to the car park.

access information

The walk starts from the car park at Rhossili, at the end of the B4247 west of the A4118.

Buses 18, 18A, 18C, 18D run to Rhossili from Swansea; call Traveline for information on 0870 6082608.

Halfway around this circular footpath, you will be rewarded with beautiful views over Rhossili Beach.

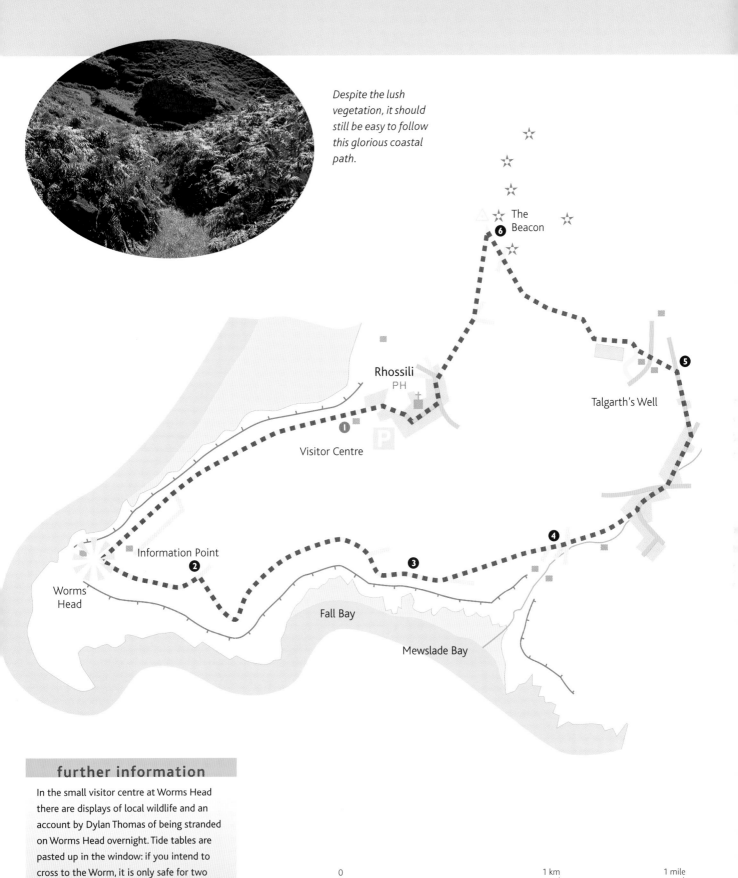

Despite the lush vegetation, it should still be easy to follow this glorious coastal path.

The Beacon

6

5

Rhossili
PH

Talgarth's Well

Visitor Centre

1

Information Point

2

4

3

Worms
Head

Fall Bay

Mewslade Bay

further information

In the small visitor centre at Worms Head there are displays of local wildlife and an account by Dylan Thomas of being stranded on Worms Head overnight. Tide tables are pasted up in the window: if you intend to cross to the Worm, it is only safe for two hours either side of low tide.

0   1 km   1 mile

▲ Map: Explorer OL 35

▲ Distance: 7 km/4¼ miles

▲ Walk ID: 1411 Pat Roberts

Difficulty rating

Time

▲ Sea, Toilets, Wildlife, Birds, Flowers, Great Views, Butterflies, Woodland

Witches' Cauldron from Moylgrove

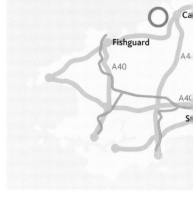

This walk is a lovely mixture of coast and countryside, taking in two woodland areas.

1 From the car park walk right along the road towards St Dogmaels. Follow the road as it climbs. Where the road swings sharply right, look for a gate on the left. Pass through the gate and walk down through Cwm Trewyddel, following the stream. The path goes over a small bridge and up to join the minor road from Moylgrove.

2 Follow the road round the bend and up the hill for about 120 m. Follow the 'Coast Path' sign on the right, and continue with the sea on your right.

3 Pwll y Wrach (The Witches' Cauldron) is a classic example of marine erosion. The path drops right down and climbs sharply back up, passing over a natural arch on the way. The sea comes in under the arch, creating the 'boiling cauldron'. Follow the path down the steps and back up the other side.

4 After the climb you come to a double stile. Leave the coast by the left-hand stile. The route continues over fields initially. After passing a ruined building, enter the woodland of Cwm Ffynnon-alwm to emerge over a stile and turn left onto a green track. This soon becomes a stony farm track climbing gradually.

5 Continue through a gate opposite Treriffith Farm where the sign points right, past the farm buildings then left up the drive. Emerge through a gate and continue to reach the Moylgrove road.

At the evocatively named Witches' Cauldron, the sea can be quite calm or spectacularly rough.

access information

Parking is in the car park at Moylgrove, a small village signed from the B4582 which is itself off the A487 Cardigan to Fishguard road.

▲ Map: Explorer OL 36

▲ Distance: 1.5 km/1 mile

▲ Walk ID: 1089 Peter Salenieks

Difficulty rating

Time

▲ Sea, Toilets, National Trust, Wildlife, Birds, Flowers, Great Views, Gift Shop, Mostly Flat, Public Transport, Ancient Monument

Martin's Haven and Marine Nature Reserve

This is a scenic circuit of the headland at Martin's Haven, offering views of Skomer Island and Skokholm Island and opportunities for watching seals within the Marine Nature Reserve.

1 Exit the National Trust car park at the far corner. Walk down a few steps, then turn left and follow the road downhill towards Martin's Haven. Just before the road bends right, go through the kissing gate and turn left. Follow a grassy path, which runs parallel to the stone wall, until you see a stile near the cliff edge, overlooking Deadman's Bay.

2 The path leads clockwise around the tip of the Marloes Peninsula. After the path bears around to the right, a natural arch can be seen, connecting two coves on the edge of the peninsula. About 200 m after the arch, the path joins a footpath, which leads to Wooltack Point, the northern tip of the peninsula.

3 Retrace your route from Wooltack Point and bear left, following the footpath along the northern edge of the peninsula, before bearing right and climbing a small hill to reach the old coastguard lookout.

4 Continue along the footpath until you reach steps leading down to the kissing gate. Go through the kissing gate and follow the road back uphill, passing Lockley Lodge Information Point, to reach the National Trust car park.

access information

The National Trust car park at Martin's Haven is accessible by road from Haverfordwest via the B4327 and a minor road through Marloes.

Martin's Haven can also be reached by the Puffin Shuttle Bus Service 400, which operates between St David's and Milford Haven.

This footpath offers both rugged cliff views and a chance to spot grey seals.

0   1 km   1 mile

▲ Map: Explorer OL 35

▲ Distance: 9 km/5½ miles

▲ Walk ID: 976 D. J. Martin

Difficulty rating

Time

▲ Sea, Toilets, National Trust, Birds, Flowers, Great Views, Café, Food Shop, Ancient Monument

Around St David's Head

This circular walk around St David's Head includes part of the Pembrokeshire Coast Path. There is a short optional diversion from the Coast Path onto Penllechwen Head, which gives extensive coastal views.

1 Leaving the car park, walk up the road, past the first turn on the left. At a marker on the right, turn left up a road. At the top, follow the main track right, towards Upper Porthmawr. After about 100 m the track turns left. Continue past the farmhouse.

2 Above the farmhouse the main track turns left. At this point, just before a small quarry, follow the path off to the right, taking in excellent views of Whitesands Bay, Ramsey Island and St Bride's Bay. At the T-junction, turn right through the gate.

3 A short distance downhill the main track continues straight on, but the walk turns left, behind a low building at a three-way marker, and immediately crosses a stile with another marker. Continue along the bottom of the field, keeping the stone wall on your right, and cross a stile. The next stile, near a farmhouse, crosses onto a track. Turn left to go to the top of the ridge. At the gate follow the track round to the right. Follow the public footpath indicated by the marker. Where the path becomes indistinct, head left of the hill and aim for a gate and stile in the top right of the field. Cross the stile and continue towards a marker.

4 Turn right and follow the track downhill, passing through a metal gate. When you reach a wooden gate, turn to the left onto a grassy track at the bottom of the field. Keep the fence on your right, ignoring side tracks.

5 At the T-junction, turn left up the hill, with a stone wall on your right. The path continues uphill and then between rocky outcrops. Descend towards the sea.

6 When you reach the Pembrokeshire Coast Path, turn left. Keep to the track that is closest to the coast. At Porthmelgan climb up the wooden steps on the path and continue back to Whitesands Bay.

access information

Take the B4583 from St David's towards Whitesands Bay. Whitesands Bay car park is at the end of this road.

A picturesque spot on the Pembrokeshire Coast Path is home to the St Justinian's lifeboat station, which serves the St David's Head area.

Markers point the way along the Coast Path to make navigation extremely easy.

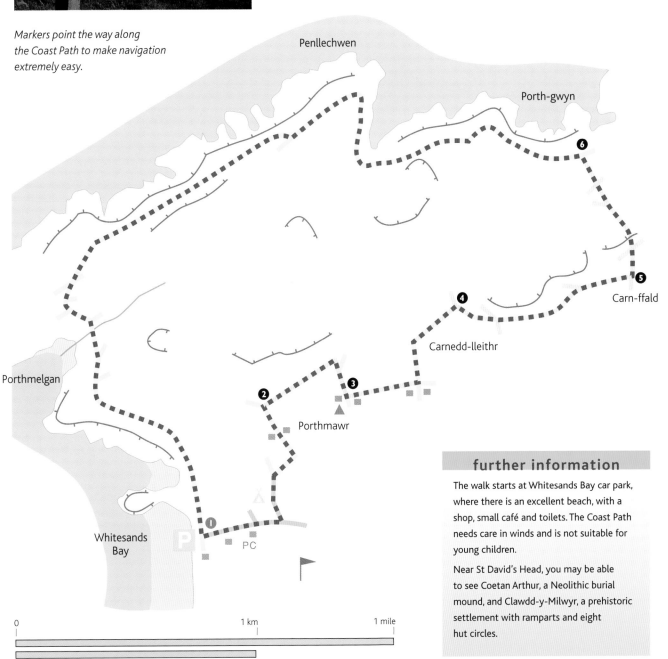

Penllechwen

Porth-gwyn

Porthmelgan

Carn-ffald

Carnedd-lleithr

Porthmawr

Whitesands Bay

PC

0   1 km   1 mile

further information

The walk starts at Whitesands Bay car park, where there is an excellent beach, with a shop, small café and toilets. The Coast Path needs care in winds and is not suitable for young children.

Near St David's Head, you may be able to see Coetan Arthur, a Neolithic burial mound, and Clawdd-y-Milwyr, a prehistoric settlement with ramparts and eight hut circles.

▲ Map: Explorer OL 35
▲ Distance: 7 km/4¼ miles
▲ Walk ID: 1414 Pat Roberts

Difficulty rating

Time

▲ Sea, Pub, Toilets, Wildlife, Birds,
Flowers, Great Views, Butterflies,
Waterfall, Woodland

Cwm Rhigian Woods from Parrog

Walk part of the Pembrokeshire Coast Path, and enjoy the wildlife in Cwm Rhigian Woods, before walking open moorland and returning to Newport and Parrog.

❶ From the car park, join the coast path by going down the slipway and left, with the sea on your right. If the tide is in, keep above the sea wall and follow the 'High Tide Route' as signed. Follow the Coast Path for over 2 km. Pass the old lifeboat station and Cat Rock. There is lovely scenery to enjoy here, and plenty of sea birds to look out for.

❷ As you drop down into the cove at Aber Rhigian, cross the stream using the footbridge and follow the footpath away from the sea. Soon recross the stream so that it is now on your right-hand side. The stream cascades down, and just after a good waterfall the path swings left, and over another footbridge. Emerge from the wood over a stile, and at a bungalow turn left up the drive. When you reach a T-Junction with another track, turn right up to the A487. Head left for 200 m.

❸ Turn right up the drive to the Hendre. After the farmhouse, go through a gate and carry on to cross a stream. Follow the sign along the left hedge of this field to another stile. Continue straight on up the track, keeping to the right of the hedge to reach a broken stile. Go straight on.

❹ Climb over the stile and continue on ahead up to a wall, which you keep on your right-hand side, soon to walk between two walls. Cross a minor road

and continue past a house and through a small gate onto open moorland. Take the left path at the signpost. When you reach the next fork, keep left to continue down a road and over, turning left over a cattle grid towards Newport.

❺ Emerge at the bottom of Mill Lane and take the short cut up the side of the church to reach the A487 at Newport. Head left for 120 m and take the signed road down to the right to the start of the walk at Parrog.

It is possible to see across Newport Sands to St Brynach's Church, home to a 4-metre Celtic cross, believed to be the finest in Wales.

further information

While walking down the long descent into Newport, notice the mill stream down on the right side of the road, and the remains of Castle Mill next to the bridge near the bottom.

access information

Park in Parrog car park, at the yacht club. Parrog is signed from the A487 in Newport.

A good bus service serves Newport from Fishguard or Cardigan.

The area is renowned for its scenery and birdlife, and at low tide it is a joy to geologists.

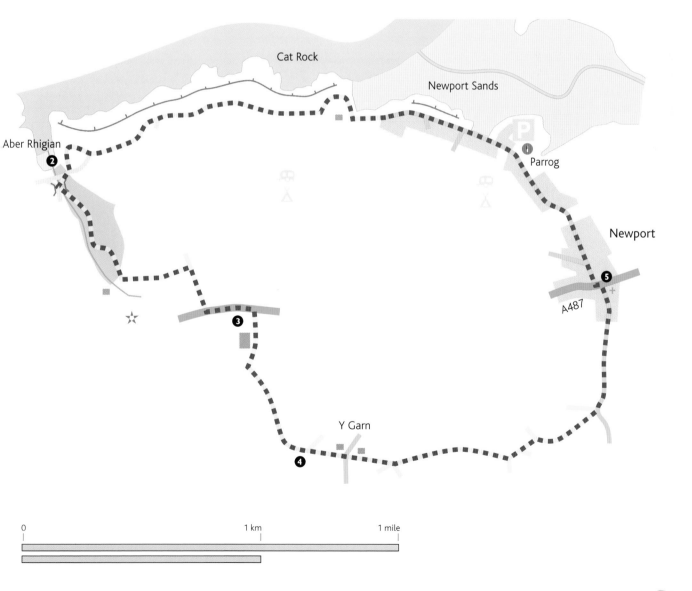

Difficulty rating

Time

▲ Hills or Fells, River, Pub, Wildlife, Birds, Great Views, Butterflies, Industrial Archaeology, Moor, Public Transport, Waterfall, Woodland

Hepste Waterfalls from Pontneddfechan

This walk gives a taste of the 'Waterfall Country' south of Ystadfellte – including Sgwd yr Eira where you can walk under the falls – with some moorland sections and great views.

1 From the car park, walk back over the bridge. After 30 m turn sharp right in front of the houses onto a gravel track. Continue along the track, ignoring turns left and right. Opposite the ruins of the Gunpowder Works cross the footbridge. Go straight ahead up a narrow path, and continue up some steps. Turn left at the signs towards Sgwd yr Eira, going through a gate and following the path between spruce trees.

2 Turn right following the 'Advised Path' signs, then left after about 50 m.

3 Turn left at the signpost to Sgwd yr Eira. The path drops steeply down some steps and then there is a short, rocky section before the falls. You can walk under the falls here. Retrace your steps back to the signpost, then follow the signs to Penderyn.

4 Bear right up the hill, keeping the fence on your left. Look out for views to the tops of the Brecon Beacons on your left. Just over the crest of the hill, cross a stile on your left but continue in the same general direction downhill for 50 m to cross another stile. Follow the well-defined track, passing some quarries on your right. Pass a stile on your left and follow the wide track (an old railway). Go through a kissing gate and follow the lane to the road. Turn right onto the road and go steeply uphill, passing a children's playground.

5 Continue ahead, ignoring a junction on your left, and follow the road downhill. Where the road turns left, go straight ahead through a gate. Follow this track for about 1.5 km.

6 The path descends past some old workings on the right and crosses a shallow valley. Ignore the path on your left and follow the path ahead. Continue down to the starting point.

On this walk the tranquillity of the countryside contrasts with the thunderous roar of the waterfalls.

access information

This walk starts at the 'waterfalls' car park in Pontneddfechan. Turn off the A465 at the A4109 junction then turn right at the lights.

The X5 bus service from Swansea goes to the car park.

It is possible to walk behind the wall of rushing water formed by the Sgwd yr Eira waterfalls.

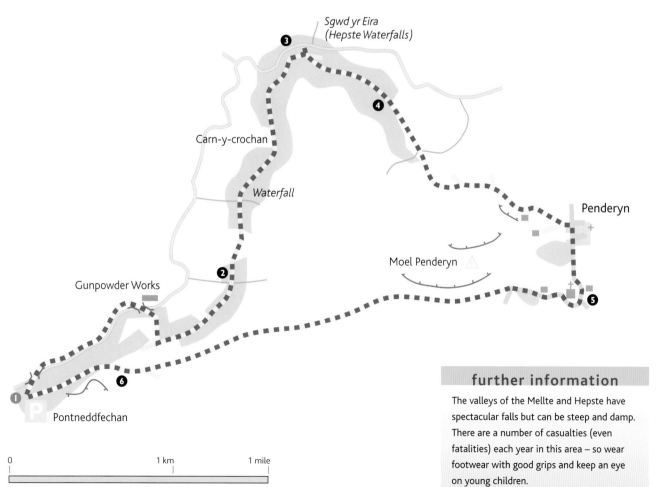

Sgwd yr Eira (Hepste Waterfalls)

Carn-y-crochan

Waterfall

Penderyn

Moel Penderyn

Gunpowder Works

Pontneddfechan

0   1 km   1 mile

further information

The valleys of the Mellte and Hepste have spectacular falls but can be steep and damp. There are a number of casualties (even fatalities) each year in this area – so wear footwear with good grips and keep an eye on young children.

The Welsh mountains and forests offer a spectacular range of landscape and wildlife. Highlights include The Precipice Walk and the Brecon Beacons Horseshoe.

▲ Map: Explorer 265

▲ Distance: 9 km/5½ miles

▲ Walk ID: 342 Jim Grindle

Difficulty rating

Time

▲ River, Pub, Toilets, Play Area, Wildlife, Flowers, Great Views, Good for Wheelchairs

Loggerheads and the Leete Path

Loggerheads is not far from Mold and is a Country Park. The walk takes you through the park and along a terrace above the River Alyn. Field paths and country lanes bring you back to the Leete Path near the start.

1 Cross the little bridge at the end of the car park. Pass by some buildings and continue to a stone bridge over the River Alyn. Go over the bridge and turn left towards a gateway at the end of the country park signposted Leete Path. The gravelled track becomes muddier and the channel of the Leete is to your right. Pass the boarding kennels and continue on their driveway past a white metal gate to a lane. Cross to another signpost.

2 You come to a diagonal crossing of tracks. Take the north-west path that keeps you on the same level. You will notice a number of mine shafts on the right and will shortly cross a bridge over the largest shaft. Another diagonal crossroads is reached and then a signposted junction with another right of way.

3 Following this you come to a lane. Turn left, downhill, and cross the road bridge. On a sharp right bend, follow the footpath sign to Pentre on the left.

4 Cross six stiles, keeping to the left-hand edge of the fields. The seventh takes you to the other side of the wire and the next down to a junction with a bridleway. Turn right and go up the hill with the cascade from a small lake on your left. You come to a lane where you turn left. Pass Wayside Cottage and turn left at the T-junction.

5 Walk for about 2 km, then look right to see the Jubilee Tower on Moel Famau. Continue until a concrete road to the left takes you down to a ford and bridge. Cross the river and climb towards a signpost 'Leete Path, Loggerheads' on the right, just where the lane bends left.

6 Take the right turn, and retrace your steps to the car park, 1.5 km away.

This footpath leads you through such tranquil countryside that it is difficult to believe that the area was once an industrial landscape of mine shafts, waterwheels and the water channel called the Leete.

access information

Loggerheads Country Park lies 5 km to the west of Mold on the A494. Parking is by the Information Centre. The Ruthin/Mold bus service calls in at the car park.

further information

The Leete was a clay-lined channel, designed to carry water that had been pumped from the lead mines in the adjacent valley to prevent flooding. It runs alongside the River Alyn for a distance of about 5 km.

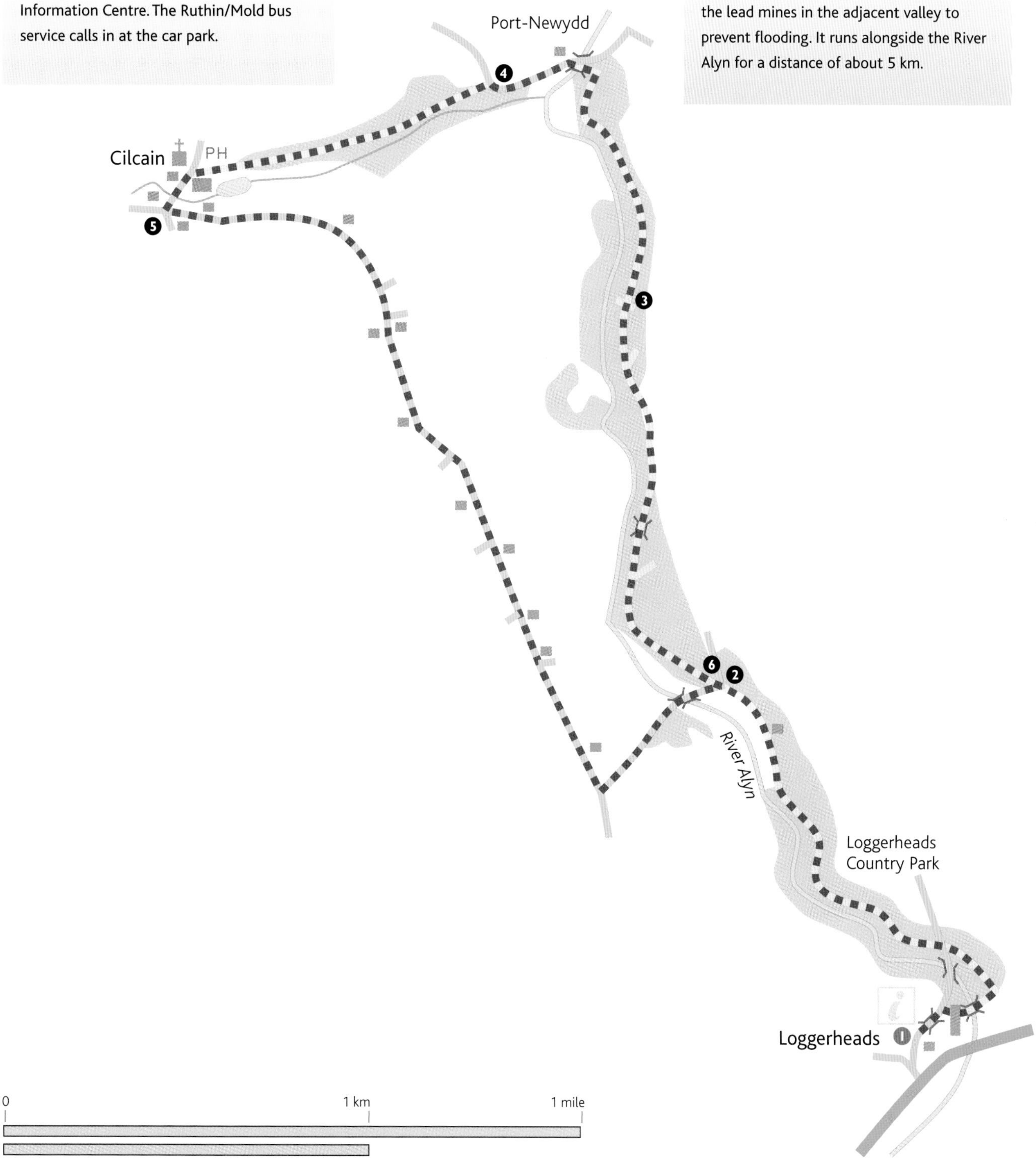

Port-Newydd

4

Cilcain

PH

5

3

6 **2**

River Alyn

Loggerheads
Country Park

Loggerheads **1**

0

1 km

1 mile

▲ Map: Explorer 256
▲ Distance: 9 km/5½ miles
▲ Walk ID: 230 Jim Grindle

Difficulty rating

Time

▲ River, Toilets, National Trust/NTS, Good for Wheelchairs (accessible for part of the way)

Erddig Hall at Wrexham Steeple

This is a short, pleasant walk through the grounds surrounding Erddig Hall, a National Trust property. It includes riverside, parkland and woodland sections and is mostly easy underfoot.

1 From the car park go back to the road and turn right. Walk towards the crossroads. Go straight across, as far as a signpost by the railings on the left. Turn right here and join a tarred track downhill. After passing a cattle grid you will see the Cup and Saucer Waterfall to your left. Continue on the track, crossing over a bridge. The path will then lead you onto a second bridge.

Erddig Hall provides a majestic backdrop to this footpath, which runs through the grounds that surround the house.

2 Cross the bridge and go through the kissing gate on the right. Follow the track by the river to reach a car park on a lane. Turn right onto the lane, and just before the road signs, turn left through a gate.

3 Follow the river bank or the hedge on the left of the fields. Watch out for a footbridge to cross. Follow the white arrows on the signposts, which lead you gradually above the river, but stay in the wood with the river below you on the right. Cross a bridge and stile near the edge of the wood and follow the track to the edge of a meadow.

4 Make for the large tree. If you look upwards you will see another signpost just past a second tree, a large oak. At the top of the slope keep to the right edge of the field – the exit is through a stile to the right.

5 Cross the stile to the lane, turn left and cross to a kissing gate. Continue on the narrow path ahead with fields on your left. You will reach a signpost. Keep straight ahead until you come to the end of the fields on the left. Turn left where the paths meet. Go left again, still with the fields on your left and the grounds of Erddig on your right.

6 Keep on the path until you come to a gate. Turn right and go through another gate. You will see ahead of you the dovecote by the car park as you return to the start of the walk.

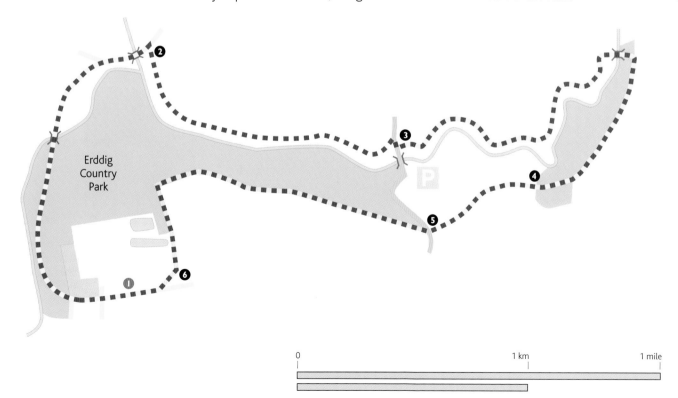

Erddig Country Park

0   1 km   1 mile

▲ Map: Explorer OL 17

▲ Distance: 14 km/8¾ miles

▲ Walk ID: 338 Haydn Williams

Difficulty rating

!!!

Time

●●●●●

▲ Pub, Castle, Great Views

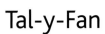

Tal-y-Fan

This walk takes you over the northern part of the Carneddau range. Allow yourself time at the summit to enjoy this glorious landscape and also views of Anglesey, Liverpool and the Conwy Valley.

❶ From the car park follow the black track for half a kilometre. The way the tracks diverge is slightly confusing, but you should turn sharp right and follow the obvious track uphill. Keep the lake to your right and continue for half a kilometre, to meet a farmer's track.

❷ Turn right on to this track and stay on it until you reach a wall on the left, following it for about 2.5 km. Cross the ford, then continue uphill, keeping the wall on the right for 200 m. Pick up the track immediately ahead. Continue for about one kilometre, from where you will see a wall 90 degrees to your right.

❸ Turning right at this wall, and by keeping it on your left, you will start a steep climb for 200 m. On reaching the summit cross the ladder stile to the trig point.

❹ At the summit enjoy the extensive views of the Menai Straits, Anglesey, Puffin Island, Conwy Bay, Great Orme, Llandudno Bay, Conwy Castle and Conwy Valley. Recross the ladder stile and go directly downhill with the wall at your back. When you reach a small cairn, turn right onto a footpath that takes you back to the wall. Follow this until you reach a distinct corner of the wall.

❺ From this point pick your own path down to the quarry heading diagonally right for half a kilometre. At the quarry take the left-hand route down. After approximately 200 m a stream drops off to the right. Continue straight on and turn right at the next obvious path.

❻ Walk past the standing stone and this path will bring you back to your original track. Turn left and follow the track back to the car park.

The windswept ridges of the Welsh mountains offer panoramic views to take the breath away.

Pengychnant

Craigytedwen

access information

Conwy is on the A55 near Llandudno. By car from Conwy town square, turn left before the arch, proceed uphill to another arch and follow the road to the right, going uphill for 2 km. Go over the cattle grid and, ignoring the small car park by the road junction, carry on uphill. After a bend on the road you will see a well-built wall with a parking sign. Turn left here into the car park. To come by public transport use the Sherpa Park & Ride.

From the highest point of this walk you will have excellent views of Conwy, with its magnificent castle and a bridge (below) built to complement the style of the fortress.

Standing Stone

Tal-y-Fan

0   1 km   1 mile

▲ Map: Explorer OL 17
▲ Distance: 8 km/5 miles
▲ Walk ID: 738 Jim Grindle

Difficulty rating

Time

▲ National Trust/NTS,
Great Views, Toilets

Bodnant Gardens and Moel Gyffylog

This walk begins at the attractive National Trust gardens at Bodnant. It covers the unclassified lanes to the east, rising to 250 m and offering outstanding views over the Conwy valley to the Carneddau range.

1 Turn left out of the car park at Bodnant. In 300 m you will come to a lane, Ffordd Bodnant. Turn left here and left again at the T-junction just ahead. The lane goes uphill for about 1.4 km to a junction just past Bodnant Ucha farm.
2 Turn right. In 350 m you reach a junction with another lane. Turn left here. Pass a junction with a lane from the left and continue to a small farm, Erw Goch. Barely 100 m further on there is another T-junction.
3 Turn right with the telephone lines on your right. At the top of the rise is another farm and 100 m beyond it you reach another T-junction. Turn left and go only 50 m, to a lane coming in from the right.
4 Turn right here for the next junction, 800 m away. Turn right at the signpost in the direction of Eglwysbach. It is 2.5 km downhill to the village, and you cross the stream by the entrance to Gyffylog farm on the way.
5 Turn right in Eglwysbach, to pass a bus stop on the left and a chapel on the right. Eight hundred metres from the junction you reach a red telephone box and a bus shelter by a crossroads in the hamlet of Graig. Bodnant is signposted on the right. Keep straight on, passing the bus shelter on your left.
6 Follow the road to Bodnant, to visit the gardens or return to the car park.

further information

The café, car park and the garden centre are free to enter but there is an entrance fee to the gardens themselves (NT members go in free). In addition to the beautiful gardens, there are many semi-wild areas and ponds. The grounds are open every day from mid-March to early November.

access information

Bodnant is on the A470 south of Llandudno and is well signposted from the A55. A bus from Conwy stops outside the gardens.

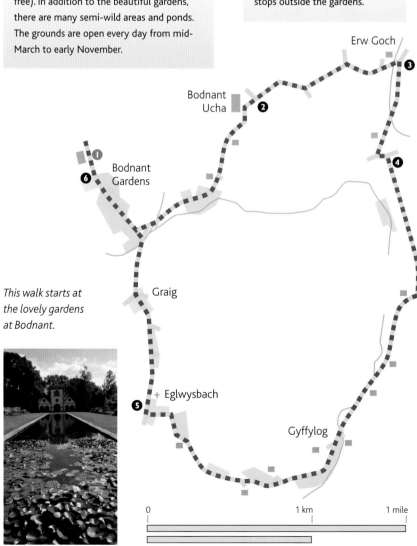

This walk starts at the lovely gardens at Bodnant.

▲ Map: Explorer OL 23
▲ Distance: 6 km/3¾ miles
▲ Walk ID: 225 Ian Morison

Difficulty rating

Time

▲ Hills or Fells, Lake/Loch, Toilets, Wildlife, Birds, Great Views

The Precipice Walk, north of Dolgellau

A classic Snowdonia walk with wonderful vistas over the Arans, Coed y Brenin Forest, the Mawddach estuary and Cader Idris. The view is one of the most beautiful panoramas in Wales, and there are perfect spots for picnics.

❶ Turn left out of the car park and follow the minor road for a short way. Turn left along the signposted track. Follow it round to the right where the track splits into two, keeping the open field to your left. Bear left as you pass the stone cottage.

❷ Cross a low ladder stile into woodland and turn right along the path. Cross the stile at the end of the wood into the open country. Follow the path round to the right. Llyn Cynwch is seen down the valley on the left.

❸ Turn right at the corner of the field following the signpost direction. Cross the ladder stile. The village of Llanfachreth is seen in the valley to your right. As you follow the stony path round to the left, Coed y Brenin Forest stretches out in front of you.

❹ The narrow path takes you along the flanks of Foel Cynwch. To the right lies the River Mawddach. The view opens out with the Mawddach estuary becoming visible to the right with distant views of Cader Idris.

❺ Climb over a ladder stile and follow the path round the hillside to the left. Cross a further ladder stile. Follow the path down towards Llyn Cynwch.

❻ Bear left, and drop onto the path by the lake. Follow the path beside the lake. Rejoin the outward route and retrace your steps to the car park.

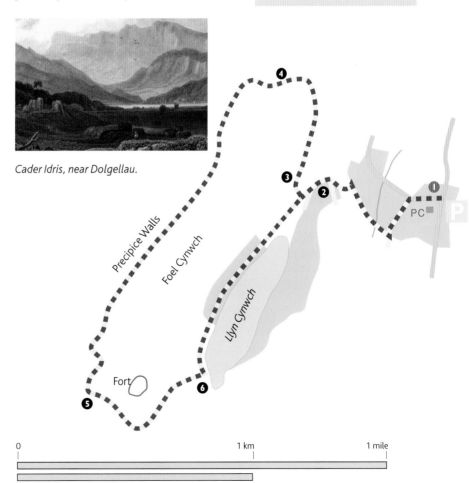

Cader Idris, near Dolgellau.

further information

The route runs high above the River Mawddach. The ground drops steeply into the valley so young children will need to be well supervised, but there are no sheer drops. The path is good, but occasionally rocky.

access information

By car only. A National Park car park is on the left-hand side of the minor road between Dolgellau, on the A470, and the village of Llanfachreth – from Dolgellau, follow signs to the Precipice Walk.

▲ Map: Explorer OL 17

▲ Distance: 6 km/3¾ miles

▲ Walk ID: 772 Haydn Williams

Difficulty rating

Time

▲ Mountains, Lake/Loch, Great Views

Beddgelert Forest

This walk through Beddgelert Forest gives great views of the surrounding mountains. It is easy to follow the route with the aid of the numbered marker poles set at regular intervals through the forest.

❶ At the top of the car park, take a shortcut to the track, through the bushes. Turn left onto the track. Turn right at the first junction, at marker pole 80. Follow the delightful little stream on your right. On your right you have views of Moel Hebog. Turn right onto the concrete bridge. Straight ahead are views of Y Garn.

❷ Look for marker pole 64 and turn left. There is a view of Yr Aran. Carry on uphill keeping the stream on your right. Ahead is the Nantlle Ridge, on the left is Moel Hebog and Moel Ogof.

❸ Turn left at the T-junction and cross a concrete bridge. Turn sharp right onto a footpath, ignoring the junction ahead. Look for a marker pole 66. Bear left onto the track at marker pole 34. Take the path to the right. Bear left at the junction, cross over a concrete bridge at marker pole 42, and carry straight on, ignoring the turning to the right.

❹ Keep bearing left, ignoring the track on your right and the grassy path ahead. Turn left and go downhill at the junction at marker pole 36.

❺ Carry on downhill. Turn right onto the main track, passing marker pole 35. Pass marker pole 34 on your left.

❻ Turn left at the junction, heading downhill. Directly ahead is Moel Hebog, marked by marker pole 33. Turn right at the junction marked by marker pole 70.

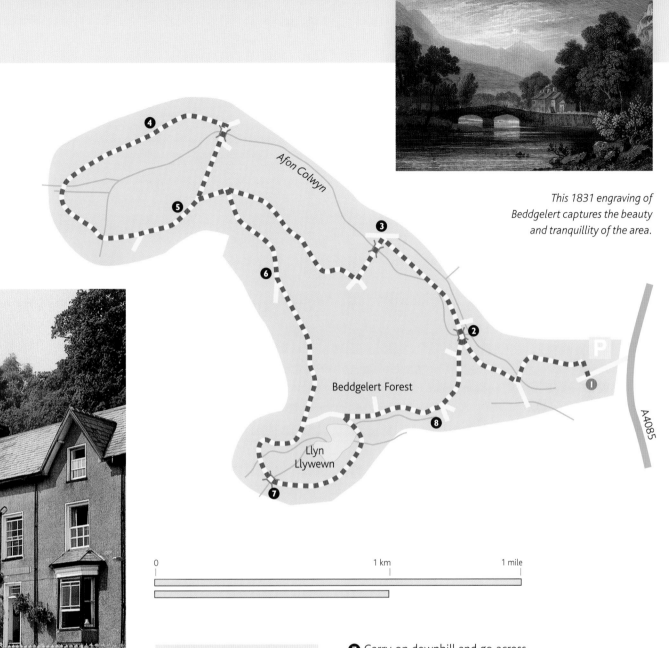

This 1831 engraving of Beddgelert captures the beauty and tranquillity of the area.

access information

Access is on the Beddgelert to Caernarfon road (A4085). Turn left into the Forestry Commission access and drive down to the car park.

The village of Beddgelert, at the confluence of the Glaslyn and Colwyn rivers, is also situated at the approaches to two mountain passes, offering access to some of the most spectacular scenery in Snowdonia.

7 Carry on downhill and go across another concrete bridge. Turn left onto the path, which borders the lake. You enter the picnic area. On leaving turn right at marker pole 69 on the edge of the lake.

8 Carry straight on at the crossroads, at marker pole 68. Turn left at junction post marker pole 67. Turn right off the main track by the trees, marker pole 65, and down the cinder path. Turn right just before the concrete bridge sending you down on the path you came up on. Turn left at marker pole 80 and proceed back to the car park.

Difficulty rating

Time

▲ Hills or Fells, Mountains, River, Toilets, Great Views, Food Shop, Moor, Tea Shop, Waterfall

Pistyll Llanrhaeadr and the Berwyns

Starting at a waterfall, this short, circular walk takes you into the fringes of the Berwyn Mountains, where there are clear views of the craggy eastern faces of the highest peaks.

❶ Go through the small wooden gate by the café and turn right towards the falls. Turn right into the woods. Pass through a gate and follow the path slightly left to a stile and gate at the edge of the wood.

❷ Follow the stony track to the steps. At the top, turn left. Look for a signpost on the left of the track. It points towards a ladder stile. To go to the falls turn left and return to continue the walk. Further up the valley the path divides.

❸ Take the lower path, on the left. The path ends but carry on to a very straight and deep stream bed. On the far side is a wire fence. Turn left, downhill to where the stream joins the main stream. Go downstream to where the water is shallower. Cross, turn right and make for the corner where the two fences meet.

❹ Cross the gate and turn left. Go to the left of the sheep pens and then turn right, following a little stream uphill until you can cross it. At the conifer trees, cross the gate and follow the fence on your left. At the top of this first rise there are good views of the Berwyns.

❺ Keep going with the fence on your left. The track eventually rises to the highest point of the walk. It then drops again and takes a sharp turn left in the first of a series of bends into the valley on your left. At the bend leave the track, using sheep tracks to reach a path

alongside a fence below you. Aim for the rowan tree. Now turn left and follow the path along the fence. Pass a stile on your right and you will come to another one leading into a wood.

❻ Follow the path through woodland and some small clearings until you see some fencing on the right below you. You will soon come back to the iron bridge. Cross it to get back to the gate.

The remote peaks of the Berwyns are wild and deserted, populated only by grazing mountain sheep.

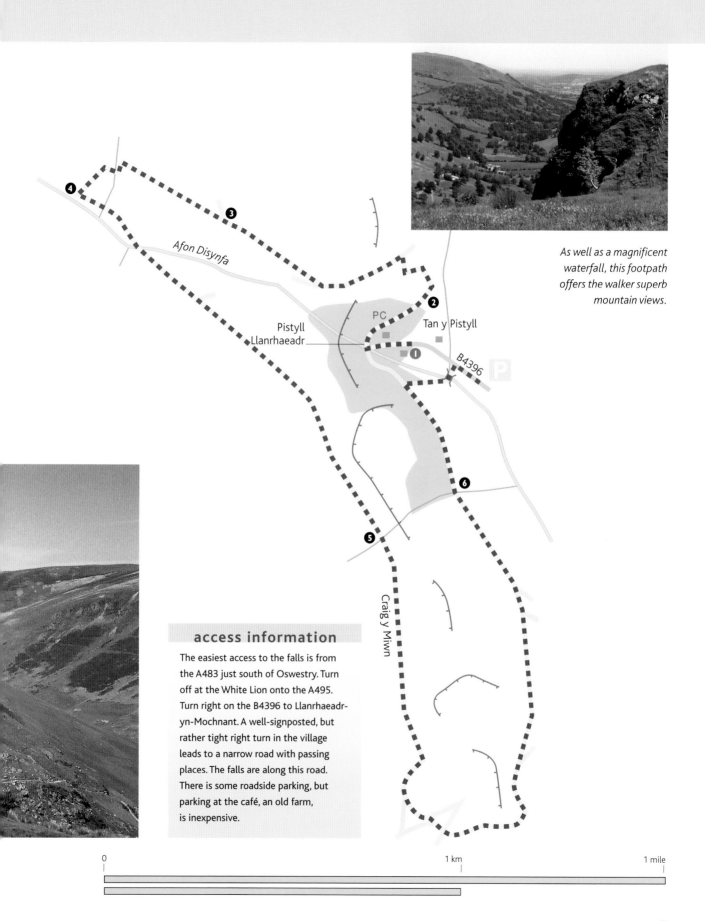

As well as a magnificent
waterfall, this footpath
offers the walker superb
mountain views.

4

3

Afon Disynfa

2

PC

Pistyll
Llanrhaeadr

Tan y Pistyll

1

B4396

6

5

Craig y Mwn

access information

The easiest access to the falls is from
the A483 just south of Oswestry. Turn
off at the White Lion onto the A495.
Turn right on the B4396 to Llanrhaeadr-
yn-Mochnant. A well-signposted, but
rather tight right turn in the village
leads to a narrow road with passing
places. The falls are along this road.
There is some roadside parking, but
parking at the café, an old farm,
is inexpensive.

0   1 km   1 mile

▲ Map: Explorer 265

▲ Distance: 4 km/2½ miles

▲ Walk ID: 1567 Jim Grindle

Difficulty rating

Time

▲ Lake/Loch, Toilets, Museum, Church, Good for Wheelchairs, Café, Food Shop, Good for Kids, Nature Trail, Restaurant, Woodland, Ancient Monument.

St Winefride's Well from Holywell

This walk in Greenfield Heritage Park includes St Winefride's Well, one of the Seven Wonders of Wales. There is one main track running through the park. Smaller paths lead to the old railway and industrial sites.

1 From the car park take the signposted path towards the Visitor Centre. Just before you reach the centre there is a path going off to the right. Follow this path. On the right there is a garden on the site of the Abbey Wire Mill. Continue on the path to the left until you reach a reservoir.

2 Take the fork to the right so that you keep by the edge of the water. A little further on the path divides. Take the right fork and stay on the path until you have to go up left to the railway track. The railway track is the level path on the right. Stay on this until you see some gravelled steps going down to the right.

3 Take the little path down the steps and stay on it until you have to go up left to the railway. Take the right branch, which is the old railway track. Look for a flight of steps going up to the left, but ignore them to stay on the track. Watch now for a split in this track.

4 Take the right fork at a red and white marker post 8JF. Just out of sight is a small gate by a larger one. Go through the small gate and drop down through an industrial area to the B5121. You will see a footpath sign on the left of the opening onto the road. Turn left.

5 About 100 m up the road is the entrance to St Winefride's Well. After visiting the famous well, go back the

way you came but stay on the old railway track. This will bring you right back to Basingwerk Abbey, passing by features you have passed earlier. The track takes you over a little bridge and then it curves down to the left to the ruins of the abbey.

6 Go through the little gate to the abbey. At the far end is a similar gate. The car park is also signposted.

The estuaries of North Wales can provide some of the most spectacular views in Britain.

Greenfield
(Maes-Glas)

Basingwerk
Abbey

❻

Holywell Visitor Centre

❷

❸

Heritage Park

B5121

❹

❺ St Winefride's Well

access information

Holywell lies between the A55 Expressway
and the A548; both Basingwerk Abbey and
St Winefride's Well are signposted. Buses
from Chester to Rhyl call at Holywell.
The car park on the B5121 is closest to the
Visitor Centre, but the car park on the A548
for the abbey can also be used.

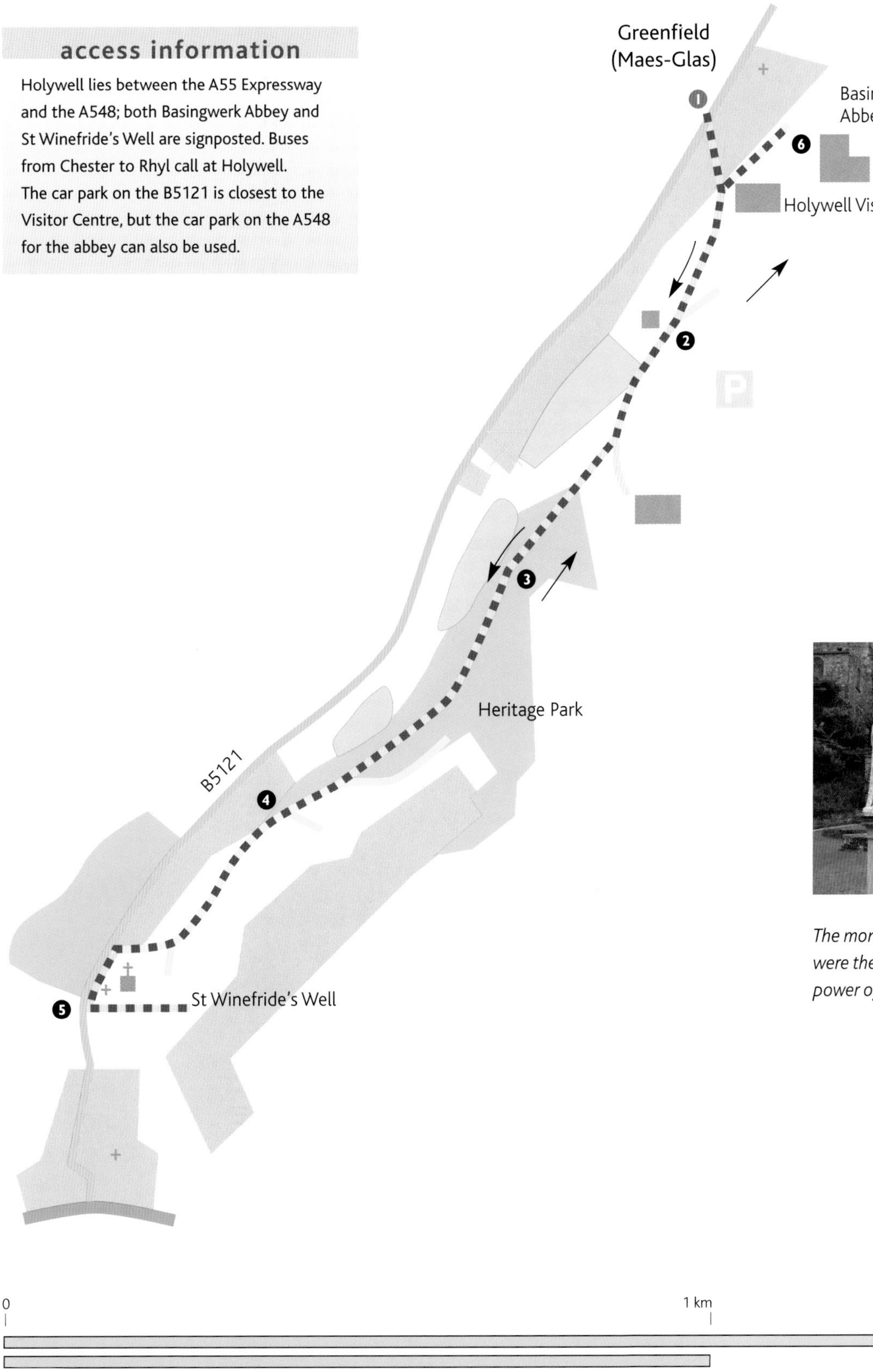

*The monks at Basingwerk Abbey
were the first to harness the
power of the nearby stream.*

0   1 km   1 mile

▲ Map: Explorer OL 14

▲ Distance: 5 km/3 miles

▲ Walk ID: 213 Peter Salenieks

Difficulty rating

Time

▲ River, Pub, Toilets, Church, Wildlife, Birds, Great Views, Café, Gift Shop, Tea Shop, Woodland

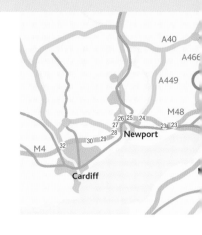

Devil's Pulpit from Tintern Abbey

This is a short walk from the atmospheric, ivy-clad ruins of Tintern Abbey along woodland paths that lead to the Devil's Pulpit, overlooking the Wye Valley. The route follows part of the Offa's Dyke Path.

❶ From the car park opposite Tintern Abbey, walk along a minor road that leads towards the River Wye. Pass the Anchor pub to reach a footpath on the left. Follow the footpath along the bank of the river. After the footpath turns towards Tintern, pass a whitewashed house on the left and continue along a minor road to reach a T-junction with the A466.

❷ Turn right and continue along the pavement, passing a hotel on your left and an art gallery on your right. Continue until you reach a minor road junction on your right, just past the Abbey Mill.

❸ Walk along the minor road towards the River Wye and cross the footbridge. Continue along the footpath, passing another footpath on the right. Follow the path on the left as it leads uphill, with several metal posts at the start. Shortly after it levels off, there is a junction. Take the right-hand path and follow it until you reach another junction marked by a wooden post with a footpath sign.

❹ Take the right-hand path. At the next junction, turn left and follow the footpath uphill. As the gradient levels off, the path bears to the right. Climb the short flight of wooden steps on the left to reach a junction marked by a wooden post with a footpath sign.

❺ Turn right and walk along the track. At the next junction bear left and follow the footpath uphill to reach Offa's Dyke Path. Turn right at the footpath sign and walk along Offa's Dyke Path until you reach a junction and a sign at a right-hand bend.

❻ Continue along Offa's Dyke Path from the footpath sign to reach the Devil's Pulpit. Retrace your route to the start.

Tintern Abbey, founded in 1131, was the first Cistercian monastery in Wales. Over the past 100 years it has undergone a continuous programme of maintenance and restoration.

access information

Tintern lies between Monmouth and Chepstow in the Wye Valley. The abbey is just off the A466, at the southern end of the village. There is a car park just off the main road. If this is full, the car park for Tintern Abbey is at the rear of the abbey, beside the River Wye.

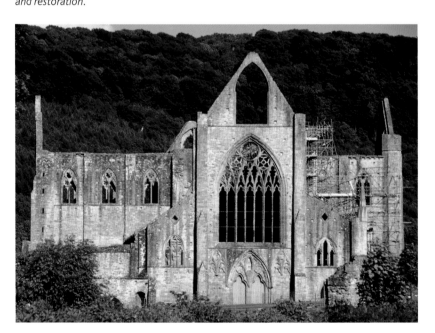

further information

This walk can be combined with a visit to Tintern Abbey. Contact the information centre on 01291 689251 for information about when the abbey is open.

The Devil's Pulpit is a small limestone rock that juts out from the cliffs. It looks down over Tintern Abbey from the hills beside Offa's Dyke on the eastern side of the River Wye. Local legend has it that the Devil stood upon the Devil's Pulpit to preach to the monks below, tempting them to desert their order.

The view of Tintern Abbey from the Devil's Pulpit takes in a vast expanse of the River Wye.

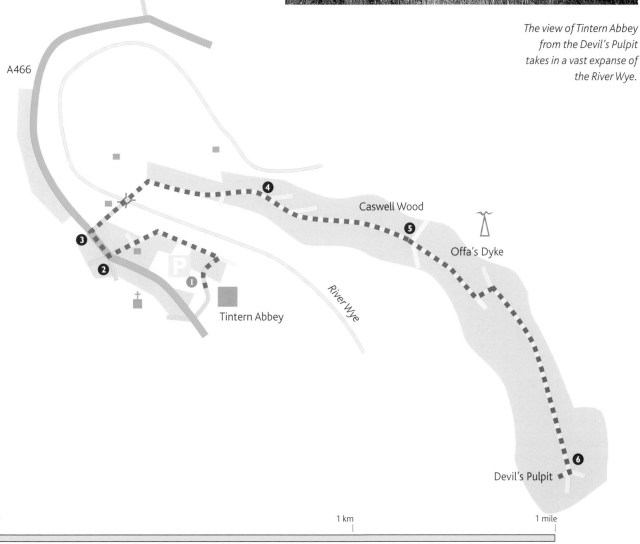

A466

Caswell Wood

Offa's Dyke

River Wye

Tintern Abbey

Devil's Pulpit

0   1 km   1 mile

▲ Map: Explorer 152

▲ Distance: 6.5 km/4 miles

▲ Walk ID: 999 John Thorn

Difficulty rating

Time

▲ Pub, Castle, Birds, Flowers, Great Views, Butterflies, Industrial Archaeology, Public Transport, Woodland, Ancient Monument

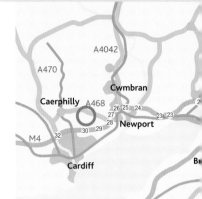

Ruperra Castle from Draethen

This is a pleasant walk that follows a route almost entirely through varied woodland, with the added interest of passing the ruins of Ruperra Castle and an Iron Age fort along the way.

1 From the centre of the village walk up the road signposted Rudry and Lisvane. At the bridle path sign, turn right up a concrete drive. At the cottage, turn left to follow the bridleway sign, through a gate, then another gate into the woods. Just after the track levels out turn right at a T-junction, then left. Emerge onto an open area with several paths.

2 Take the gravel track slightly to the left. Almost immediately take a hard-to-see path that drops down steeply to the left. Towards the bottom of the valley, where the path turns right and the woods open out a little, turn left past a ruined cottage. Cross the road by going left then right down a drive marked 'The Retreat'. Go between the houses. Do not turn left into a gate, but cross a gravelled area, go down some steps and cross a footbridge. Take the left-hand path up through the woods. Cross a track and continue. Pass a steel barn on your left, go through the gate and turn left onto a road. Just past a cottage, bear right, keeping the woods on the left and the field on the right.

3 At the end of the field, go through the kissing gate and follow the wall, crossing two stiles. At the end of the wall, turn left to a gateway for a view of Ruperra Castle. Retrace your steps back to the kissing gate, then turn right past the gateway marked 'Ruperra Castle Farm'.

Bear left, slightly uphill, for another view of the castle.

4 Before you reach a gateway in the wall, turn left uphill following yellow arrows. When you reach another path, turn right to climb the ridge to the top of the Iron Age hill fort. When the track turns sharp right, follow it down, then left.

5 Turn right at a junction then right at the next junction to return to point 4. Climb away from the wall but continue across the next path, following the arrows. Turn right at a wider track.

6 Turn left onto a narrow path. Continue down through the woodland. Go through a kissing gate into a field. Follow the right-hand side of the field down into the valley. Turn right at the stile to reach the starting point.

further information

As the path levels out at point 4 there are fine views of the castle, Cardiff, the Bristol Channel and the Quantocks.

The original 17th-century castle of Ruperra was twice destroyed by fire and was rebuilt once. It is now nothing more than a romantic ruin.

access information

This walk starts in Draethen. In the centre of the village, opposite the post and telephone boxes, turn towards the Hollybush Inn but instead of crossing either of the bridges turn sharp left onto a gravelled area in front of an old stone barn.

Buses from Caerphilly to Newport stop in Lower Machen, on the A468.

Ruperra Castle was built to command views across a swathe of countryside.

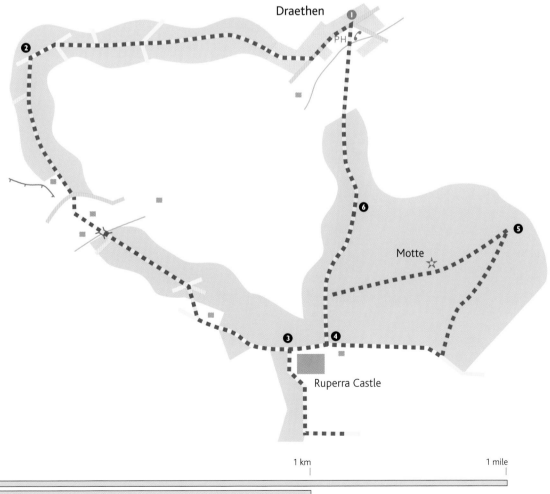

▲ Map: Explorer OL 35
▲ Distance: 11 km/6¾ miles
▲ Walk ID: 1323 Pat Roberts

Difficulty rating

Time

▲ Mountains, Wildlife, Birds, Flowers, Great Views, Butterflies, Moor, Tea Shop, Woodland

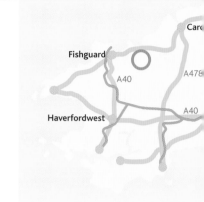

Carningli from Sychbant

This walk climbs to Bedd Morris, then onto Carningli, for incredible views of the Wicklow Hills in Ireland, the Welsh coast and the Preseli Hills, to return down through the Gwaun Valley.

❶ From the car park walk up the drive to Ffald-y-Brenin (Sychbant on the map). Where the drive swings left, go over the marked stile to the left of the gate. Continue up a field to pass through another gate. Turn left to reach a gate with blue arrows. Go through the gate and turn right up a green lane. Go over two stiles in quick succession to enter the forest. An information board tells us that this is the 'Penlan Project'. Follow the arrow to the right, to Carningli. After about 1 km bear left towards Bedd Morris and emerge from the forest on a stony track.

❷ At Bedd Morris, with the stone behind you, walk ahead on a path that follows a raised bank in an easterly direction, leaving the bank to curve slightly left over the top of Mynydd Caregog. After passing above the forest, a fence comes in from the right. Follow the grassy path, keeping the fence on your right. As you come level with Carn Edward, a large rocky outcrop on the right, take the left fork, then turn immediately left again.

❸ Keep heading towards Carningli, following any of the small paths. Once you are within 150 m of the outcrop, head for the northern end, and you will see a well-used route up onto the top.

❹ At the top of Carningli there are fantastic views. Retrace your steps off the outcrop, and turn right. Take the most suitable path round the rocks. Descend on the narrow but good path heading east. Follow the path down to the Dolrannog road.

❺ On reaching the road turn right. Go through the farmyard and walk through a metal gate to pass Dolrannog Uchaf.

❻ At the end of the road go through the gate to the left of the bungalow. Follow the bridle path down through the woods to reach Llanerch and the valley road. Turn right to return to the start.

further information

There are many legends attached to Bedd Morris, but it is most likely a Bronze Age standing stone and is now one of the markers standing on Newport Parish Boundary.

An ancient copper-beech tree presides over the Preseli Hills like a monument to the enduring power of nature.

access information

Parking is at the Sychbant Picnic Site on a minor road off the B4313 out of Fishguard. Look for the sign for 'Ffald-y-Brenin' at a bend in the road. This house is marked on the Ordnance Survey® map as 'Sychbant' and is next to the car park.

With its weather-beaten rocks, standing stones and ancient legends, Carningli is not a place for the faint-hearted.

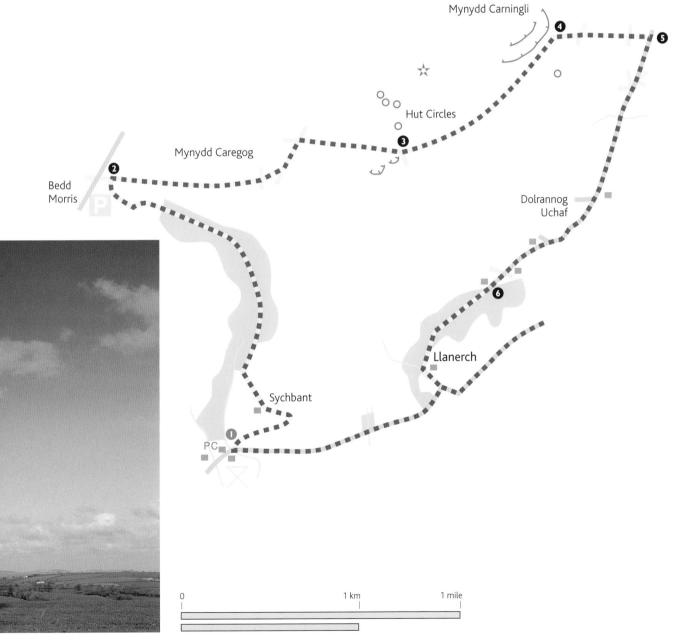

Mynydd Carningli

Hut Circles

Mynydd Caregog

Bedd Morris

Dolrannog Uchaf

Llanerch

Sychbant

P C

0   1 km   1 mile

▲ Map: Explorer OL 12

▲ Distance: 11 km/6¾ miles

▲ Walk ID: 1290 John Thorn

Difficulty rating

Time

▲ Mountains, Reservoir, National Trust, Wildlife, Birds, Flowers, Great Views

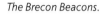

Brecon Beacons Horseshoe

This walk to the top of the Brecon Beacons has stupendous views from almost every point.

❶ Do not go through the gate but turn up to the right to reach a track. Cross the stile and walk between the two fences. When the fence on your right turns right follow it up. As you approach the trees bear left to join the rough track. Turn left onto the Roman road. Go down a steep dip and up the other side, bearing right. Follow the track to the top of the pass.

❷ At the top, cross the stile on your left and bear left on the well-defined path that climbs around the shoulder of Cribyn. At the saddle between Cribyn and Pen y Fan, continue ahead climbing steeply. Look over your right shoulder for views of Cribyn, Llangorse Lake, the Black Mountains and, later, the Sugar Loaf.

❸ The summit of Pen y Fan has commanding views in all directions. Descend towards the flat top of Corn Du, but at the saddle bear left. At the next saddle bear left again, climbing slightly to follow the escarpment for about 3 km. You pass to the left of a large cairn, following the edge. Pass another large cairn and ignore the steep path down to your left in a fold in the mountain.

❹ Turn right to start a steep descent, aiming for the end of the dam. Go though the gate, walk along the dam then veer off to the right to cross a bridge. Go through the gate to reach the starting point.

access information

Start at the parking area by the dam of the lower Neuadd reservoir. Access is from the minor road between Vaynor/Merthyr and Talybont off the A465.

The Brecon Beacons.

further information

Pen y Fan (see photo on page 218) is the highest point in South Wales. Do not attempt this walk in poor visibility. Most of the paths on the first part are well defined but less so after leaving Corn Du, and parts of the route can be muddy or boggy.

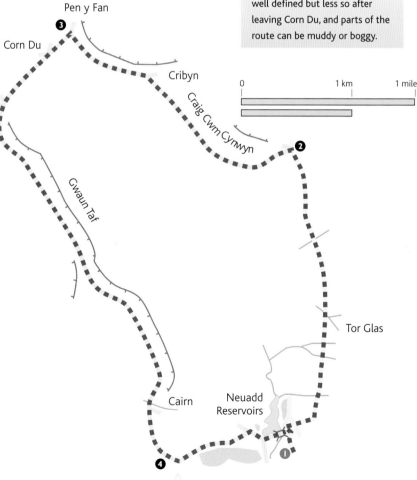

▲ Map: Explorer 200

▲ Distance: 9 km/5½ miles

▲ Walk ID: 951 Pete Brett

Difficulty rating

Time

▲ Hills or Fells, Reservoir, Toilets, Play Area, Church, Wildlife, Birds, Flowers, Great Views, Good for Wheelchairs, Nature Trail, Tea Shop, Woodland

Garreg-ddu Reservoir from Elan Valley

This relatively short walk offers the walker peace and tranquillity amid superb scenery.

1 Leave the car park taking the ascending path to a cinder track and turn left towards Caban Coch Dam. Remain on the track beside the reservoir until reaching the arched road bridge.

2 Cross the road by Foel Tower and rejoin the track. (If time permits you can turn left over the road bridge and visit Nantgwyllt Church on the far bank.) Leave the track through the gate and continue on the grass verge beside the road for 200 m to the bridle path on the right. Climb the bridle path steeply at first then over the stream, ignoring any small side tracks.

3 Where the path branches left, continue straight ahead towards high ground for all-round views. From the viewpoint return to this point and descend the path, following small posts and signs to reach a metal gate.

4 At the gate turn right and continue to descend, following little yellow markers until you reach a wire fence. Turn left and follow the fence to the gates of the water treatment buildings. Go through the gates and down steps to the road.

5 Cross the road. Behind the houses, cross the footbridge over the river. Turn right and follow the river through the Elan estate to pass the toilets on the left. Go through a white gate beside the bridges into Cnwch woods and continue on the path through the trees.

6 Go behind the first turbine house and cross the bridge in front of the dam. Head behind the second turbine house to return to the visitor centre car park.

The bridge over the majestic Caban Coch Dam forms an integral part of this walk.

access information

From Rhayader take the B4518 road heading south-west (follow signs to Elan Valley Reservoirs) and park at the Elan Valley Visitor Centre.

further information

Wheelchair users can follow the route alongside the reservoirs, returning to the visitor centre the same way.

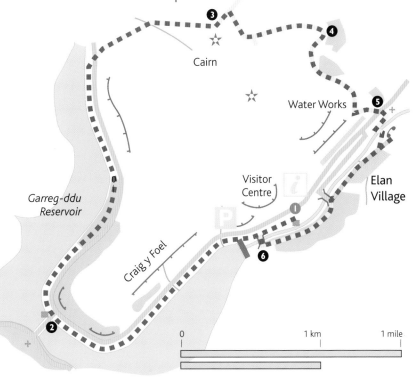

▲ Map: Explorer OL 13	Difficulty rating	Time	▲ Mountains, Pub, Wildlife, Birds, Great

▲ Map: Explorer OL 13
▲ Distance: 10 km/6¼ miles
▲ Walk ID: 1511 Pat Roberts

Difficulty rating

Time

▲ Mountains, Pub, Wildlife, Birds, Great Views, Industrial Archaeology, Ancient Monument

Blaenavon from Foxhunter Car Park

This walk in the Blaenavon heritage area takes in a visit to the Ironworks, as well as views of Big Pit and Coity Mountain. The return route is across opencast landscape, past old mines with fine views of the Brecon Beacons and the Black Mountains.

1 From the car park walk to the minor road by the masts and go right for a short distance. Take the narrow path on the left towards the telegraph poles. Just above a covered reservoir join a gravel path to reach the B4246. Turn left towards Blaenavon. As you reach the 30 mph signs, cross the road.

2 Opposite the Riflemans Arms, take a path through a car park and picnic area, to emerge on a road. Cross over to reach the footpath and head downhill. Soon take a right turn, just after a left bend, where you can see the ironworks on the right. Just after the bend, go down the steps in front of York House. Cross over to join another road with the ironworks' railings on your right. Continue down the road to visit the ironworks.

3 Head down the hill and take the first turn on the right. Follow this road to join the B4248 road to Brynmawr. Turn left and continue until you reach a bus shelter on your right.

4 Just past the bus shelter, take the lane up towards two houses. Where the lane swings right, continue ahead on a track. Go over another stepped gate and through another gate to follow the track up into the open hillside.

5 You will come across a square chimney stack with a tree growing out of the top. To each side you will see fenced-off areas. Continue on the track

to reach another fenced square. Ignore a yellow arrow pointing straight on and head for the incline on the right.

6 At the ridge there are views of Brecon Beacons and the Black Mountains. Take the right-hand path towards the masts. Maintain direction, heading just right of the masts, until you reach the B4246. You should emerge opposite the side road leading to the masts and car park.

access information

Park at the Foxhunter car park, near the masts on the Blorenge. Take the B4246 road from Abergavenny to Blaenavon, and turn off near the Keeper's Pond at the top, heading for the two big masts. These should also help you to navigate the walk.

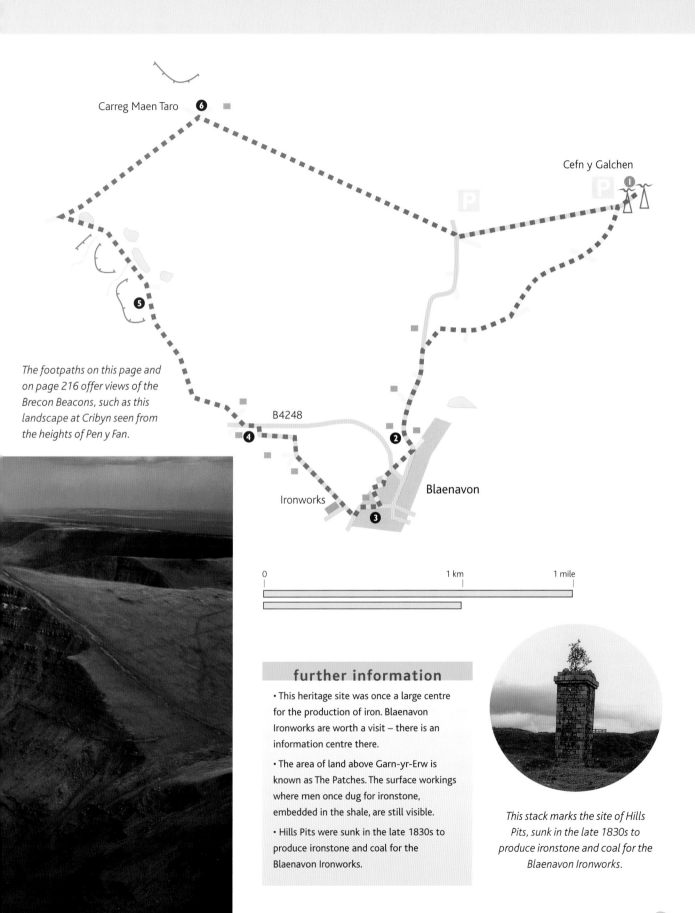

Carreg Maen Taro **6**

Cefn y Galchen **1**

5

The footpaths on this page and on page 216 offer views of the Brecon Beacons, such as this landscape at Cribyn seen from the heights of Pen y Fan.

B4248

4

2

Ironworks

Blaenavon

3

0   1 km   1 mile

further information

• This heritage site was once a large centre for the production of iron. Blaenavon Ironworks are worth a visit – there is an information centre there.

• The area of land above Garn-yr-Erw is known as The Patches. The surface workings where men once dug for ironstone, embedded in the shale, are still visible.

• Hills Pits were sunk in the late 1830s to produce ironstone and coal for the Blaenavon Ironworks.

This stack marks the site of Hills Pits, sunk in the late 1830s to produce ironstone and coal for the Blaenavon Ironworks.

▲ Map: Explorer OL 13
▲ Distance: 13 km/8 miles
▲ Walk ID: 1270 Pat Roberts

Difficulty rating

Time

▲ Mountains, Church, Wildlife, Birds, Flowers, Great Views, Butterflies, Waterfall

Revenge Stone from Pont Esgob

This route combines two ridge walks with a visit to an attractive old church, a memorial stone with a very unusual name, an Iron Age hill fort and a walk in the Grwyne Valley.

1 Take the minor road signed Partrishow and Crickhowell. Keep right at the fork and follow the road, ignoring the road on the left. Just below the church, approach the Holy Well of St Issui by paving stones on the right.

2 Walk through the churchyard and through a gate onto the hillside. Join a track, and, above the farmhouse on the right, head right and down, keeping the wall on your left. Pass between the buildings to reach a track. Go through the first gate on the left and cross a field to a stile. Continue down the next field to a stile and then left and down past ruins to reach another stile by the road.

3 Cross the road and continue down the minor road. Pass the chapel and keep to the road. Keep to the right of the farm and buildings and keep to the main track leading gently upwards. At the farm, keep to the right of the farmhouse to reach a gate, which leads to a sunken stony path. Continue through another gate, keeping to the right wall. As the wall swings right, go straight up to the ridge and the memorial stone.

4 At Dial Garreg (The Revenge Stone), turn right to walk the ridge. At the fork, take the left path to reach a wide, grassy track, heading towards Twyn y Gaer. As the wall and track start to swing away from the fort, and there is a junction of paths, continue on the central green track up to the top of Twyn y Gaer.

5 Retrace your steps down from the top and at a crosspaths fork left, keeping to the fence on your left.
Cross the stile and head down, across grass and then on an old drovers' road between two old walls.

6 At a break in the wall, keep to the right of the wall to reach a stile onto another stony track. Continue bearing left and down to join a road, then right and down, eventually to reach the starting point of the walk.

further information

The Revenge Stone marks the spot where the Norman Marcher Lord, Richard de Clare, was attacked and killed by Morgan ap Owen in 1135.

Twyn y Gaer is a fine Iron Age fort with extensive views.

Seen here from a point near Crickhowell, Powys, the Black Mountains provide a majestic background to the landscape.

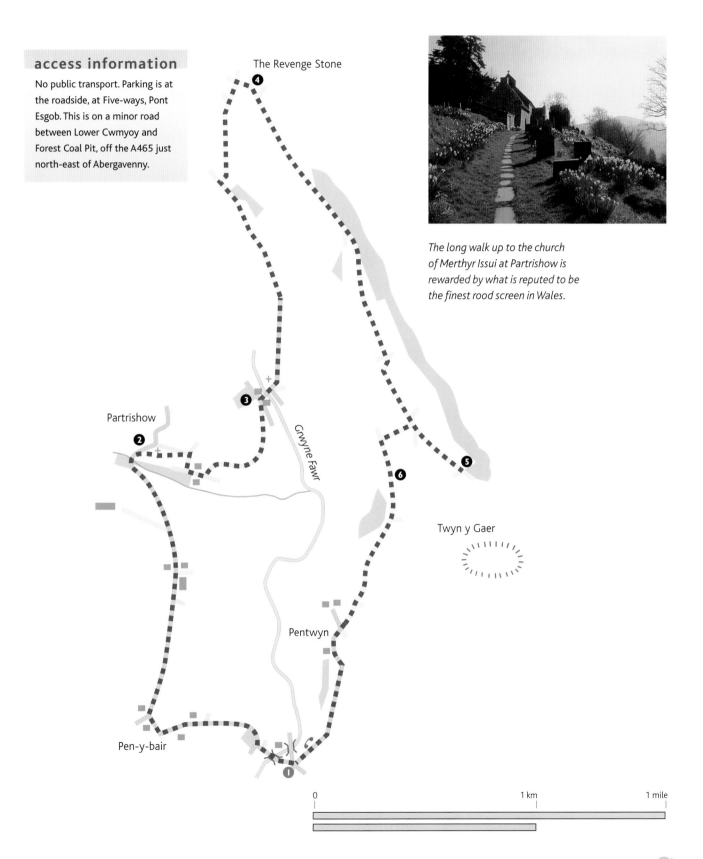

access information

No public transport. Parking is at the roadside, at Five-ways, Pont Esgob. This is on a minor road between Lower Cwmyoy and Forest Coal Pit, off the A465 just north-east of Abergavenny.

The Revenge Stone

4

Partrishow

2

3

Grwyne Fawr

5

6

Twyn y Gaer

Pentwyn

Pen-y-bair

1

The long walk up to the church of Merthyr Issui at Partrishow is rewarded by what is reputed to be the finest rood screen in Wales.

| 0 | 1 km | 1 mile |

▲ Map: Explorer OL 13

▲ Distance: 8 km/5 miles

▲ Walk ID: 307 Peter Salenieks

Difficulty rating

Time

▲ Hills or Fells, Mountains, Pub, Toilets, Church, Great Views

Hatterrall Hill from Llanthony Priory

This is a short circular walk set in the heart of the Black Mountains, with fine views of the surrounding hills and plains. At the start or end of your walk, you can wander among the Gothic arches of the ruined Llanthony Priory.

1 As you leave the car park walk straight ahead, keeping the Abbey Hotel and Llanthony Priory on your right. A short distance ahead, there is a footpath sign next to a gate and a stile. Cross the stile and turn right. Keep the Abbey Hotel on your right and walk for about 100 m.

2 Cross the stile and follow the sign to Offa's Dyke. The footpath leads along a track across a field. Close to a small stream, turn left at the National Park marker and walk a few metres to cross the first of a series of five stiles. The path leads gently uphill across fields towards Loxidge Tump. There is a National Park sign next to the fifth stile, which includes a map of Hatterrall Hill. Now the path climbs through bracken, before bearing right and zigzagging to gain the ridge. Cross open ground along a path, which passes a small cairn before joining Offa's Dyke Path at a milestone (signed Llanthony).

3 Turn right at the milestone and walk along Offa's Dyke Path for about 3 km. The path dips into a col, where another milestone points to Longtown and Llanthony.

4 Turn right and follow the footpath down towards Llanthony, taking in the views of the Vale of Ewyas. Continue for about 1.5 km along this footpath until you reach a junction with a footpath

sign and a stile on the left, together with a National Park sign.

5 Cross the stile and follow the footpath downhill, keeping the fence on your left. Cross another stile and enter Wiral Wood. The footpath bears right then left at a small stream, before crossing another stile at the edge of the woods. Cross the field to a stile in the bottom right corner.

6 Cross the stile and follow the dry-stone wall, keeping Llanthony Priory to your left, until you reach the stile at point 2. Cross the stile and retrace your route to the start.

access information

Approach the start by road from Abergavenny or Hereford along the A465 to Llanvihangel Crucorney. Then follow minor roads for 10 km to reach Llanthony. Park in the free car park at Llanthony Priory.

Abandoned by the Augustinian monks in 1134, Llanthony Priory's ruined skeleton stands forlornly in the shadow of the Black Mountains.

Pony trekking can be arranged at Court Farm, which is immediately adjacent to the Abbey Hotel.

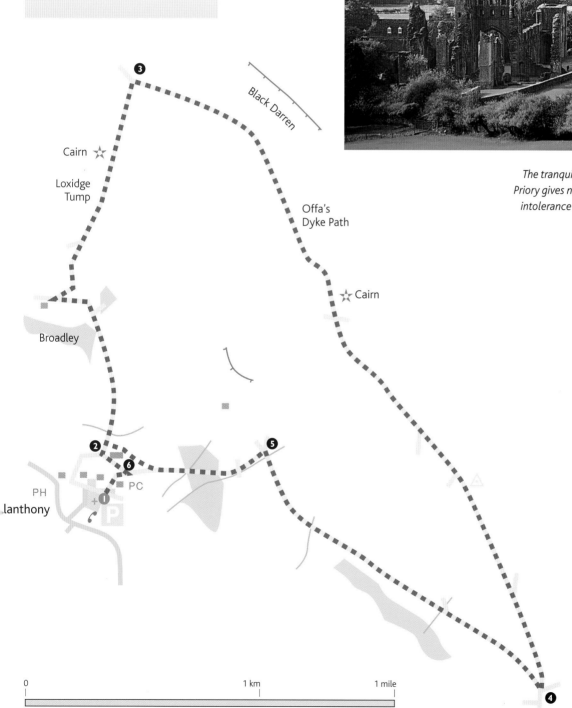

The tranquil setting of Llanthony Priory gives no hint of the religious intolerance and persecution that led to its decline.

Black Darren

Cairn ☆

Loxidge Tump

Offa's Dyke Path

☆ Cairn

Broadley

PH

PC

Llanthony

0   1 km   1 mile

South-west England

Coastal & Waterside

This is a region of delightful bays and secret coves, with monuments that invoke all manner of myths and legends. Highlights include Tintagel, Lulworth Cove and Old Harry.

▲ Map: Explorer OL 20
▲ Distance: 5 km/3 miles
▲ Walk ID: 1131 Dennis Blackford

Difficulty rating

Time

▲ Hills or Fells, Sea, National Trust/
NTS, Wildlife, Birds, Flowers, Great
Views, Butterflies, Public Transport

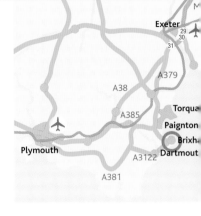

Man Sands from Sharkham Head

This is an easy-to-follow circular walk that passes along tracks and quiet Devonshire country lanes to Man Sands before returning to Sharkham Head along the beautiful South West Coast Path.

❶ From the far end of the car park, cross the stile and follow the grit track. After about 100 m, at the first bend, take the path off to the right. Follow the path through a pair of stone gateposts (it can be muddy at times).

❷ At the end of the path, turn right and follow the farm track.

❸ The track exits into a country road through South Bay Holiday Camp before joining the road to the car park. Turn left onto the road for about 50 m and, immediately past the entrance to the holiday camp, go up the path to the right of the wall. The path widens to become a farm track. Follow the track uphill until arriving at a T-junction. Turn left.

❹ The track ends at a country road. Turn left to follow the road. After about 800 m, the road ends at Southdown Barns. To the left of the gates to a large house, join a wooded lane leading downhill to Man Sands. About 500 m down, where the lane bends to the right, continue on down the smaller path off the bend.

❺ The path now leads out on the grass area above the beach. After spending time at the beach, take the coast path up the steep hill to the left.

❻ After about 2 km the path goes over a stone stile into a field. Continue along the coast side of the field. At the end of the field, go over the wooden stile and turn left through the gap, which will lead back to the car park.

Sharkham Head is a Site of Special Scientific Interest.

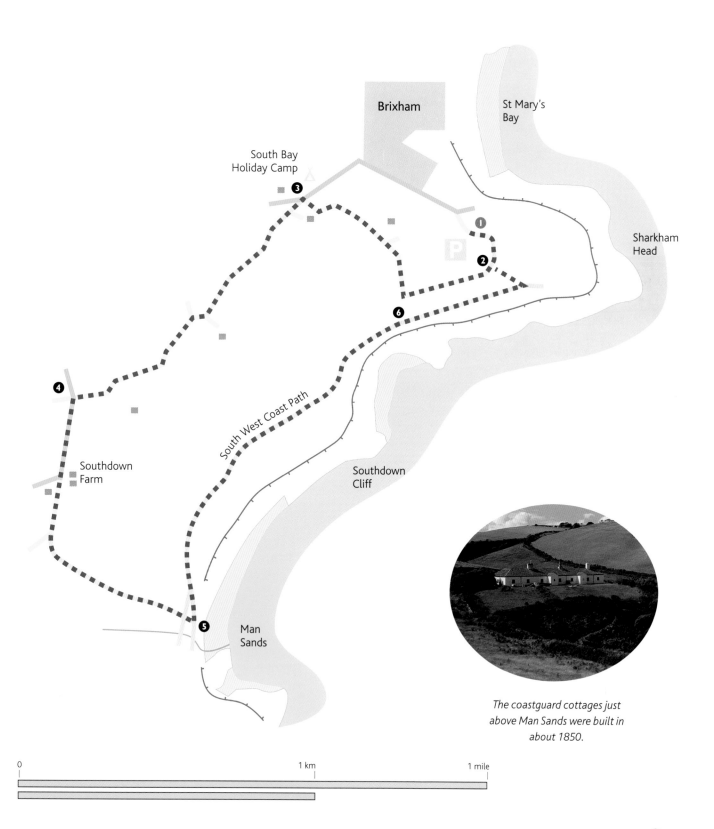

Brixham

St Mary's
Bay

South Bay
Holiday Camp

❸

❶

P

❷

Sharkham
Head

❻

South West Coast Path

❹

Southdown
Farm

Southdown
Cliff

❺

Man
Sands

*The coastguard cottages just
above Man Sands were built in
about 1850.*

0   1 km   1 mile

▲ Map: Explorer OL 20

▲ Distance: 4 km/2½ miles

▲ Walk ID: 995 Dennis Blackford

Difficulty rating

Time

▲ Hills or Fells, Sea, Wildlife, Birds,
Flowers, Great Views, Butterflies,
Industrial Archaeology

Scabbacombe Coast – Two Bays Walk

This is another pleasant walk taking in part of the South West Coast Path and visiting the two bays of Man Sands and Scabbacombe Sands. It is a fairly short walk, so you will have plenty of time to relax on the beach if you wish.

1 Leave the car park and turn right into the road. Follow the road down about 1 km to Man Sands car park. Continue past Man Sands car park. The tarmac road now continues as a stony track. As you near the beach, the path branches to the right. Continue straight on to Man Sands Beach. Return to the branch and walk up a side-shoot for about 100 m to reach a stile on your right. The stone structure that you pass on the way to the beach is an old limekiln where lime was baked to make fertilizer.

2 Go into the field via the stile. The path is clearly signposted and passes behind the old coastguard cottages. Walk up the path and through the gap in the wall.

3 Take the path up the hill to the top of the field. Walk south along the South West Coast Path, bearing around to your right and along to the gate.

4 Pass through the gate or over the stile and follow the coast path for about another kilometre to reach another gate and stile.

5 After passing through the gate, continue along the coast path for about 400 m until you come to a stile over the fence, leading to Scabbacombe Beach. After spending some time on the beach, return up the path to the stile. Walk back along the coast about 200 m and slightly up to the left, until you come to an isolated stile with no fence. Turn left here and follow the sheep path to the main gate leading into the farm track.

6 Pass through the gate or over the stile onto the farm track. At the top of the farm track, pass the large gate and go through the kissing gate back to the car park.

access information

By car, take the Brixham to Kingswear road. About 1.5 km from the small roundabout, halfway down a hill past the holiday camp, turn left, signposted 'Kingston, Boohay, Woodhuish and Brownstone'. After about 1.5 km, this lane branches into two lanes with dead-end signs. Take the left-hand one. Just under 1 km away, an opening in the hedgerow on the right leads into the car park.

By bus, take the Brixham to Kingswear bus to the end of the above lane. It is about 2 km from the bus stop to the car park.

further information

The left-hand end of Scabbacombe is a 'clothes optional' beach.

The rugged coastline between Brixham and Scabbacombe.

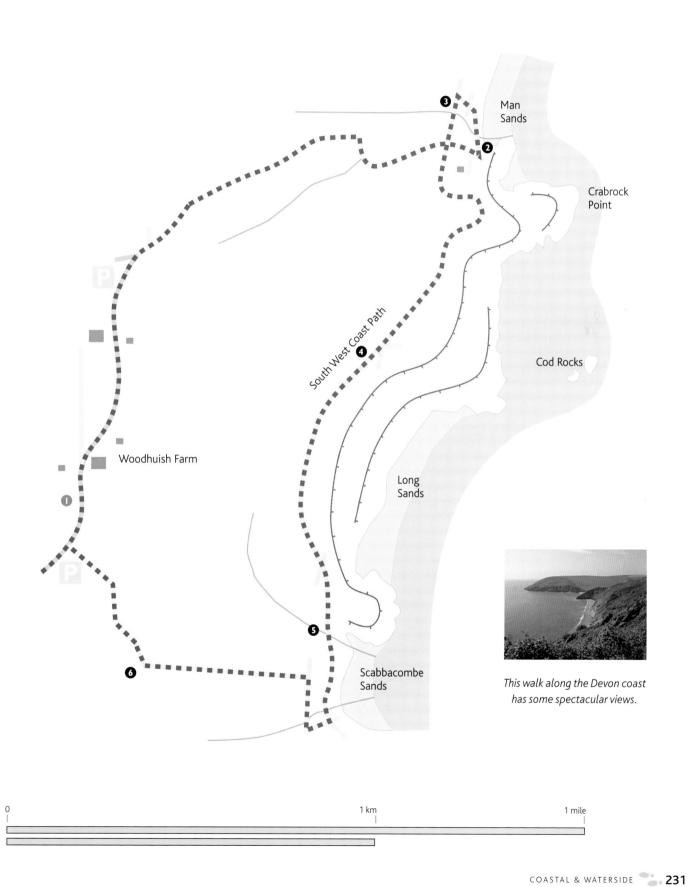

Man
Sands

Crabrock
Point

Cod Rocks

South West Coast Path

Long
Sands

Woodhuish Farm

Scabbacombe
Sands

*This walk along the Devon coast
has some spectacular views.*

0   1 km   1 mile

▲ Map: Explorer 106

▲ Distance: 11 km/6¾ miles

▲ Walk ID: 699 Pete Brett

Difficulty rating

Time

▲ Sea, Pub, Toilets, Museum, Church, Stately Home, Wildlife, Flowers, Great Views, Food Shop, Good for Kids, Tea Shop

South West Coast Path from Padstow

further information

The Elizabethan manor house of Prideaux Place has a deer park and is open to visitors in summer.

The church of St Petroc, dating mainly from the 15th century, and the Shipwreck Museum can both be found in Padstow.

This is a circular walk from the Cornish fishing port of Padstow, with long stretches of sandy beach ideal for swimming, and dramatic cliff-top views.

1 Leave the car park on the path to the left of the toilet block and descend to the north side of the harbour. Join the South West Coast Path, which starts near the tourist information centre. The path ascends to the War Memorial with extensive views back towards Padstow and the Camel Estuary. Follow the path around Gun Point to the beautiful sandy Harbour Cove.

2 Cross the sands to rejoin the path. At Hawker's Cove the path joins a short stretch of track behind the beach and skirts the old lifeboat house and terraced pilots' houses.

3 Ascend from the pilots' houses over the stile and take the right path to Stone Daymark. Continue on the coast path above dramatic cliffs with outstanding views.

4 At the stile, turn left inland to reach a road. Follow the road to the village of Crugmeer and curve round to the left at the junction. Pass the cottages on the left and take the next left turn.

5 Take the footpath on the right, just past Little Crugmeer Farm. Cross the stile into the field. Cross diagonally over seven fields with slate stiles to a stile leading onto the road. Turn right along the road and under the arch to Prideaux Place. Continue down the road and turn left at the hotel into Fentonluna Lane. Descend through the town to the harbour. From the harbour return to the start via the road.

access information

Follow the A39 south from Wadebridge then take the A389 to Padstow. Do not descend into the town but continue for 200 m and turn into the top car park.

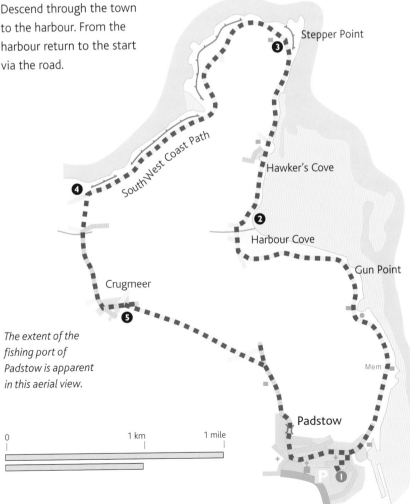

South West Coast Path

Stepper Point

Hawker's Cove

Harbour Cove

Gun Point

Crugmeer

Mem

Padstow

0   1 km   1 mile

The extent of the fishing port of Padstow is apparent in this aerial view.

▲ Map: Explorer 111
▲ Distance: 3 km/1¾ miles
▲ Walk ID: 1095 Dennis Blackford

Difficulty rating

👣👣👣

Time

⬤⬤⬤

▲ Hills or Fells, Sea, Toilets, Castle, National Trust, Wildlife, Birds, Flowers, Great Views, Butterflies, Restaurant, Tea Shop, Monument

Tintagel Castle and Coast

This walk goes through Tintagel and along the cliff path to visit the legendary castle of King Arthur and Merlin's Cave, with wonderful views and a wealth of wildlife.

❶ From the car park, turn right onto the main road and walk into Tintagel village. Walk through the village until reaching the 'No Through Road' at the side of the Cornishman's Inn. Follow this road down to the car park at the end.

❷ Follow the church wall around to the right and onto the coast path, looking out for the ruins of the castle below. Follow the path down.

❸ On reaching the paved path to the castle, take the path to your right which zigzags down to the Visitor Centre. At low tide you can go down to the beach and visit Merlin's Cave.

❹ Cross over the bridge and climb the steps to continue on the coast path up the other side of the valley. About 200 m further on, after crossing a little wooden bridge, follow the left-hand path up to Barras Nose, with its spectacular view over the cove and the castle. Continue on the coast path. About 1 km further on, pass through a gate which will lead you to Willapark. Pass through the gap in the wall and take the left-hand fork to the point. Return to the junction and

With natural and man-made rock formations, it is no wonder Tintagel is a place of legends.

continue on the path to the right of the gap, heading down into the valley.

❺ Take the steps up the other side of the valley and cross the stile down to the track. Turn right to return to the starting point.

access information

Tintagel is on the B3263 off the A39. From Tintagel, take the Boscastle road for about 1 km to Bossiney car park on your left.

There are also bus services to take you to Tintagel.

further information

At waymark 5, instead of turning right, you could turn left to detour down into the secluded cove of Bossiney Haven, which is popular for swimming at low tide.

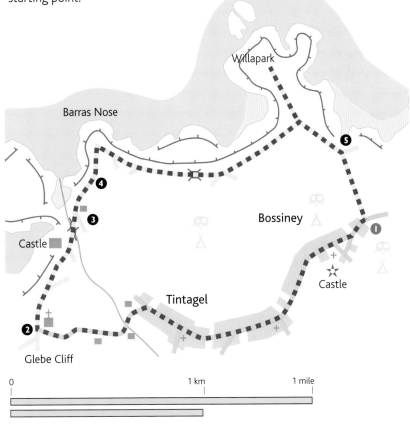

▲ Map: Explorer 105

▲ Distance: 7 km/4¼ miles

▲ Walk ID: 1513 Jim Grindle

Difficulty rating

Time

▲ River, Toilets, Stately Home, National Trust, Wildlife, Birds, Good for Kids, Nature Trail, Restaurant, Tea Shop, Woodland, Ancient Monument

Lamouth Creek from Trelissick Garden

You begin by entering the park and dropping down to follow the river through woods to King Harry Ferry. The walk offers open views of the estuary before a gentle climb through the park back to the start.

❶ Take the path next to the car park, signposted 'Woodland Walks'. Go through a gate next to a cattle grid and follow the path to a junction. Turn right onto the driveway and continue to the edge of a wood.

❷ Go through the gate to the left of the cattle grid, then turn to the right on a path going uphill. Pass the lodge and go through the green gate. Cross the road and go through the gate on the other side. Follow a gravel track that zigzags downhill. When it straightens out there is a stream on the left.

❸ Turn left and cross the stream. On the other side take the right fork, following Lamouth Creek, which is below you on your right. Continue as the woods thin out, until you reach the entrance to the next wood, marked by two low stone banks. Take the right fork, heading over the ditch and then straight through the rampart of the Iron Age fort before joining another track. Turn right. Just before the quay, go down a few steps and emerge into the open.

❹ Visit Roundwood Quay, then retrace your steps back to point 3. Continue with the river now on your left for 1.5 km. You will reach a steep flight of steps leading down to the road you crossed earlier. The ferry is just to your left, and opposite is a white house with a flight of steps going up on its right.

❺ At Bosanko's Cottage, take the track that continues on the far side. Only one track branches off to the right away from the river and your way is signposted. About 1.5 km from the ferry you leave the woods by a kissing gate. Go up the hill, keeping the iron fence on your right.

❻ At the top cross the drive that enters Trelissick House. You will soon reach the exit from the car park. Go through the gate and back to the start.

access information

Trelissick is 6 km south of Truro on the B3289, east of the A39. Buses T7 and 89B run from Truro, where there is a railway station.

This footpath will lead you past cosy woodland cottages to the much grander residence of Trelissick House.

further information

The first house was built here in about 1750 and went through many hands, with much development of the gardens which were acquired by The National Trust in 1955.

Roundwood Quay was built in the 18th century to ship tin and copper, and in past days there were buildings for smelting and refining and many wharves. There was a malt house, limekilns and ship-building yards, a busy place compared to the tranquillity that you will find there now.

Since 1888 the King Harry Steam Ferry Company has operated a ferry that pulls itself across the Fal by chains, although the motive power is now diesel. It is thought that a ferry has existed here since the Norman Conquest.

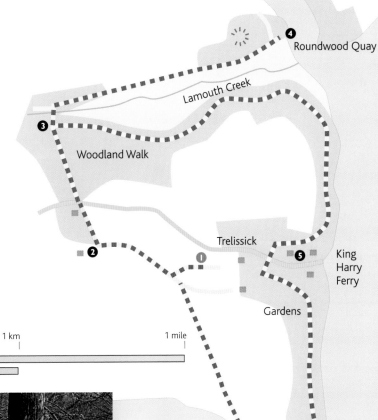

▲ Map: Explorer OL 22

▲ Distance: 6 km/3¾ miles

▲ Walk ID: 719 Peter Salenieks

Difficulty rating

Time

▲ Sea, Toilets, Wildlife, Birds, Great Views

Hengistbury Head

The route of this popular walk takes in historic Hengistbury Head, a nature reserve and the beach at Sandspit. There are lovely views over Christchurch Harbour and across to the Isle of Wight.

1 Start with the Ranger Office and Land Train terminus behind you and walk about 50 m along the road until you reach a junction with the track just before the Double Dykes. Bear right and go along the track. At end of the Double Dykes turn left and follow a path that goes along the cliff top heading towards Hengistbury Head. Continue past Barn Field and two paths on your left. Climb steadily, keeping the wildlife pond on your right, to reach the top of Warren Hill. Walk along a gravel track, past the coastguard lookout station and, later, a junction on the left.

2 At the crossroads turn right and follow the track along the cliff top, passing the southern end of the wildlife pond in the old quarry on your left. Follow the track to the southern tip of Hengistbury Head, before turning left to reach broad steps that lead down to the beach.

further information

Hengistbury Head has witnessed 11,000 years of human history, including a Stone Age camp on Warren Hill, an Iron Age port and 18th-century quarrying. Today it is a popular tourist spot, including a nature reserve, which is home to a variety of birds, insects and small mammals.

Hengistbury Head is a magnificent setting for a footpath. It has a variety of wildlife as well as a wealth of ancient archaeological sites.

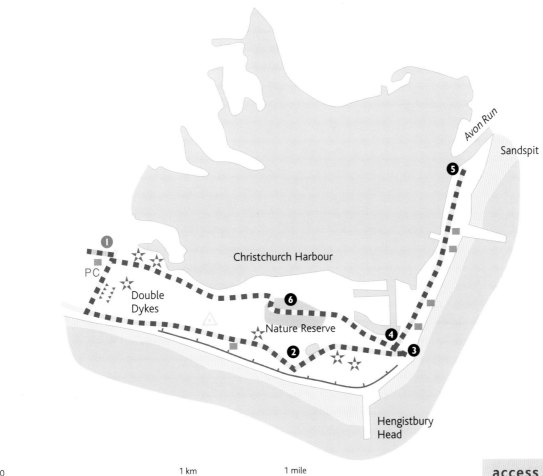

Christchurch Harbour

Avon Run

Sandspit

5

1

PC

Double
Dykes

Nature Reserve

6

2

4

3

Hengistbury
Head

0		1 km		1 mile

3 Descend the steps and bear left to pick up a broad path, which leads inland from the beach huts at Sandspit, until you reach the road.

4 Turn right and follow the road towards Sandspit. Pass the Land Train terminus and the pontoon for the ferry to Mudeford Quay on your left. When you reach the Hut Café, cross between it and the beach office to reach the seaward side of Sandspit and walk towards the end of the spit, where Avon Run marks the outflow from Christchurch Harbour into the sea.

5 Retrace your route from Avon Run and head right along the road, passing Holloway's Dock, which is a Site of Special Scientific Interest, on your right. Pass a track on your left before entering woodland. Continue until you see a wooded track on your left which leads gently uphill.

6 Follow the track about 50 m uphill for an optional detour to the wildlife pond, then go back to the road to return to your starting point.

access information

Cars can be parked in Hengistbury Head car park. This is approached from the A35, turning south onto the B3059 and then east onto the Broadway to the west of Tuckton.

Hengistbury Head is also accessible by bus during the summer. Open Top Coastal Service 12 runs between Sandbanks and Christchurch Quay from the end of May to the end of September. Telephone Yellow Buses (01202) 636060 for further information or visit www.yellowbuses.co.uk.

▲ Map: Explorer OL 15
▲ Distance: 15 km/9¼ miles
▲ Walk ID: 389 Al Rodger

Difficulty rating

Time

▲ Hills or Fells, Sea, Pub, Toilets, Wildlife, Great Views

Lulworth and White Nothe Coastal Tour

Starting on the ridge above Ringstead, the route first crosses downland to West Lulworth and the magnificent coast at Lulworth Cove and Durdle Door, to return along the cliff-top path.

1 Exit the car park over the stile at the far end and continue down the track. Where the track bears sharp right, cross the stile and continue up the track. Keep straight ahead through two more stiles and a gate.

2 At the second gate, keep straight ahead over the next two rises. As the path rises for a third time, turn right over the stile at the signpost to Newlands Farm Camp Site. Go through Newlands Farm and continue past West Lulworth Church and down to Lulworth Cove.

3 The walk resumes from the pay-and-display car park up Hambury Tout on the stone path, dropping down to the cliff above Durdle Door, then over the small hill to Scratchy Bottom.

4 From Scratchy Bottom cross the stile at the foot of Swyre Head and follow the path diagonally uphill. Cross the stile at the top, to reach a well-used path. Follow the path until reaching the obelisk.

5 At the obelisk, take one of the paths round the hillside and over the summit to the coastguard cottages at White Nothe. Continue along the cliff top, with Weymouth Bay in sight ahead. Cross the stile and descend the field onto a track at the next stile.

6 Follow the track uphill, bearing left at a post box. Continue ahead to the car park.

The stretch of coastline between Durdle Door and Lulworth Cove is possibly the most impressive in the whole of Dorset.

access information

This walk starts from the Ringstead Bay National Trust car park on the ridge above Ringstead. Take the Ringstead turning off the A353 between Poxwell and Osmington. Follow the road ahead to the car park, parking towards the far end.

No practical access by public transport.

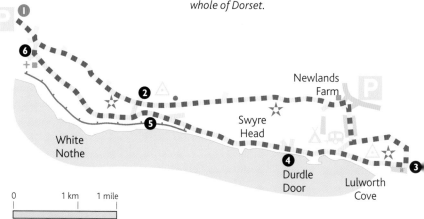

▲ Map: Explorer 102

▲ Distance: 6½ km/4 miles

▲ Walk ID: 124 Colin Ward

Difficulty rating

Time

▲ Sea, Pub, Great Views

Lamorna Cove from Mousehole

This walk takes you from the picturesque fishing village of Mousehole to Lamorna, returning along the South West Coast Path.

1 From the harbour, take the lane past the Lobster Pot restaurant to the Methodist chapel. Walk up the hill, out of the village, to the point where it bears to the right. Keep on the road for about 100 m, and follow the footpath sign to take a path on the left.

2 Turn right into the field and walk round the edge, until you reach the stile on the far side. Continue walking across the field to reach the farm at Kemyel Drea. The path passes to the right of the first building, and then between the large sheds. Once through the farm, follow the hedge and pick up the path that leads into the hedges beyond.

3 Walk to the stile and turn left. Continue straight up the lane past the farmhouses, and the gate marked with a Caravan Club sign. Cross the stile, and continue across the fields to the farmhouses of Kemyel Wartha. Follow the track through the hamlet, as it bears right to the footpath sign. Take the path on the left down to the quarry. Continue past the quarry to Lamorna Cove.

4 Take the obvious path up to Carn-du and continue round the coast for 3 km. Eventually you will come to the road, where you should continue straight on, and down into Mousehole.

further information

The disused quarry on the way to Lamorna Cove supplied the stone for London Bridge. The cove was once used for shipping the stone, but the difficult task of navigating the harbour rendered it redundant in the last century.

The South West Coast Path goes through a small wooded nature reserve.

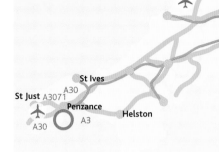

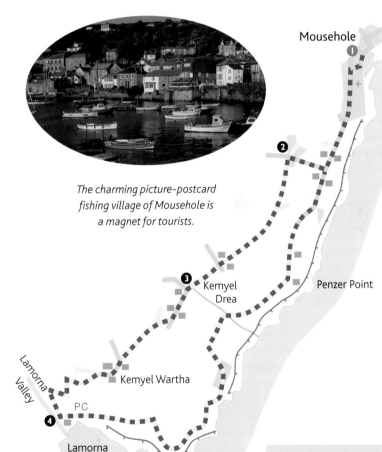

The charming picture-postcard fishing village of Mousehole is a magnet for tourists.

access information

Mousehole is off the B3315 south of the A30 Penzance to Land's End road. Parking is in the village and around the harbour. Buses run from Penzance.

0   1 km   1 mile

▲ Map: Explorer OL 15

▲ Distance: 10 km/6¼ miles

▲ Walk ID: 365 Al Rodger

Difficulty rating

Time

▲ Sea, Toilets, Church, National Trust, Wildlife, Birds, Flowers, Great Views

Old Harry and Ballard Down from Studland

A circular walk from Studland to Old Harry passing Studland's Norman church en route. Continuing up the coast and along the top of Ballard Down, the route returns to Studland via Agglestone Rock.

1 Exit the car park away from the beach, immediately turning left at the road junction past the car park sign. Turn right at the road junction by the Manor House Hotel. Turn left through the gate and follow the path past St Nicholas's Church and continue straight ahead to the marker post. Turn left down the road and where the road bends left, continue up the track straight ahead to the right of the public toilets. Keep straight ahead to Old Harry, where tracks join at a marker stone.

2 The route continues up the cliff path. Keep outside the fenced area ahead and pause to sample the views behind you. Continue along the South West Coast Path. Keep left at the marker stone, taking in the superior views as you go.

3 At the fence line coming in from the right, bear right away from the cliff and go through the gate and gap in the ancient dyke. Continue along the crest of Ballard Down.

4 At the obelisk, continue straight ahead through the gate and down the track that bends to the right down to the road. Turn left down the road. Take the path on the right. Go over two stiles and through the woods, straight over the golf course to reach the stile onto the road.

access information

Studland is on the B3351 east of the A351. The walk starts from Middle Beach car park, situated at the end of Beach Road, the northern of the two side roads heading towards the beach.

A bus runs hourly from Bournemouth to Swanage over the ferry and stops at the end of Beach Road.

This chalk arch and stack form a spectacular view at the heart of Studland Bay.

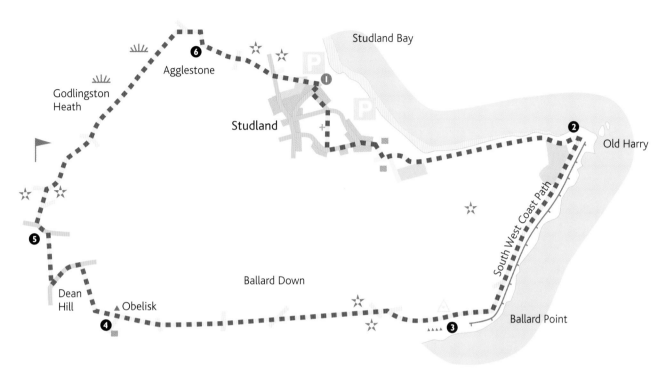

Studland Bay

6

Agglestone

Godlingston
Heath

Studland

1

2

Old Harry

South West Coast Path

Ballard Down

5

Dean
Hill

▲ Obelisk

4

3

Ballard Point

0	1 km	1 mile

*The Agglestone Rock
(composed of sandstone
in an area of limestone)
is said to have been thrown
by the Devil from the Isle
of Wight at Corfe Castle.*

5 Meander left and then right. Pass
through two gates onto the good path.
Keep straight ahead at the first two
marker stones making for Agglestone
Studland Heath. Turn left onto a bridle
path just before the 'No Entry' signs,
skirting the edge of the golf course. At
the gate continue straight ahead on
towards Agglestone. From Agglestone,
the route continues down into the
valley, ascending the far side before
bearing right and descending again. At
the main track, turn right downhill. The
track turns sharply to the right and
crosses a ford.

6 Continue up the track and through
the gate, turning right at the main road.
Cross the road and follow the path on
the left through the gully to Beach Road.
Turn left to return to the car park.

Woodland & Hillside

Woodland and hillside footpaths reveal historic West Country monuments, and idyllic Cotswold villages. Highlights include Nancledra, Hardy's Chess Piece and Glastonbury Tor.

▲ Map: Explorer OL 28

▲ Distance: 15 km/9¼ miles

▲ Walk ID: 1428 Paul Edney

Difficulty rating

Time

▲ Hills or Fells, Pub, Church, Great Views, Café, Moor, Tea Shop, Ancient Monument

Grimspound from Widecombe

This walk from Widecombe takes in the Bronze Age enclosure at Grimspound, and includes spectacular views all along the top of Hameldown. The route also includes the remains of a medieval village.

1 From the car park, turn right along the path on the other side of the fence. Join the road on the other side of the village green. After 200 m turn left up the path signed Grimspound via Hameldown. Keep right and continue up a stony track. Go through the gate and take the path up the hillside.

2 The wall on your right turns right, where your path joins the Two Moors Way. Turn right and keep to the path just above the wall. Where the wall turns right again, head across open ground. Take either path to the top of Hameldown. Eventually, just to the left of the path, cross to the trig point at Hameldown Tor. Continue downhill towards Grimspound.

3 In the middle of the compound, turn right and follow the path towards the road at Natsworthy. Go through the gate onto the road, head left for 10 m, then turn right onto the bridle path. Go through the gate where the bridle path meets the road. Go past Jay's Grave, cross the road, and continue through the gate opposite onto the bridle path and over the hill.

4 Where the bridle path meets another road, with Bowerman's Nose to the left, turn right and follow the road towards Hound Tor.

5 At the crossroads, turn left and cross the grass to Hound Tor. Go down into the remains of the medieval village. Pick up the path over the shoulder of the hill to the right of Greator Rocks. Go through the right-hand gate in the wall and take the right-hand path to Bonehill Down. At the top go through a gap in the wall and continue on the path downhill. Ignore the path to the left and continue to a gate.

6 Go through the gate and turn left onto the road, down to the river. Cross the cattle grid and head to the right, across the down. Take the left fork at the junction. Over the rise, Bell Tor is on your right.

7 Join the road and turn right, to reach a T-junction. Turn right to return to Widecombe.

further information

From the trig point at Hameldown Tor you have a bird's eye view of Grimspound, which is probably the best preserved Bronze Age enclosure on the moor.

Since 1860, when Kitty Jay's grave was discovered and restored, there have always been fresh flowers on the grave, although no one admits to putting them there.

Bowerman's Nose is only a few minutes off the route and is worth a visit. Legend has it that the shape is due to a bowman who discovered a coven of witches. They turned him and his hounds to stone. The hounds can be seen at Hound Tor.

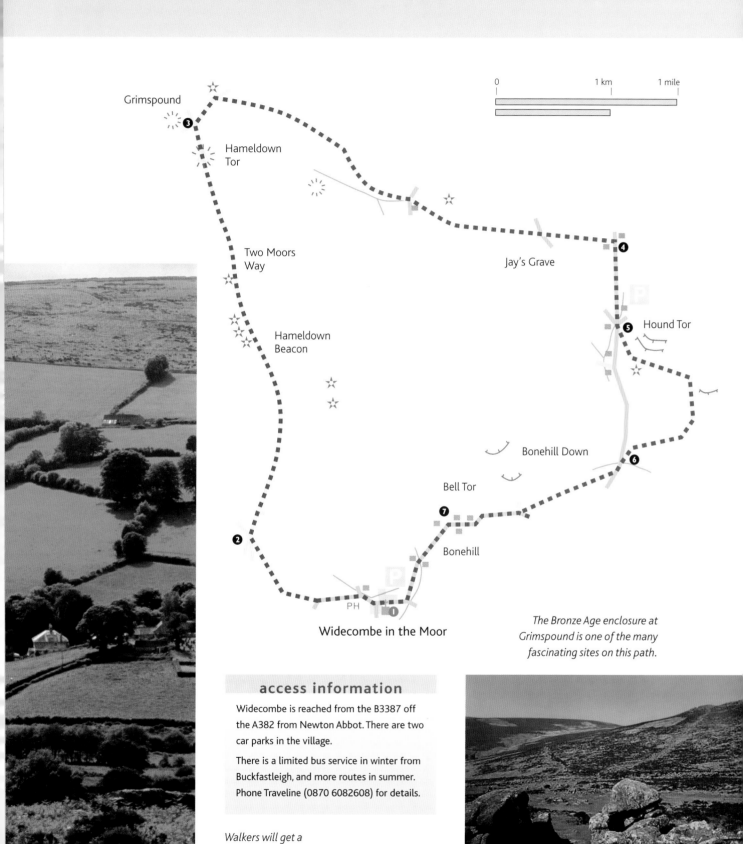

Grimspound

Hameldown
Tor

Two Moors
Way

Hameldown
Beacon

3

2

0   1 km   1 mile

Jay's Grave

4

Hound Tor

5

Bonehill Down

6

Bell Tor

7

Bonehill

P H

1

Widecombe in the Moor

*The Bronze Age enclosure at
Grimspound is one of the many
fascinating sites on this path.*

access information

Widecombe is reached from the B3387 off
the A382 from Newton Abbot. There are two
car parks in the village.

There is a limited bus service in winter from
Buckfastleigh, and more routes in summer.
Phone Traveline (0870 6082608) for details.

*Walkers will get a
spectacular view over
Widecombe from the
top of Hameldown.*

▲ Map: Explorer 116
▲ Distance: 10 km/6¼ miles
▲ Walk ID: 997 Al Rodger

Difficulty rating

Time

▲ Pub, Church, Wildlife, Birds, Great Views, Butterflies, Woodland

Symondsbury from North Chideock

This is a circular walk through countryside west of Bridport, starting from the village of Chideock, home of the Chideock Martyrs. The route illustrates the charm of West Dorset at its best, and there are wonderful views to enjoy.

❶ Take the track with a cul-de-sac sign beside the cottage. Proceed uphill in a field with a fence on the left. Descend straight down the second field.

❷ Turn right up the hedged track. At the top of the hill continue down the Symondsbury track. Take the road to the left at the school.

❸ Beyond Symondsbury, turn right onto a track. Cross into a field on the left and make for the far-left corner. Cross the bridge and turn right, following the edge of the field to a gate. Cross the track into the field opposite. Cross the field half-left up to the corner of the hedge. Continue with the hedge on your right. At the hole through the hedge, take the path through the trees. Turn right at the junction. On the brow of the hill, turn left for rewarding views.

❹ Continue clockwise round the edge of the hilltop. Take the left path at the first junction. Continue down the steps towards the road and turn left. Turn right up the path between the housing and the hospital. Cross to the right-hand field. Keep ahead to cross back to the left-hand field at the gateway. Continue with the hedge on your right-hand side for two fields.

further information

John Cornelius, the Catholic chaplain of Lady Arundell, was arrested when visiting Chideock in 1594, along with two servants from Chideock and another visitor. The four were found guilty of treason. Refusing to embrace Protestantism, they were executed three months after their arrest.

A cross on the site of Chideock Castle commemorates these martyrs, and two others, Thomas Pilchard and Hugh Green.

The chiselled headlands around Lyme Regis create quite a distinctive coastline that is a fascinating place to explore.

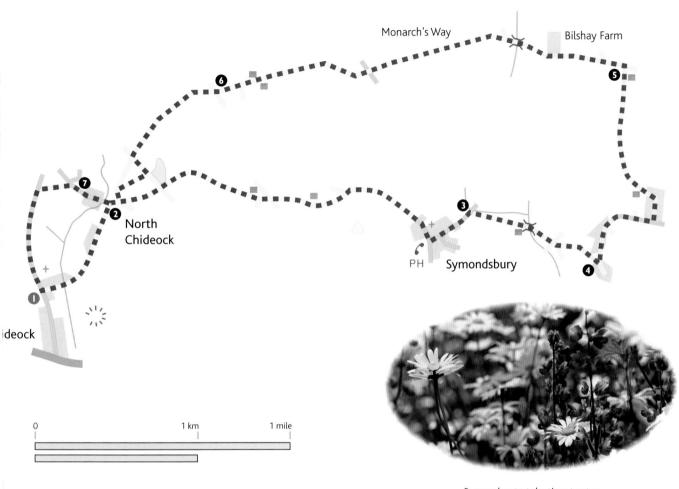

Map labels:
- Monarch's Way
- Bilshay Farm
- **6**
- **5**
- **7**
- **2** North Chideock
- **3**
- PH Symondsbury
- **4**
- **1**
- ideock

Scale: 0 — 1 km — 1 mile

Remember to take time to stop on your walk and 'smell the flowers'.

5 At the cottage turn left and follow the hedge. Cross the field to the right-hand of two gates into the next field. Head left towards the electricity pylon. Go over the stile into a garden, following the fence. Descend the field to a gate at the end of a line of posts. Cross the bridge and keep to the right side of the field. Go through the gap in the hedge into the next field. Follow the track up the left side to continue on the Monarch's Way.

6 Go through both gates. Continue down the field and round the thicket on the sheep path. Follow the path and continue down the field towards the hedge, keeping the hedge on the right. Cross the bottom field to the left to reach a stile by a gate. Turn right to follow a track becoming a tarmac lane.

7 Just before the junction, turn up the path on the left. Cross the field to a stile leading down to a path. Turn left at the road and continue back to the start.

access information

Turn north off the A35 in Chideock, west of Bridport, by the church on the road signed North Chideock. Just past the lane with the lodge on the corner, park on the side of the road with a slight verge.

A good bus service runs between Bridport and Lyme Regis and stops in Chideock, not far from the start.

▲ Map: Explorer OL 14
▲ Distance: 5 km/3 miles
▲ Walk ID: 1426 Pat Roberts

Difficulty rating

Time

▲ Wildlife, Birds, Flowers, Great Views, Butterflies, Mostly Flat, Woodland

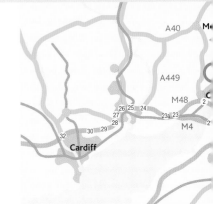

Poors Allotment and the Jubilee Stone from Tidenham Chase

This easy, fairly level walk rewards you with fine views over the Severn Estuary to the Cotswolds to visit the Jubilee Stone.

1 Leave the car park and turn left onto the road. After 120 m, at the footpath sign, go right and continue through a series of gates to reach a minor road. Turn right.

2 Where the road swings sharply right, take the gate next to the footpath signs and follow the sign on the left. Head diagonally left, towards a stile in a fence. Cross the stile onto Poors Allotment, taking in the views over the Severn Estuary to the left.

3 Cross a small stream. Just before the large holly tree, the main path swings to the right. Ignore this path and head left, then turn left into the wood. Emerge from the wood into open ground and swing sharp right to reach a yellow marker post and then cross a stile onto a road. Turn left. After about 150 m, head right, past a barrier and into heathland, small trees and gorse. As the Gloucester Way comes in from the left, continue with it on the path furthest on the left.

4 At the Jubilee Stone, turn right and continue, ignoring any minor paths until you reach a clearing. At the clearing, ignore the track that comes in from the left and take the narrow path that goes off to the right. Follow this path through the wood. Ignore paths off to the left and the main road. When you reach a minor road, turn left.

5 Just before the main road take the stone stile on the right onto Poors Allotment. Stay on this grass track as it moves away from the trees and road on your left.

6 At the junction of paths, take the left fork, heading towards the trees and into the wood. Emerge from the wood through a metal kissing gate at the roadside opposite the car park.

access information

Parking is in an area adjoining the B4228, north-east of Chepstow. There is a roadside sign to Offa's Dyke.

A view of the Severn Bridge, built across the Severn Estuary to provide a link between Wales and England, can be enjoyed during this walk.

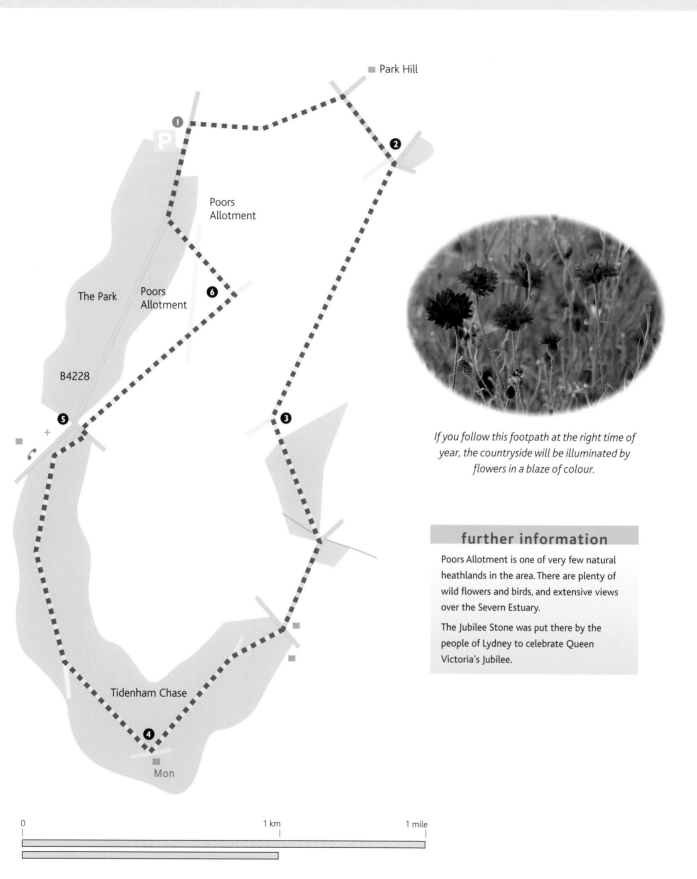

Park Hill

P

❶

❷

Poors
Allotment

The Park

Poors
Allotment

❻

B4228

❺

❸

*If you follow this footpath at the right time of
year, the countryside will be illuminated by
flowers in a blaze of colour.*

further information

Poors Allotment is one of very few natural
heathlands in the area. There are plenty of
wild flowers and birds, and extensive views
over the Severn Estuary.

The Jubilee Stone was put there by the
people of Lydney to celebrate Queen
Victoria's Jubilee.

Tidenham Chase

❹

Mon

0   1 km   1 mile

South & South-east England

Coastal & Waterside

The waterside walks of South and South-east England take in historic coasts, marshlands teeming with wildlife, and splendid canals. Highlights include the Saxon Shore Way and Virginia Water.

▲ Map: Explorer 163
▲ Distance: 5.64 km/3½ miles
▲ Walk ID: 873 Ian Elmes

Difficulty rating

Time

▲ River, Pub, Toilets, Castle,
Great Views, Food Shop

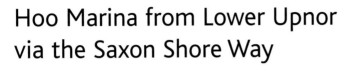

Hoo Marina from Lower Upnor via the Saxon Shore Way

This walk begins in the delightful village of Lower Upnor, then follows part of the Saxon Shore Way along the River Medway. The route continues into Hoo, then back across open fields to Lower Upnor.

1 From the car park, turn right towards the Medway Yacht Club. At the gate, bear right and follow the footpath to the end. Drop down to the beach and follow the Saxon Shore Way. Follow the raised footpath at the Wilsonian Sailing Club, then continue along the beach, following the line of the river.

2 When you reach a raised footpath, follow this to the Hoo Ness Yacht Club. Go through the gateway and follow the track ahead, bearing right just before the white gate. Follow this path until you reach a car parking area. Follow the high metal fence, then walk along the road past the Marina Office.

3 Continue straight ahead, along a gravel track then a footpath. Out in the open, bear right, following the 'Saxon Shore' marker post. Walk past the yachts to the end of the path. By the fence, turn right to cross the road and walk between the bus depot and the steel works.

4 Cross the road and follow the footpath left of Whitton Marina, coming out opposite a factory. Turn left along the road. Take the footpath directly ahead of you towards three distant houses. Before you reach the houses, bear left onto another path to the road.

5 Turn left at the main road, then right on the farm track by Church Farm Lodge. Follow the track up the hill. Go through the gate at the top. At the crossroads, go straight on, following the track to an enclosed footpath past some houses.

6 Turn left and follow the road up the hill. At the top, follow the enclosed footpath straight ahead. Ignoring the footpath to the right, carry straight on, following the footpath down towards the river, bearing left at the yellow marker post. At the bottom, follow the road back to the car park.

access information

Lower Upnor lies just off the A228 north of Rochester. The walk starts at the car park.

further information

The village of Lower Upnor is ideal for spending relaxed evenings, with two pubs, great views across to Chatham Historic Dockyard, and a steady stream of yachts going up and down the river. Nearby Upper Upnor also has two pubs and a castle.

A scene of peace and tranquillity is often the reward when taking this riverside walk.

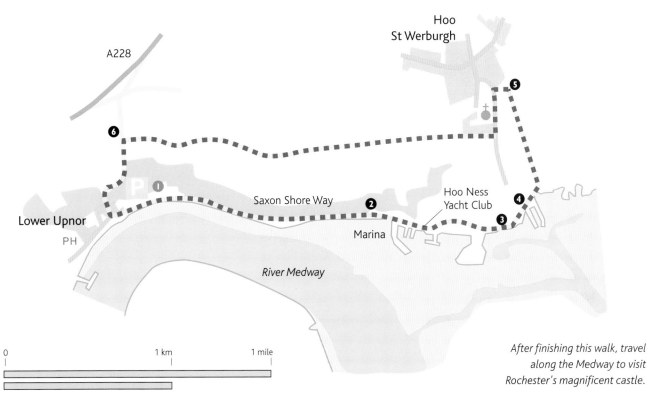

A228

Hoo
St Werburgh

6

5

P **1**

Saxon Shore Way

2

Hoo Ness
Yacht Club

4

Marina

3

Lower Upnor

PH

River Medway

0   1 km   1 mile

*After finishing this walk, travel
along the Medway to visit
Rochester's magnificent castle.*

▲ Map: Explorer 159

▲ Distance: 9.66 km/6 miles

▲ Walk ID: 688 Tony Brotherton

Difficulty rating

Time

▲ Hills, River, Lake, Pub, Toilets, Museum, Church, Wildlife, Birds, Flowers, Great Views

The Kennet & Avon Canal and Padworth Lock from Aldermaston

This circular walk covers a section of the Kennet & Avon Canal and the River Kennet, together with fields, woods and gentle inclines to the south, combining the bustle and colour of canal locks and longboats with quiet rural interludes.

1 From the car park, cross the road and turn left. Go through a gate to the canal at Aldermaston Wharf. Turn left along the bank and over the bridge at the road. Follow the path to Froudes Bridge. Leave the path, cross the bridge and rejoin the path on the opposite bank.

2 Follow the canal to the river. Turn right and proceed through the woods to cross Wickham Knights Bridge. Turn left along the opposite riverbank. Follow the footpath diversion through the woods to rejoin the river where it meets the canal.

3 Walk on, then follow an arrow diagonally right across a field. Cross a stream and bear right towards a footbridge leading into a small car park. Cross the A340 and turn left. Take a footpath to the right just before Aldermaston Bridge.

4 Go through double gates into a poplar copse. At the 'Wasing Estate' sign, follow a right-hand path through the copse to a footbridge and squeeze-stile. Cross three fields over footbridges to a wide track. Turn left. Turn right over the next stile and follow the footpath over a series of stiles. Climb a stile to the road.

5 Turn left. At the top of the hill, turn left. Follow the footpath to a stile. Bear half-right to another stile. Cross the next field, to descend to a stile into woodland. Follow the path left, then right at a pond, and leave the woods. Before a gate, climb a stile to the left to a fenced strip. At the top, go through the gate. Follow the left-hand meadow boundary. Climb a stile into a lane.

6 Turn left. After the right bend, turn left through woods. Cross a footbridge over a stream. Leaving the woods, cross to the next footbridge. Go straight ahead. At Padworth Mill, cross the river, the island and more water, to a lane. Turn left, then right before the first house. Follow the lakeside path to the canal. Turn left. At Padworth Lock, cross and return to Aldermaston Wharf.

access information

Aldermaston lies on the A340 Basingstoke to Reading road.

Trains between Reading and Newbury stop at Aldermaston about once an hour, Monday to Saturday. For information, phone National Rail Enquiries on 08457 484950 or visit www.railtrack.co.uk.

further information

The Canal Visitors' Centre (0118 971 2868) near the end of the walk has exhibitions and information, plus some refreshments. It is open April to October, Mon–Sat 10 a.m. to 5 p.m. and Sun 2–5 p.m.

As well as wildlife and birds, an encounter with a gently puffing steam barge is likely on a walk alongside the Kennet & Avon canal.

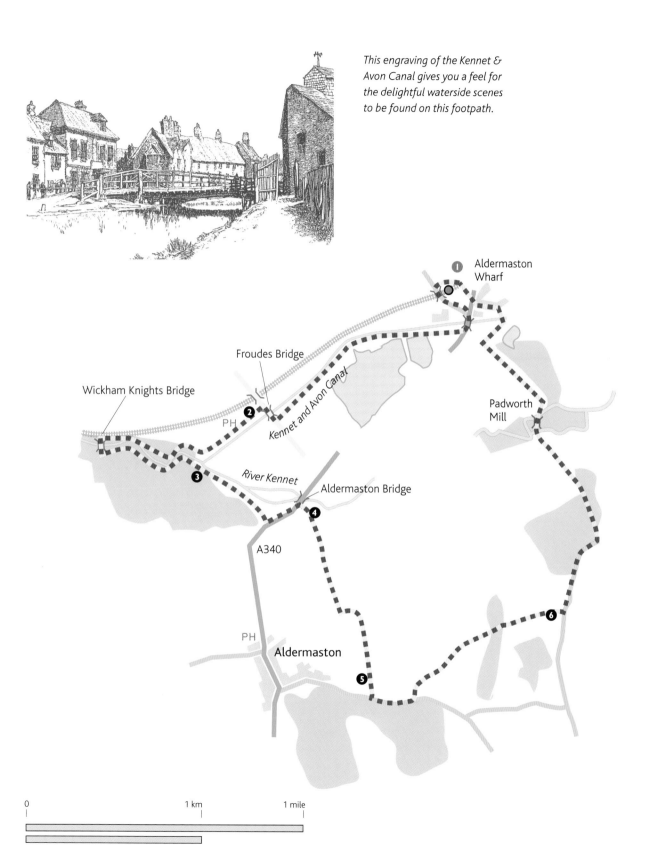

This engraving of the Kennet &
Avon Canal gives you a feel for
the delightful waterside scenes
to be found on this footpath.

Aldermaston
Wharf

Froudes Bridge

Wickham Knights Bridge

Kennet and Avon Canal

PH

Padworth
Mill

River Kennet

Aldermaston Bridge

A340

PH

Aldermaston

0   1 km   1 mile

▲ Map: Explorer 171

▲ Distance: 7 km/4¼ miles

▲ Walk ID: 81 Liz and David Fishlock

Difficulty rating

Time

▲ Weir, Mill, River, Pub, Toilets, Church, Great Views

Aston and Remenham from Mill End

This walk crosses the Thames beside Hambleden Weir and Hambleden Mill, follows an open ridge with views across the Thames Valley to the Chiltern Hills, drops down to Remenham and follows the riverside path back to the weir.

1 From the car park, turn right. Just before the junction with the A4155, take the pavement on the right. Cross the road carefully to the footpath that runs between houses on the other side. Follow the footpath signs to pass to the left of Hambleden Mill.

2 Take the footbridge across the weir and then across the lock. Turn left onto the Thames Path. Ignore the right turn shortly after and carry on ahead through the gate to follow the Thames Path, keeping the riverbank on your left.

3 Where the path meets a lane, turn right. At the road junction by the Flower Pot Hotel, turn left and follow the lane to Aston, ignoring a Thames Path sign on your left.

4 Immediately after Highway Cottage, take the path to the right, which crosses a stile then passes to the left of a house to reach a track. Carry on ahead, following the direction of the footpath sign. The clearly defined track crosses open fields to reach a road.

This gentle stroll crosses the weir at Hambleden Mill and provides fine views of the river.

5 Turn right along the road and at the next junction turn left, with Remenham Church on your right. Keeping the church wall on your right, carry on past the lychgate and turn right at the footpath sign, walking along the road until you reach the riverbank.

6 Turn right at the riverbank. Follow the path back to Hambleden Lock, then retrace your steps to the car park.

access information

Mill End lies just east of Henley-on-Thames on the A4155 Henley to Marlow road. Turn left at Mill End towards Hambleden and Skirmett. After about 300 m/328 yards, turn left into the car park.

further information

The picturesque Hambleden Mill has been much photographed, and the walkway that crosses the weir gives beautiful views of the river. From the riverside path on the return route, there are views of Temple Island, which marks the start of the famous Henley Royal Regatta course.

▲ Map: Explorer OL 29, 22

▲ Distance: 7.89 km/5 miles

▲ Walk ID: 1327 Graham Hollier

Difficulty rating

Time

▲ Lake, Pub, Toilets, Castle, Wildlife, Birds, Great Views, Butterflies, Mostly Flat, Ancient Monument

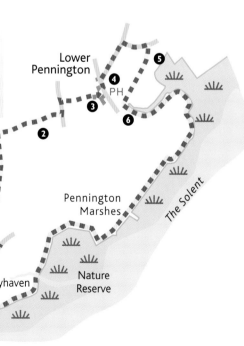

Pennington Marshes from Keyhaven

This bracing walk passes through farmland, much of which has been reclaimed from landfill and quarry sites, to pick up the Solent Way for a glorious coastal walk. There is abundant birdlife and wildlife, and wonderful views across to the Isle of Wight.

1 From the car park, follow a lane almost opposite the Gun Inn, passing Keyhaven Harbour to your right. At a large green gate on your left, cross a broken stile and follow the lane to a council amenity tip. Cross a stile, cross the service road to the tip, and follow the track opposite to a metal gate.

2 Go past the gate and follow the metalled roadway to another metal gate. Go through a gap to the road. Turn left for a short distance, then cross a stile through the hedge on your right. Follow the footpath, keeping the field edge on your right, to cross another stile towards some houses.

3 Before you reach the houses, climb a stile in the hedge on your right. Immediately turn left, heading for a path to the left of the fence in front of you. Cross a stile, carry on and cross the next stile. Head for a metalled driveway leading to a road.

4 Turn left, passing the Chequers pub. Fork right and walk along Platoff Road for a short distance to a bench on your right. Turn right here, signposted 'Maiden Lane', and leading to Normandy Lane. At the next junction, turn right into Maiden Lane.

5 Follow the road around to the right, through a yacht club yard, passing the clubhouse on the left. Continue on to follow the Solent Way. Carry on along an unmade road, which turns into a path through small trees and shrubs, coming out at a clearing.

6 Passing a house on your right, turn immediately left over a stile to follow a pathway, keeping the waterway on your left. When you reach a stile, cross it and head for a pair of lock gates. From the gates, follow the sea defence wall back to the start of the walk.

access information

Soon after leaving Lymington on the A337 Lymington to New Milton road, branch left towards Lower Pennington and Keyhaven. The walk starts at the car park on the right in Keyhaven, just before the Gun Inn on your left.

Keep watch for birds and wildlife as you gaze out across the Pennington Marshes.

further information

You can extend your walk to include a visit to Hurst Castle, one of the many coastal defences built by Henry VIII. The castle is reached by ferry, which is just a short walk from the car park. Alternatively, you can walk or drive to the start of the shingle spit and walk out to the castle.

▲ Map: Explorer 145
▲ Distance: 15 km/9¼ miles
▲ Walk ID: 667 Barrie England

Difficulty rating

Time

▲ Lake, Pub, Birds, Great Views

Basingstoke Canal and Surrounding Countryside

Beginning and ending at Winchfield's Barley Mow pub, this walk follows part of the Basingstoke Canal and crosses open countryside. The stretch at Step 6 can be difficult after heavy rain, so an alternative is given in the 'further information'.

1 From the car park, turn left and follow the canal, walking under Blacksmith's Bridge and Double Bridge. Immediately before Chequers Bridge turn left, walk through Crookham Wharf car park, cross the road carefully and turn left, facing the oncoming traffic.

2 Turn left into Stroud Lane. After Willow Cottage, turn left and cross a stream and a stile. Cross the field diagonally left. Cross another stile. Follow the path up across the field, between the pylon and the woods, then down into woodland and across a stream to join a track.

3 Follow the track between the houses. Turn left over a stile and follow the signposted path across the field to two stiles among trees, then onto a track. Continue over another stile. Follow the narrow path between two fences. Cross a left-hand stile into a field and head to the right of a pylon. Follow the path to the road.

4 Cross over and follow the path opposite, beside Double Bridge Farm. Cross a stile and follow the track over Blacksmith's Bridge and down to climb another stile. Turn right, then left to walk beside Tundry Pond. At the bridge, bear left. Cross a stile and after a short distance cross another stile on the right.

5 Fork left and follow the path up across a field towards the barn on the horizon. Follow a track past the barn to the summit, then down past woods and Dogmersfield Lake on the right. Go slightly uphill and across another track to reach two lodges.

6 Turn right immediately after the lodges and follow the path through the woods to the canal. Turn left and follow the path to turn right across the canal bridge. Turn right again and down to follow the canal all the way back to Barley Mow Bridge. Walk under it and turn left to the car park.

further information

After heavy rain, at Step 6 continue walking to the main A287. Turn right and walk with great care on the right side of the road. After 750 m take the first right at the roundabout and follow this narrow road through Broad Oak to the bridge over the canal.

▲ Map: Explorer 121
▲ Distance: 7 km/4¼ miles
▲ Walk ID: 76 Nicholas Rudd-Jones

Difficulty rating

Time

▲ River, Pub, Church, Wildlife,
Great Views

Arundel Castle.

Houghton and River Arun

This is a circular walk around the River Arun, taking in the delightful villages of North Stoke and South Stoke on the Sussex Downs above Arundel. If you have time, you can take a detour into Arundel Park.

1 From the small road next to the phone box and post box, take a footpath to the right. Climb two stiles, cross a track and continue on the grassy path downhill. At the bottom of the field, the path becomes gravelled. Cross the footbridge and follow the path as it swings right. Climb the stile and turn left at the river.

2 Climb the next stile to turn right and cross the bridge. Follow the track past the houses and St Leonard's Church in South Stoke. Join the road and swing left past the barn on the right. Turn right off the road and follow the bridleway behind the barn.

3 At the next bridleway signpost, turn left to follow the stony track. Go through a gate and turn right to follow the path around the field edge. Pass the gate back into the woods. Continue past a metal gate leading into Arundel Park on the left. Follow the path along the river, passing under white cliffs.

4 Go through a metal gate at the end of the path and follow the road uphill into Houghton village. At the crossroads, cross the B2139 and follow the minor road signposted to Bury across the fields.

5 Turn right when the South Downs Way crosses the road. At the river, follow the path round to the right to Amberley Bridge. Turn left over the bridge and take the footpath halfway across the bridge

on the right, heading towards North Stoke.

6 Cross a subsidiary bridge, then turn right, back alongside the river. Climb a stile and shortly afterwards take the path to the left. On reaching the North Stoke Road, turn right and return to the start.

further information

The River Arun is tidal and very prone to flooding, so it is a good idea to check the condition before you start out. At Step 4, there is a path alongside the river straight to Houghton Bridge, which can be used to shorten the route in dry weather.

access information

North Stoke lies south of Amberley Station, off the B2139 from Storrington. Parking is available near the phone box in North Stoke. You can also take a train to Amberley (on the Pulborough line from London) and start the walk from there.

▲ Map: Explorer 15
▲ Distance: 12 km/7½ miles
▲ Walk ID: 2078 David Stewart

Difficulty rating

!!!

Time

●●●◖

▲ Sea, Pub, Toilets, Play Area, National Trust/NTS, Birds, Great Views, Butterflies, Café, Good for Kids

Osmington and Ringstead

This is an enjoyable, family-friendly walk covering a delightful stretch of the Dorset coast and surrounding countryside.

❶ Come out through the car park entrance and walk back along the road for about 1 km. Take the footpath on the right and walk downhill. Follow the track through the farm and uphill again until you emerge at the A352.

❷ Cross the road to the footpath directly opposite and proceed uphill. Further on the path crosses a field and is harder to follow – head to the left of the mobile phone mast. Pass through the gate at the bottom and cross the track from Poxwell Manor (on your right). Walk up towards the mast, following the sign for the Hardy Way. Once at the mast, veer to the left and follow the ancient trackway to White Horse Hill.

❸ Just short of the summit and the gated stile, there is a left turn signposted to Osmington. Follow this stony track downhill to the village. Turn round on your way down to admire the White Horse on the hillside behind you.

❹ At Osmington, turn left onto Village Street, which is signposted to Osmington Mills. The street bends sharply to the right before joining the main road at the Sun Ray pub. Turn left onto the road and walk for about 125 m before crossing. Proceed along the footpath by the cottage. When you reach the stile by the busy dairy farm, cross over and go through the gate opposite. (If the farmer is moving cattle

the path may appear barred.) Follow the path as it veers to the left until you emerge into an open field.

❺ Make your way to the field boundary by the campsite. Follow the hedge to the far corner and climb the stile to join the coast path. Walk along the boards through the trees to the quiet road. Turn right and walk for a couple of hundred metres to the Smuggler's Inn.

❻ Walk round the left-hand side of the pub to find the coastal path. Pass through the kissing gate by the white house and then on up to the next kissing gate to follow the coastal path to Ringstead, where the path veers inland.

The White Horse, cut into the turf to reveal the chalk, at White Horse Hill.

access information

The walk begins at the South Down car park at Ringstead, just off the A352 east of Weymouth.

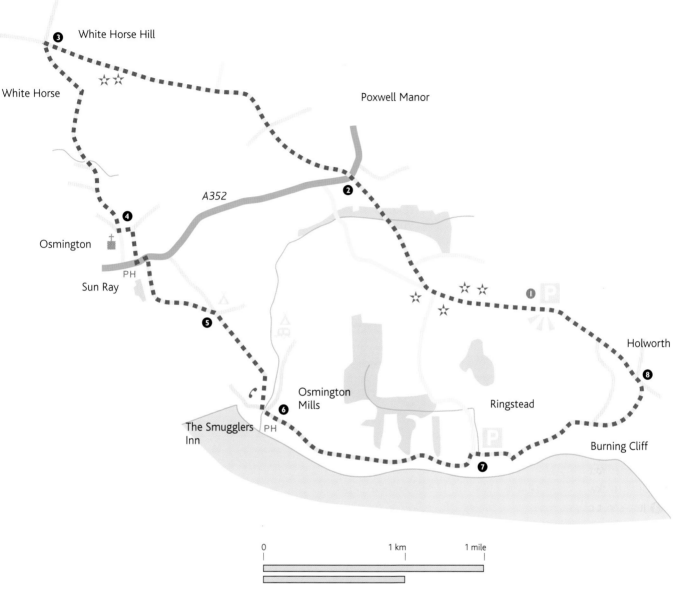

White Horse Hill

❸

White Horse

☆ ☆

Poxwell Manor

A352

❹

Osmington

✝

PH

Sun Ray

❷

❺

☆ ☆
☆
☆

❶ P

Holworth

❽

Osmington
Mills

❻

Ringstead

The Smugglers
Inn

PH

P

❼

Burning Cliff

0		1 km	1 mile

❼ As you come up to the car park, take the right-hand turn for the coastal path, signposted to White Nothe. After a while, cross the stile on the right, walk through the meadow to the beach and walk along to the steps, at the top of which you rejoin the coastal path at Burning Cliff. Continue on the coastal path to Holworth, climbing steadily and veering left.

❽ Where the track forks, keep to the left and head back to your car.

further information

This is a child-friendly section of coast, with few dangers and an opportunity to spend time on the beach.

There are toilets, a beach shop and refreshment facilities at Ringstead.

The Smuggler's Inn serves food and has a children's play area.

▲ Map: Explorer 145

▲ Distance: 8.53 km/5¼ miles

▲ Walk ID: 468 Nina Thornhill

Difficulty rating

Time

▲ Pub, Toilets, Wildlife, Birds, Visitor Centre

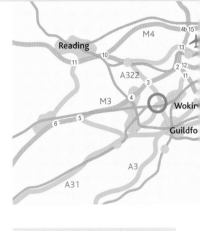

Brookwood to Aldershot

This walk takes in varied stretches of the Basingstoke Canal. You pass the Deepcut Locks to reach the Great Heath. The canal then runs through the wooded Deepcut Cutting. At the Frimley Aqueduct, the canal widens and barges hug the banks.

1 At Brookwood station, turn left and cross the road into a side road by the Brookwood Hotel. Cross over the A324 at the end and go down Sheets Heath Lane. At the bridge, cross over and turn left, keeping to the towpath on the left, not the bridleway. At Pirbright Bridge, go up the slope on the right and then cross the road.

2 Walk to the first of the Deepcut Locks and cross over it, as the towpath continues on the opposite bank from this point. Keep ahead on the towpath at two more bridges. After passing Frimley Lock (no. 28) and cottage, you reach Deepcut Cutting.

3 Keep ahead along this straight stretch of canal, then walk under a white bridge. After crossing the Frimley Aqueduct, keep ahead at the gate until you reach a fork. You can take either path here, as they both lead to the B3012 ahead.

4 When you reach the road, turn right and go over the bridge. Cross the road just before the King's Head pub and turn left along the towpath. Continue to follow the towpath, with Frimley Lodge Park on your right. If you wish to visit the Basingstoke Canal Visitor Centre further on, cross over to it via a small swing bridge. Otherwise, just keep walking ahead.

5 Pass under Mytchett Place Bridge, then under Canal Bridge, which comes out by Mytchett Lake. Walk on, passing under two railway bridges. Just after the second of these, you come to a gap on your right. Turn right through the gap into Ash Vale station car park.

access information

The walk runs from Brookwood to Ash Vale railway stations, and can be followed in either direction. Both stations are on the Waterloo to Alton line and car parking is available at both, although Brookwood is larger.

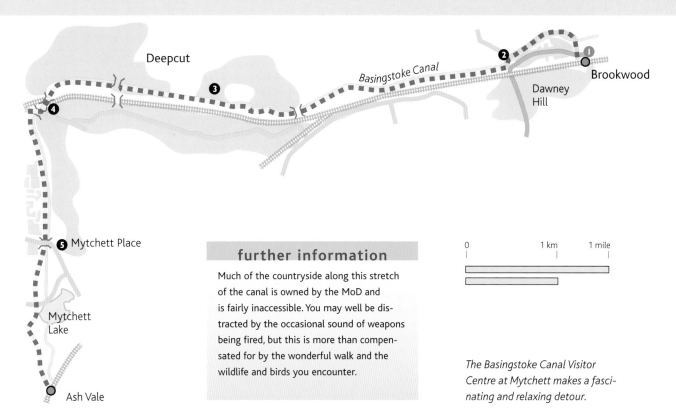

Deepcut

Basingstoke Canal

❷ Brookwood

Dawney
Hill

❸

❹

❺ Mytchett Place

Mytchett
Lake

Ash Vale

further information

Much of the countryside along this stretch
of the canal is owned by the MoD and
is fairly inaccessible. You may well be dis-
tracted by the occasional sound of weapons
being fired, but this is more than compensated for by the wonderful walk and the
wildlife and birds you encounter.

0   1 km   1 mile

*The Basingstoke Canal Visitor
Centre at Mytchett makes a fascinating and relaxing detour.*

▲ Map: Explorer 160
▲ Distance: 8.86 km/5½ miles
▲ Walk ID: 736 Tony Brotherton

Difficulty rating

Time

▲ Lake, Pub, Toilets, Wildlife, Birds, Flowers, Great Views

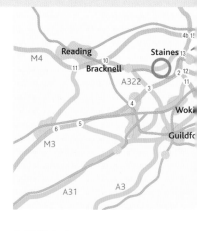

Around Virginia Water

This walk around Virginia Water, in Windsor Great Park, has some stunning vistas. The Valley Gardens are among the world's best woodland gardens. Detours from the main route given here will reveal many interesting features and landmarks.

1 From Blacknest car park, walk ahead on the broad woodland path to reach the lake opposite the stone bridge. Turn right to follow the lakeside path, eventually passing the 'ruins' to your right. Walk on to the cascade, and continue downhill.

2 Cross the stone bridge and look out for the 'hidden' path between the rhododendrons on the left. Climb a short path to rejoin the lakeside path and walk past the Wheatsheaf car park. Carry on alongside the lake to the totem-pole. From here, take the sand and gravel path uphill towards Valley Gardens.

3 Near the top of the gardens, turn right to reach a signpost at a cross-paths. Follow the 'Savill Gardens' sign through parkland to a five-fingered signpost. Take the path to Obelisk Pond. Follow the path around the pond, then continue to cross a balustraded bridge.

4 When the path gives way to grass, bear half-left between trees to follow the edge of a wood on your left. Heading towards the equestrian statue, reach the crossroads at the corner of Smith's Lawn. Turn left, and follow the rail fence, with the grandstand ahead.

5 Go left at the 'Guards Polo Club' sign. Bear right to re-enter Valley Gardens and continue to the heather garden entrance. Go into the heather garden and bear left along the broad grass path. Leave the

garden through either of two gates, taking the path to the right back to the five-fingered signpost. Follow the sandy path half-right into woods, then a broad grassy swathe back to the lake path.

6 Follow the lake path, finally turning left to join the road between the main lake and Johnson's Pond. Leave the road to walk alongside the horse gallop, then rejoin the road to cross the stone bridge. Bear left on the path back to the lakeside. Go ahead on the woodland path to Blacknest car park, or turn left for the Wheatsheaf car park.

further information

There are no stiles, brambles or nettles on this walk – just a few gentle slopes, rhododendrons, azaleas and magnolias in spring, and a fantastic variety of birdlife both on and around the lake. Look out for green woodpeckers, kingfishers, herons and great crested grebes, as well as exotic ducks and geese.

Enjoy the abundant floral delights in the peaceful surroundings of Virginia Water.

The route passes close to the three main car parks that serve the park. They are at Blacknest (current charge £1.50), Wheatsheaf (current charge £3.50) and Savill Gardens (current charge £2.00). There is free verge car parking at Mill Lane. Wheatsheaf car park is accessible by buses between Bagshot and Egham.

Visit the nearby Windsor Castle, the splendid royal residence of Queen Elizabeth II.

▲ Map: Explorer 161
▲ Distance: 14 km/8¾ miles
▲ Walk ID: 511 Oliver O'Brien

Difficulty rating

●●●

Time

●●●●

▲ River, Pub, Toilets, Museum, Play
Area, Stately Home, Botanic Gardens,
Wildlife, Birds, Flowers, Great Views

Richmond and Kew

This circular walk takes in a meander of the Thames, so that most of it is beside the river. Starting at Mortlake, the route joins the Thames Path. The return leg takes in the north end of Richmond Park, with a short stretch through a residential

❶ From the station, walk into Mortlake Green and take the path to the left across the park. Cross the road and follow the Budweiser Brewery access road ahead, signposted 'Thames Cycle Route'. Pass The Ship pub and turn left towards Kew Bridge to follow the path beside the river.

❷ Staying on the path when it bears away from the road, pass under Chiswick Bridge and continue past the Public Record Office. Pass under Kew Rail Bridge and carry on past Kew Gardens Pier and under Kew Road Bridge.

❸ Just after Kew Bridge, pass the sign indicating the Kew Gardens entrance, and another pier. Continue along the towpath beside the river, passing another entrance to the gardens. Crossing the Meridian Line, the route continues along the path, with water on both sides.

❹ Pass Richmond Lock, cross the Meridian Line again, and continue along the path, passing under Twickenham Bridge, a railway bridge and Richmond Bridge. When the path leaves the river, follow it through a small park and pass a small flight of steps on the left.

❺ Go straight ahead, through a set of gates and across a field. After a house, turn left and cross the main road. Follow the path opposite steeply uphill. At the top, turn right on another road.

access information

This walk starts at Mortlake railway station, which is served by South Western trains and is accessible from central London. If you are travelling by car, there is very limited parking at the station. An alternative is to park in Richmond town centre and head west across Richmond Green to the river.

An enchanting glimpse of the River Thames across the lush countryside from Richmond Hill.

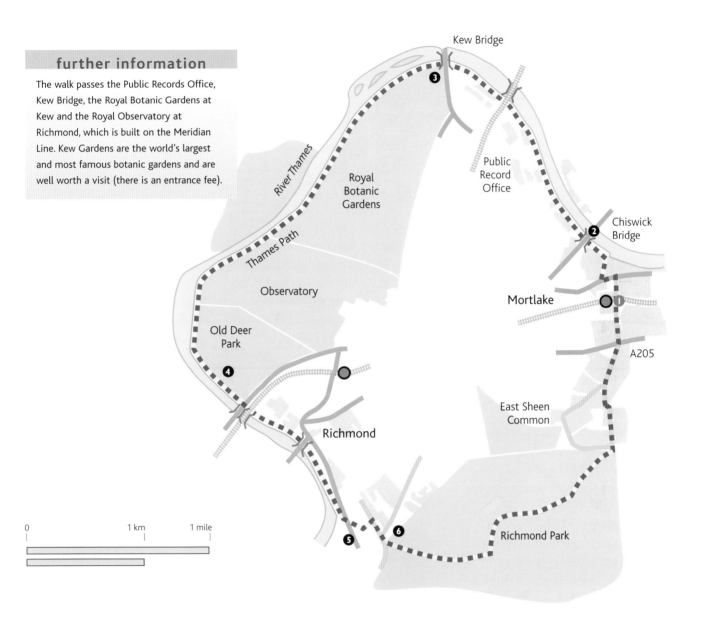

further information

The walk passes the Public Records Office,
Kew Bridge, the Royal Botanic Gardens at
Kew and the Royal Observatory at
Richmond, which is built on the Meridian
Line. Kew Gardens are the world's largest
and most famous botanic gardens and are
well worth a visit (there is an entrance fee).

Kew Bridge

❸

River Thames

Royal
Botanic
Gardens

Public
Record
Office

❷ Chiswick
Bridge

Thames Path

Observatory

Mortlake ❶

A205

Old Deer
Park

❹

East Sheen
Common

Richmond

❺ ❻

Richmond Park

0   1 km   1 mile

❻ Carry on ahead at the first mini-
roundabout, then turn left at the next
into Richmond Park. Go straight on at
the next mini-roundabout and follow
the path to the left of the road. Turn
left towards Holly Lodge (Bog Lodge),
then bear right just before the lodge
and follow the path to Sheen Gate.
Walk up Sheen Lane (B351), cross
Upper Richmond Road West (A205) at
the traffic lights, and continue along
Sheen Lane back to Mortlake station.

*When passing through
the picturesque
Richmond Park, herds of
deer are a common sight.*

▲ Map: Explorer 192
▲ Distance: 8.05 km/5 miles
▲ Walk ID: 1183 Brian and Anne Sandland

Difficulty rating

Time

▲ Pub, Toilets, Church, Wildlife, Birds, Flowers, Butterflies, Great Views, Industrial Archaeology

The Grand Union Canal and Great Brickhill from Three Locks Inn

From the Three Locks Inn, this walk follows the towpath of the Grand Union Canal, then crosses fields to Great Brickhill village on a ridge with great views. From here, the route follows a bridleway to rejoin the towpath and return to the start point.

1 From the car park, cross the road and go down to the canal towpath. Follow the path to the first bridge, then cross the canal and continue on the opposite bank. Pass the lock at Stoke Hammond and carry on under the bridge. Continue for some distance to the next bridge. Look for an exit to the right and climb the steps to the road.

2 Turn right and follow the road. Cross the river bridges, then Lower Rectory Farm on your right. Opposite the entrance to Westfield Farm on your left, turn right onto a signposted path. Go through the metal gate and follow the broad path diagonally left across the field, then bear right to follow trees and a hedge on your left. Cross a fence and bear left.

3 Follow an old wall on your left, cross a stile by a metal gate, then head for the further of two Scots pines to reach another gate just after a yellow way-mark. Beyond the gate, follow a track between hedges. Go through another gate and turn left onto the tarmacked lane, past Great Brickhill Church. At the T-junction, turn right into Lower Way.

The Grand Union Canal is a modern man-made wonder and is enjoyed today for a variety of leisure activities.

access information

The Three Locks car park and picnic site is on the east side of the A4146 between Bletchley and Leighton Buzzard.

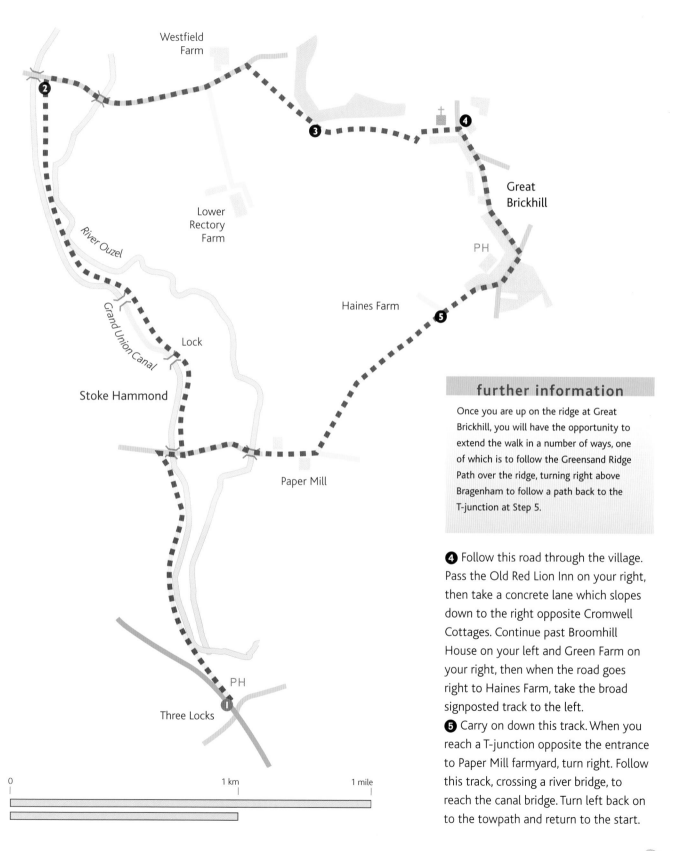

Westfield
Farm

Lower
Rectory
Farm

River Ouzel

Grand Union Canal

Lock

Stoke Hammond

Paper Mill

Great
Brickhill

PH

Haines Farm

PH

Three Locks

0   1 km   1 mile

further information

Once you are up on the ridge at Great
Brickhill, you will have the opportunity to
extend the walk in a number of ways, one
of which is to follow the Greensand Ridge
Path over the ridge, turning right above
Bragenham to follow a path back to the
T-junction at Step 5.

❹ Follow this road through the village.
Pass the Old Red Lion Inn on your right,
then take a concrete lane which slopes
down to the right opposite Cromwell
Cottages. Continue past Broomhill
House on your left and Green Farm on
your right, then when the road goes
right to Haines Farm, take the broad
signposted track to the left.

❺ Carry on down this track. When you
reach a T-junction opposite the entrance
to Paper Mill farmyard, turn right. Follow
this track, crossing a river bridge, to
reach the canal bridge. Turn left back on
to the towpath and return to the start.

The Naze and Cormorant Creek from Walton Station

 Map: Explorer 184
Distance: 8.05 km/5 miles
Walk ID: 1125 Brian and Anne Sandland

Difficulty rating

Time

River, Sea, Toilets, Play Area, Church, Wildlife, Birds, Flowers, Great Views, Butterflies, Café, Gift Shop, Food Shop, Public Transport, Restaurant

This circular walk starts beside the sea, going through the little resort of Walton, then across the open space of the Naze. You then turn alongside Cormorant Creek to reach the backwater of Walton Channel and return beside Walton Hall Marshes.

1 From the station, follow the road to the seafront, then continue ahead with the sea on your right.

2 Continue along the coast, and turn right into East Terrace to stay close to the sea. When the road ends, just after the coastguard station and the old lifeboat house, take the tarmacked path, then Cliff Parade. When this road ends, continue on the grass, rising slightly but still staying close to the sea. Just after a shelter on your right, bear right.

3 Head initially towards the sea, but bear left along a path to the seaward side of bungalows to follow a footpath above the sea. Bear left again when you reach steps down, then after a short distance go right on a broad gravel track to head towards a tall brick tower.

4 Continue, still close to the cliff-edge, along a wide area of mown grass. The mown path bears left and right around a cliff fall, then continues ahead in the direction of Felixstowe.

5 Carry on between bushes on a very narrow path close to the cliff-edge, but when this ends turn inland for a short distance to another, wider path and turn right, still heading towards Felixstowe. When you reach a raised bank, climb this and turn left onto tarmac.

6 At the end of the tarmac bear left, still on the raised bank. Follow the path alongside Cormorant Creek, then along the backwater of Walton Channel, with Walton Hall Marshes on your left. The riverbank eventually brings you to a bend on a road via a field-edge path. Turn right and follow the road back towards the town centre. Retrace your steps along the seafront and back to the station.

A dramatic view of the Naze Nature Reserve, an area rich in its diversity of indigenous and migratory birds.

Walton is a small, old-fashioned seaside resort just north of Clacton and Frinton. The Naze on which it stands is an area of open land fronting the North Sea. There is much wildlife here, and a great variety of birdlife. The cliffs on the seaward edge of the Naze are a favourite haunt of geologists and fossil hunters.

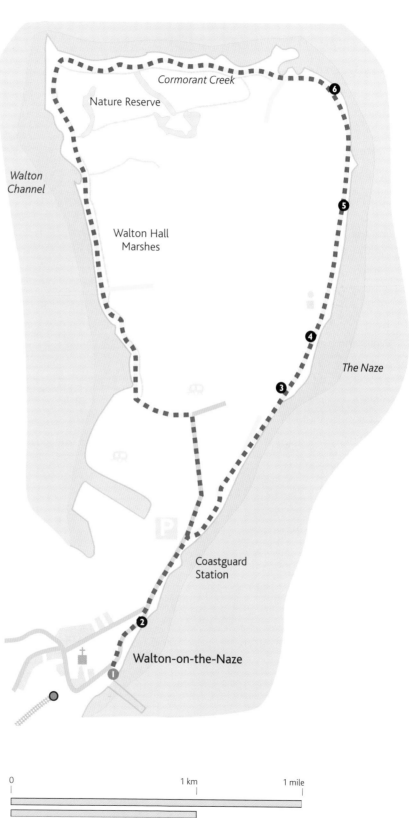

Cormorant Creek

Nature Reserve

Walton Channel

Walton Hall Marshes

The Naze

Coastguard Station

Walton-on-the-Naze

0   1 km   1 mile

▲ Map: Explorer 184

▲ Distance: 9.66 km/6 miles

▲ Walk ID: 1028 Brian and Anne Sandland

Difficulty rating

Time

▲ River, Lake, Pub, Church, Wildlife, Birds, Flowers, Great Views, Butterflies, Food Shop, Industrial Archaeology, Mostly Flat, Tea Shop, Woodland

River Colne and Alresford Creek from Wivenhoe

This walk starts at Wivenhoe and follows the River Colne seawards, mainly along a former railway track enticingly known as the 'Crab and Winkle Line'. The route then turns away from the river and returns to Wivenhoe through fields and woodland.

① From the station, walk along West Street, then turn right into Bath Street. Turn left at the quay and walk on, keeping the river to your right. Take the concrete path to the left of the rusting shipbuilding shed, then bear right along a tarmac road, passing the Colne Barrier.

② Follow the gravel path past Wivenhoe Sailing Club. Go through a gate and follow the raised path by the river. Cross a stile, walk through the trees, then continue parallel to the river. Where the path forks, bear left, with Alresford Creek to your right, to meet a road.

③ Turn left and walk past the sand and gravel workings. At the brow of the hill, turn left along a signposted bridleway. At the next junction, continue on the track to the right beside the concrete road. After passing Marsh Farm, turn right and continue along the road.

④ Follow a signposted path left over a stile. Cross the railway, then turn left to reach a sandy track. After a short distance, take a right-hand path through the trees, crossing a stream to follow it on your left. Cross a bridge, then climb and descend steps. Follow the stream to a stile and a lane.

Wivenhoe and the River Colne, popular with boat lovers of all tastes.

access information

The walk starts at Wivenhoe railway station. Wivenhoe is on the London Liverpool Street to Clacton line and there is an hourly service in both directions.

Wivenhoe lies south of the A133 from Colchester to Clacton. Turn right onto the B1027, then fork right onto the B1028.

further information

Wivenhoe was formerly a shipbuilding town and the walk passes the site of the old shipyard. There is also an impressive barrage, built to prevent tidal surges reaching Wivenhoe and Colchester, further upriver. The water-filled pits of disused sand and gravel workings provide homes for a variety of wildfowl and wildlife.

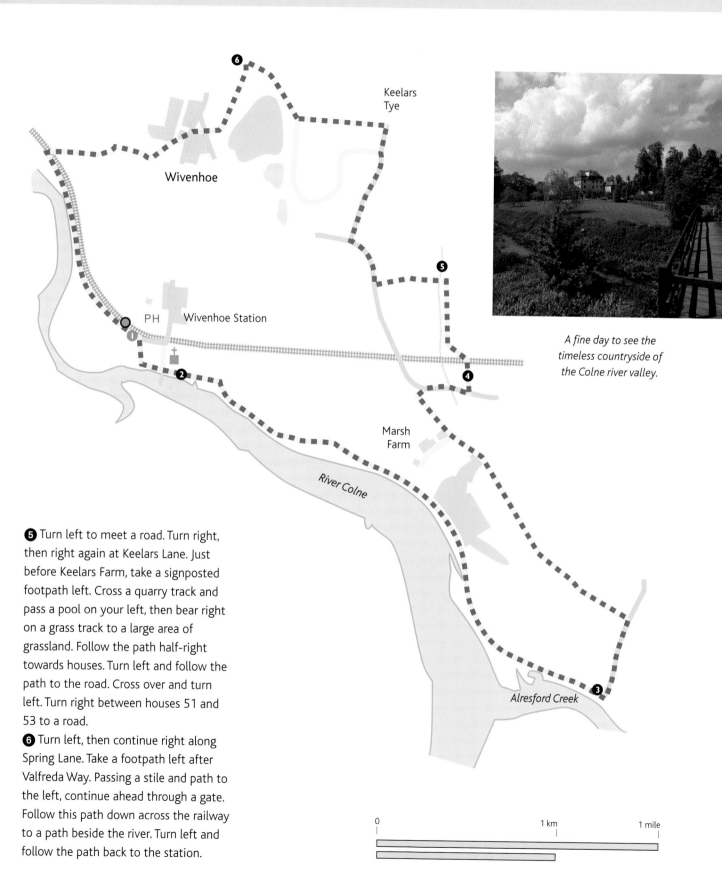

Keelars
Tye

Wivenhoe

6

5

PH   Wivenhoe Station

2

4

Marsh
Farm

River Colne

Alresford Creek

3

*A fine day to see the
timeless countryside of
the Colne river valley.*

5 Turn left to meet a road. Turn right, then right again at Keelars Lane. Just before Keelars Farm, take a signposted footpath left. Cross a quarry track and pass a pool on your left, then bear right on a grass track to a large area of grassland. Follow the path half-right towards houses. Turn left and follow the path to the road. Cross over and turn left. Turn right between houses 51 and 53 to a road.

6 Turn left, then continue right along Spring Lane. Take a footpath left after Valfreda Way. Passing a stile and path to the left, continue ahead through a gate. Follow this path down across the railway to a path beside the river. Turn left and follow the path back to the station.

0   1 km   1 mile

Woodland & Hillside

The woodland and hillside walks of South and South-east England reveal downland and deer parks, ancient battlegrounds and eerie monuments. Highlights include Avebury Ring and the 1066 Walk.

▲ Map: Explorer 184

▲ Distance: 6.44 km/4 miles

▲ Walk ID: 1213 Brian and Anne Sandland

Difficulty rating

Time

▲ Toilets, Play Area, Church, Wildlife, Birds, Flowers, Butterflies, Mostly Flat, Public Transport, Restaurant, Tea Shop, Ancient Monument

Frating Abbey and Aingers Green from Great Bentley

Great Bentley is a charming village with the largest village green in the country, where cricket is played in summer. This walk follows field paths to Frating Abbey, then lanes and more field and woodland tracks and paths all the way back.

❶ From the station, walk towards the village, then fork left at the village green towards the church. Walk through the churchyard, keeping the church on your left. Go through a gate in the hedge and turn left. Go through two more gates then turn right with a wire fence on your right.

❷ Follow a fence then a ditch bearing left. Cross the ditch over a concrete bridge and turn left. Bear right for a short distance by the embankment, then cross a stile on the left to continue along a narrow path. At the foot crossing, go over the railway, then a stile.

❸ Walk between fields with a ditch on your right. Cross the ditch and continue with the ditch on your left. When the ditch ends, turn right towards farm buildings. Follow the farm track to the road and turn left, past Frating Abbey. Continue to a signposted path left.

❹ Cross the field to the far side, then follow the arrow to cross two bridges, then a stile. Cross a narrow field and another stile. After a short distance, turn left on a path curving right to a grass path. Follow the grass path up the rise.

❺ At the woodland, turn right, then left over a track to a track between the trees. Follow this to a road at Aingers Green. Cross to follow Weeley Road to a

junction, and take a left turn signposted Tendring. Follow the lane to St Mary's Farm and turn left, passing the farm on a signposted footpath.

❻ Follow the path towards the railway. Just before the railway, turn left, then right over a footbridge. Cross a narrow section of field, then the railway. Follow a tarmacked path to a road and bear right on Pine Close. At a junction, bear right again to a footpath between fences. At the road, turn left and walk beside the village green to the Plough Inn. Turn left to the station.

Great Bentley village green and the very essence of English life – a game of cricket.

access information

Great Bentley lies south of the A133 Colchester to Clacton Road. The walk starts at the railway station, which is served by trains from London Liverpool Street. Car parking is available outside the station. Great Bentley is also accessible by buses running between Colchester and Clacton.

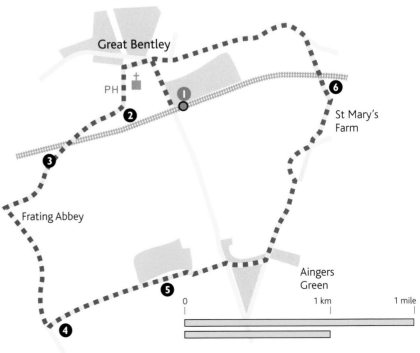

▲ Map: Explorer 138
▲ Distance: 7 km/4¼ miles
▲ Walk ID: 1048 Ian Elmes

Difficulty rating

Time

▲ Wildlife, Birds, Flowers, Great Views, Butterflies

Castle Hill

Ancient meets modern on this short circular walk above Folkestone, which begins at a viewpoint, then takes a pleasant route along part of the North Downs Way, taking in views of the English Channel and overlooking the Channel Tunnel Terminal.

The English Channel with the impressive Channel Tunnel in the foreground.

1 From the viewpoint, go through the kissing gate and turn left. Follow signs for the North Downs Way and Saxon Shore Way. Continue along the footpath, alongside the road, then follow the signs through a gate heading towards Castle Lane. Passing a stile on the left, continue along the footpath.

2 Go through a kissing gate and follow the path to the top of Castle Lane. Turn right for a short distance down Castle Hill, then take a footpath to the left. Follow the path round to the left, through kissing gates and up the hill past the pylon.

3 At the next waymark, keep left on the North Downs Way. Follow the path, and at the next waymark, keep straight ahead. At the bottom of the path, where the road meets the footpath, go through the right-hand gate and keep to the path bearing right.

4 Walk up and over the hill and down the other side. Keep to the fence on your left. At the bottom, turn right, following the footpath down and then up some steps. Follow the path, keeping right at the waymarks, signposted Countryside Project. Carry on downhill for some distance, then turn right at the next waymark.

5 Follow the path up the steps and diagonally left to the next waymark, following more steep winding steps. At the next waymark, turn left, following the blue arrow. This path crosses the A20. Follow the path round to the kissing gate.

access information

Leave the M20 at Junction 13 and follow the signs for Folkestone (A259). At the third roundabout left onto Canterbury Road, continue up the hill and turn left on the Pilgrims Way. Follow the road along and into Crete Road West. The viewpoint is on the left by a lay-by.

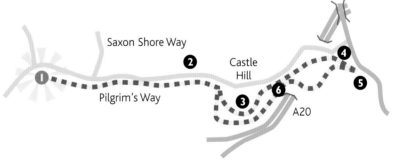

6 Turn left at the kissing gate, following the path towards Castle Hill and Caesar's Camp, then follow the lower path on the left to the bottom of Castle Hill. At the end of the path, go through the gate and turn right up the road, then right again up Castle Hill. At the top, turn left and return to the viewpoint.

▲ Map: Explorer 196

▲ Distance: 12.88 km/8 miles

▲ Walk ID: 1352 Brian and Anne Sandland

Difficulty rating

Time

▲ Lake, Church, Wildlife, Birds, Flowers, Great Views, Butterflies, Mostly Flat, Woodland

Tye Green and Rivers Hall from Boxted

The beginning and end of this walk follow sections of the Essex Way through delightful countryside in an area of outstanding natural beauty, giving superb views at various points.

A summer scene stretching below Langham Church near Boxted.

❶ From the car park, walk back towards the road, then turn right to take the signposted path. At the field end, bear right, passing wooden barns, then fork left by a pond. Follow a track past Boxted Hall, then turn left at a road. Take the right turn at the T-junction with Church Road and continue.

❷ Turn left on a footpath opposite Kerseys. At the field end, cross a footbridge. Follow the track ahead to Green Lane. Turn right, then left on a footpath. Follow the right field edge to a signpost in a hollow. Turn right across the field to pass through Holly Lodge Farm to the road. Turn left and walk through Tye Green.

❸ Turn left on a footpath opposite Preen View. Just before farm buildings, bear diagonally left across a field. Cross a track. Go through a hedge, then a field, a hedge and a field to pass Barritts Farm on the right. Follow the drive to a road. Turn left.

❹ Turn right at the next signposted path, which bears right to another road. Turn left. Turn right on the footpath opposite a pond. Follow the field edge to a telegraph pole, then bear right to pass Plains Farm on your left. Continue ahead across the field. Turn left into Cage Lane, turning left at the sharp bend.

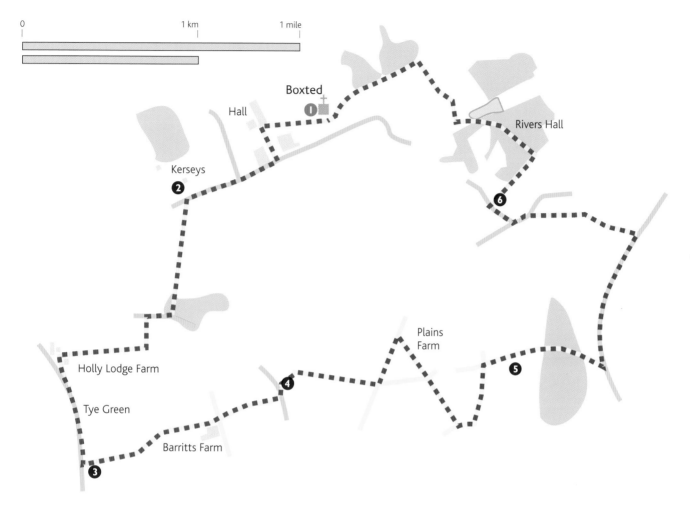

0   1 km   1 mile

Boxted

Hall

Rivers Hall

Kerseys

2

6

Plains Farm

Holly Lodge Farm

5

Tye Green

4

Barritts Farm

3

5 Turn right and follow a track signed 'Unsuitable for Motor Vehicles' through trees and across to a road. Turn left and follow the road down through woodland then up. At the top of the hill, follow a footpath left across two fields to Dedham Road. Turn left, then right into Cooks Hill.

6 Turn right and follow the footpath to meet a track. Turn left towards Rivers Hall. Follow the footpath left then right around the outbuildings. When you meet the drive by the moat, turn left downhill through woodland, past a lake, then up. Turn left along Church Street to Boxted. At the bend by Aubrey Cottages, follow the path ahead back to the start.

further information

At Step 2 you pass an interesting vineyard with opportunities for wine-tasting and/or purchase. The walk can be shortened by turning left at the end of Step 3, then following a signposted footpath left at Boxted British Legion Hut, past a lake and back to the start point.

access information

Boxted lies east of the A134 Colchester to Sudbury road, and can be reached via a number of signposted turnings. Follow signs to the village and park in the car park by the church and school.

Take time to visit the 12th-century Church of St Peter's in Boxted, with its splendid square Norman tower and dormer windows.

▲ Map: Explorer OL 29

▲ Distance: 8 km/5 miles

▲ Walk ID: 546 David L. White

Difficulty rating

Time

▲ Hills, Sea, Pub, Toilets, Church,
Wildlife, Birds, Flowers, Great Views

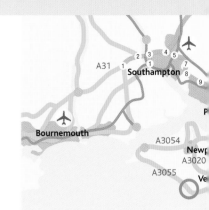

Niton and St Catherine's Down from Blackgang

This walk is in an area with a seafaring history, with three lighthouses from different periods and a smuggling tradition around Blackgang and Niton. Blackgang now clings precariously to the cliff-edge, slowly disappearing as the cliff erodes.

1 From the seaward side of the car park, climb up some steps and follow the path to the cliff top. Turn left towards Niton and follow the path past the radio mast station. After the second stile beyond the radio station, turn immediately left over another stile, heading inland.

The southern coastline of the Isle of Wight with Blackgang and most of the walk area visible.

2 Keeping the fence on your right, walk across the field to a stile at the far side. Cross a small meadow, bearing slightly left, to climb another stile. Walk through a coppice path to the main road. Follow the road to the right until it bears left, marked 'Through traffic', to the church. At the lychgate, turn left and go up Pan Lane. When the lane becomes a bridle path, carry on, turning left at a junction of paths.

access information

Blackgang lies just off the southern tip of the Isle of Wight, off the A3055. There is a large car park. The nearest bus stop is Blackgang. If you are travelling by ferry from the mainland, the best crossings are the Portsmouth/Ryde catamaran, the Southsea/Ryde hovercraft and the Portsmouth/Fishbourne car ferry.

③ Go through a metal gate and follow a blue arrow straight ahead. Go through another metal gate at the far side of the field. (At this point you can turn right and walk across the field, bearing slightly right towards a signpost, then follow a bridleway to Hoy's Monument. Return to the gate to continue the walk at Step 4.)

④ Turn immediately left and climb to the summit of the hill, where the Old Oratory stands, for fantastic views. The Old Oratory was one of the original lighthouses, built in 1314. From the Old Oratory, cross the field, heading towards the sea, to climb a stile. Follow the path down to the start of the walk.

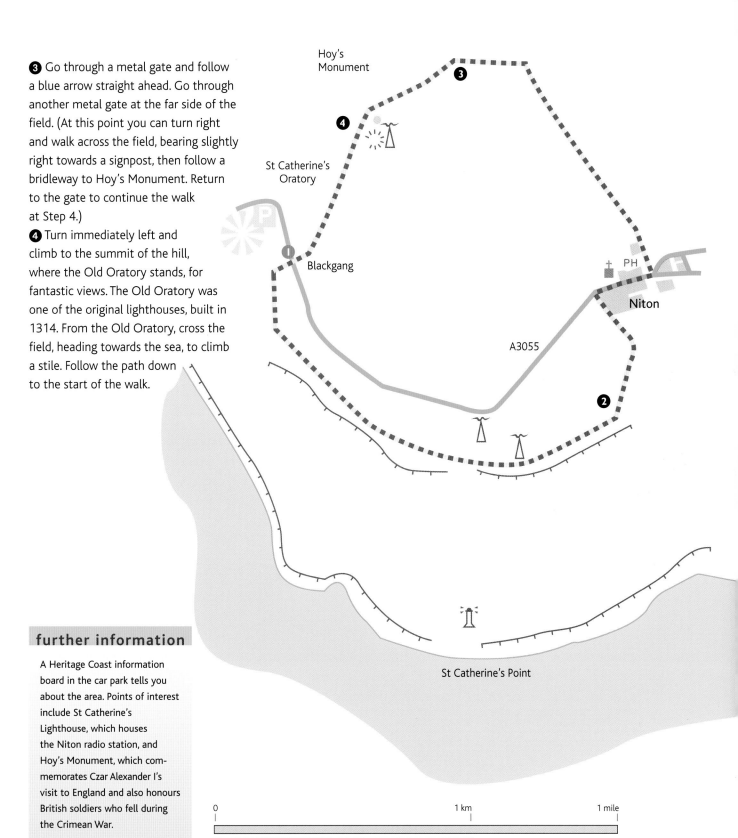

Hoy's Monument

St Catherine's Oratory

Blackgang

Niton

PH

A3055

St Catherine's Point

further information

A Heritage Coast information board in the car park tells you about the area. Points of interest include St Catherine's Lighthouse, which houses the Niton radio station, and Hoy's Monument, which commemorates Czar Alexander I's visit to England and also honours British soldiers who fell during the Crimean War.

0   1 km   1 mile

▲ Map: Explorer 144

▲ Distance: 10 km/6¼ miles

▲ Walk ID: 1348 David Stewart

Difficulty rating

Time

▲ Pub, Church, Great Views

North Oakley and Hannington from White Hill

This circular walk has very little climbing, but really fantastic views nonetheless. The route follows the Wayfarers Walk, then a combination of paths, tracks and small country roads. The last section along the escarpment makes a great finale.

1 Take the Wayfarers Walk from beside the car park entrance. The path crosses some fields then bears right, down to a road. Turn left on the road, then right on a track past Walkeridge Farm. Go into a field used as a caravan site and walk on down the slope.

2 Go through a gate and continue ahead along the grassy path until you meet a track. Turn left to walk into North Oakley. Turn left at the road junction, then left again up a driveway, following the footpath sign, and climb a stile. Cross a patch of grass diagonally right to the corner. Cross two more stiles, then head across the field. Bear left at the end. After a short distance bear right across the next field.

3 Follow the path through the hedge to the road, and turn left into Hannington. Cross the village green and follow the lane right of the churchyard. Follow the footpath on your right, signposted alongside a barn, to a gate onto an open field. Turn right and follow the field edge to the road. Turn right.

4 Almost immediately, turn left on a signposted footpath. At the corner of the field, turn sharp left up the hill, then bear right by the woods. Follow the path over the hill, down into the valley and up again. At a prominent water tank,

continue straight ahead.

5 Follow the track when it bends left, climbing a stile to a path around the contour of the hill through woodland. At a fork, turn left, continuing around the hill to reach a field boundary at the radio mast. Drop down to the right a little and follow the path just outside the field below the mast.

6 Climb a stile signposted to the left and walk straight up the hill. At the top of the field, turn right at a junction of paths and follow the field edge. Cross a stile and bear left slightly. Follow the path down to rejoin the Wayfarers Way and return to the car park.

access information

The White Hill car park is on the B3051 between Overton and Kingsclere, south of the A339.

further information

The Vine in Hannington, a combined pub and restaurant, makes a good stopping point at around the halfway point.

Among the magnificent sights worth visiting on the Wayfarers Walk is the spine-chilling Combe Gibbet at Inkpen Hill.

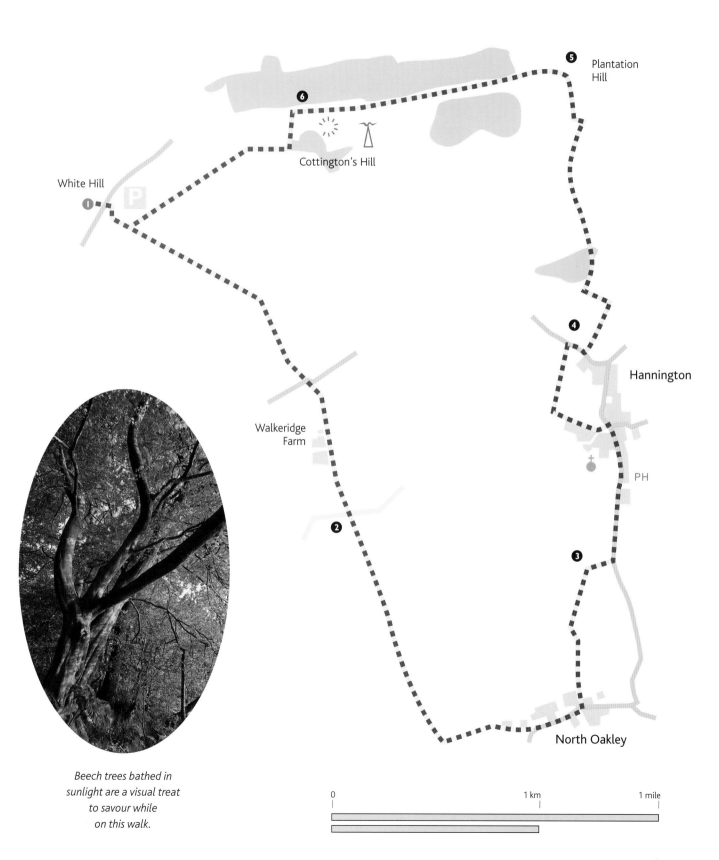

White Hill

1

P

Cottington's Hill

6

5 Plantation Hill

Walkeridge Farm

2

4

Hannington

PH

3

North Oakley

Beech trees bathed in sunlight are a visual treat to savour while on this walk.

0   1 km   1 mile

▲ Map: Explorer 118

▲ Distance: 10.7 km/6¾ miles

▲ Walk ID: 486 Al Rodger

Difficulty rating

Time

● ● ●

▲ Hills, Pub, Church, Birds, Great Views

Win Green and Tollard Royal

This peaceful circular walk starts at Win Green Hill, the highest point on Cranborne Chase, with exceptional views. The route follows a tree-lined dry valley to Tollard Royal, then returns on a mostly gradual climb to the main ridgeway.

1 From the car park, walk towards the clump of trees, passing either side of them to reach the ridgeway. Around the first corner, climb a stile over the right-hand fence into the trees and descend the steep hillside on the path slanting right. The path becomes somewhat indistinct, but aim to keep up from the valley bottom until turning right as the side valley comes in from the right.

2 Follow the main track over the rise and down the valley, following the marker posts. (The path passes through a cottage garden but to avoid upsetting the occupants, bypass the cottage on the track.) Where the main track bends right, turn left down to the fence, crossing two stiles and going up through a gate to the track along the left side of the valley.

3 When you meet another track, either walk down into Tollard Royal or head up the track, then turn right and cross a stile to follow a footpath pointer. The path slants left up the hill then crosses fields over the top of the hill.

access information

From the A30 Shaftesbury to Salisbury road, turn right in Ludwell at the signpost to the Larmer Tree Garden. As you climb onto the Chase, look for a signpost Byway to Win Green on the left, and follow the pot-holed road to the car park.

further information

Cranborne Chase was originally a royal hunting ground, popular with King John, and run by the Lord of the Chase. Privately owned from the 1600s to 1830, the Lord of the Chase owned the deer and game which, along with the woods they bred in, were protected. Tolls were charged during fawning and crop damage caused by hunters went uncompensated.

4 Cross a stile beside a gate and follow the path slanting down the hill to the left to join a track in the valley bottom. Go through a gate and climb up the track ahead. At the next fence line, follow the track round to the right and through a gate alongside trees, keeping out of the field.

5 Emerging from the wood, follow the route left off the track, then right into the field, heading for the gap in the trees on the skyline. At the crossroads on the top of the ridge, turn left. When the road begins to drop off the ridge, fork left on the track.

6 At the junction of tracks and road, walk straight on and take the track rising over the hill ahead, meeting the outward route and following the track back to the car park.

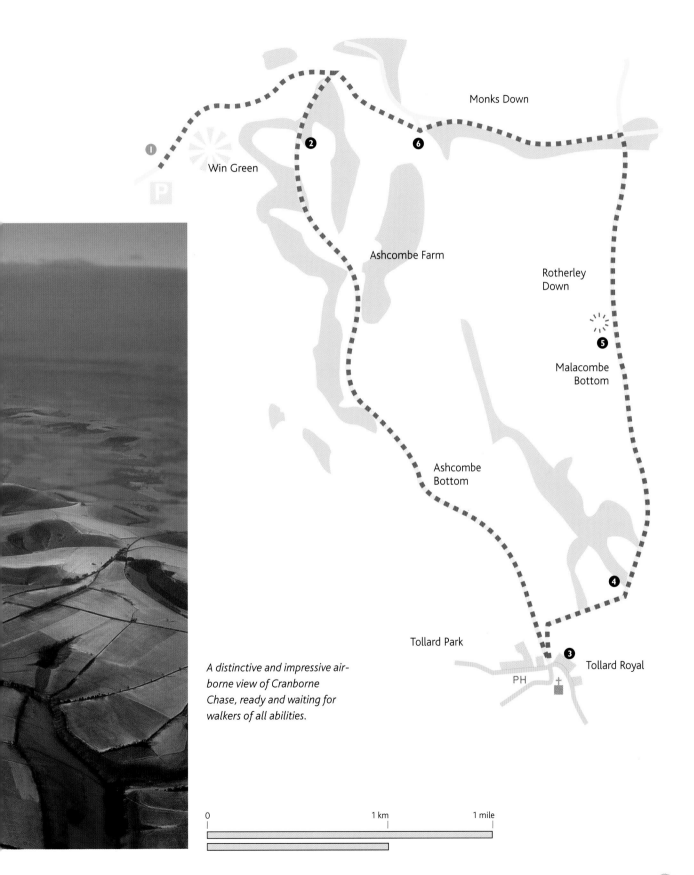

Win Green

Monks Down

Ashcombe Farm

Rotherley
Down

Malacombe
Bottom

Ashcombe
Bottom

Tollard Park

Tollard Royal

PH

*A distinctive and impressive air-
borne view of Cranborne
Chase, ready and waiting for
walkers of all abilities.*

0   1 km   1 mile

▲ Map: Explorer 157
▲ Distance: 8.5 km/5¼ miles
▲ Walk ID: 68 David Stewart

Difficulty rating

Time

▲ Pub, Museum, National Trust/NTS, Gift Shop, Restaurant, Great Views

The Sanctuary, West Kennet Long Barrow and Silbury Hill from Avebury

From the Avebury stone circle, this walk goes along the Stone Avenue and up to the Ridgeway with its views of 'hedgehogs' and curious burial mounds. The route then visits The Sanctuary, the West Kennet Long Barrow and Silbury Hill burial ground.

❶ From the car park, follow the signs to Avebury village. At the road, turn right into the ring. Follow the ring round to the left. Cross the main road into the next part of the ring. Bear right and climb up onto the bank. Go down the other side towards a gate. Cross the road into the field. Walk down Stone Avenue between the stones.

❷ At the end of Stone Avenue go through a gate, cross the road, and follow the path opposite. Keeping on the same side of the hedge, cross into the next field. Follow the left-hand field edge slightly uphill to the next field boundary.

❸ Turn right on the track leading towards the 'hedgehogs', a clump of trees on the horizon. Follow the path as it bears left after the hedgehogs, then turn right and follow the Ridgeway down to cross the main road.

❹ Visit The Sanctuary on the right, then follow the path signed 'Byway', directly opposite the end of the Ridgeway. Just before the path turns left and crosses a bridge, turn right and follow the path alongside the river to a road.

access information

Avebury lies halfway between Marlborough and Calne, just off the A4. The National Trust provides a free car park just before reaching Avebury village on the A4361. Buses are available from Devizes, Marlborough and Swindon (Wiltshire Bus Line, 0845 7090899).

A fine aerial view of Avebury village. Strong shadows throw the ancient stone circle into relief.

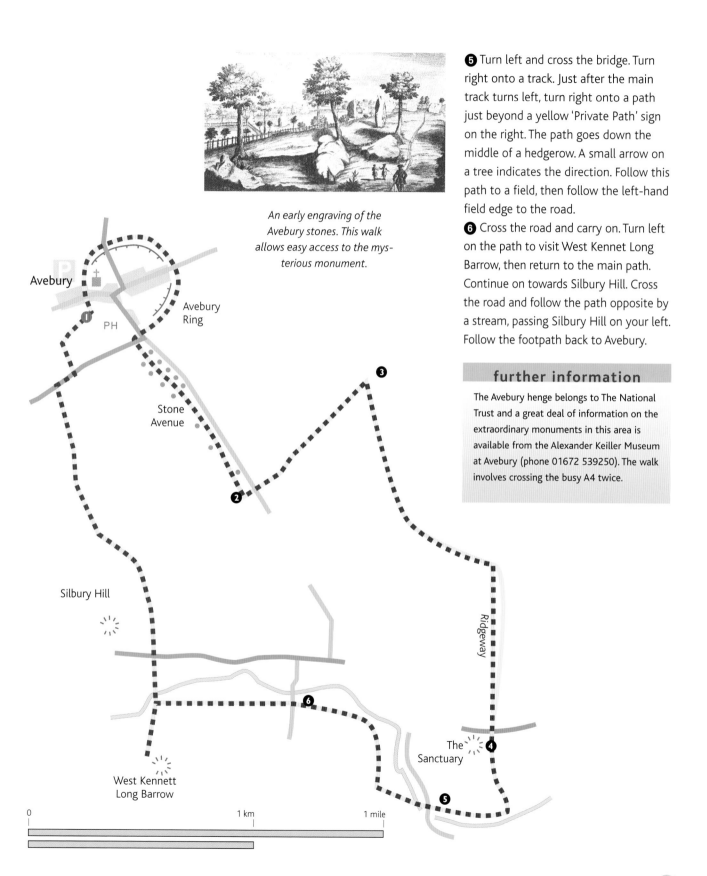

An early engraving of the Avebury stones. This walk allows easy access to the mysterious monument.

5 Turn left and cross the bridge. Turn right onto a track. Just after the main track turns left, turn right onto a path just beyond a yellow 'Private Path' sign on the right. The path goes down the middle of a hedgerow. A small arrow on a tree indicates the direction. Follow this path to a field, then follow the left-hand field edge to the road.

6 Cross the road and carry on. Turn left on the path to visit West Kennet Long Barrow, then return to the main path. Continue on towards Silbury Hill. Cross the road and follow the path opposite by a stream, passing Silbury Hill on your left. Follow the footpath back to Avebury.

further information

The Avebury henge belongs to The National Trust and a great deal of information on the extraordinary monuments in this area is available from the Alexander Keiller Museum at Avebury (phone 01672 539250). The walk involves crossing the busy A4 twice.

Avebury

Avebury Ring

PH

Stone Avenue

Silbury Hill

West Kennett Long Barrow

The Sanctuary

Ridgeway

0   1 km   1 mile

▲ Map: Explorer 135	Difficulty rating	Time
▲ Distance: 9.5 km/6 miles		
▲ Walk ID: 1076 Matthew Mayer		

▲ Lake, Pub, Toilets, Birds, Food Shop, Public Transport, Tea Shop, Woodland

Horsted Keynes to Sheffield Park

This walk starts at the Bluebell Railway station at Horsted Keynes. The route passes through this pretty village, then through woods and farmland, following part of the West Sussex Border Path, to Sheffield Park station. Return in style by steam train.

1 From the station, turn left. Follow the road behind the car park. Take the first right turn towards wooden gates. Go through the kissing gates alongside, and down a wooded path. Climb a stile and follow the footpath to another stile. At the road, turn left and cross over. Walk up the drive of Leamlands Barn.

2 Go through the metal gate and turn right. At the field boundary, cross into the next field and follow the path around to the left and over a stile. At a crossroads, follow the footpath straight on. Cross a small bridge, then three more bridges to a track. Turn right, passing a lake.

3 At the crossroads, follow the red arrow across the fields, climbing a stile. At the road, turn right. Go straight across at the junction. Cross the main road in Horsted Keynes. Fork left down Chapel Lane. Cross to Wyatts Lane. Follow the West Sussex Border Path through a small wood and up a hill. Turn left along the Border Path.

4 Turn right along the rough road to a T-junction. Fork left to reach the main road. Turn right, then left towards Kidborough Farm. Fork right at the 'No Horses' sign. Follow the field edge. Go through the wood and cross two fields to a road. Turn right, then left after Town Place. Follow the left-hand field edge. Cross a stile and bridge and turn right.

5 Follow a footpath sign across the railway bridge. Cross the field to a stile. Cross two more stiles to the road. Turn left and then left again to Bacon Wish. Cross a stile. Follow the marked West Sussex Border Path through the wood.

6 Passing the main path to the right, follow another yellow arrow right, down the slope. Cross a stile and turn left along the field edge, crossing to skirt the next wood. Cross another stile. Turn right across the grass through the wooden gate. Fork left at the road to the main road. Turn left to Sheffield Park station.

further information

The Bluebell Railway uses original steam locomotives to give today's visitors a taste of the Age of Steam. From Sheffield Park, it is possible to return to Horsted Keynes for about £4. If you are planning to travel on the Bluebell Railway, check the timetable by phoning 01825 722370 (24 hours) or visit www.bluebell-railway.co.uk.

A truly spectacular view across a reflective lily pond to the imposing Sheffield Park.

Horsted Keynes Station

Horsted Keynes

PH

Wyatts

West Sussex Border Path

Kidborough Farm

Town Place

PH

Sheffield Park

A rare treat for everyone: the age of steam revisited on the Bluebell Railway that runs from Sheffield Park to Horsted Keynes stations.

0   1 km   1 mile

▲ Map: Explorer 123
▲ Distance: 6.44 km/4 miles
▲ Walk ID: 590 Martin Heaps

Difficulty rating

Time

▲ Sea, Pub, Toilets, National Trust/NTS, Great Views

East Dean Round

This is an easy walk on grassy downland paths and farm tracks. There are wonderful views from the start of the walk over Eastbourne and further east towards Pevensey Marshes and Hastings, and later from Went Hill.

1 From the bus stop, follow the well-defined grassy path, which starts near by, towards the sea. When the triangulation point comes into view with the dew pond near by, bear right towards the road and keep to the right.

2 Cross the road carefully and go through the gate on the far side. Follow the path, which can get muddy, past Crapham Down and into East Hale Bottom, passing a pumping station. Walk on through the next gate and past a group of farm buildings to join a concrete track at Cornish Farm.

3 Follow the track round to the left, heading towards Belle Tout, a disused lighthouse now converted to a residential home. When you reach the road, cross over to join the path and turn right towards Birling Gap.

4 When the road alongside turns almost back on itself to the right, walk on through the car park towards the toilet block, and turn left onto the stony track. Follow the track as it bears right up Went Hill.

5 Where the path forks left, turn right downhill towards East Dean. The path bears right to a gate, then passes several houses and becomes a narrow road. The road emerges on the village green.

6 Facing the Tiger Inn, walk to the left and onto the main road. At the road, turn right and then left when you reach Downsview Lane. This track runs parallel to the road through the golf course and back to the start of the walk.

further information

The energetic can access the start point from the town centre along the A259 towards Brighton. The climb up East Dean Hill can be somewhat taxing, but is certainly rewarding for the views.

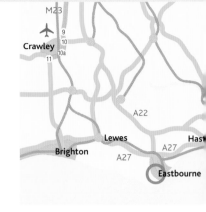

access information

The start and end point is easily accessible from Eastbourne town centre, with a bus stop only a short distance away.

0   1 km   1 mile

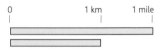

Glimpses of the evocative chalk hills of the South Downs are to be enjoyed on the coastal part of the journey.

▲ Map: Explorer 121

▲ Distance: 8.5 km/5¼ miles

▲ Walk ID: 75 Nicholas Rudd-Jones

Difficulty rating

Time

▲ Hills, Pub, Church, National Trust/NTS, Wildlife, Birds, Great Views, Woodland

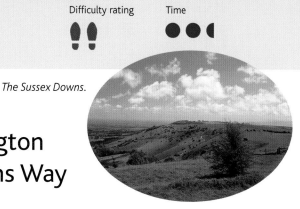

The Sussex Downs.

Sutton, Barlavington and South Downs Way

This varied walk climbs to the top of the South Downs, where there are great views of the Downs and the south coast. Much of the walk follows lovely woodland paths.

1 From the car park, walk up through the gate and alongside the stone wall. Turn right through the gate, climb the stone steps and turn right behind the building. Cross the garden to the kissing gate. Cross the field diagonally left to the far edge. Follow the grassy path straight ahead. At the meadow corner, walk straight ahead though the woods.

2 Cross a stream and a stile. Turn right towards a gate. Climb a stile and turn left to Barlavington. Turn left along the track. Go through gates into the churchyard and out at the far side. Follow the road round to the left. At the junction, follow the bridleway uphill and into the woods, swinging left. At a small bench, follow the chalky right-hand path. Leave the woods and turn left.

3 At the crossroads, follow the path uphill across the field. Go through the gate, the woods and another gate, then between fields to more woods. At the next junction, turn right uphill, then immediately left uphill. At the blue waymark, join the track uphill to the left. Keep left, following the National Trust sign to the Bignor Hill car park. Walk downhill past the 'Roman Villa' sign.

4 Turn left on a steep signposted footpath. Later, join a track to the right then immediately turn left, leaving the woods. Follow the field edge, climb a stile, and cross the fields. Ignore a yellow waymarked stile and swing right along the track into woods. Pass a house on your left and at the road turn left to walk into Bignor.

5 Go through the gate to the left of the next house and follow the path into woods. Cross a footbridge. Follow the path to another footbridge. Bear right at the footpath sign. Cross a footbridge and a stile. Head for the footpath sign across the meadow then uphill to a stile. Cross the field to Sutton. Follow the path between trees back to the pub.

access information

Sutton lies between the A285 Petworth to Chichester road and the A29 Pulborough to Bognor Regis road. Parking is available at the White Horse Pub in Sutton (patrons only, so if you park here it is necessary to patronize at some point).

further information

There is much evidence of the area's long history along this route, which passes several tumuli and a Neolithic camp. At Bignor, there are the remains of a Roman villa. The raised bank crossing the track at Step 3 is Stane Street, a Roman road.

▲ Map: Explorer 145
▲ Distance: 12.1 km/7½ miles
▲ Walk ID: 67 Liz and David Fishlock

Difficulty rating

Time

▲ River, Pub, Toilets, Museum, Play Area, Wildlife, Birds

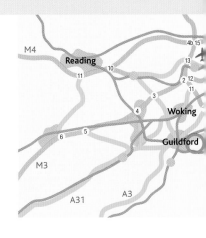

Netley Heath and Shere from Newlands Corner

This walk has two sections. The first follows the North Downs Way for 5 km/3 miles through woodland, while the second crosses open grassland before the final ascent back to the start. If you have time, explore Shere village on the River Tillingbourne.

1 From the car park, walk back towards the road, then follow the North Downs Way off to the right, signposted with a blue arrow. Cross the road, then follow the path ahead. At the West Hangar car park, carry on ahead to meet a minor road. Turn right, then fork left on a path leading to a surfaced track. Bear left to a junction of tracks.

2 Turn left, passing a house and stables. At a crossing track, carry on ahead through the woods, to a junction of tracks by a bench marked Gravelhill Gate. Turn right, leaving the North Downs Way, to pass Colekitchen Farm.

3 At the top of the hill, follow a bridleway on your right near a white 'Private Drive' sign. Near the top of the hill, soon after a left-hand path, fork left through wooden barriers. Follow the path round to the left and down to cross the main road. Turn left, then right into Queen Street.

4 Turn right into Gravelpits Lane. At Gravelpits Farmhouse, follow the path to the right of the house. At a crossing track, turn right to Shere. Turn left into the village. Turn right, then left into Lower Street. Follow the road round to the right, crossing a ford.

5 Turn left on an enclosed footpath beside the Old Rectory wall. Cross the lane and carry on. Go through a kissing gate. Cross the field and walk through the wood. Cross a stile. Follow the left-hand field edge, then walk ahead to a stile. Follow the track to a road. Cross over and follow the right-hand field edge. Cross a stile into woodland. Where the path emerges, cross a driveway. Continue straight ahead.

6 Cross a stile to the right of Timbercroft and carry on ahead. When you reach cottages, follow a track to the right of the driveway down to a T-junction. Turn right. Follow this main track to turn left at a bridleway sign back to the car park.

further information

The North Downs Way is some 240 km long and travellers have used this ancient track since the Stone Age. To read about the flora and fauna associated with the chalk hills of the North Downs, visit the Countryside Information Centre (open weekends and Bank Holidays) in the car park.

access information

Park at Newlands Corner, which is signposted on the A25 Guildford to Dorking road. If you are travelling by bus or train, start the walk at Step 4 after turning down Queen Street from the main A25. The route crosses the A25 close to the bus stop here, and Gomshall railway station is 5 minutes' walk away (exit the station and walk along the A25 towards Guildford).

This walk passes the exquisite Shere Church in the village of Shere.

The rolling countryside of the North Downs provides a beautiful backdrop for this lovely walk.

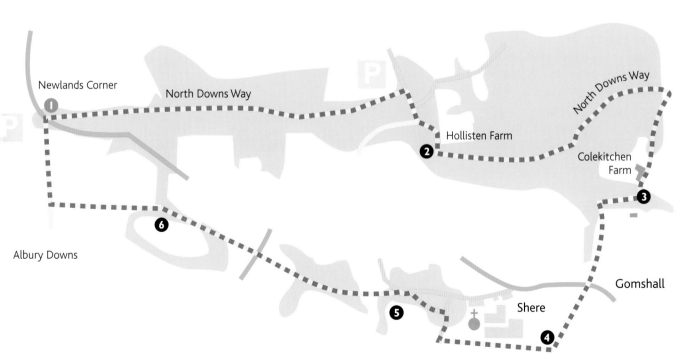

Newlands Corner

North Downs Way

North Downs Way

Hollisten Farm

2

Colekitchen Farm

3

Albury Downs

6

Gomshall

5

Shere

4

▲ Map: Explorer 124

▲ Distance: 8.5 km/5¼ miles

▲ Walk ID: 206 Jacky Rix-Brown

Difficulty rating

Time

▲ River, Sea, Toilets, Museum, Church, Castle, Wildlife, Birds, Flowers, Great Views

1066 Walk – Battle to Bexhill

This spur of the 1066 Walk from Pevensey to Rye via Battle takes you from Battle to Bexhill-on-Sea. It starts at Battle Abbey and heads south through rolling hills, the Fore Wood Nature Reserve and the village of Crowhurst on the way to Bexhill.

❶ From the Abbey, walk past the Pilgrim's Rest restaurant. At the track, follow the 1066 walk symbol. When the track divides, fork left to Bexhill, past the wood, over a hill and across a stream. Carry on, crossing a tarmacked track, and climb a stile to follow the path parallel to a road.

❷ Climb the stile and cross the road carefully to Talham Lane opposite. Fork right to Peppering Eye Farm and follow the path straight ahead up the hill. At the junction of paths near a cottage, fork left through the woods, following the 1066 symbol. Turn left downhill with the footpath. Cross the stream into another wood.

❸ Bend right on the main track and follow it through the wood. Just past a pond on the left, fork right to the stile at the edge of the wood. Follow the 1066 symbol across the field, bear left up the hill and continue to the road.

❹ Turn right to Crowhurst. Turn right, past the church, down the hill and follow the road through the village (keeping left at fork). Where the road bends sharp left, turn right over a stile to follow the footpath beside a stream.

❺ Just past Adam's Farm, follow the 1066 sign to the right. Follow the zigzag path to cross two bridges, then continue across the marshland to climb an inconspicuous stile. Continue beside the hedge, then across the field, converging

with the railway embankment. Cross the disused railway. Follow the track past Little Worsham Farm. Turn right at the T-junction, then left at another junction to Upper Worsham Farm.

❻ Where the tracks fork, climb a stile in between and follow the path, crossing a stream, to reach the A2036. Cross to follow a footpath between gardens to a road. Following the 1066 signs, turn left to the next junction, then right along a road leading to a footpath and bridge which crosses the A259 and continues to a road leading to the car park.

access information

Battle lies at the junction of the A271 with the A2100 between Hastings and Hailsham. Bexhill is on the A259. Parking is difficult in Battle, so it is easier to start in the car park in Bexhill, where the walk ends, and catch the no. 328 bus from Town Hall Square to Battle (for information, phone Traveline 0870 6082608). Bexhill is on the railway line between Hastings and Eastbourne, and Battle is on the main Hastings to London line, but not all trains stop there.

further information

The 1066 walk commemorates the Battle of Hastings, where William the Conqueror famously defeated King Harold on Senlac Hill. There are plenty of places of interest to visit along the walk, including Battle Abbey, the ancient church and centuries-old yew tree in Crowhurst and the museum and ruins of a manor in Bexhill.

Battle Abbey was built on the site of the defining battle between William the Conqueror and King Harold.

0   1 km   1 mile

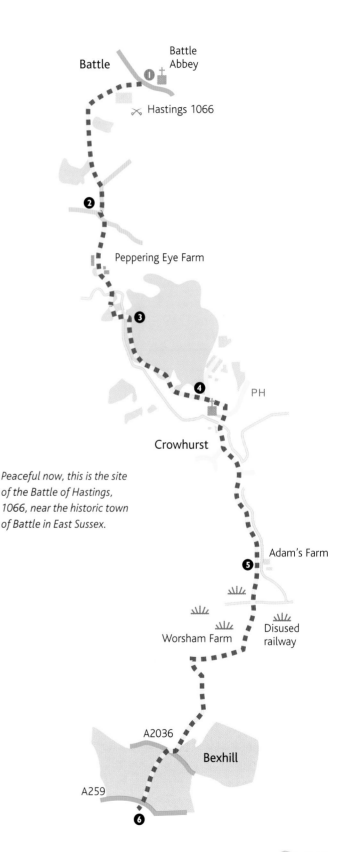

Peaceful now, this is the site of the Battle of Hastings, 1066, near the historic town of Battle in East Sussex.

▲ Map: Explorer 133
▲ Distance: 9.02 km/5½ miles
▲ Walk ID: 1289 Ray Clarke

Difficulty rating

Time

▲ Toilets, Wildlife, Flowers, Great Views, Café

Butser Hill Trail

This is a satisfying walk, which gets the heart pumping as you climb the hill. Look for birds, rabbits, sheep, the occasional fox, flowers and fine views of the South Downs. On a clear day, you can see as far as the Isle of Wight.

1 From the car park, return to the entrance and walk under the bridge beneath the main road.

2 After a short distance, cross the car park access road at the fingerpost sign and follow the blue horseshoe signs. Go through a gate and follow the path up the hill, passing between two belts of woodland and heading roughly in the direction of the radio mast. Go through a gate halfway up.

3 Carry on through another gate and bear round to the left towards a small circular building that resembles an Iron Age house. Follow the road past the building and out of the car park, passing the pay-and-display meter. After a short distance, turn right to follow a broad track down the hill. Where the track forks at Butser Hill, bear left, passing woodland on your right. The track bears right and left, passing Leythe House on the right to reach a lane.

4 Turn right along the lane. When you reach a crossroads with the Ramsdean road signposted to the left, follow the track to the right.

5 After a short distance, climb a stile on the left and follow the track, passing first through woodland then climbing up the spine of the hill, heading just to the right of the radio mast. Continue along the path until you meet the road back to the car park.

6 Cross straight over the road, then turn left and retrace your steps through the gate and back down the hill to the first gate. Return to the car park.

This breathtaking view across the ancient countryside of Hampshire is from Butser Hill near Petersfield.

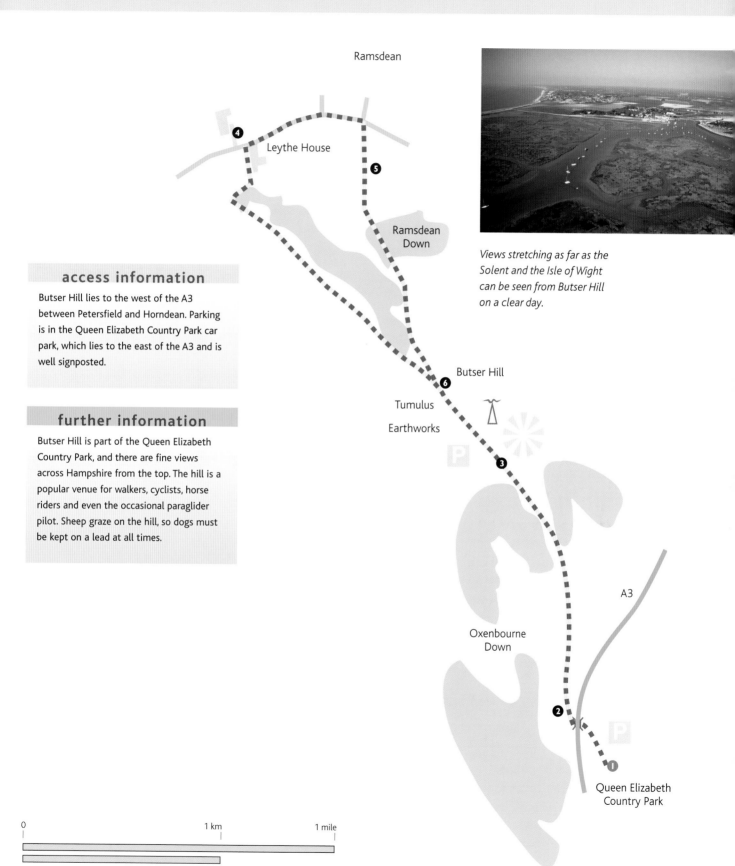

Ramsdean

4

Leythe House

5

Ramsdean
Down

*Views stretching as far as the
Solent and the Isle of Wight
can be seen from Butser Hill
on a clear day.*

access information

Butser Hill lies to the west of the A3
between Petersfield and Horndean. Parking
is in the Queen Elizabeth Country Park car
park, which lies to the east of the A3 and is
well signposted.

further information

Butser Hill is part of the Queen Elizabeth
Country Park, and there are fine views
across Hampshire from the top. The hill is a
popular venue for walkers, cyclists, horse
riders and even the occasional paraglider
pilot. Sheep graze on the hill, so dogs must
be kept on a lead at all times.

Butser Hill

6

Tumulus

Earthworks

3

A3

Oxenbourne
Down

2

1

Queen Elizabeth
Country Park

0   1 km   1 mile

▲ Map: Explorer 192

▲ Distance: 8.86 km/5½ miles

▲ Walk ID: 1122 Tony Brotherton

Difficulty rating

Time

▲ Hills, Lake, Pub, Toilets, Play Area, Church, Stately Home, Wildlife, Birds, Flowers, Great Views, Butterflies, Food Shop

Around Woburn

This is a gentle circular walk from the village of Woburn, crossing the Bedford Estate with its deer park, then looping around through farmland on the Greensand Ridge Walk to return across the park with a fine view of the glorious Woburn Abbey.

1 From the car park, turn right down Park Street. Take the signposted footpath immediately right after the lodge. Follow the drive through Park Farm and over staggered cross-paths to walk to the left of the water. Walk diagonally left across the parkland to a small rise. At the vehicle entrance to Woburn, walk downhill to the estate gates.

2 Fork right towards Milton Bryan. At Hills End Cottages, turn left on the footpath. Climb the stile and cross the field to an orange-topped waymark post. Keep ahead, and at the next post turn right. Cross a footbridge and cross the next field straight ahead. Cross a stile to a gravel drive leading to a lane.

3 Turn left past Helford House, then turn right on a footpath. Follow the left-hand field edge to a hedged path. Follow the right-hand hedge in the next field. After the next waymark post, turn right and follow the Greensand Ridge Walk to the road at Church End, Eversholt.

4 Walk through the village. At the T-junction, turn right. Just before the road bends, turn right through a gate and follow the Greensand Ridge Walk sign diagonally across the field. Cross a stream at a double stile to reach cross-paths and a signpost, with the lake on your right.

5 Follow the Greensand Ridge Walk, crossing the stream again, to a stile. Follow the path across a field and through trees, then uphill through a plantation. The path continues uphill and into the deer park, then downhill to a path junction after the Abbey entrance.

6 Keep ahead. At the crossing track, continue ahead on a narrow causeway between ponds and cross the parkland, following occasional small posts. Go through a gate at the corner of the woods to a fenced path to the road ahead. Turn right to Woburn village, then right into Park Street to the car park.

When walking through Woburn Park, look out for herds of deer or an encounter with the occasional shy lone animal.

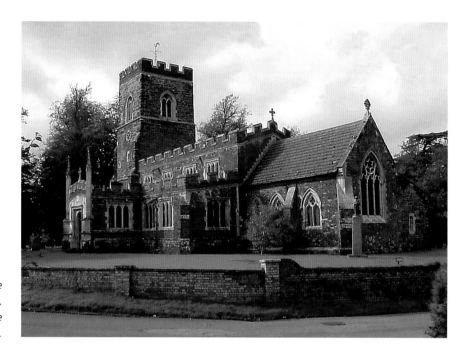

About halfway round the walk, the route passes Church End, Eversholt, before striking out towards the Greensand Ridge Walk.

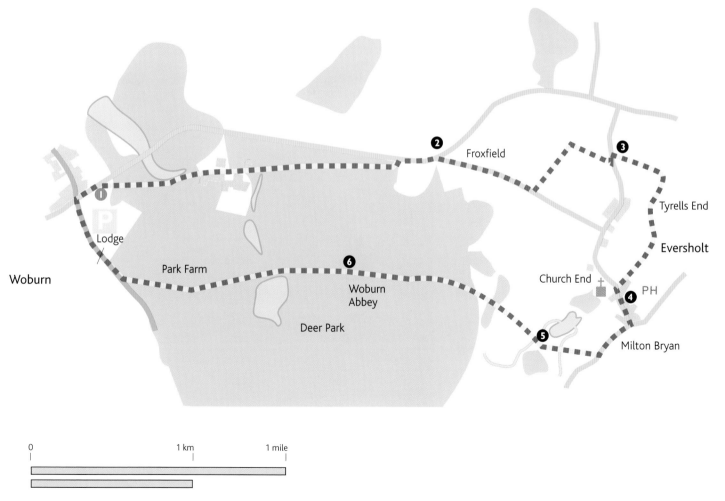

▲ Map: Explorer 180

▲ Distance: 8.45 km/5¼ miles

▲ Walk ID: 1234 Ron and Jenny Glynn

Difficulty rating

Time

▲ Lake, Church, Stately Home, Wildlife, Birds, Flowers, Great Views, Butterflies, Woodland

Wotton Underwood from Ludgershall

This gentle walk begins in Ludgershall and wanders through Buckinghamshire on a mixture of footpaths, bridleways and quiet country roads. The route passes through the beautiful parkland surrounding the magnificent Wotton House.

1 Take the minor road, just before the church at Peartree Farm, signed to Wotton, and walk along to the junction. Walk over to the narrow path at Wotton End, and follow the hedge line to cross a brook. Fork right over common ground to an opening.

2 Walk past the stile on the left at a junction of paths, and follow the left-hand hedge in ridge and furrow meadowland. Climb a stile and cross the next two fields, with woodland over to the left. Cross a double stile and footbridge. Turn right on a bridleway, with the hedge on your right. Go through a walkers' gate and then another gate.

3 Cross the road and another stile. Cross a large field, with farm buildings on your right, gradually climbing uphill. Head slightly right over two stiles. Climb a stile in the corner of the field to a hard track. Walk over and cross the stile to the left of the white gate to Middle Farm. Follow the field edge until you reach a metal kissing gate.

4 Turn right through a wooden gate and pass the back of a farmhouse to a hard path, passing through a wild flower meadow and crossing a miniature railway track. Pass a red-brick house, then turn right through a gate to walk by Wotton House. The path runs downhill.

5 Walk ahead over a large green to join the road, and follow it along between trees and hedgerows. Turn right past Lawn Farm. Just before the railway, fork right towards Ludgershall and Kingswood on a narrow road through woodland.

6 At the junction at the end of the woodland, follow the lane ahead to Ludgershall. Turn left into Church Lane, and retrace your steps to the start.

After Middle Farm the walk passes the grandiose Wotton House, in Wotton Underwood, seen here with the 'ha-ha' in the foreground.

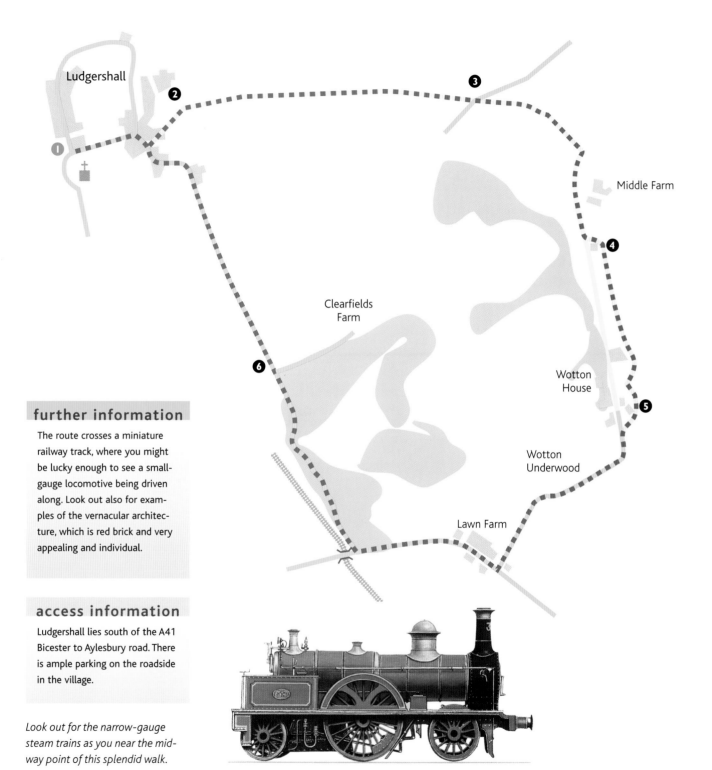

Ludgershall

❶

❷

❸

Middle Farm

❹

Clearfields
Farm

Wotton
House

❺

❻

Wotton
Underwood

Lawn Farm

further information

The route crosses a miniature
railway track, where you might
be lucky enough to see a small-
gauge locomotive being driven
along. Look out also for examples of the vernacular architecture, which is red brick and very
appealing and individual.

access information

Ludgershall lies south of the A41
Bicester to Aylesbury road. There
is ample parking on the roadside
in the village.

*Look out for the narrow-gauge
steam trains as you near the mid-
way point of this splendid walk.*

0   1 km   1 mile

Difficulty rating

Time

▲ Pub, Birds, Flowers, Great Views

Windmill Walk from Parslows Hillock

This is a flat, open walk with just one steep climb in the final stages. The Pink and Lily pub at the start was a favourite haunt of the World War I poet, Rupert Brooke. Allow extra time to visit the windmill at Lacey Green, believed to date from 1650.

access information

From the A4010 Aylesbury to High Wycombe Road, turn into a road called Woodhay, about 750 m/820 yards from the southern outskirts of Princes Risborough (on your right if you are heading towards Princes Risborough, or left if you are leaving Princes Risborough). Follow the road to the cross-roads at the Whip Inn, then turn left into Pink Road. Park in the lay-by on the left, just before the Pink & Lily pub.

① Walk past the pub and down Lily Bottom Lane to Hillock Cottages. Turn right up the Chiltern Way, then climb a right-hand stile and cross the field diagonally left. Cross the stile and the field towards a gate. Climb another stile and follow the fenced path, ignoring a farm track and a stile on your right.

② Climb the next stile and cross the field diagonally right. Climb another stile. At the hedgerow corner, follow the right-hand field edge. Cross another stile and follow the right-hand field edge. Cross a stile and a field to the main road. Turn right, then right into Pink Road.

③ Cross the road at Widmer Farm and climb the stile. Cross the field. Before the power line pole, climb a stile on your right. Turn left, then cross another stile on your right and turn left. Go under the power lines and cross another stile. Follow the left-hand field edge.

④ Cross the corner stile and turn right. Cross a stile and walk down to the road. Turn right. Cross to Wardrobes Lane. Cross the stile and the field corner. Cross a stile, and bear diagonally left. Cross a stile and follow the right-hand field edge. Carry on, crossing the farm drive.

⑤ Where the field edge bears right, go straight ahead. At the rise, carry on across two stiles, a field and a stile. Go under the power lines, then follow the left-hand field edge. Just before the wood on your left, turn right across the field. Cross a stile. Turn left along the lane, then right at the road.

⑥ At the right bend, turn left over a stile. Walk to another stile. Follow the left-hand field edge to a stile into the wood. Follow the steep path up through the wood, then turn right on a crossing track. Exit through a gate. Turn left along the driveway, then right at the road to the start.

The fascinating windmill at Lacey Green.

▲ Map: Explorer 192
▲ Distance: 5 km/3 miles
▲ Walk ID: 237 Gill Perkins

Difficulty rating

Time

▲ Hills, Pub, Church, Wildlife, Birds, Great Views

A breathtaking viewpoint.

Quainton Hill

Although fairly short, this circular walk is very rewarding, beginning in the unspoilt village of Quainton, then climbing to the top of Quainton Hill for panoramic views of the Chilterns, the Cotswolds and north Buckinghamshire.

❶ From the entrance to St Mary's Church, walk downhill, with the church on your right, for a short distance to cross two stiles into a field. Walk straight ahead to the next stile in the hedge. The footpath is marked Matthew's Way and Swan's Way.

❷ Climb the stile and cross to the gate in the hedge. Go through the gate and follow the track up the hill towards a telecommunications mast, going through another gate halfway up.

❸ From the top of the hill, with the mast on your right, go through a gate straight ahead and follow the path downhill. Go through another gate and immediately turn left. Continue ahead to climb a stile. Walk through some rough land for a short distance, then cross another stile onto open rolling hills.

❹ Walk across the hills, following the grassy track which runs parallel to the hedge on your left. Climb another stile

further information

Quainton Windmill, built around 1830 with bricks made on the site, is 20 m/60 ft high and has six floors. It is occasionally open to the public (for information, phone local Tourist Information). St Mary's Church in Quainton contains monuments to various famous people. The market cross at the top of the green dates from the 15th century.

access information

Quainton lies north of the A41 between Aylesbury and Bicester. Car parking is available either in Church Street by the almshouses, or anywhere around the church. Trains between Aylesbury and London run frequently. Bus nos. 16, 17 and 18 run from Aylesbury to Quainton every day except Sunday (for information, go to www.pindar.co.uk/bucks/tt/ayndx.htm).

at a junction of paths, and continue ahead on the track. As you walk over the hills, you see Quainton Windmill and the village ahead of you.

❺ When you reach a stile next to a gate, climb the stile. If you like, climb the hill to enjoy the views, then walk back down to continue. Turn left to follow the path round the base of the hill and towards the village rooftops, with the windmill on your left, to a kissing gate.

❻ Cross the sleeper bridge through the gate and pass down a narrow track between two houses to the village. Turn left on Lower Street and walk towards the village green. Walk along the top of the village green, then continue walking down Church Street to return to your car.

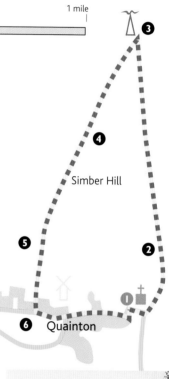

A spectacular reward for the short climb to the top of Quainton Hill – the Chilterns in all their glory.

Central England

Coastal & Waterside

The waterside walks of Central England embrace Norfolk's shores and marshes, Cambridgeshire fens and Oxford's tow-paths. Highlights include Ludham Marshes, Houghton Mill and Calcutt Locks.

▲ Map: Explorer 25
▲ Distance: 9.66 km/6 miles
▲ Walk ID: 812 Stephanie Kedik

Difficulty rating

Time

▲ Hills, Cliffs, Sea, Pub, Toilets,
National Trust/NTS, Birds, Great Views,
Gift Shop, Food Shop, Nature Trail,
Tea Shop, Woodland

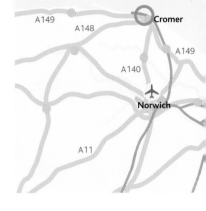

East and West Runton

This is a walk of great variety, centred around a beautiful part of the North Norfolk coast. The route takes in the pretty village of East Runton, beaches, woodland paths and stunning views from Beeston Regis cliffs.

❶ From the car park, turn right and go down to the beach. Turn left and walk along the beach, past a curious pointed rock formation, to some steep wooden steps. Climb the steps to the cliff top, turn right and walk across the camp site towards 'Beeston Bump'. Alternatively, follow the detour described in 'further information'.

❷ Leaving the camp site, turn left and follow the National Trail 'acorn' sign down a grassy track and across the level crossing. Cross the main road and take the lane to your left, towards 'The Roman Camp'. Follow the lane, which turns from shingle to dirt track, through Hall Farm and up to the woods.

❸ At the woods, turn left at the 'Beeston Regis Heath' sign. Where the track forks, follow the 'Coast Path' sign

further information

If you wish to avoid the steep steps in step 1, walk further along the beach to Sheringham. As you leave the beach and enter the town, head back along the cliff, over the hill called 'Beeston Bump', and reconnect with the walk at Step 2. This detour will add about 30–45 minutes to the walk. At high tide, the beach area can be stony, so walking shoes, or walking at low tide, are recommended. For tidal information, phone Cromer Tourist Information, 01263 512497.

through a gate. Take the small footpath through the woods and go through another gate. At the junction, carry on through the woods, along a shingle track and past a caravan park. Carry on, following the larger shingle road round to your left.

❹ At a road junction, go straight across and take the 'acorn' path to your left. Pass a caravan site entrance and follow the bridleway to your right. At a junction of paths, take the bridleway towards Cromer. Go through a kissing gate, along the side of a field, through another gate and over a stream.

❺ Across the track, turn right, following the Coastal Path 'acorn' sign. Ignoring the two entrances to fields, take the small wooded track in the centre. Follow this through the trees to a farm track corner. Go straight down this track.

❻ At the junction with the road, turn left towards East Runton, past the village green and duck pond and round to your right. Continue under the viaducts and past the village sign. At the junction with the A149, turn right, cross over, and go down Beach Road to the car park.

access information

The Bittern Line runs from Norwich to the coast via Cromer and finishes at Sheringham, and also has an accessible station at West Runton (for information, phone Anglia Railways 01473 693333).

By car, West Runton can be reached via the A140 from Norwich/A149 coast road. The walk begins at a pay-and-display car park that operates every day, all year round.

For information on buses, phone Norfolk Bus Information on 0845 300 6116, or Traveline on 0870 6082608.

The imposing cliffs and grey waters of the North Norfolk coast provide the backdrop to a section of this varied walk.

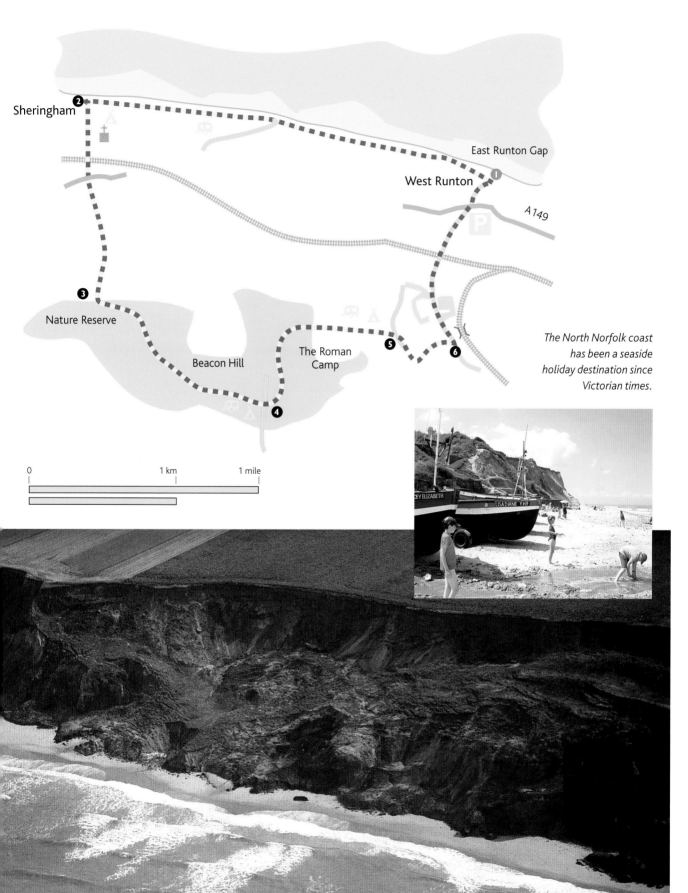

Sheringham

East Runton Gap

West Runton

A149

Nature Reserve

Beacon Hill

The Roman
Camp

*The North Norfolk coast
has been a seaside
holiday destination since
Victorian times.*

0   1 km   1 mile

▲ Map: Explorer OL 40
▲ Distance: 5.5 km/3½ miles
▲ Walk ID: 800 Stephanie Kedik

Difficulty rating

Time

▲ River, Pub, Toilets, Play Area, Church, Wildlife, Birds, Flowers, Butterflies, Gift Shop, Food Shop, Good for Kids, Nature Trail, Tea Shop

Ludham Marshes

access information

Ludham can be reached by car from Norwich (A1151/A1062) or by bus (for information, phone Norfolk Bus Information on 0845 300 6116 or Traveline on 0870 6082608).

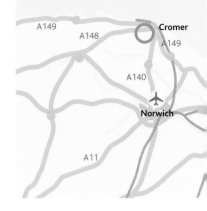

This picturesque stroll starts in the beautiful village of Ludham and takes in Ludham Marshes Nature Reserve. Renowned for their abundance of wildlife, the marshes sit alongside the River Thurne, where boatyards are dotted along the banks.

❶ From the centre of Ludham, take the main Yarmouth Road past the Ludham village sign at Bakers Arms Green. Further down, on the right, is a little path leading off and running alongside the road. Follow this until you reach a right turn where Horse Fen Road meets the Yarmouth Road.

❷ Turn right into Horse Fen Road. Continue along the lane, past Womack Water boat hire and camp site. Follow the public bridleway down on to Ludham Marshes National Nature Reserve.

❸ As you take the path round the corner and into the reserve, you will pass first a garden and then a wood on your left beyond the drainage ditch (deer are sometimes seen in the wood). On your right, the marshes stretch out across to the River Thurne. Follow the footpath through the reserve.

❹ Where you meet the gravel track, take a turn to the right through the gate (which says 'Danger – Unstable road!'). Continue along this track and go through another gate.

❺ When you reach Horse Fen pumping station, turn right to follow the green footpath sign. Across the bridge, follow the footpath along the river, keeping the river on your left. Although this stretch can be a bit overgrown in summer, it is compensated by the views of the river.

❻ Follow the footpath back from the river, up the creek, and out of the reserve at the side of Hunters Yard. Walk back up Horse Fen Road, past Womack Water and the boatyard. At the top of Horse Fen Road, turn left and follow the road leading back into Ludham village.

The marshes are renowned for their wildlife and provide a peaceful environment for sailors of small craft.

further information

In the summer months Ludham Marshes Nature Reserve buzzes with insects and butterflies, and there are many varieties of birds to be seen all year round. Deer are also sometimes spotted in the nearby wood. The undergrowth along the riverbank can grow quite high, so leg-covering is recommended. Boats can be hired by the day from the marina in the village.

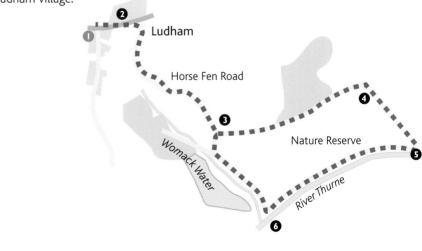

▲ Map: Explorer 23
▲ Distance: 8.86 km/5½ miles
▲ Walk ID: 810 J. and C. Boldero

Difficulty rating

Time

▲ Sea, Pub, Toilets, Churches,
Roman Fort, Wildlife, Birds, Flowers,
Great Views, Butterflies

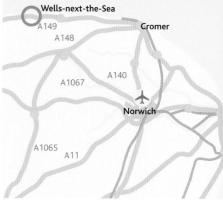

St Mary's Church, Burnham Deepdale.

Burnham Deepdale

This circular walk takes in part of the North Norfolk Coastal Path, passing tidal creeks with mussel beds and a wide variety of wading and sea birds. The return route passes the site of a 3rd-century Roman fort, then crosses Barrow Common.

1 Starting with the garage on your left, walk along the road for a very short distance, then turn right along a 'No Through Road'. Follow the signed footpath that runs between the trees. When you reach the finger signpost, turn left along the coastal path, with the creeks on your right. Follow this winding path to the end at Brancaster Staithe, where you pass between brick sheds by a cottage.

2 Turn left along the track, then almost immediately right, following the yellow arrow on the wall. Go along a narrow path between a fence and a brick wall, then through a gate. Follow the board walk to the end at Brancaster.

3 Turn left along a country lane, then at the main road turn left again by the church, with the Ship Inn opposite. Turn left along London Road, then right along the narrow lane just before the last house on the right (if you reach a footpath, you have gone too far). At the end of the lane, turn right along the gravel path, then left along a country lane, following the path round the site of the Roman fort.

4 When you reach the main road, cross it and turn left along the pavement, which is hidden between the grass and the hedge. Almost immediately, turn right up a wide, hedged track, and at the top turn right again along a grassy track.

5 Go through the gate onto Barrow Common, ignoring the path on the left. When you reach the open space, keep to the right-hand path, which later veers left with the wood on the right. At the country lane, turn right for a very short distance, then left along another country lane. At the T-junction in Burnham Deepdale, turn right to the lay-by and the start of the walk.

access information

There is a coastal bus route (for more information, phone 0845 3006116 or Traveline on 0870 6082608). There is parking in the long lay-by opposite the garage and by the church at Burnham Deepdale, which is situated on the A149, 11.25 km west of Wells-next-the-Sea in North Norfolk.

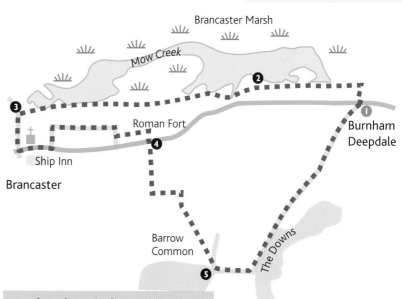

further information

Burnham Deepdale Church has an Anglo-Saxon tower and a font with a Norman bowl. At St Mary's in Brancaster, look out for a carving of a man with his head at a very strange angle. Brancaster Staithe has been a fishing port since Roman times.

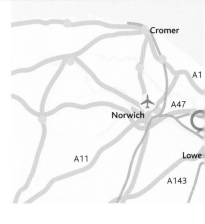

▲ Map: Explorer OL 40

▲ Distance: 12.08 km/7½ miles

▲ Walk ID: 1372 J. and C. Boldero

Difficulty rating

Time

▲ River, Pub, Toilets, Wildlife, Birds, Great Views, Food Shop

Halvergate Marshes

This walk through Halvergate Marshes follows tracks and crosses meadows, passing Breydon Water and running alongside the River Yare. The marshes have a unique and very special atmosphere, desolate in summer and even more so in winter.

❶ From where you parked your car, walk along the tarmac lane, which becomes a rough track. Follow the track as it winds along, going through gates and over stiles until you reach a concrete lane.

❷ Turn right along the concrete track marked 'Weavers Way' and continue to follow it to the railway crossing. Cross the lines with care. With the building on your right, keep right until you reach a stile and a notice board.

❸ Climb the stile and turn left along the bank, with Breydon Water on your left. Continue to follow the path, passing the Berney Arms pub and windmill on your right.

❹ At the windmill, turn right down the steps, climb the stile, and continue along the gravel path. Turn left to two white posts by the sign 'Railway Station'. Go through the gate and cross the meadow, aiming for the white gates ahead.

❺ At the railway station, cross the lines, then go through the gate, turn right over the stile, and turn left across the meadow. Continue across the meadows, going through or over the gates. The ditch is now on your right. When you reach the gate with a 'Weavers Way' sign on it, go through it.

❻ Go over the earth bridge on your right, then turn left along the grass track. Climb the stile and cross the meadows to the barriers ahead. Continue through

or over more gates and over another earth bridge. Climb the next stile and continue along the path heading towards the windmill, where the path goes left. Go through a small gate, and continue along the path. Go round to the stile, climb it, then turn left to return to your car.

access information

By car, from the A47 turn off to Halvergate 4 km/2½ miles east of Acle. At the right-hand bend, turn left at the Weavers Way sign along a tarmac lane, and park on the verge just after passing farm buildings. By train, go by Anglia Railways to Berney Arms station, and follow the walk route from Step 5 (for information, phone 0845 748 4950, a 24-hour service, or local call Norwich 01603 764776, open daily 8 a.m. to 10 p.m.).

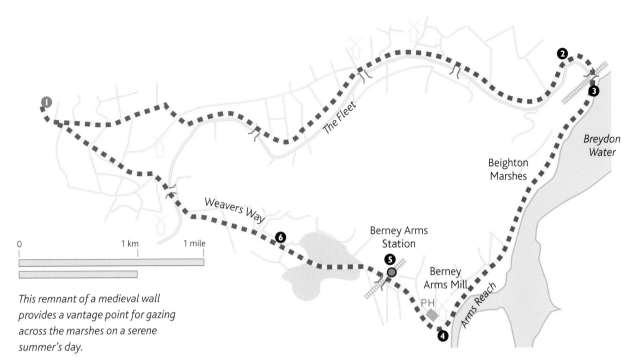

This remnant of a medieval wall provides a vantage point for gazing across the marshes on a serene summer's day.

This walk leads to the most charming riverside views along the River Yare.

further information

The Berney Arms windmill, built in the 1800s for the Berney family, is said to be the finest and tallest on the Broads, and is usually open to the public. Cattle and sheep graze on Halvergate Marshes, so dogs should be kept on leads.

Difficulty rating

Time

▲ Pub, Toilets, Play Area, National Trust/NTS, Wildlife, Birds, Flowers, Great Views, Accessible for Wheelchairs

Sizewell and Minsmere from Dunwich

This walk from Dunwich crosses heath and woodland, passing through Eastbridge before taking in the majestic forest of Sizewell Belts. An alternative is to visit the dazzling dome of the Sizewell Power Station, before returning via the seashore.

1 From the car park, go through the gap between the pine trees to the right of the toilets. Follow this wide track left over the heath (do not take the track which rises to the right). Continue until you enter woodland at a stile.

2 Climb the stile and continue in the same direction. At a T-junction of tracks, turn left. When you reach a narrow road, cross straight over and carry on, with fields to both sides of the track.

3 Enter more woodland and descend to meet another narrow road on a bend. Go straight ahead along the road, bearing left at a house. Cross the bridge over the Minsmere, and keep going, passing the Eel's Foot on your left.

4 Continue along the road to a footpath on the left, leading to an abandoned cottage. At the cottage, turn right along a broad track between hedges. Follow the track gently downhill, then up again.

5 At the belt of trees on your left, look for a wide gate and a stile. Climb the stile and follow the track through the left-hand edge of the trees. When the trees become denser on the left, you begin to descend slightly. At the bottom, bear right along the main track, following the black arrow on a post.

6 Continue, following two more black arrows close to each other. Another black arrow sends you right at a fork. The track suddenly veers left, away from the power station, and here you turn right at another black arrow. Go over two bridges and a wooden walkway. At the next black arrow, turn left and follow the path to the end of the mound on your right. At the large concrete blocks, turn left along a wide grass track. Follow this path, parallel to the sea, all the way back to the car park at Dunwich.

access information

Take the unclassified road eastwards off the A12, just north-east of Yoxford, signposted to Westleton/Dunwich. In Westleton, turn left along the B1125 signposted Blythburgh/ Dunwich, then after 100 m take the turn right signposted Minsmere/Dunwich. Follow signs to Dunwich Heath (right after the track to Mount Pleasant Farm on the right). Park in the National Trust car park.

further information

In addition to the visitor centre at Sizewell, there are plenty of places of interest in this area, including Dunwich Heath, owned by The National Trust; the small village of Dunwich, which was once a large and influential town and now lies mostly below the sea; and the renowned RSPB reserve at Minsmere.

The RSPB reserve at Minsmere, with its wide variety of birdlife, is an internationally famous site.

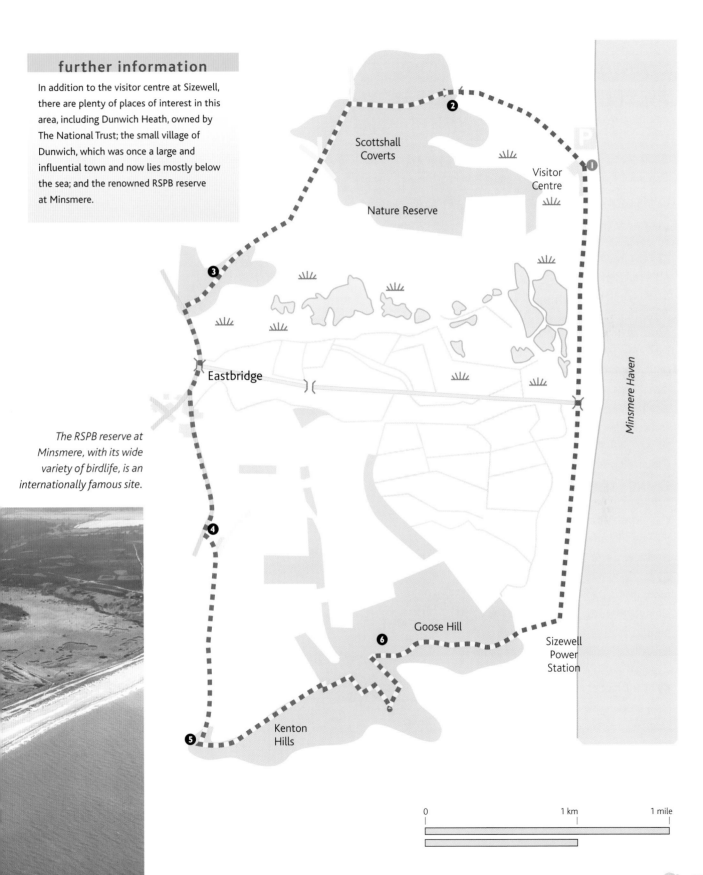

Scottshall Coverts

Visitor Centre

Nature Reserve

Minsmere Haven

Eastbridge

Goose Hill

Sizewell Power Station

Kenton Hills

0   1 km   1 mile

▲ Map: Explorer 212

▲ Distance: 11.27 km/7 miles

▲ Walk ID: 1359 B. and A. Sandland

Difficulty rating

Time

● ● ●

▲ Sea, Pub, Toilets, Museum, Play Area, Church, Castle, National Trust/NTS, Birds, Great Views, Good for Kids, Restaurant, Tea Shop, Ancient Monument

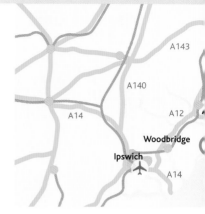

Orford and the Rivers Ore and Butley

This walk is perfect for experiencing the vastness of the sky and seascapes of East Anglia. There are superb views of Orford Ness and Havergate Island across the River Ore, and the route takes in a medieval castle at Orford.

❶ From the car park, walk to the quay, then turn right and soon bear right again. Climb the steps to the riverbank. Turn left and follow the path along the bank. When you reach the Butley River, turn inland with it, climbing another stile but still on the raised bank. Continue past the ferry landing then cross another stile near some huts. Soon after, descend to a track on your right.

❷ Carry on along the track with a paddock on your left, then a cottage on your right. The track then turns left and right. Continue to follow it, passing Gedgrave Hall on your left. Just before Richmond Farm, take the path to the left by the postbox.

❸ Just before the track bends to the right, take a signposted path right. After climbing the steps, enter a field. The path ahead crosses several fields, heading straight for Orford Castle. Cross a drive and continue ahead.

❹ At the castle, carry on to the road, then on the road head for the church. By the King's Head, go slightly left to enter the churchyard. Keeping the church porch on your left, go right to another gate and exit the churchyard, turning left on a road.

❺ Continue on this road to Brundish Lane. Follow Brundish Lane, bearing right

at a junction then turning right again at a T-junction after the Rectory on your left. Just before a large house with a high brick wall, turn left onto a signposted track.

❻ After the gate, follow the grass path which heads initially for the lighthouse. At the end of a deep ditch on the right, bear half right to cross a field. At the far side, cross a stile and climb steps to the river bank. Follow the path back to your starting point.

access information

From the A12 (London to Great Yarmouth), turn onto the A1152 at Woodbridge. Just after Wilford Bridge, take the B1084, signposted to Orford. In Orford, park in the pay-and-display car park near the quay.

The route provides superb views of Orford Ness across the River Ore.

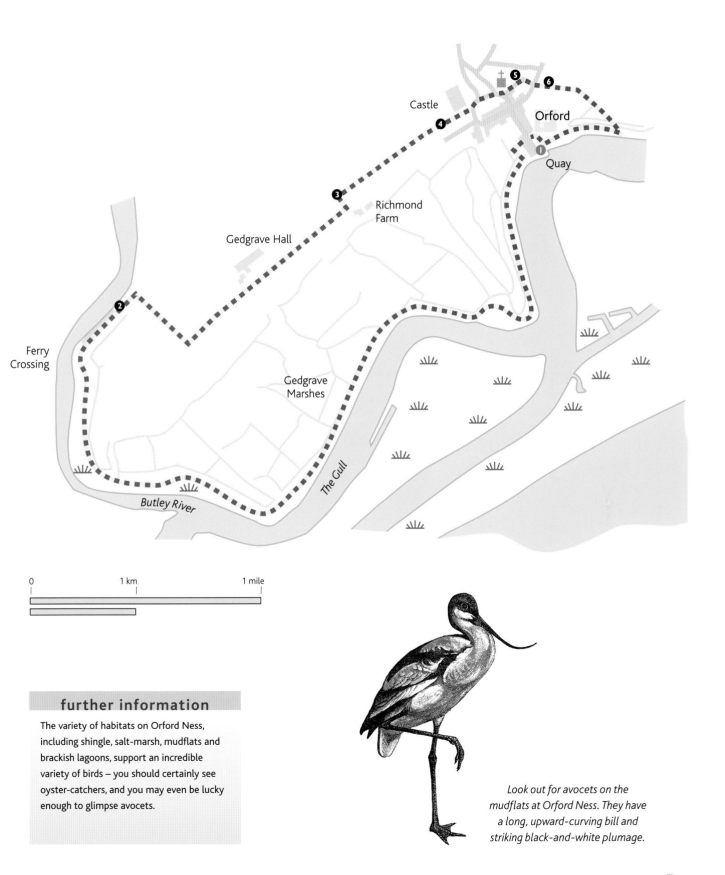

Castle

Orford

4

5

6

3

Richmond
Farm

Gedgrave Hall

Quay

1

2

Ferry
Crossing

Gedgrave
Marshes

The Gull

Butley River

0   1 km   1 mile

further information

The variety of habitats on Orford Ness,
including shingle, salt-marsh, mudflats and
brackish lagoons, support an incredible
variety of birds – you should certainly see
oyster-catchers, and you may even be lucky
enough to glimpse avocets.

*Look out for avocets on the
mudflats at Orford Ness. They have
a long, upward-curving bill and
striking black-and-white plumage.*

▲ Map: Explorer 225

▲ Distance: 9 km/5½ miles

▲ Walk ID: 106 Nicholas Rudd-Jones

Difficulty rating

Time

▲ River, Pub, Mill, National Trust Tea Room, Picnic Site, Nature Reserve, Museum, Good for Kids

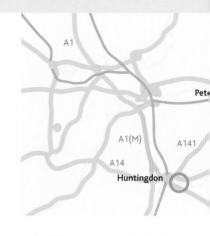

St Ives and Hemingford Grey from Hemingford Abbots

This is a charming riverside walk in the Cambridgeshire fens, taking in the delightful villages of Hemingford Abbots and Hemingford Grey as well as the historic town of St Ives. If time permits, there is a working flour mill and a nature reserve in an ancient osier bed to visit en route.

Twelfth-century Hemingford Grey Manor, reputedly one of the oldest continuously inhabited houses in Britain.

1 From the Axe and Compass pub, take the minor road to the left of the pub. Turn right at the postbox into Meadow Lane. Cross the bridge, then turn right, through the gate and across Hemingford meadow.

2 Cross the bridge over the lock, then turn left and over the rollers, heading right on the tarmac path. Turn left over a small bridge to Houghton Mill. Follow the Ouse Valley Way footpath sign. Go through the gates and turn right along the gravel path.

3 Passing the National Trust Tea Room on the right, follow the yellow waymarks across the field, past the caravan site. Carry on until you reach a kissing gate on your left. Go through, then turn right along the gravel path by a brick wall. At the junction, turn left and then right along a minor road.

further information

Houghton Mill is open weekends and bank holidays April–September, 2–5.30 p.m. Punts are available for hire at weekends 10 a.m.– 6 p.m. and weekdays during school holidays 2–6 p.m. For info, phone 01480 468184. Holt Island Nature Reserve is open on Sundays April–September 10.30 a.m.– 5 p.m. For info, phone 01480 388442.

❹ As the tarmac road swings left, take a small footbridge across the river and follow this road. Pass through St Ives thicket, emerging by the river. At the next junction, go straight ahead (signposted 'Ouse Valley Way'). The path continues through gardens, coming out opposite the church.

❺ Go through the churchyard and out via the iron gates. Follow the road to the Jubilee monument and fork right. Turn right at the end of the road and cross the town bridge. Take the first right turn, following the footpath to Hemingford Grey. Go through a gate and cross the meadows on the left-hand path.

❻ Go through the gate and join a track. Immediately, take the path to the left to join a road. At the next junction, take the footpath straight ahead. Turn right at the road, then left onto the footpath by the church. Follow the path back to the village. At the road, turn right and return to the Axe and Compass.

Houghton Mill is a major historic attraction along the route of this walk.

access information

Hemingford Abbots is just off the A14 from Huntingdon to Cambridge, between the junctions for Huntingdon and St Ives.

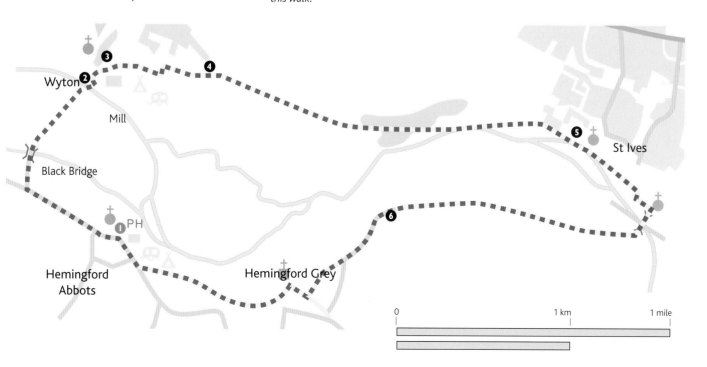

▲ Map: Explorer 227

▲ Distance: 10 km/6¼ miles

▲ Walk ID: 38 Nicholas Rudd-Jones

Difficulty rating

Time

▲ Steam Train, Country Park, Model Train Rides, Lake, River, Boat Trips in Summer, Toilets, Museum, Play Area, Wildlife, Birds, Flowers, Great Views

[Map showing roads: A1, A16, Market Deeping, A47, Pete[r], A605, A14, A1(M), Huntingdon]

Nene Valley Railway and Ferry Meadows

Take a nostalgic trip on the Nene Valley Railway, a preserved steam train running from Wansford to Ferry Meadows, then walk back to Wansford through an area of great historic interest, following the meandering River Nene.

❶ From the station, follow the platform towards the level crossing. Cross the road and take the path between the trees to the left. Follow the path by the driveway into Ferry Meadows Country Park. Walk either side of Overton Lake and cross the bridge at the far corner.

❷ Turn left at the junction and follow the path by Gunwade Lake. At the next junction, take the right path, bearing left by the river. Turn right over the ferry bridge. Immediately turn left, go through the gate and follow the path by the river.

❸ At the junction with Landy Green Way, continue alongside the river to the railway bridge. At the Nene Valley Railway bridge, take the steep path up to the railway track and cross over, back to the riverside path.

❹ The footpath is blocked here, so cross the first footbridge and return over the second. At the old mill follow Mill Road, turning left at the footpath sign onto a narrow fenced path. Climb the stile and follow the track beside the fence. Climb the next stile, and turn left across the field to the footbridge.

❺ Cross the bridge and the field to the right of the oxbow lake. Then follow the path by the river. Cross another bridge and pass a row of pollarded trees. Climb the stile and cross a third footbridge. Go past the bridge to Water Newton, pass the gate and stile and carry on.

❻ At a small weir, climb the stile waymarked 'Nene Way', and follow the edge of the field. At the corner, turn right towards the pylon. Climb the stile and follow the field edge, parallel to the railway track. Climb another stile and carry on. At Wansford station, go down the wooden steps, turn right and follow the path to the bridge.

The meandering course of the River Nene accompanies the walker along most of this route.

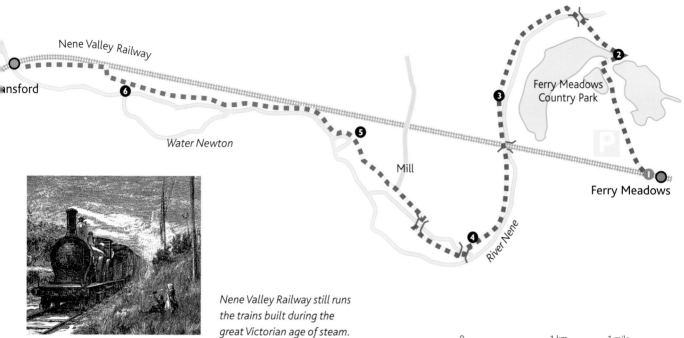

Nene Valley Railway

Wansford

Water Newton

Mill

Ferry Meadows
Country Park

River Nene

Ferry Meadows

Nene Valley Railway still runs the trains built during the great Victorian age of steam.

0   1 km   1 mile

▲ Map: Explorer 245
▲ Distance: 8.75 km/5½ miles
▲ Walk ID: 647 Jude Howat

Difficulty rating

Time

▲ Canal, River, Pubs, Wildlife, Birds, Great Views

Aston-on-Trent and the Trent and Mersey Canal

This delightful circular walk begins on good tow-paths by the Trent and Mersey Canal, then crosses over open land to follow a small section of the River Derwent before returning to the canal path.

1 From the lay-by, head down the track towards the canal. Cross over the bridge and follow the tow-path to the left. Shortly after passing a pub on the opposite side, the path runs closer to the canal bank. Go under a bridge and carry on to a lock just before a high bridge over the River Trent.

2 Go onto the bridge to see the canal merging with the rivers Trent and Derwent, then retrace your steps to the lock and very carefully cross the canal. On the far side, follow a footpath leading from the canal to the River Derwent. After passing between two ponds, the path becomes unclear, but aim towards the large tree by the river.

3 At the tree, the path becomes clear again. Follow the riverbank until you reach the first bridge. Do not cross the bridge, but turn left and follow the path across the fields towards the houses, to a metalled track.

4 Join the metalled road and follow it round a sharp bend and past a converted church. Turn right off this road just before a bridge over the canal. Aim towards a white pub in the distance. Just after the pub, the road bends sharply to the left. Follow the road to reach a small lane off to the right.

5 Go through the lane, then follow the road on the far side. When you reach a T-junction, turn right. At this point, you can see the pub you passed earlier on the walk. Cross the road and go through the pub car park and to the left of the building to the canal.

6 Carefully cross the canal via one of the locks. Turn right at the far side, and follow the canal tow-path back to the start of the walk.

A barge progresses sedately along the calm waters of the Trent and Mersey Canal as it makes its way through the peaceful countryside to its junction with the Trent and Derwent rivers.

access information

Aston-on-Trent is just south of the A50 between Derby and Nottingham. There is lay-by parking close to the start of the walk, and also a community centre car park nearby.

further information

As long as they are closely supervised, this is a good route for young children – the tow-path is easy to walk, and there are usually fishermen sitting on the banks, with all kinds of fascinating grubs squirming in tins! The path between the canal and the river can get quite damp after rain, so wellies and old clothes are recommended for little people who enjoy jumping in puddles.

Many properties near the water's edge have their own narrowboat moorings.

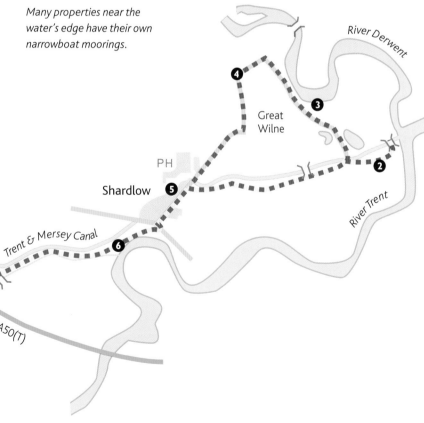

▲ Map: Explorer 15

▲ Distance: 7 km/4¼ miles

▲ Walk ID: 27 Nicholas Rudd-Jones

Difficulty rating

Time

▲ River, Pub, Church, Birds, Flowers, Great Views

Harringworth Viaduct and Seaton

The Welland Valley is one of the most rewarding places to walk in an otherwise rather flat landscape. The walk first hugs the pretty River Welland, then climbs to the ridge to give fine views of the valley.

❶ At Harringworth, go through the church gates and follow the path on the south side to another gate. Turn right through a riding centre and carry on to the road. Turn left along a path by the side of the road for a short distance.

❷ Follow a footpath to the left, through a gate and immediately over a stile. Head diagonally to the right across the field to the river. Turn right and follow the river to the Turtle Bridge. Turn left over the bridge along a stone track, which soon crosses a disued railway line. Follow the track up the slope to the road.

❸ Turn left and follow the road to the next junction. Turn left again and follow the road to Seaton village. As you come into the village, look for a pub ahead on the right. Turn left just after it in front of the church and head down this road to where a path leads back into the fields. Climb a stile and head diagonally left across the fields towards a railway embankment which rises visibly ahead.

❹ Go up the steps in the embankment – carefully, as they are in poor repair – and go down the other side. Cross the road and follow the footpath down a track leading to a private house. Just before the house, skirt round to the left, then veer right. Cross a little footbridge, then immediately climb a stile on the left. Follow the path diagonally left over the fields.

❺ Head towards the viaduct, which you will pass under. At the end of the field, just beyond the viaduct, there is a gate and a stile. Climb the stile. You are now back in Harringworth village. Turn left and at the White Swan pub turn left again to your car.

further information

For information on the Harringworth viaduct, go to http://www.skynet.co.uk/maurice/northants/nviaduct.htm.

The White Swan pub in Harringworth has good food and welcomes children.

As you will see on this walk, river valleys are home to some of Britain's prettiest wild flowers.

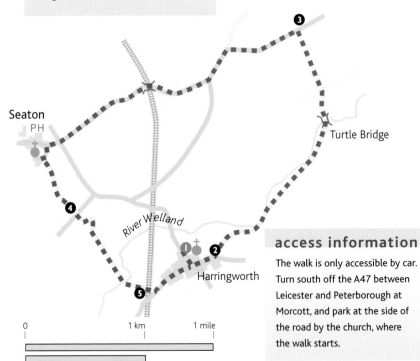

access information

The walk is only accessible by car. Turn south off the A47 between Leicester and Peterborough at Morcott, and park at the side of the road by the church, where the walk starts.

▲ Map: Explorer 234

▲ Distance: 4.19 km/2½ miles

▲ Walk ID: 65 Nicholas Rudd-Jones

Difficulty rating

Time

▲ River, Pub, Toilets, Museum, Church, Wildlife, Birds, Flowers, Great Views

The River Welland.

Stamford to the end of the meadows and back

This short, easy walk captures all the magic of the meadows, and gives a splendid view of the town. History lovers can relish standing on the spot where the feisty Celtic warrior queen Boudicca challenged the Roman 9th Legion in AD 61.

❶ From the car park, cross a small bridge across a tributary and head south-west across the meadow towards a gate. Go through the gate and then follow the path beside the River Welland. When you reach the stone seat with Boudicca's plaque on it, look back to enjoy the splendid view of Stamford.

❷ From here, continue to follow the path beside the meandering river for a few hundred metres until you reach the metal Broadeng footbridge, which marks the furthest point of the walk.

❸ Setting back towards Stamford, follow the path that bisects the meadow, and at a fork take the left path leading towards a gate. Go through the gate, leaving the meadows.

❹ Once through the gate, follow Melancholy Walk, which begins just in front of you. It is a raised path next to a water channel. To your right are good views across the meadow, while on your left are some of Stamford's well-established allotment gardens. At the end of Melancholy Walk, past a small row of houses on your right, turn left up the hill. When you reach Austin Street, turn right.

❺ Carry on along Austin Street – calling in for refreshments at St Peter's Inn via its back entrance, if you like – until you reach the cobbled King's Mill Lane. Turn right downhill and return to the car park at the start of the walk. Near here is another pub, The George, a famous coaching inn.

access information

Parking is available in the car park at Stamford meadows.

There is a regular train service to Stamford station – the start of the walk is two minutes from the station. Go to www.railtrack.co.uk for information on train times.

further information

This is an excellent walk for children as it is easy and not too long – take some bread with you to feed the ducks. Look out for the remains of the castle wall at the start of the walk, and for the plaque on a small stone seat beside the river commemorating Queen Boudicca. For further information, go to the Stamford website www.stamford.co.uk.

▲ Map: Explorer 207
▲ Distance: 13.69 km/8½ miles
▲ Walk ID: 1301 R. and J. Glynn

Difficulty rating

Time

▲ River, Pub, Church, Wildlife, Birds, Flowers, Great Views, Butterflies, Food Shop

Nether Heyford from Weedon

This diverse walk follows the Nene Way, then the tow-path beside the Grand Union Canal, before following footpaths through fields and meadows to the pretty village of Nether Heyford. The route continues through a beautiful rural landscape, passing Bugbrooke Mill and village before rejoining the canal tow-path.

❶ From Weedon Post Office, follow the road to the railway bridge. Past St Peter's churchyard, turn right on the Nene Way. Cross the road and carry on. Fork right off the old Wharf House drive. Cross the canal at bridge 25, go down the steps, then turn left along the tow-path. Turn left at bridge 27 and left along the road.
❷ Turn right at the footpath, crossing two fields, then a third, bearing slightly right. Cross a footbridge, a stile and more meadows to a footbridge into a field. Cross a hard track and climb the stile to the right, then cross another field. Climb the stile, and follow the path, turning right by a wall into Nether Heyford.
❸ Turn left into Church Lane. Go through the church gate, then turn left. Follow the footpath between trees, then two walls. Cross a narrow road and follow the path opposite. Cross the estate road and carry on. Opposite Brookside Close, turn right.
❹ Turn left on the Kislingbury footpath. Cross the river, then go through the kissing gate on the left and follow the field edge. Turn left through another gate, following the field edge to the right. Go through two more gates. Following the hedge line, enter a small copse. Follow the River Nene for a short distance, then take the hard track away.

❺ Turn right on the footpath across the fields to Bugbrooke. Climb the stile, follow a narrow path to the road and turn right. At the junction, turn right into Church Lane. Passing the church, turn right towards Weedon, then left on the Old Crown footpath.
❻ Turn right at the canal bridge and follow the towpath. Soon after Flore Lane Bridge, climb the stile and follow a track through meadowland. Cross a large field towards a white building. Climb the stile in the corner. Walk up to the road and cross over. Join the Nene Way opposite, and walk along to the canal bridge. Return to the start point.

further information

The walk recalls a time when the Grand Union Canal was an essential route, along which boatmen and their families would travel to and from London with their cargoes. Flour is still produced at Bugbrooke Mill, and in the graveyard of Bugbrooke Church look out for an inscription from Longfellow on a tree.

access information

Weedon lies south of the A5 between Daventry and Northampton. Street parking is available in the village.

The Grand Union Canal, which crosses this route, is a semi-permanent home for houseboat-dwellers.

Weedon

① ②

Grand Union Canal

Nether
Heyford

③

④

R. Nene

Nene Way

⑤ Bugbrooke
Mill

⑥

Bugbrooke

0   1 km   1 mile

*This walk takes in a
beautiful English church.*

▲ Map: Explorer 191
▲ Distance: 8.86 km/5½ miles
▲ Walk ID: 858 R. and J. Glynn

Difficulty rating

Time

▲ Church, Wildlife, Birds, Flowers,
Great Views, Butterflies

Nell Bridge and Kings Sutton from Twyford Wharf

This walk emphasises the peace and tranquillity of the canal environment. Willows droop lazily at the water's edge, and there are lovely renovated cottages and pretty gardens. Look out for the old-fashioned drawbridges, a characteristic of this canal.

1 From the bridge at Twyford Wharf, go down onto the canal tow-path and turn left to walk under the bridge. As you walk, you will see the silhouette of Kings Sutton Church and spire. Continue along the tow-path.

2 At Nell Bridge Lock, leave the canal, turning left by the road bridge to walk alongside the road, crossing the border into Northamptonshire. Turn left to follow a minor road towards the village of Kings Sutton.

3 Follow the first footpath sign on the left across a field. Go through a gap in the hedge, and cross another field. Climb a stile and head diagonally right, towards an ivy-clad dead tree, where a footbridge crosses a stream. Climb another stile and carry on, towards a weighted wooden gate. Cross a track and go through two more gates.

4 Carry on, with the lovely setting of the Manor House and Kings Sutton Church on your right. Head towards a kissing gate, hidden under a clump of trees. Do not go through the gate, but turn left to walk beside the stone wall beneath the spreading oaks.

5 Turn right down a bank on a signed footpath, above the railway station. Walk over rough ground towards the village street. Cross, and follow the footpath

The elegant spire of Kings Sutton Church provides a walker's landmark.

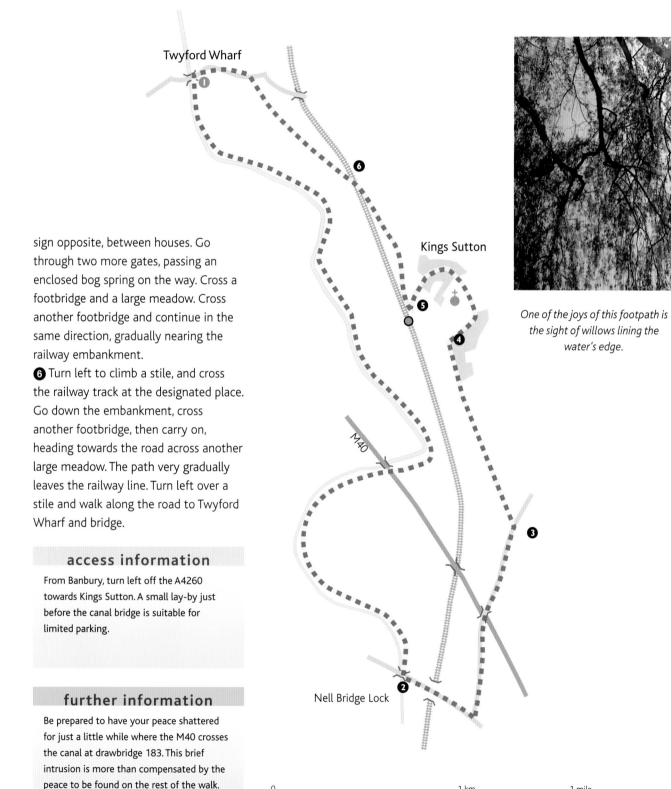

Twyford Wharf

Kings Sutton

Nell Bridge Lock

M40

sign opposite, between houses. Go through two more gates, passing an enclosed bog spring on the way. Cross a footbridge and a large meadow. Cross another footbridge and continue in the same direction, gradually nearing the railway embankment.

❻ Turn left to climb a stile, and cross the railway track at the designated place. Go down the embankment, cross another footbridge, then carry on, heading towards the road across another large meadow. The path very gradually leaves the railway line. Turn left over a stile and walk along the road to Twyford Wharf and bridge.

access information

From Banbury, turn left off the A4260 towards Kings Sutton. A small lay-by just before the canal bridge is suitable for limited parking.

further information

Be prepared to have your peace shattered for just a little while where the M40 crosses the canal at drawbridge 183. This brief intrusion is more than compensated by the peace to be found on the rest of the walk.

One of the joys of this footpath is the sight of willows lining the water's edge.

0   1 km   1 mile

▲ Map: Explorer 180

▲ Distance: 12 km/7½ miles

▲ Walk ID: 269 Oliver O'Brien

Difficulty rating

Time

▲ River, Pub, Canal, Toilets, Museum, Church, Wildlife, Birds, Flowers, Great Views

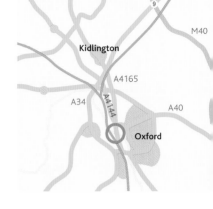

Oxford, Godstow and Port Meadow

From the heart of Oxford, this is a complete circuit of Port Meadow. The first half follows the Thames Path National Trail to Godstow, with its lock, ruined abbey and famous Trout Inn. The return walk follows the Oxford Canal back to the city centre.

1 From the traffic lights by Folly Bridge, follow the Thames Path west, passing a barrier and crossing a small bridge. Pass an old crane and bear right where the path meets the road, staying by the Thames bank. Cross under a bridge and continue along the path right on the river bank.

2 Immediately after the railway bridges, cross a bridge over a tributary and continue alongside the main river. Pass through Osney Lock and carry on. Bear left slightly and cross a footbridge. Crossing the road with care, cross the bridge on the pavement. On the other side, continue along the signposted Thames Path.

3 At the next bridge, take the signposted path to the left, following the Thames. Cross a bright red bridge over the river and carry on, passing a boatyard to the left. Pass through a small gate and continue on the Thames Path.

4 Pass Godstow Lock and the abbey ruins. Bear slightly right off the main path up to the road. Go through the gate, and turn right over the narrow bridge. Follow the road through Wolvercote. Crossing the big road bridge, follow a path down about halfway along on the left, and bear right. Pass Wolvercote Lock and under the bridges, then follow the tow-path.

5 Cross the black-and-white bridge on to an 'island'. Continue along the path. When the canal ends, cross the busy road, turn right and cross a bridge. Immediately, follow a path signposted 'Mill Stream Walk', which crosses another busy road. The path eventually turns into a road which bears round to the left. Turn left at the next junction.

6 Turn right and walk along Queen Street to Carfax. Turn right and walk right down St Aldates. Continue down the road, passing two sets of traffic lights, and cross Folly Bridge to the start of the walk.

access information

Oxford's bus and train stations are both in the city centre, so are near the start and finish of the walk.

Oxford is difficult to get around by car, and parking is extremely difficult. Either park in a suburb of Oxford and walk in, or use the park-and-ride service.

In time-honoured tradition, rowers make their regular progress along the River Cherwell at Oxford.

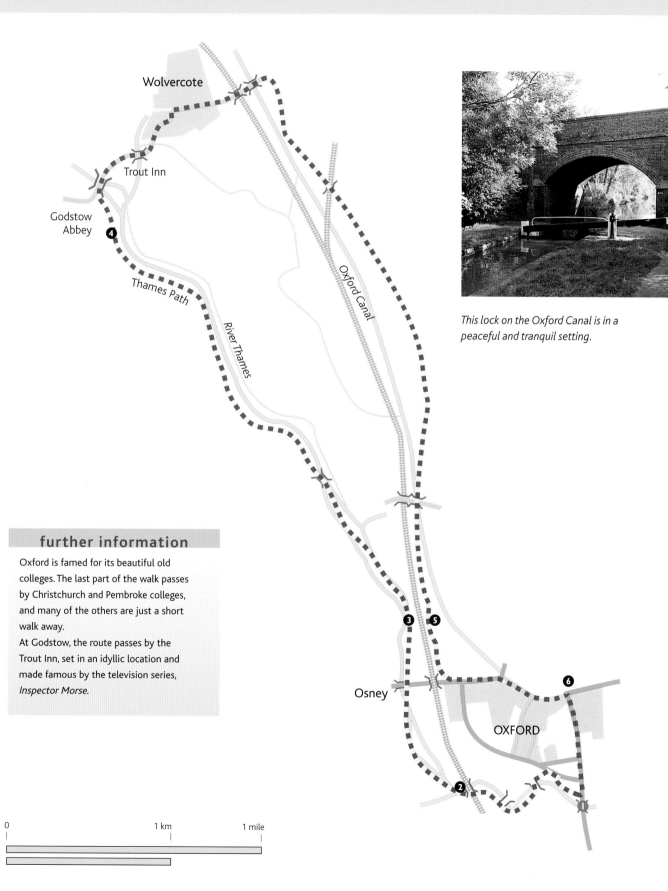

Wolvercote

Trout Inn

Godstow
Abbey

4

Thames Path

River Thames

Oxford Canal

3 **5**

6

Osney

2

OXFORD

*This lock on the Oxford Canal is in a
peaceful and tranquil setting.*

further information

Oxford is famed for its beautiful old
colleges. The last part of the walk passes
by Christchurch and Pembroke colleges,
and many of the others are just a short
walk away.

At Godstow, the route passes by the
Trout Inn, set in an idyllic location and
made famous by the television series,
Inspector Morse.

0   1 km   1 mile

▲ Map: Explorer 191
▲ Distance: 12.88 km/8 miles
▲ Walk ID: 367 R. and J. Glynn

Difficulty rating

Time

▲ River, Pub, Church, Birds, Great Views

The Heyfords from Somerton

Starting from the beautiful village of Somerton, this walk gives fine views across the Cherwell Valley. The Heyfords are charming and interesting villages alongside the Southern Oxford Canal.

❶ Cross the canal bridge and walk under the railway bridge and uphill into the village of Somerton. When you reach the junction with the Ardley road at Yew Tree Cottage, turn left and follow the road for some distance.

❷ Turn right onto a bridleway leading to Upper Heyford. Walk past a farm, bearing left to follow the track in the same direction, then walk along the perimeter fence of the now disused Heyford Airbase. Continue to follow the fence as the path turns right and then left.

❸ Turn right across a field, heading for a gap, and come out on the road. Turn left towards the houses, passing the Barley Mow pub on your left. Turn right into the High Street and walk through the village of Upper Heyford. Take the left fork into School Lane and walk along to the church.

❹ Take the path on the left, through a kissing gate and across the meadow to another gate. Turn left, then right along a hard track, through a gate and along to the sewage works. Climb a stile on the left and walk with the hedge on your right. Follow the fence when it turns

right, then turn left away from it along the edge of the field. Follow this path, with the canal on your right, to Lower Heyford village hall.

❺ Turn right onto the road to cross the drawbridge, then turn right onto the canal tow-path. You now have the canal on your right and the River Cherwell on your left. Continue the walk back along the tow-path, through the flood meadows, and leave the path at bridge 96 to return to the start of the walk.

further information

The flood meadows of the River Cherwell run alongside the tow-path of part of the Southern Oxford Canal, and when flooded can look like a vast lake. Locks and graceful arched bridges add charm and interest as the walk meanders back along the canal.

This bank along the route of the River Cherwell is the perfect picnic place.

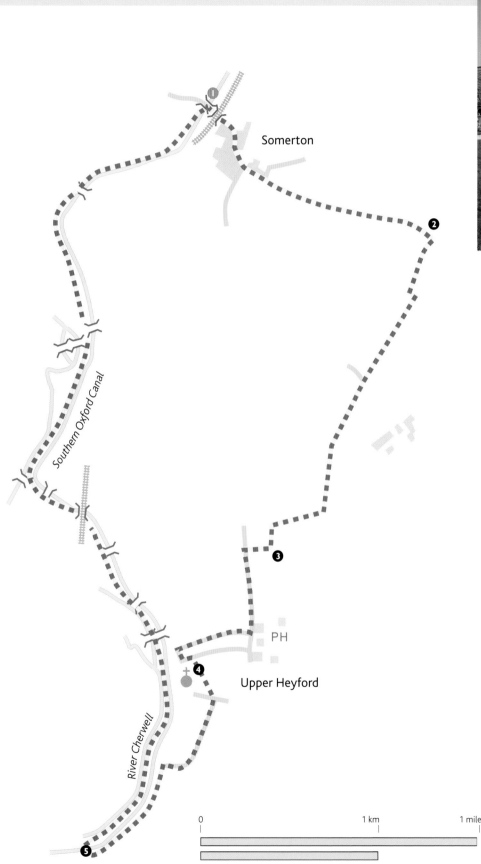

Somerton

Southern Oxford Canal

PH

Upper Heyford

River Cherwell

The city of Oxford provides a magnificent urban backdrop for the Cherwell.

access information

Take the turning to North Aston and Somerton off the A4260 main Banbury to Oxford road. Park near the canal bridge just before the village of Somerton.

0   1 km   1 mile

▲ Map: Explorer 221

▲ Distance: 8.86 km/5½ miles

▲ Walk ID: 992 R. and J. Glynn

Difficulty rating

Time

▲ Pub, Stately Home, Birds, Flowers, Great Views, Butterflies, Food Shop, Woodland

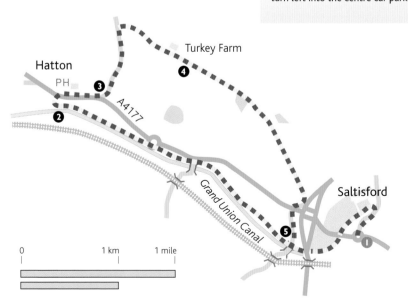

Hatton Locks at Warwick.

Saltisford Basin and Hatton Locks

Much of this walk is on the Grand Union Canal tow-path, following the dramatic climb of the 21 Hatton Locks. The walk then follows a fine bridleway through very pleasant flat farmland, before rejoining the canal to return to Saltisford Basin.

1 From the car park, turn right, go through the metal gates, then turn left at the end of Budbrooke Road to walk over the canal bridge. Turn left on the footpath opposite the cemetery. After a short distance, veer left off the footpath and go through a gap down onto the canal tow-path. Turn right and walk along the path, passing the first of the 21 Hatton Locks at Hatton Bottom, and then 'Ugly Bridge'.

2 At bridge 54, the route leaves the canal. Walk with the large white house on your right, and go through the kissing gate in the corner, beneath a tree. Walk uphill to pass the Waterman pub, turning right beside it. Turn right onto the pavement along the road, then cross the road to take the left fork to Beausale.

3 After a short distance, turn left onto a minor road, which gradually climbs to reach Ashwood Lodge. Turn right on a bridleway towards Turkey Farm House. Go through the metal gate beside the farmhouse and carry on, passing a pond. Turn right at a marker and walk around the field edge.

4 Go through a gap on the left, beside an oak tree, and follow the edge of the field on a permissive path to the far corner, turning right into the next field. Walk on with Blackbrake Plantation on the left and a wooded area on the right, still following the field edges, which zigzag before Wedgnock Farm. Pass the farm on a track to the right and follow the track to the road. Cross by the traffic lights, and walk along Budbrooke Road ahead, passing the Fire Safety Headquarters before reaching the canal bridge.

5 Turn right over the road and then go down onto the canal footpath and turn left. Retrace your steps to the Saltisford Basin car park.

further information

The 21 Hatton Locks are a spectacular sight, with their tall, white-topped paddles, white-tipped gates and white edging around the lock entrances. Once a hubbub of working narrow boats, the locks are now used only by leisure craft, and the sight of a loaded pair of boats, crewed by the boatman and his family, has gone for ever.

access information

From the A425 between Warwick and Birmingham, follow the sign to Canal Centre, Saltisford, and turn left into the centre car park.

▲ Map: Explorer 222
▲ Distance: 9.66 km/6 miles
▲ Walk ID: 1481 R. and J. Glynn

Difficulty rating

👣👣

Time

⬤⬤⬤

▲ Lake, Pub, Church, Wildlife, Birds, Flowers, Great Views, Butterflies, Food Shop

Calcutt Locks from Stockton

This great little walk can almost be entitled 'a marina walk', as it visits three – Ventnor Farm Marina and Calcutt Marina, both on the Grand Union Canal, and Napton Marina, on the North Oxford Canal.

❶ Following the Napton road, cross the sports field to a gap in the far corner. Follow the field edge to the stile. Turn left on the road. At the metal gate, turn right and cross a field diagonally left, then a large meadow, following the hedge. Cross another meadow, then climb two stiles through pasture, heading for the top left corner.

❷ Turn left on a track, then right at the road. Turn left through the gate opposite Hill Cottage onto a bridleway. Go through another gate and follow the path. Turn left over Tomlow Bridge, left on to the tow-path, and left again under the bridge to walk beside the Grand Union Canal.

❸ At Calcutt Locks, walk to the top of the flight. Cross the top lock gate, then a footbridge by the shop, turning left by the railings. Turn right over the footbridge, then left. Turn right through an opening between the two sections of reservoir. Crossing a wooden bridge, turn left.

❹ Turn right through a signed gap in the fence and cross the meadow to a gap in the hedge. Cross another meadow. Enter another field, aiming for a stile at the top. Walk over to a metal gate and on to the North Oxford Canal tow-path. Turn right under the bridge and walk to bridge 111. Turn right through a gate to the road.

❺ Turn immediately right through a gate and cross two fields. Cross a stile, a footbridge, and three more fields. Climb the stile and follow the edge of two more fields. When the hedge turns away, walk on, cross a stile and a footbridge, and head towards the sewage works. Cross the next field to the stile in the corner. Turn left onto a track, then right on a private road. Follow the road back into Stockton.

Taking a narrowboat down the Grand Union Canal.

further information

The paths across the fields and meadows are well-defined and easy to follow. The Napton Reservoir is surrounded by natural meadowland, where wonderful wild flowers grow. There is also a huge reed bed near the point at which you head away from the reservoir. As you walk, look out for the Napton Windmill – it comes into view near the start of the route, and again at the reservoir.

access information

From the A423 Banbury to Coventry road, take the A426 towards Rugby, and turn off on an unclassified road to the village of Stockton.

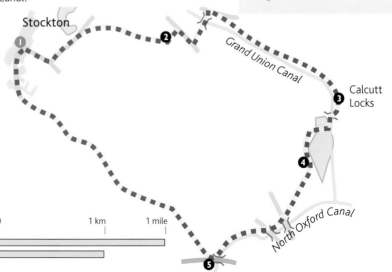

Woodland & Hillside

The woodland and hillside walks of Central England reveal Herefordshire hills, the Peak District and the Lincolnshire Wolds. Highlights include Barnack Hills and Holes, Long Melford and Gradbach Wood.

▲ Map: Explorer 14
▲ Distance: 11.27 km/7 miles
▲ Walk ID: 974 Pat Roberts

Difficulty rating

Time

▲ Hills, Pub, Toilets, National Trust/NTS, Wildlife, Birds, Great Views, Butterflies, Gift Shop, Nature Trail, Tea Shop, Woodland

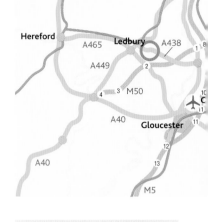

Herefordshire Beacon and Midsummer Hill from Hollybush NT

This is an energetic but historically interesting walk, taking in two Iron Age hill forts – the British Camp on the Herefordshire Beacon, and Midsummer Hill – as well as the intriguing Giant's Cave. The route is in an area of Special Scientific Interest.

1 From the car park entrance, follow the signposted Worcestershire Way, which turns from a metalled road to a rougher track as it goes uphill. Carry on until you reach a fingerpost and a kissing gate.

2 Go through the gate and take the path second from the left to the Obelisk. Return to the Worcestershire Way and continue to follow the path north. At the top of a hill where the ruts in the path become deeper, climb a stile on the right.

3 Follow the path through the wood to the road at the bottom. Turn left, and after a short distance cross the road to follow the Worcestershire Way markers past a house to a wood. Where the drive bears right, take the path through the wood. Climb a stile into open ground and reach another three-fingered post.

4 Turn right, signed 'British Camp Car Park' and follow the path through the trees. Cross the A449, and take the hard path to the right of the car park. Zigzag up the hill, following the signs for the British Camp to the top.

5 Head south along the ridge to a steep stone path, and go down carefully, heading for a marker in the dip. At the marker, take the path to the right signposted 'Giant's Cave'. At the cave,

carry on to a T-junction. Take the right-hand path on to Swinyard Hill and follow the ridge until it starts to drop.

6 Follow the right-hand path, signposted 'Obelisk' and 'Midsummer Hill', to the Worcestershire Way. Turn left, and at the fingerpost and kissing gate follow Worcestershire Way South. Take a path on the left to climb to the top of Midsummer Hill. Head south, gradually losing height, and drop down through a wood to the open ground above the car park.

access information

Hollybush is on the A438 south of Great Malvern. There is a private car park just outside Hollybush belonging to the Eastnor Castle Company. Most of the paths belong to the estate but the public may use the facilities with certain restrictions on cars and bikes. There is a bus service.

The Malverns are noted for their many varieties of butterfly.

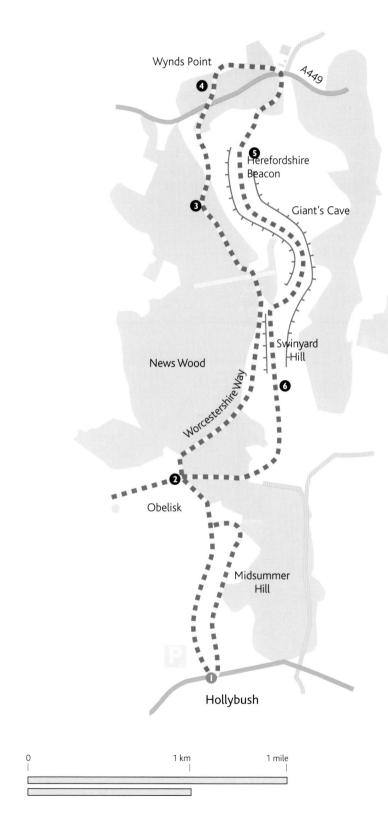

Wynds Point

A449

❹

❺ Herefordshire
Beacon

Giant's Cave

❸

News Wood

Swinyard
Hill

❻

Worcestershire Way

❷

Obelisk

Midsummer
Hill

P

❶

Hollybush

0   1 km   1 mile

further information

The outward leg of the route includes a
detour to see an Obelisk, but as the detour
returns to the same point, this can be
omitted if time is limited. The walk also
passes the Giant's Cave. Although the origins
of the cave are unknown, legend has linked it
with John Oldcastle and Owen Glendower,
or it may have been occupied by a hermit.

▲ Map: Explorer 245
▲ Distance: 4.8 km/3 miles
▲ Walk ID: 920 Jude Howat

Difficulty rating

Time

▲ Lake, Pub, Toilets, Museum,
Church, Stately Home, Gift Shop,
Food Shop, Good for Kids, Public
Transport, Restaurant, Woodland

Woodland in Melbourne Parks.

Melbourne Parks

This simple countryside walk begins and ends in the ancient village of Melbourne. The parish church is one of the finest surviving examples of Norman ecclesiastical architecture in the country, and dates from the mid-12th century.

❶ Starting at the junction into Melbourne Hall and park, follow Blackwell Lane out of Melbourne. Just before the road bends to the right, there is a footpath sign on the right. Follow the footpath into the fields. Almost immediately bear half left to a stile and follow the path diagonally across the fields. The next stile is under the trees. Continue across the fields to the main track from the park.

❷ Cross the cattle grid and then a stile, just off to the left. Follow the path diagonally across two fields up the hill towards a big tree and a farmhouse on the horizon. Leave the fields and go through a gap in the trees ahead of you. Follow the path through the next field, going down to join Green Lane.

❸ Turn right and follow the lane until it bends sharply right. Branch left to follow the bridleway. Cross a small stream and carry on. Turn right where the path splits, and head up the hill towards the trees. Follow the path through the woods and come out in a small field.

❹ Cross the field to another plantation of trees, called Paddock Pool. Cross a small bridge over a stream and come out of the woods into another field. Cross the field to its far diagonal corner. Turn right and cross the stile. The path continues along a grassy lane.

❺ As the lane bends left to the farmhouse, keep right and aim for the trees ahead. Climb a few steps to a stile, then continue on the right-hand edge of the next field. Follow the footpath signs through the fields.

❻ Leaving the last field, join the metalled track through Melbourne Park. Turn left and walk towards the Melbourne Pool. Following this track, return to the start of the walk.

access information

Melbourne is off the A514 south of Derby. Pass through Stanton-by-Bridge and take the B587 towards Melbourne. In Melbourne, follow signs for Melbourne Hall. There is limited parking outside the church.

further information

Melbourne is the second largest town in South Derbyshire, with a population of around 5,000. This ancient town is in the centre of a fertile market-gardening area.

Melbourne

Melbourne Parks

0   1 km   1 mile

▲ Map: Explorer 234

▲ Distance: 6 km/3¾ miles

▲ Walk ID: 32 Nicholas Rudd-Jones

Difficulty rating

Time

▲ Pub, Church, Wildlife, Birds, Flowers

Barnack Hills and Holes

This simple stroll starts at the enchanting and aptly named Barnack Hills and Holes, where ragstone was quarried to build Peterborough Cathedral in the 12th century – you will see a few lumps in the road at Southorpe village.

1 Choose one of the many paths across the nature reserve and head for the south-west edge. Go through a wooden gate alongside the big stone wall of Walcot Hall.

2 Follow the path between the wall and a field. At the end of the wall, where the path meets the road, turn left onto a gravelled track marked 'Public Bridleway', passing Walcot Hall on your left. At the next corner of the park wall, continue ahead on another gravelled track.

3 When the track veers left, keep straight on to the right of a low stone wall ahead of you and take the path along the field edge. Pass through a wooden gate and follow the field edge, heading for a metal gate to the right of two oak trees.

4 Go through the gate and head for the road, keeping the wall on your right. Turn left onto the road to Southorpe. Where the road starts to veer right at the end of the village, by Hall Farm, climb a stile into a field. Head for a gate and another stile at the far side of the field, then aim for a small group of cottages.

5 At the cottages, cross the road and go through a wooden gate into fields. Walk towards the left-hand corner of the thin hedge ahead of you. Keep the hedge on your right and follow the path into Barnack village, past the bowling green and cricket ground on your left,

alongside a stone wall, and then between trees. At the road, turn left. Follow the road round to the right at the Fox and Hounds pub and take the next left. Shortly afterwards, turn left again, passing the Millstone pub on the way back to the car.

The soaring architecture of Peterborough Cathedral.

further information

The nature reserve is home to Marbled White butterflies in June and July, the Pasque flower at Easter, nine species of orchid, and magical glow-worms on summer evenings. Walcot Hall, which was used in the BBC dramatization of *Middlemarch*, is not open to the public, but there are spectacular views of the house from the walk.

access information

Barnack is south of the A16 from Stamford to Market Deeping. Park in a little lay-by at the main entrance to the nature reserve.

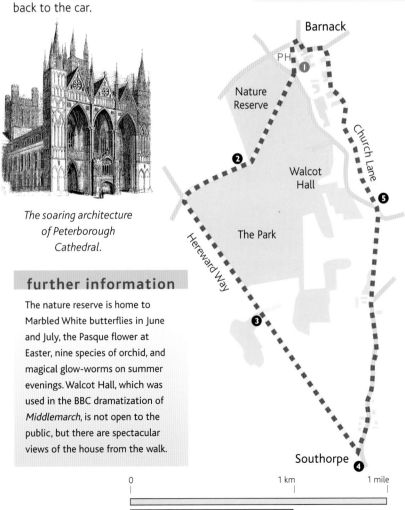

▲ Map: Explorer OL 24
▲ Distance: 10 km/6¼ miles
▲ Walk ID: 1545 Jim Grindle

Difficulty rating

Time

▲ Hills or Fells, Pubs, Toilets, Church, National Trust/NTS, Wildlife, Flowers, Great Views, Butterflies, Good for Kids, Public Transport, Woodland, Ancient Monument

The Nine Ladies and Robin Hood's Stride from Winster

This wonderfully varied walk takes you up hill and down dale, although not too steeply. Along the way, there is a prehistoric stone circle known as the Nine Ladies. There are rocks to climb up and through, and pleasant views of the Peak District.

❶ From the junction near the car park, take the right-hand road to the village. Walk up the lane opposite the Market House and a little to the left. Climb a stile into a field on the left. Follow the left-hand flagged path to a fence with two stiles.

❷ Climb the right-hand stile and follow the path uphill and through the trees. Cross over the next track, through the gate and up the hill. Where four paths meet, go straight on past the barn and follow the field edge to the lane. Climb the stile, turn right, and climb another stile on the left.

❸ Fork right towards a rock tower. At the next stile, turn left, following the fence to a tower. Passing the tower, climb a stile on the left and walk to the stone circle. Turn left and follow a broad track to a crossing track by a hut circle. Turn right, walk to the lane and turn left.

❹ Walk across the car park opposite the quarry buildings. Go between two sculptures to follow the path beyond through the trees to Birchover. Turn right along a 'No Through Road'. Follow the stony track at the end, going straight on at the next two crossing tracks.

❺ Climb the stile and head left over the field to another stile. Turn left and at a junction with a narrow lane turn right up a gravelled farm track. At a gap in a wall, follow the left field-edge. Go through a gate and follow the fence on your left. Climb the stile to Robin Hood's Stride.

❻ Retrace your steps and follow the narrow lane. At the junction, cross over and follow the gravelled track to the next road junction. Turn left and head for the next junction. Cross the green strip and follow the lane opposite to the car park.

access information

Winster is 6.5 km west of Matlock on the B5057. The no 172 bus runs from Matlock to the village.

The gently undulating path takes the walker past the prehistoric stone circles known as the Nine Ladies.

Stone Circle

Stanton Moor
Plantation

Birchover

Robin
Hood's
Stride

PH

Barn
Farm

Winster

PH

The route provides far-reaching views of moorland given over to pasture.

0   1 km   1 mile

▲ Map: Explorer 234

▲ Distance: 8 km/5 miles

▲ Walk ID: 9 Nicholas Rudd-Jones

Difficulty rating

Time

▲ River, Pub, Toilets, Museum, Church, Wildlife, Birds, Flowers, Great Views

Easton on the Hill from Stamford

This splendid walk begins in Stamford Meadows and carries on to give fine views of the Welland Valley. The route passes through Easton, a typical Welland Valley village, and returns to Stamford through glorious countryside and woodland.

❶ From the car park, cross a bridge across a tributary and cross the meadow to a gate. Go through and follow the path across the meadow. Pass the stone seat with a plaque commemorating Queen Boudicca, and follow the river to the Broadeng Bridge. Cross over and continue to follow the river.

❷ Follow a marked path slightly to the left and go through the tunnel under the A1. Cross a bridge and a field, and climb the wooden steps up and over the railway crossing. On the other side, walk through an overgrown stretch into a long field. Follow the path leading up towards the Easton slope.

❸ At the corner of the field, go through a gap in the hedge and cross the field to a stile. Climb this stile and the next one and carry on to Easton, coming out in Church Street. Turn left at the church into the village. After the War Memorial, turn left to the A43 and turn left again for a short distance. Cross carefully to a signed footpath.

❹ Follow this track, passing first between two fields and then through the woods. With the Wothorpe ruins on your right, walk down a stone track then climb a stile to a footpath on your right. Walk down towards the A1.

❺ Go through the tunnel under the A1 and immediately turn right, following the field edge to the next field. Turn left towards Stamford. Climb a stile, cross the field and climb another stile.

❻ Follow the path between houses then walk along an entrance road. The path continues between two hedges to the left of a Victorian house. At the next field, cross diagonally left to a bridge over a stream. Cross another field to the main road. Cross straight over and walk back to the meadows.

The resident deer at Stamford's Burghley Park are just a small part of the wildlife interest in this area.

further information

There are many types of butterflies to be seen in the woods on this walk, particularly Peacocks, Red Admirals, Small Tortoiseshells and Speckled Woods. A good time to see butterflies is late September when the ivy comes into flower, a valuable source of nectar for the long winter months ahead.

access information

Parking is available in the car park at Stamford Meadows.

There is a regular train service to Stamford station – the start of the walk is two minutes from the station. Go to www.railtrack.co.uk for information on train times.

The Peacock (far left) and the Red Admiral (left) are just two of the many types of butterfly that can be found in the woods along this walk.

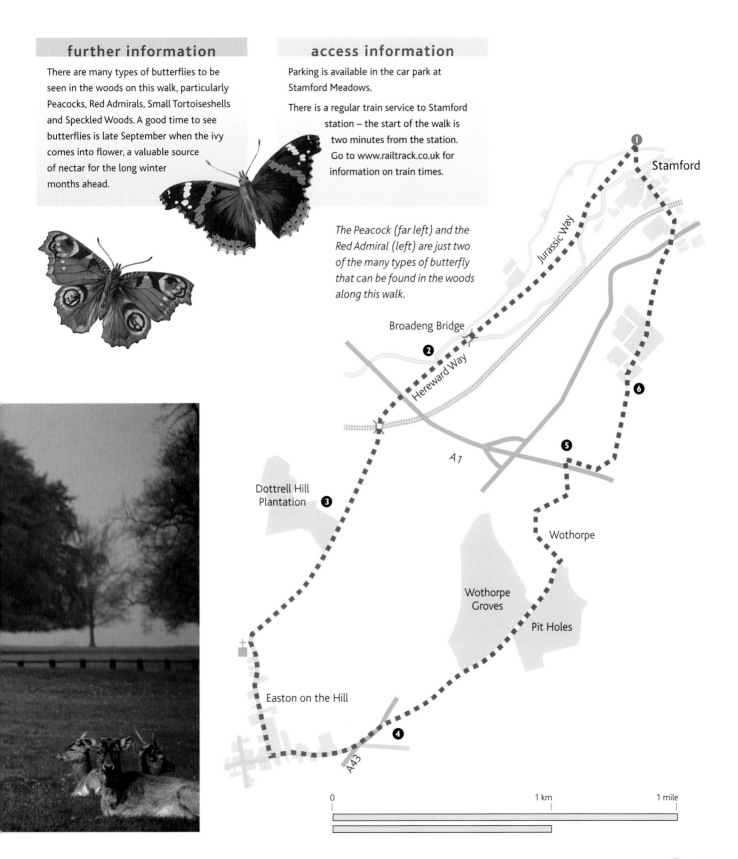

Stamford

Jurassic Way

Broadeng Bridge

Hereward Way

2

6

A1

5

Dottrell Hill Plantation 3

Wothorpe

Wothorpe Groves

Pit Holes

Easton on the Hill

4

A43

0   1 km   1 mile

▲ Map: Explorer 273

▲ Distance: 13.69 km/8½ miles

▲ Walk ID: 473 E. Hutchinson

Difficulty rating

Time

▲ Hills, Pub, Churches, Wildlife, Birds, Flowers, Great Views

Tetford and Worlaby from Maidenwell

This walk in the Lincolnshire Wolds descends to Farforth and follows a wonderful deserted valley to Oxcombe. From Tetford there is a steep climb, skirting Worlaby to Ruckland. If time permits, visit the churches at Oxcombe, Tetford and Ruckland.

❶ From the starting point, go through the gate and walk diagonally left across the field towards some trees. The path joins a track which leads to a metal footpath sign. Turn right, keeping the hedge on your left. Follow the path, descending first to pass a wood then following the valley to Oxcombe. If you wish, make a detour to the church.

❷ Turn right and walk along the lane to the first waymark on the left. Cross a small paddock to another lane and turn left. At the next junction, turn right towards Belchford, then turn left on the bridleway towards Glebe Farm Low Yard. After a short distance turn left at another waymark and follow the bridleway to Tetford.

❸ At Tetford, go straight ahead and bear left at the first junction. Visit the church if you like, then follow the lane to the left of the church. At the end go through the cottage entrance. Cross a stile left of the greenhouse. Follow the path across a small paddock, over a stile and up and over the hill. Follow the path through a paddock.

❹ Climb another stile and turn left on the track, then diagonally right across the field. Turn right and cross the road. Beside the gate to Worlaby Farm, cross the stile, the paddock and another stile to follow the well-waymarked farm road through the estate grounds.

❺ At the end of the estate road, turn right. Detour to Ruckland Church if you wish. The walk route turns left at the top of a bank. Follow the path, which is clearly waymarked all the way to Farforth. At Farforth, turn right onto the lane and then left by some fencing. Follow the track ahead to rejoin the track you started out on.

The typical orange-red earth of the Lincolnshire Wolds, with the town of Louth in the background.

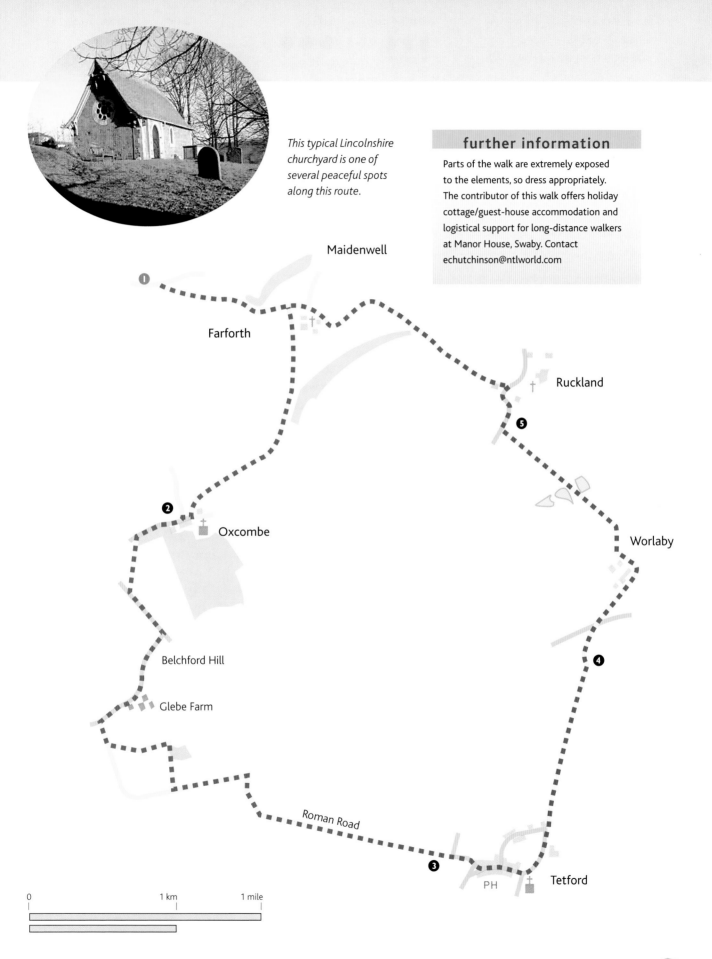

This typical Lincolnshire churchyard is one of several peaceful spots along this route.

further information

Parts of the walk are extremely exposed to the elements, so dress appropriately. The contributor of this walk offers holiday cottage/guest-house accommodation and logistical support for long-distance walkers at Manor House, Swaby. Contact echutchinson@ntlworld.com

Maidenwell

❶

Farforth

Ruckland

❺

❷

Oxcombe

Worlaby

Belchford Hill

❹

Glebe Farm

Roman Road

❸

PH

Tetford

0 1 km 1 mile

▲ Map: Explorer 196
▲ Distance: 12.88 km/8 miles
▲ Walk ID: 1090 B. and A. Sandland

Difficulty rating

🥾🥾

Time

⬤ ⬤ ⬤

▲ River, Pub, Toilets, Church, Stately Home, National Trust/NTS, Wildlife, Birds, Flowers, Great Views, Restaurant, Tea Shop, Woodland, Ancient Monument

The Stour Valley Way and Glemsford from Long Melford

This walk begins in Long Melford, an idyllic Suffolk village surrounded by sweeping parkland and rolling countryside. There are several great manor houses, including the Tudor Long Melford Hall and the moated Kentwell Hall.

❶ From the car park, turn left. Cross the A1092 to the church. Turn left in the churchyard, go through a gateway, then cross a stile. Turn right across another stile and a paddock. Cross two more stiles, passing woodland to a third stile. Walk across to another stile and turn towards Kentwell Hall. Just before the gates, turn left. Go through two gates, then bear right. Follow the track, passing fields then woodland.

❷ Turn left. Follow the path, with woodland then a ditch and field on your left. When you reach trees ahead and a gap on the left, turn right. Where the track goes left to a farm, carry on and cross a footbridge. Follow the track to the road. Turn right, then left at Mill Farmhouse.

❸ Cross a metal footbridge then turn half right to a bridge over a ditch. Turn right with the ditch on your right. At the end of the field on your left, turn left and walk on to meet Park Lane. Turn left, then turn right along the left side of a field. At the end, turn left along a signposted footpath.

further information

At Kentwell Hall, there are frequent reconstructions of life as it would have been when the house was built in 1564. Authentic clothing is worn, and there are demonstrations of cooking, weaving and spinning in Tudor style.

access information

Long Melford lies slightly north of Sudbury and just west of the A134 from Sudbury to Bury St Edmunds. The walk starts from the free car park opposite Melford Hall, and there is plenty of additional parking.

This view of the village of Nayland, in the Stour Valley, has remained unchanged for centuries.

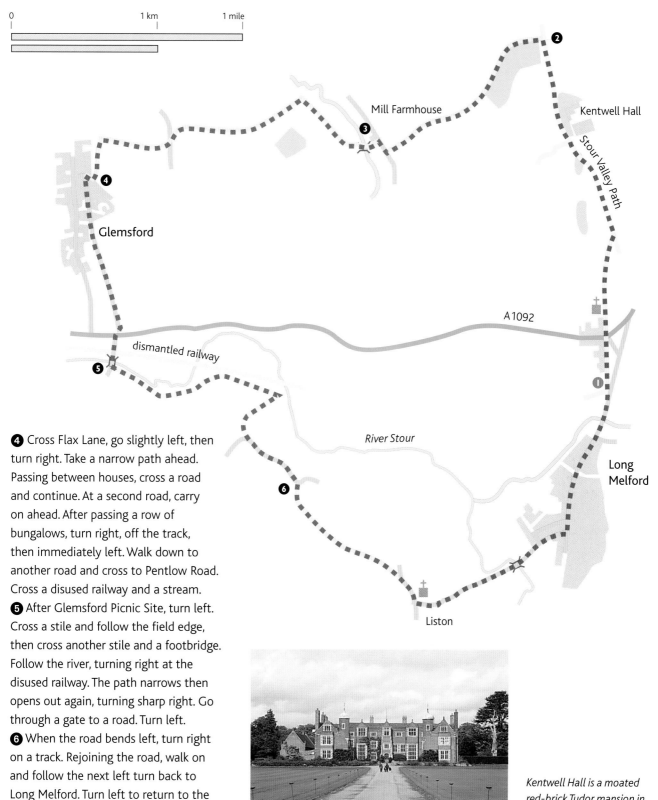

4 Cross Flax Lane, go slightly left, then turn right. Take a narrow path ahead. Passing between houses, cross a road and continue. At a second road, carry on ahead. After passing a row of bungalows, turn right, off the track, then immediately left. Walk down to another road and cross to Pentlow Road. Cross a disused railway and a stream.

5 After Glemsford Picnic Site, turn left. Cross a stile and follow the field edge, then cross another stile and a footbridge. Follow the river, turning right at the disused railway. The path narrows then opens out again, turning sharp right. Go through a gate to a road. Turn left.

6 When the road bends left, turn right on a track. Rejoining the road, walk on and follow the next left turn back to Long Melford. Turn left to return to the car park.

Kentwell Hall is a moated red-brick Tudor mansion in a parkland setting.

▲ Map: Explorer 229 and 230W
▲ Distance: 6.44 km/4 miles
▲ Walk ID: 219 J. and C. Boldero

Difficulty rating

Time

▲ River, Toilets, Wildlife, Birds, Flowers,
Good for Wheelchairs

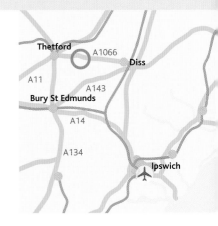

Knettishall Heath Country Park

This walk begins in Knettishall Heath Country Park, the meeting place of Peddars Way, Icknield Way and Angles Way. The route follows the River Little Ouse for a short way, before crossing heathland and running through woodland.

1 From the entrance to the country park, walk westwards along the track, with the river on your right and the picnic area on your left. Immediately after the toilet block, turn right along the path signed with a blue arrow and three waves. Ignore the path that turns to the left at a bend.

2 Take the path to the left beside the river and follow it until it turns left away from the river. Cross a bridge, ignoring the path on the left with a blue arrow, and keep straight ahead. At the T-junction, keep right, walking into woodland.

3 At the next T-junction of tracks, turn left along Peddars Way. Go round the barrier, cross the road, and cross the car park opposite. Go through the open gateway onto the Icknield Way. Carry straight along the path, which narrows between trees.

4 At the end of the woodland to your left, and at the fingerpost sign, turn left through woodland and continue along the wide path between the crops, which becomes a track. At the end, turn left along a country lane.

5 Where two roads join, and just after a Suffolk County Council notice, turn left across the grass to a sign 'Horse riders'. Continue along the woodland path. As the path goes downhill, turn right at a post with a sign on the other side, still in the wood.

6 When the path forks left, take the narrower path straight ahead under trees. At the next T-junction of paths, turn right for a very short distance. Turn left at a yellow arrow marker, still in the wood. Follow the arrows (one is white) through the woods. At the T-junction of paths, turn right, go through the barrier, and cross over to the car park.

access information

There is free parking at Knettishall Heath Country Park, which is situated 9.7 km east of Thetford off the A1066. Follow the 'Country Park' signs along a country lane for about 1.5 km to just beyond the river bridge.

For information about public transport, contact Traveline on 0870 6082608.

further information

The country park is 'wheelchair friendly', with the wheelchair symbol clearly indicated on posts. The heathland is grazed by Exmoor ponies, fallow deer and Hebredian sheep, enabling rare wild flowers to grow, such as dropwort and tormentil, as well as the more common foxglove, gorse, harebell and heather.

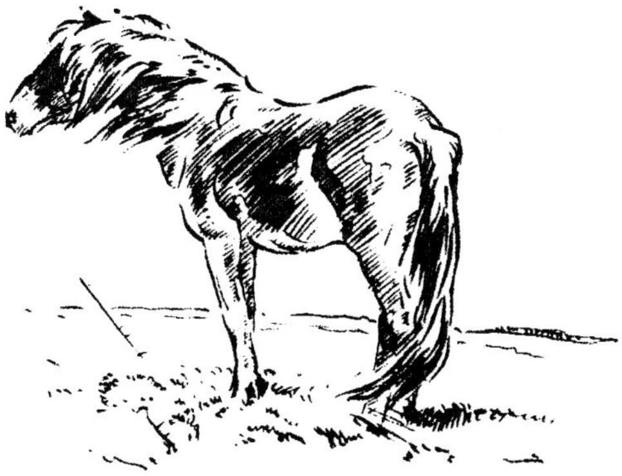

The hardy Exmoor pony is one of the best-known residents of this area.

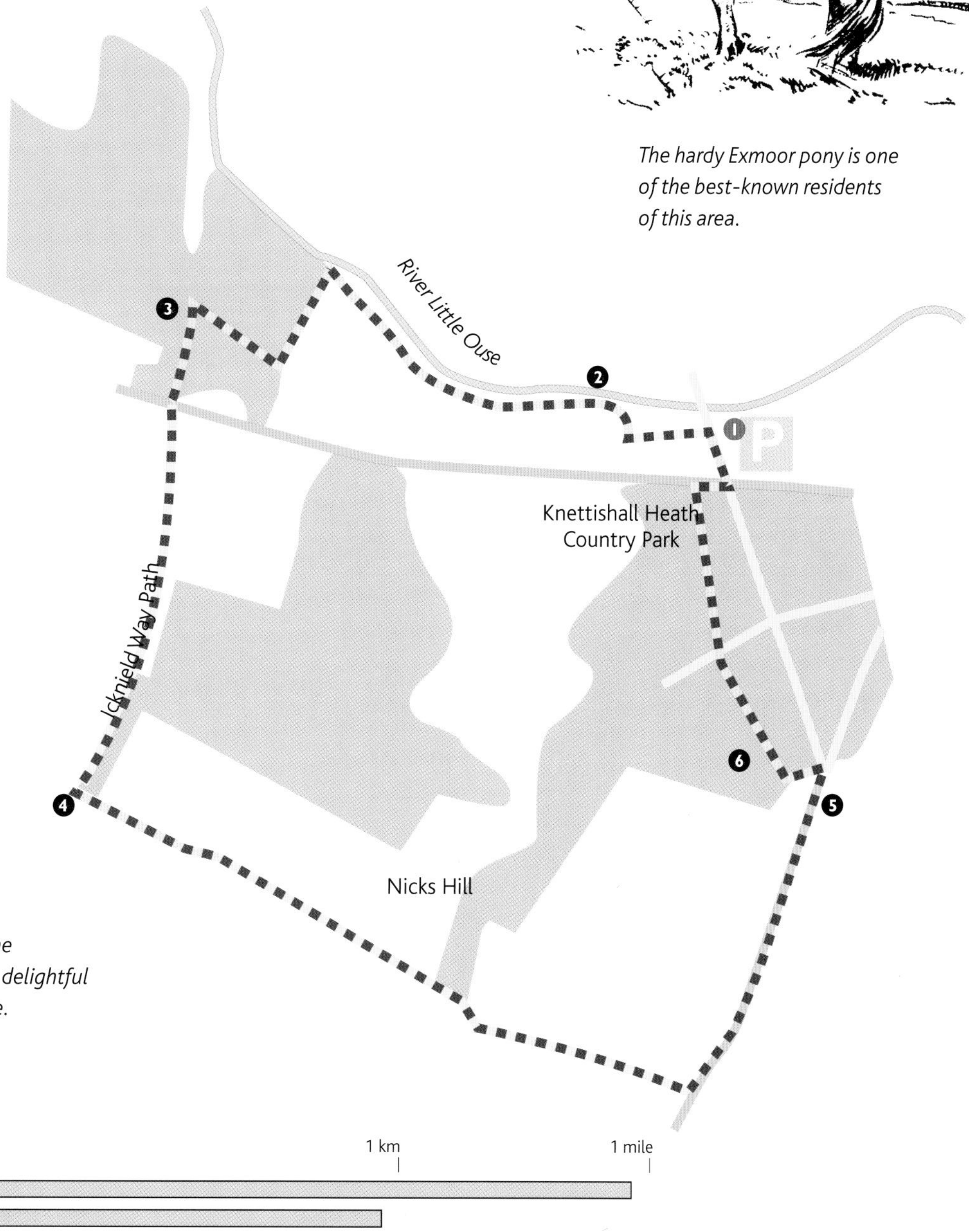
River Little Ouse
Icknield Way Path
Knettishall Heath Country Park
Nicks Hill
P
1
2
3
4
5
6
0
1 km
1 mile

A windmill provides the finishing touch to this delightful view of the Little Ouse.

▲ Map: Explorer OL 24
▲ Distance: 11 km/6¾ miles
▲ Walk ID: 1041 Barry Smith

Difficulty rating

Time

▲ Hills or Fells, River, Wildlife, Great Views, Moor, Woodland

Gradbach Wood and The Roaches from Gradbach

This is a magnificent walk with plenty of contrast. From Gradbach, you follow the beautiful River Dane and Black Brook, followed by forest paths in deep woodland, before climbing to The Roaches, a rocky moorland ridge.

① Turn right out of the car park and fork right to the Youth Hostel. Follow a short lane on the left of the Hostel car park to the corner. Go up the steps and path and climb the stile. The path widens into a farm track. Climb the stile in the wall ahead and turn right downhill to Castors Bridge. Cross the footbridge into Forest Bottom, and follow the sign left.

② Continue up the path beside Black Brook and through Gradbach Wood. At the next fork in the path, take the lower one to continue beside, but above, Black Brook. Join a wider path coming from the right, and continue left.

③ At the top of a hill, take the sign for Roach End over a small stream. Follow the path, mostly uphill, into open countryside. Cross a stile, then another squeeze stile almost immediately on the left leading to a road.

④ Cross the road and follow the path opposite, uphill and by a wall, onto The Roaches. Climb to the trig point and carry on. At the deep cleft in the ridge on your right, follow a path going down to the next left turn. Follow the path along the base of the cliff to the end.

⑤ Ignore the steps to the right and take the path downhill into the col, towards the gate and path leading to Hen Cloud.

Ascend Hen Cloud if you wish. If not, turn left and follow the main path straight ahead. After a farm track, you reach a minor road.

⑥ Follow the road to the right, then turn left opposite Newstone Farm. At the next junction, bear left, then follow the green lane signposted to Gradbach across the fields. Turn right, passing the fork to the Youth Hostel, and return to the car park.

access information

From Buxton, take the A53 Leek road for about 8 km. At the sign for Flash, turn right on a minor road, bearing left for Gradbach after 0.5 km. In another 3.5 km. turn left, signed for Gradbach Youth Hostel, then turn right into the car park.

The spectacular view from The Roaches is well worth the climb.

further information

This area is rich in myths and legends. There are stories of a headless rider and a tall man dressed in green, which could be folk recollections of the story of Sir Gawain in Arthurian legend. Lud's Church, a cave on The Roaches estate, is said to be the legendary Green Chapel in a 14th-century poem reciting Sir Gawain's story.

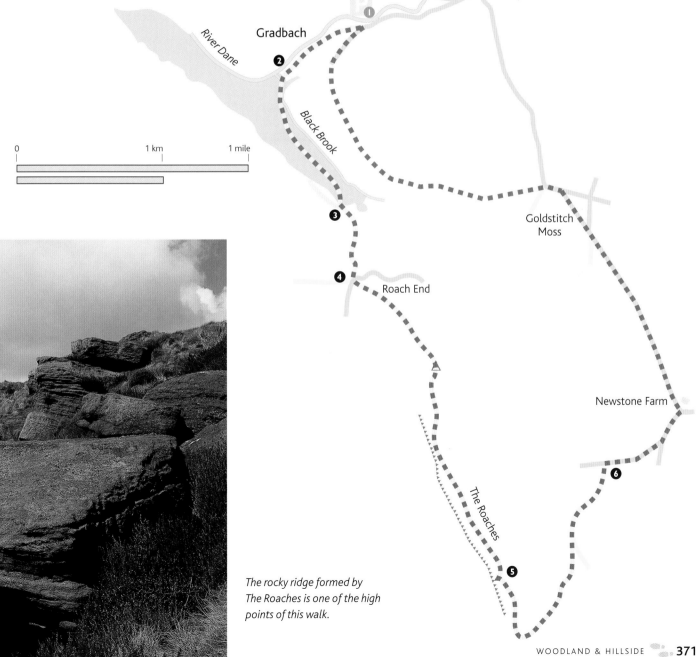

River Dane

Gradbach

Black Brook

0   1 km   1 mile

Goldstitch Moss

Roach End

Newstone Farm

The Roaches

The rocky ridge formed by The Roaches is one of the high points of this walk.

▲ Map: Explorer 206
▲ Distance: 6.44 km/4 miles
▲ Walk ID: 1011 R. and J. Glynn

Difficulty rating

Time

▲ Hills, Lake, Pub, Toilets, Church, Stately Home, Wildlife, Birds, Flowers, Great Views, Butterflies, Food Shop, Woodland

Church Charwelton from Woodford Halse

This simple but rewarding walk is in the midst of lovely rural Northamptonshire agricultural land. It visits the site of the medieval village of Charwelton, with its beautiful little church, before returning along part of the Jurassic Way.

❶ From St Mary the Virgin Church, walk along School Street past the library. Turn left opposite Old Barn onto a hard track that crosses the River Cherwell and climb steps up to the road. Follow the path opposite, through the white barrier rails, and continue between a fence and bushes, then with the hedge on the right only. Keep to the edge of fields over two stiles and look for an oak tree with a sign on it to bear diagonally left.

❷ Follow this sign and head for a gap, to cut off the top corner of the field. Cross the footbridge and walk on. Climb a stile into the next field and follow the hedge on the right, eventually turning right through a metal gate. Follow the fence on the right, turning right with the fence line, then follow the hedge on the right to a stile ahead. Walk across the next field, then bear left to a gap in the hedge. Cross the footbridge, and follow the left-hand field edge.

access information

Woodford Halse lies east of the A361 between Banbury and Daventry. At Byfield, take the road signed to Woodford Halse, drive into the village, and park in the vicinity of the church.

The spire of the medieval Church of St Mary the Virgin in the village of Woodford Halse dominates the winter landscape.

further information

Unfortunately the church at Charwelton is kept locked, but it is well worth going into the porch and peering through the grids in the door to admire the beautiful interior.

❸ Turn left through a metal gate and cross the medieval village site, bearing right of the farm buildings. Go through two gates to the church. Follow the Jurassic Way marker, bearing right towards the far fence line. Follow the fence to a footbridge and a gate. Bear left towards the railway bridge. Near the bridge, go through a metal gate onto a path, crossing it to continue along the field edges. Go through a wooden gate and walk on uphill.

❹ At the Ramblers' Millennium fingerpost, walk on, following the hard track between woodland and fields. At the end of the track turn left along the road, following the pavement for a short distance. Turn right onto a woodland path, the Jurassic Way, crossing a bridge to turn left into Castle Road. Turn left at the top of the road, and walk back to the church.

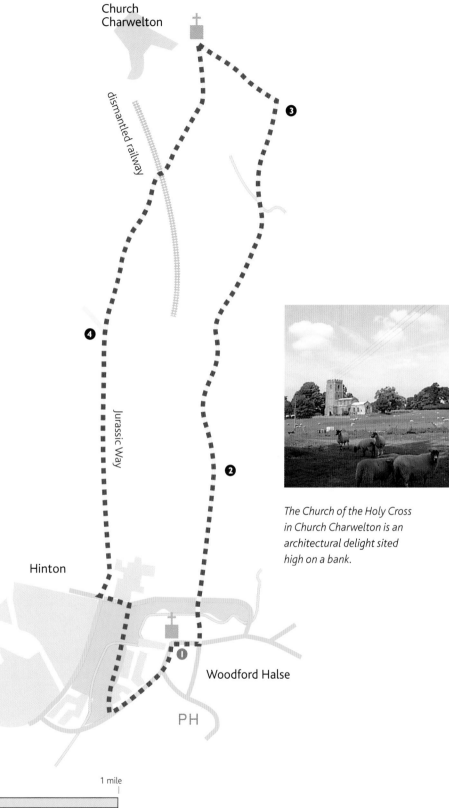

Church Charwelton

dismantled railway

Jurassic Way

❸

❹

❷

Hinton

Woodford Halse

❶

PH

The Church of the Holy Cross in Church Charwelton is an architectural delight sited high on a bank.

0   1 km   1 mile

▲ Map: Explorer 180
▲ Distance: 12.08 km/7½ miles
▲ Walk ID: 1181 R. and J. Glynn

Difficulty rating

Time

▲ River, Lake, Pub, Toilets, Church, Wildlife, Birds, Flowers, Great Views, Food Shop, Woodland, Ancient Monument

Finstock from Charlbury

This walk on the edge of the Cotswolds follows lanes, bridleways and footpaths through beautiful surroundings. The route encircles the Cornbury Estate, on part of the Oxfordshire Way, edges the Wychwood Forest, and returns via Cornbury Park.

❶ From the car park, turn right opposite the fountain and walk along Browns Lane, passing the Bull Inn. Turn right and walk down the road past the Library and Post Office. Turn left past the Chapel on Dyers Hill and walk on, over the river, past the station and over a road bridge.

❷ Turn right on a bridleway signed to Walcot and follow the path past Cotswold stone cottages, Top Barn (further on), then uphill and downhill. Turn left on a minor road called Catsham Lane.

❸ At the next junction, follow the road opposite along the edge of Wychwood Forest, signed to Leafield. Pass Ranger's Lodge, staying on the road at the entrance to Cornbury Park, and walk with woodland on either side. Turn left opposite Watermans Farm and follow the sign onto a woodland path.

❹ Come out in a clearing and turn right to join a track which passes some old huts. The path drops down to a lake and turns left by a metal gate and a fence. Climb up Patch Hill through woodland, to a clearing. Continue along the edge of the wood and come out in meadowland.

❺ Turn left along the Witney road through Finstock and beyond, then turn left to follow a bridleway signed to Cornbury Park Fishery. Cross the bridge over the lake and take the right of two gates ahead. Passing South Hill Lodge, follow the fence line of Cornbury Park.

❻ Go through a wooden gate and turn right between the pillars of a wide river bridge. Cross a smaller railway bridge later on. At North Lodge Gate, turn left into Charlbury. Passing St Mary's Church, follow the road to the Bell Inn in Church Street. At the junction, cross the road and walk back to the start.

The Church of St Mary at Charlbury is a typical Cotswold church, built of grey stone with an imposing square tower.

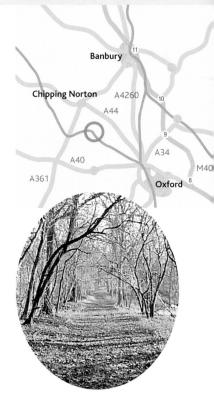

This tree-lined walk has a warm, golden beauty in the dying days of autumn.

access information

Charlbury is at the crossroads of the B4437 and the B4022 just north of Witney. Free car parking is available at the Spendlove Centre in the village, where the walk starts.

further information

Peace and tranquillity prevail in this area of outstanding natural beauty. The woodland path through part of the Wychwood Forest is magical, with mature trees giving refuge to many different birds species, while Cornbury Park is spectacular with its herd of deer roaming freely through the majestic trees.

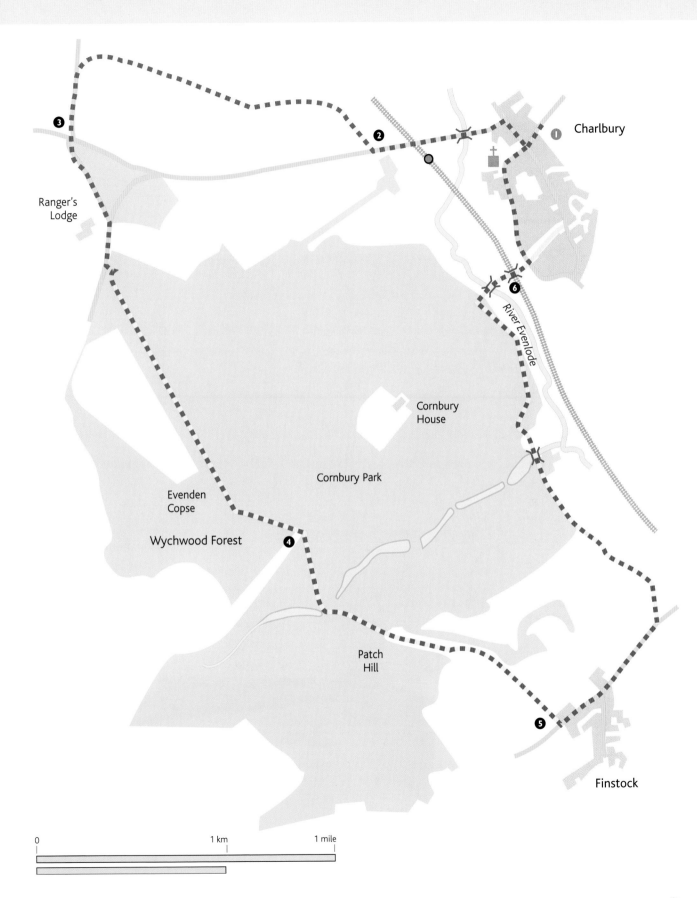

Charlbury

Ranger's
Lodge

Cornbury
House

Cornbury Park

Evenden
Copse

Wychwood Forest

River Evenlode

Patch
Hill

Finstock

0   1 km   1 mile

▲ Map: Explorer 191
▲ Distance: 7.65 km/4¾ miles
▲ Walk ID: 523 R. and J. Glynn

Difficulty rating

Time

▲ Parkland, Castle, Moat, Church, Fulling Mill, Stream, Great Views

Lower Tadmarton from Broughton

This walk starts in the grounds of Broughton Castle, with a splendid view of this fairy-tale moated castle and the delightful church beside it. You also pass a fulling mill, a legacy of the days when plush weaving was a flourishing local industry.

1 Just within the castle entrance, climb a stone stile, following the left-hand path. Walk uphill over parkland with the castle and moat on your left. At the brow of the hill, bear right towards a copse. Walk to the right of the copse towards a stile.

2 Cross the stile and walk with the fence on your left. Turn left over two stiles, passing some farm buildings, and walk with the fence and a hedge on your right, across two fields. Go through a metal gate and turn left. Walk down past the fulling mill.

3 Go through a metal gate and turn left to a tree on the bank. Go through another gate and walk across two fields. Go through a wide gap into the next field and head diagonally right. Go through the gap in a hedge and follow the hedge on your right for a short distance.

4 Take the narrow path to the right, walking between a hedge and a copse. Carry on to a metal gate leading through a kennels, and follow the track to the road. Turn left and walk to the main road junction. Cross and turn left again.

5 Turn right towards Bloxham. After Oak Tree Farm, turn left on a bridleway. Go through a walkers' gate, now with a spinney on your right. Go through the second metal gate on the left and the walkers' gate immediately on the right,

and follow the path with Nayland Farm on your right. Stay on the path around two field edges.

6 Go through a walkers' gate to the main road. Turn right and walk towards Broughton. Just before a house, turn left on a stone path leading to Broughton Church, crossing the footbridge into the churchyard. Leave by the wooden gate and follow the drive back to the start.

access information

Broughton is on the B4035 just south-west of Banbury. Park on a small lay-by adjacent to the main entrance to Broughton Castle.

The Oxfordshire countryside is a tranquil landscape for walkers.

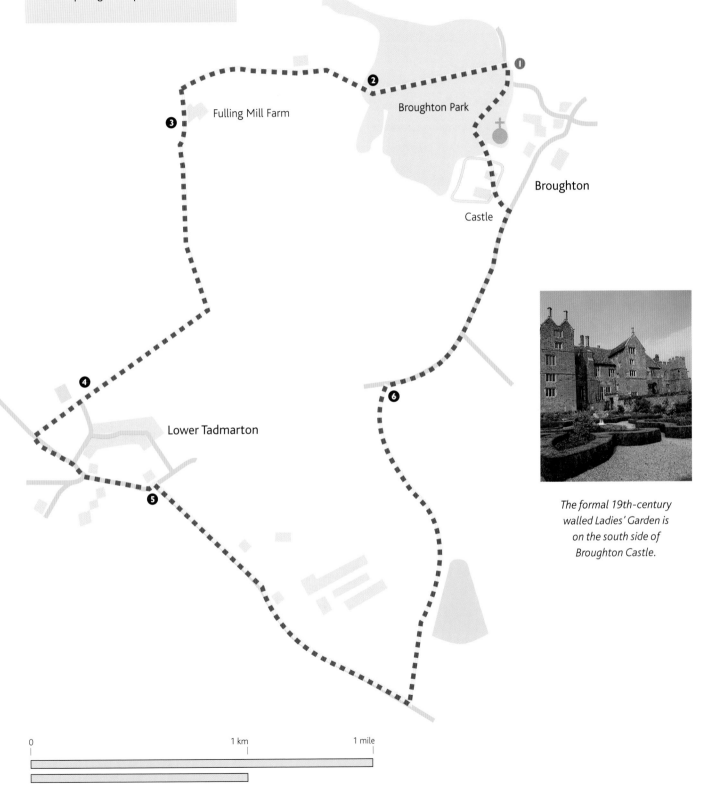

Broughton Park

1

2

Fulling Mill Farm

3

Broughton

Castle

4

Lower Tadmarton

6

5

*The formal 19th-century
walled Ladies' Garden is
on the south side of
Broughton Castle.*

0   1 km   1 mile

▲ Map: Explorer 271
▲ Distance: 9.66 km/6 miles
▲ Walk ID: 1440 David Berry

Difficulty rating

Time

▲ Pub, Toilets, Museum, Church, Wildlife, Great Views

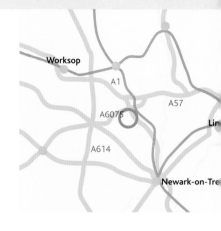

Laxton from Egmanton

From Egmanton, this walk initially climbs gently on farm tracks before taking to field footpaths leading to Laxton and a circular return to the start. Laxton is England's last open-field farming village with an ancient strip-field system.

1 From the Old Plough Inn, turn right. Fork right along Weston Road, then turn right up Wood Lane, which becomes a stone track. Follow the track to skirt the edge of Egmanton Wood. When the track ends, continue ahead on a path across a field to a hedge, and turn left.

2 Go through a gap in the hedge, turn left and follow the field edge. Turn right to follow the footpath, which has an electricity pole and two large trees on it, to the far side of the field. Go through a gateway and turn right along a track.

3 Turn left and follow the footpath to a playing field. Go past the pavilion and through the hedge. Turn right, then left through the hedge and under a wooden bar. Cross the field diagonally to a footpath sign. Follow the left edge of the next field to a stile. Follow the footpath to the road and turn right through Laxton.

4 Fork right along the 'No Through Road'. By a bungalow, turn right, following the footpath across the field to the left, then to the corner. Climb the stile and go through the gateway beyond. Walk down this field to climb a stile on the left, then follow the hedge, turning left at the ditch. Cross a footbridge and a stile.

5 Follow the path ahead. Where the path diverges from the hedge on your right, head towards a communications tower. When the path ends, climb the mound and turn right along a track for a short distance. Go through a gateway, but follow the tractor tracks parallel to the hedge instead of the yellow arrow.

6 As the track goes downhill, follow the footpath proper to a fingerpost in the far hedge. Climb the stile, turn right and follow the fence. In the right-hand corner, climb the stile and follow a straight line, keeping the hedge on your left. At the last field, go through the gate to a short track, then turn right to Egmanton.

further information

At Step 5/6, there is a yellow arrow across a field, apparently indicating the direction of the footpath across the crop. However, previous walkers have followed tractor tracks which run parallel to the hedge and about 30 m into the field, bending to the left and then curving right with the hedge.

access information

Egmanton lies between the A6075 Ollerton to Tuxford road and the A616 Newark to Ollerton road. It is only a short distance off the A1 – northbound, leave at Tuxford, southbound, leave at Markham Moor. Car parking is available on the village roads.

There are bus services to Egmanton village from Tuxford, Newark, Ollerton and Retford.

Laxton parish church, with its mellow walls and overgrown graveyard, has a timeless air.

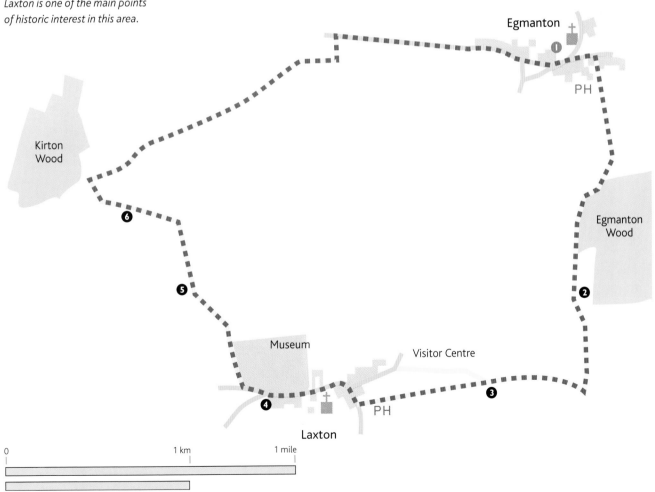

This view of the renowned strip farming of England's last medieval open-field system at Laxton is one of the main points of historic interest in this area.

Egmanton

Kirton Wood

Egmanton Wood

Museum

Visitor Centre

Laxton

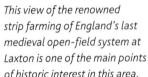

0   1 km   1 mile

▲ Map: Explorer 205
▲ Distance: 8 km/5 miles
▲ Walk ID: 1431 Wendy Pickler

Difficulty rating

Time

▲ River, Pub, Toilets, Church, Café, Public Transport

Oversley and Exhall from Alcester

This short walk begins in the old Roman town of Alcester (Alauna) and meets up with both the Arden and the Heart of England Way. The route touches the pretty village of Exhall before climbing up to pass by Oversley Castle.

1 With your back to the church entrance, turn left. Cross over to walk down Malt Mill Lane, bearing right, then taking a left-hand path across a green. Cross the main road and follow signs for the Arden Way and Heart of England Way. At Oversley Green, cross the river and bear left. Look for a footpath sign on the right soon after passing 'Polkerris' on the left.

2 Climb the stile. Cross the field diagonally right, then another stile, and pass a golf driving range. Go through a gate, following the left-hand field edge. Turn right at the corner. Go through another gate. Follow the track to a gate and stile. Carry on through two more gates to a lane. Turn right and go under the bridge.

3 Bear left and climb a stile by a gate, following a waymark track beside the wood. Go through a gateway, keeping ahead along the track. Go through a gate and keep ahead, with a hedge on the left. Go through another gate, with the hedge on the right. Go through two more gates and a farmyard to the road.

4 Turn right, then immediately right again on a tarmac track. After Rosehall Farm go through a gate to a track. Go through another gateway to reach Oversley Wood. Turn left, following signs for the Arden Way. As the Arden Way turns right, leave it by keeping on ahead.

5 At a T-junction below Oversley Castle, turn right towards Primrose Hill. Just past the two silos on top, follow the track right and down the hill, across a stile on the left and over the bypass on the pedestrian bridge. Follow Primrose Lane to a T-junction and turn left.

6 By the caravan park, follow a footpath sign on the left to a path on the right. Cross the footbridge over the river. Carry on until you come out opposite the High Street, then return to the church.

access information

Alcester lies some 13 km north of Stratford-upon-Avon, and the town centre is well signposted from all directions. Park in the free car park behind the Swan pub, which is along the old main Stratford road, not far from the small roundabout with a metal globe in the middle.

This black-and-white half-timbered building is a relatively modern one in the ancient Roman town of Alcester.

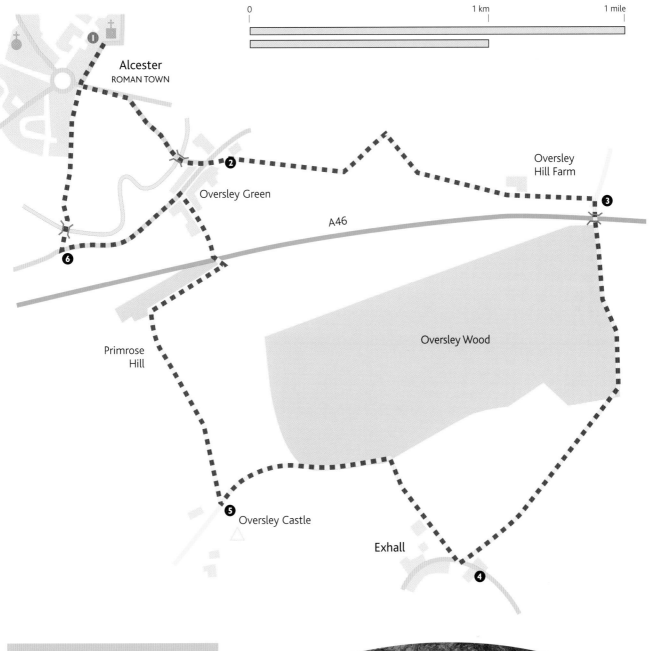

0　　　　　　　　　　　　　　　1 km　　　　　　　1 mile

Alcester
ROMAN TOWN

❶

❷

Oversley Green

Oversley
Hill Farm

❸

A46

❻

Oversley Wood

Primrose
Hill

5

Oversley Castle

Exhall

4

further information

The walk gives views of Ragley Hall, the
home of the Marquess and Marchioness of
Hertford. The house is open to the public.

With its varied woodland,
Britain is an inspiration to
walkers and artists alike.

Index

acknowledgements

The publishers wish to thank the following for the use of pictures: JOY
& CHARLES BOLDERO: p.364. TONY BROTHERTON: pp.15, 264, 324.
CAMERON COLLECTION: p.275. COLLECTIONS: pp.14 Dennis Barnes,
88 Graeme Peacock, 124, 126 Lawrence Englesberg, 148 Sam Walsh,
228 Angela Hampton, 266 David Davies, 269 Jill Swainson, 272/3,
276T, 278, 282 Robert Deane, 284 David M Hughes, 288, 294 Robert
Hales Mann, 295 Robert Estall, 298 Robin Weaver, 189 Robert Pilgrim,
310 Philip Craven, 312 + 316 Robert Pilgrim, 318 David Davies, 319T +
319B David Martyn Hughes, 332 Liz Starrs, 338 Robin Weaver, 344 Yuri
Lewinski, 345 Alan Barnes, 358 Robin Weaver, 365 George Wright,
370/1 + 371 Robin Weaver, 372 David McGill, 376 David McGill, 377
Yuri Lewinski, 380 Colin Underhill. CORBIS: pp.112 Ric Ergenbright, 24
Roger Tidman, 28 Peter Hulme/Ecoscene, 32 Niall Benvie, 38 Ric
Ergenbright, 44 Adam Wolfitt, 50 Niall Benvie, 58/9 Jason Hawkes, 60
Niall Benvie, 62 Macduff Everton, 64/5 Steve Austin/Papillio, 79
Kennan Ward, 80 Ric Ergenbright, 84 Michael Busselle, 85 Julie
Meech/Ecoscene, 86 Eddie Ryle-Hodges, Sandro Vannini, 96 Michael
Busselle, 98/9 Ric Ergenbright, 104 Michael Busselle, 105 Peter
Hulme/Ecoscene, 106 Michael Busselle, 106/7 Wildcountry, 110 Patrick
Ward, 113 Michael Boys, 115 + 116 Peter M Wilson, 120 Patrick Ward,
124 Sandy Stockwell, 166 John Heseltine, 167 Eye Ubiquitous, 168
John Heseltine, 170 Eric Crichton, 173 John Noble, 174 John Heseltine,
176 Derek Croucher, 132 Richard Klune, 136 + 140 Jon Sparks, 142
Andrew Brown/Ecoscene, 144/5 Patrick Ward, 198 Eric Crichton, 200
John Heseltine, 202 Alan Towse/Ecoscene, 208 Adam Woolfitt, 150/1
Michael Busselle, 152 Wildcountry, 156 Andrew Milliken/Cordaiy Photo
Library, 161 Michael Busselle, 188 Wildcountry, 189 Michael Busselle,
190 Robert Estall, 230 Roy Westlake, 232 Jason Hawkes, 233 Bob Krist,
234/5 Michael Boys, 239 Bob Krist, 238 Adam Woolfitt, 240 Michael
Busselle, 241 John Farmer, 214/5 Chinch Gryniewicz, 217 Peter Hulme,
218/9 Andrew Brown/Ecoscene, 220 Derek Coucher, 246 Bob Krist,
250 Michael Busselle, 252 Robert Estall, 255 Bob Krist, 256 David
Dixon/Papillio, 263 Adam Woolfitt, 273 John Heseltine, 274 Adam
Woolfitt, 276B John Heseltine, 286/7 Robert Estall, 289, 293, 296 John
Farmar/Cordaiy Photo Library Ltd., 300/1 Angelo Hornak, 302 Yann
Arthus-Bertrand, 304 Roger Antrobus, 305 WA.Sharman/Milepost, 313
John Farmar/Ecoscene, 324 + 327 Roger Tidman, 328/9 Robert Estall,
330/1 David Hoskins, 334 Michael Boys, 335 John Heseltine, 336/7
Bryan Pickering/Eye Ubiquitous, 340 Jason Hawkes, 342/3 Greenhalf
Photography, 346 Annie Griffiths Belt, 348 + 349 Chris Andrews, 350
Buddy Mays, 351 Colin Garratt/Milepost, 355 Robert Estall, 360 + 361
Michael S Yamashita, 366 + 368 Robert Estall, 374L Ric Ergenbright,
378 Robert Holmes, 379 Michael St.Maur Sheil. IAN CORDINER: pp.27,
29, 66, 67. PAUL EDNEY: p.247. JULIA EWART: pp.204, 205. GETTY
IMAGES: pp.16 Graeme Norways/Stone, 46 Chris Close/The Image
Bank, 48 David Paterson/Stone, 76/7 Chris Close/The Image Bank, 77
Trevor Wood/Stone, 118 + 122/23 Colin Raw/Stone, 132 Walter
Bibikov, 236 Michael Busselle/Stone, 244 Chris Simpson/Stone. RON
AND JENNY GLYNN: pp.343, 373, 374R. DAN GRANT: pp.34, 37, 39, 63.
JIM GRINDLE: pp.172, 135, 196, 206, 196, 206/7, 209, 155T, 160, 359.
GRAHAM HOLLIER: p.267. HUTCHISON PICTURE LIBRARY: pp.32,
178/9 Bernard Gerard, 222 Robert Francis, 254, 280, 307, 308, 363.
JEAN HARDMAN: pp.117, 122. JOYCE AND DOUG HOWAT: p.158.
JUDE HOWAT: pp.18, 19, 21, 38, 54, 82, 83, 87, 89, 108, 109. STEWART
HOWAT: pp.339, 3567. STEPHANIE KEDIK: pp.325, 326. WILLIAM
KEMBERY: pp. 119 both, 149. ALAN KINGSLAND: p.253. OLIVER
O'BRIEN: pp.22, 23, 52, 53, 279, 281, 347. MICHAEL PARKIN: pp.90, 91,
112. PAT ROBERTS: pp. 186, 191, 215, 219, 221, 257. NICHOLAS RUDD
JONES: pp.184, 185, 341. PETER SALENIEKS: pp.187, 210, 211, 223.
BRIAN & ANNE SANDLAND: p.367. COLIN AND JOANNE SIMPSON:
pp.20, 30, 31, 40, 41, 56, 57, 69. BARRY SMITH: p.125 all. MIKE TAYLOR:
p.57. JOHN THORN: pp.102, 103, 180, 181, 182, 183, 192, 193, 212,
213, 216. KAREN WALTON: p.127. DAVID L.WHITE p. 297.